WELLINGTON'S VOICE

WELLINGTON'S VOICE

The Candid Letters of
Lieutenant Colonel John Fremantle,
Coldstream Guards 1808–1837

Edited by Gareth Glover

Foreword by Charles Fremantle

Frontline Books, London

Wellington's Voice

This edition published in 2012 by Frontline Books,
an imprint of
Pen & Sword Books Limited, 47 Church Street,
Barnsley, S. Yorkshire, S70 2AS
www.frontline-books.com
email info@frontline-books.com

ISBN: 978-1-84832-573-9

A CIP data record for this title is available from the British Library.

For more information on our books, please visit
www.frontline-books.com, email info@frontline-books.com
or write to us at the above address.

Typeset by Palindrome in Stempel Garamond 10½/12 pt

Printed by CPI Group (UK) Ltd, Croydon, CR0 4YY

CONTENTS

LIST OF ILLUSTRATIONS

FOREWORD

My discovery of John Fremantle's letters came about during research I was undertaking for an article on the Adriatic Campaign under the command of his uncle, Rear-Admiral Thomas Fremantle. All of the Fremantles of the Napoleonic War period wrote frequent letters to William Fremantle MP, their brother or uncle. William was a Grenville (Whig) supporter in Parliament and close to Lord Buckingham, later the 1st duke. Buckingham did his best to promote the Fremantle careers.

There were three Fremantle brothers at war during the late eighteenth century. In the 1790s Tom was building an impressive naval career, while William's eldest brother, John, a colonel in the Coldstream Guards, served with the Duke of York in the Low Countries. Stephen, young John's father was fighting in the West Indies; William had also served as an ADC to Buckingham when he was Lord Lieutenant of Ireland in 1789. He continued his career as a civil servant and politician, under the patronage of Buckingham and the Grenvilles.

The Fremantles were a classic upwardly mobile family of the eighteenth century. They started as tenant farmers in Moreton Pinkney in Northamptonshire, after moving from Hampshire. A son John went to Lisbon and became a merchant and his son married a de Castro in Seville and became a minor diplomat before returning to England to become an important figure within Customs and Excise. The only son, again a John, eloped with an heiress, Frances Edwards, who bore him four sons and three daughters. Her wealth helped to move the family into the fringes of the aristocracy.

The eldest son John married Catherine, daughter of Lord Ongley; the second son, Stephen, married Albinia, daughter of Sir John Jefferies of Blarney Castle; the third son, Thomas, married Betsy Wynne, the diarist who was an heiress, and the fourth son, William, married Selina the widow of Felton Hervey, and closely connected to the Hervey and Bathurst dynasties. The daughters married into the Wells, Cathcart and Bishop families, who were important within the shipbuilding, diplomatic and legal professions. Frances's sisters, Lady Cave and Mrs Preston, were also influential, and eventually their wealth inherited by Thomas, 1st Baron Cottesloe, helped the family's progress in the nineteenth century.

The effect on John, who was the only son of Stephen, was to give him entrée to 'Society', through both the Anglo-Irish connections and his aunts and uncles in England. The English ones looked after the education of John and his three sisters, Georgiana, Albinia and Frances (Fanny), after his father's death in 1794 and his mother's remarriage. His Irish ones made him a blood relation of the Duke of Wellington, who also knew his father and uncles from Dublin society in the 1790s.

William became the proxy father to John, who was four years old when his father died. Stephen had left a little money but he lost all support from his mother after she remarried Colonel Taylor (Connaught Rangers) of Castle Taylor, Co. Galway. William earmarked John for a military career and sent him to Harrow, the military academy and to Germany for languages. He became guide and mentor for John's career until 1819 when John broke free, and the regular letters cease.

John's nickname was 'Jolly Jack' and as a popular member of Wellington's 'family' he was a hard-working, hard-playing and valued member of Wellington's Staff. He believed that he had earned this success by his own merit and not solely due to Uncle William's influence.

His career then became a mixture of regimental and semi-diplomatic postings with a period as deputy adjutant general in Jamaica, and accompanying Sir Charles Stuart on Canning's diplomatic mission to Portugal and Brazil in 1825. In 1827 he again served as ADC to Wellington when commander-in-chief.

In January 1829 he married an heiress with £50,000 after a whirlwind courtship in Brighton. She was Agnes Lyon, whose father David had made a fortune in Jamaica; John had met her brother when serving there. Wellington was first witness at their wedding in St George's, Hanover Square, and Fitzroy Somerset was also a witness. Their first two sons were named Arthur and Fitzroy after them.

By the end of 1832 John was a colonel, ADC to King William IV and in command of the 1st Battalion of the Coldstream Guards. The battalion went to Dublin and King William IV ordered him to Ireland after he had delayed joining his battalion for personal reasons. However, this minor scandal petered out and did not actually damage his career. He also became an ADC to Queen Victoria.

Ill health eventually forced him to retire at the end of 1839 and on 23 April 1841 he became a major general on half pay. He died in London in 1845.

John's children were successful in their military and marital careers.

Arthur became a full general and governor of Malta; Fitzroy, a major general, served in the Crimea under his father's old friend Fitzroy Somerset, now Lord Raglan; and Delvin's early death cut short a promising naval career but his daughter Leila married my grandfather, Admiral Sir Sydney Fremantle (a descendant of the naval Fremantles which include Charles, after whom the city of Fremantle in Australia is named). The marriage combined the naval and military strands of the family. A fourth son, John also, died young. Daughter Augusta married General Hall of the Coldstream Guards and their daughter Frances married into the great legal and military Thesiger family. Leila's and Frances's descendants are all that survive today. I was the last of the naval ones, while Peter, my nephew, has been serving with the army in Afghanistan.

John's stepbrother, Felton Hervey Bathurst, a dashing cavalry officer, was John's particular friend and mentor. Felton lost an arm at Oporto, but went on to become Wellington's military secretary in 1815 and thus John's boss. This caused problems in their friendship which were aggravated by the arrival of the Caton sisters from America, who stole the hearts of both Felton and Wellington and upset the normal routine of the headquarters at Cambrai. John lost Felton to Louisa Caton, and messed up his own chance of an engagement to Emma Long, the sister of Catherine, who was married to Wellington's nephew William (Wicked William). His relations with the rest of the Staff worsened during 1818 as John always felt that he had failed to achieve the social distinction he was due. Felton and his Uncle Tom were given baronetcies, Fitzroy Somerset became Lord Raglan, his stepfather Taylor became a general and gained a knighthood, and most of his fellow ADCs were sons of the peerage. John lacked their money and close family connections with those in power, and this frustration does show through in his later correspondence.

Charles Fremantle

PREFACE

The letters of John Fremantle of the Coldstream Guards and aide-de-camp to the Duke of Wellington are of immense interest and of great historical significance. Hailing from the junior ranks of the nobility John Fremantle relied on influential friends and family to propel his career. By a number of lucky coincidences his Uncle William had made some very useful connections with men who then became very senior figures in the army when his nephew joined nearly two decades later.

The letters written by John to William while serving on the Staff of General Cradock in 1808 are revealing regarding that much maligned officer and the situation of the small Army of Portugal at that time. Those written when he served with the 1st Battalion of the Coldstream Guards as adjutant for the next four years between 1809 and late 1812 are useful as another source of material on life as a subaltern Guards officer, particularly as he describes as an eyewitness the battles and sieges of Oporto, Talavera, Bussaco, Fuentes d'Oñoro, Ciudad Rodrigo, Salamanca, Madrid and Burgos.

However, the second half of the letters are of significantly greater importance; for John Fremantle finally joined Wellington's 'family' of Staff officers as an aide-de-camp and became firmly embroiled within the machinations of these young officers, all desperate to gain their commander's eye. In his new role, John witnessed the Battle of Vitoria and was given the honour of carrying the despatch and trophies of war home to lay them before the Prince Regent; however he did not gain immediate promotion within the army in the time-honoured fashion, but was given hope that it would soon come his way. On returning to Spain, having missed the Battle of Sorauren and the capture of San Sebastian, he was back in time to witness the advance into France, including the crossing of the Bidassoa and the Battles of Nivelle, the Nive and Orthes. John carried home the despatch for the Battle of Orthes and as such missed the final battle of the war at Toulouse. However, he was present with the Duke of Wellington during the following peace negotiations at Paris and at the

Congress of Vienna, where he was the Duke's right-hand man.

With war breaking out again, John accompanied Wellington to Brussels and fully participated in the Waterloo campaign, having a horse shot beneath him at the Battle of Quatre Bras, but he survived the campaign without a scratch. He then remained with the Duke's headquarters throughout the period of the Army of Occupation in France and was furnished with full powers by the Duke to ratify the Convention of Paris on 7 July 1815.

During this six years within Wellington's 'family', John wrote candid letters to his uncle, constantly carping at his fellow Staff officers, describing in great detail the bitchiness, the back-stabbing, the one-upmanship and the intriguing that went on: a far cry from the idyllic portrait of Wellington's 'family' that has been peddled for nearly two centuries.

The foibles of the great man himself are not hidden: the duke's philandering is now notorious but is confirmed here in full; his irascible nature and his own petty intrigues and jealousies are exposed.

John himself was not without sin, however; short-tempered, quick to take offence and prone to ill-considered outbursts, his own relationship with these individuals was turbulent and his constant complaining over what he perceived as unfair treatment of others was undoubtedly wearing. He had many good friends but undoubtedly also encountered some who disliked him intensely.

His opinions of other general officers are honest and consistent; Hill and Cradock receive ample praise but others, especially Clinton, whom he describes as 'greatly disliked', and Fermor, who was apparently a 'complete old woman', receive less favourable reviews.

John also writes much on the current political situation and future plans of campaign and such matters, giving a more rounded view of circumstances and the reasoning behind key decisions of the duke.

His letters, written with immediacy and without the dreaded 'hindsight', are therefore of great interest to both the military historian and those more inclined towards the social aspects of life in the upper echelons of the army and particularly of high society in the early years of the nineteenth century.

Gareth Glover

ACKNOWLEDGEMENTS

Two years ago I received a communication from Charles Fremantle informing me of his discovery of over 300 letters written by John Fremantle, aide-de-camp to the Duke of Wellington during the Peninsular War and the Waterloo campaign. They were then held by Buckinghamshire Archives, but the three leather-bound journals enclosing the letters had kindly been loaned to Charles by his cousins, John, 5th Baron Cottesloe, and his son Tom, who were very happy for them to be transcribed and published.

Charles had mentioned this discovery to Professor Chris Woolgar, Head of Special Collections at Southampton University, who oversees the Wellington papers which are housed there. Chris was already aware of my work in publishing manuscript material written by soldiers of the British army during the Napoleonic Wars and kindly advised Charles to liaise with me in bringing the material to print.

I am therefore very grateful to Charles Fremantle and Professor Woolgar for giving me the wonderful opportunity to work on these fascinating letters and doubly so to Charles and his lovely wife, Caroline, who so diligently transcribed all of the letters for me over a long period of time.

Charles has been plagued ever since by questions from me, yet always helped and advised me with great patience, knowledge and humour. Caroline also must receive ample thanks for putting up with my frequent invasions of their home, my interminable questioning of passages with Charles and generally tying up her husband's time – yet always welcoming me with genuine warmth and hospitality. Caroline is a wonderful host and Charles has indeed made the smoking of trout an art form!

This project has probably been the biggest I have undertaken to date and has been greatly aided by the members of the Napoleon Series Forum, who prove that the Napoleonic fraternity is full of individuals with a vast spectrum of speciality knowledge, who are always only too happy to give of their time to help and advise fellow enthusiasts, and I thank them all for their invaluable contributions. The discussion which eventually proved that John was indeed awarded the Order of the Tower and the Sword, despite what the official records said, turned into a major discussion of its own and drew in contributions from numerous experts from across the world and showed the community at its very best.

I must also thank Richard Fremantle, Lord Cottesloe and Sir John Hervey-Bathurst for kindly supplying digital images of the Fremantle family portraits in their possession; the Picture Library of the Royal Collection for providing permission to publish an image of the figure of John Fremantle; Robert Jones, Collection Officer for the Government Art Collection for obtaining copies of the print of Heaphy's great painting and the attached key which enabled me to identify John and also kindly granting permission to publish it in this volume; and English Heritage for permission to publish the image of the Duke with his Staff at Soignies which is held at Apsley House.

I must also thank the unfailing support, encouragement and tolerance of my wife Mary and my adult offspring, Sarah and Michael.

Gareth Glover

BEGINNINGS

John Fremantle was the only son of Colonel Stephen Fremantle, lieutenant colonel of the 39th (East Middlesex) Regiment of Foot, a well-connected man in Ireland, being the MP for Fore in Westmeath at the same time as one Arthur Wellesley (later to become famous as the Duke of Wellington) was also sitting as an MP in the Irish parliament for Trim in Meath.

The Fremantles were connected to some of the first families of both Ireland and England, including the Wellesleys, Fitzgibbons, Beresfords, Cradocks, Nugents, Herveys, Bathursts and Cathcarts and thus exerted great influence and patronage in an era when such things were virtually everything.

William Fremantle had been on the staff of the Marquess of Buckingham with Wellesley and John Cradock in 1789 and there remain in his records at Buckinghamshire Archives a few very revealing letters from the young Arthur Wellesley, and John Cradock, who wrote about the young Arthur, showing clearly that he was not at this age the stern, iron-fisted authoritarian that he came to be known as, and that his well-known proclivity for beautiful women was developed early!

John Cradock wrote:

10 July 1789

My dear Fremantle,
The day before I received yours I had heard of my good fortune; therefore your letter wanted the aid and [dramatics?] of a first announcement of good news; yet, believe me, it was fully made up by the pleasure I felt at your warm and affectionate manner of writing. I really think that my event, of whatsoever advantage, must lose much of its gratification of the few friends that live most together and should love each other best. In this light I hope we shall always stand and that when circumstance of advantage arise to you I may make appear equal sentiment of satisfaction; there are some of his in Lord Buckingham's family, who, I hope and answer, will ever live on the terms of the

highest friendship for I look upon the honour of his protection and support, as a strong bond and cement of union.

I think there is nothing worth communicating from here, except it may be of poor Wellesley, whose propensity to fall in love you are aware of; and he is now more in love with Mrs Stretford than I can describe, all his minor loves before are quite forgot, don't give me up as your author for this. I shall thank you to deliver the enclosed, and believe me, yours most truly,

    J. Cradock

A month later, a letter was received from the young Arthur Wellesley, languishing on detachment.

Black Rock,* 4 August 1789

My dear Fremantle,

I received your letter the other day & will certainly obey Lord Buckingham's orders with regard to the detachments. I suppose he knows that they do not come up to town till winter; in case he should not, I beg you will inform him of it as at that time of the year *he* may want me. I am very happy to hear that he is so nearly recovered, indeed I was sure all along that such a strong man as he is could not be long in the way he was, when the proper remedy should be applied. I don't understand what you mean by the fresh flame you say I have. I know that there are people in Dublin ready enough to circulate reports to my or anybody's disadvantage, but I beg you will give them no credit until I tell you of them myself. I shall also be much obliged to you if you will tell me the name of the person whom you suppose I *burn* for. You will see Williams soon, he will I dare say tell you the truth. I have been living at the Black Rock for this some time past. It was very pleasant but now that Lady Fitzroy Gibbon has left Merrion & is gone to the North of Ireland I am afraid it will languish very much. I wished to have a room in the house which you inhabited but Dean Butler, upon my applying for it, gave me to understand that he would do it if he could with propriety, but his wife & daughter were in the house. He certainly cannot think me such an irresistible man as Williams. I hinted to him that I would not touch his wife, if she would let me & that I would do all I could to harden his daughter from falling in love with me.

---

* Blackrock is now a suburb of Dublin, two miles north-west of Dún Laoghaire. The area was notorious for highway robberies and the detachment may well have been placed there in an attempt to prevent them.

He would not hear of it, therefore I was obliged to take a lodging. I am yours sincerely,
  A. Wesley*

It would seem that Arthur had greatly displeased his seniors.

Ballyfin,† 1 September 1789

My dear Fremantle,
Your letter of the 25th of August, I did not receive till yesterday & it surprised me so much that I am rather inclined to think it a joke. If it should be true, I beg you will be so kind as to inform his Excellency that I will more readily obey his orders, however harsh they may seem from the unknown cause of them, but that I hope he will be so good as to inform me what part of my conduct has displeased him, that I may remedy it, & who are my accusers, that I may prove them to be false. As to disobeying his two former orders, I beg leave again to state, that when Lord Buckingham left Ireland he gave me the choice of going to my regiment or to stay in town. I chose the former not only on account of my own wish but on account of his. Afterwards my commission in the 12th Dragoons‡ was sent over to England & was expected to return every day & Colonel Gordon who his Excellency particularly wished me to be under left the regiment. I could not go down in the expectation of staying only one week at most, more especially so as his object in wishing me to go was defeated. As for joining the detachment, he must know that as a light dragoon officer it is impossible at present, so that I could not disobey that order if I wished it. Lord Buckingham's mind must have been terribly poisoned against me lately, as in your two former letters you state that he approved of my reasons for not joining my regiment. All I request is that before he totally withdraws his regard from me, he will be so kind as to ask the people I have mostly lived with, how I have behaved myself since his departure. The chancellor & Mr Hobart are not people who would countenance a man behaving dishonourably or wrong in any particular. The house of the former has been my home lately & in the first part of Lord Buckingham's

---

* Arthur Wesley did not change the spelling of his surname to the old spelling of Wellesley until 1798.
† Ballyfinn House in Co. Laois (previously Queen's County), was owned by the Wellesley-Poles and is regarded as the most lavish Regency property in Ireland. It has recently been refurbished and is now a hotel.
‡ The Duke of Wellington is rarely associated with the cavalry arm; however, during his period of regiment-hopping to gain rapid promotion between 1787 and 1793, he exchanged regiments no less than seven times. This included a two-year period (1789–91) as a lieutenant in the 12th Dragoons.

absence from this country I lived mostly at the park. His Excellency has confidence in them both & it will be but fair to make enquiries from them. I thank you for the kind expressions in your letter & I am my dear Fremantle, yours most sincerely, A. Wesley.

I send this to town by Mr Packenham [*sic*] who has been here for some time past. Direct your answer to the castle & it will be sent to me wherever I may be. Not being quite certain as to the *truth* of your letter I shall delay going to my regiment till I receive it & I beg you will prevail upon his Excellency to sign it.

William left the army that year and became Deputy Teller of the Exchequer in Dublin and, when his job closed with the Act of Union in 1801, he became a Westminster MP. He was a Whig and Grenvillite by inclination and he had a very comfortable living, Selina Hervey, his wife, being very rich: she was an heiress, daughter of Sir John Elwell and Selina Bathurst, Countess Ranelagh, and widow of Felton Hervey, grandson of the Marquess of Bristol. He maintained his close connection with Arthur Wellesley and John Cradock and they both helped his nephew John Fremantle in due course.

John Fremantle was born on 17 January 1790 but his early years were not to be happy ones, as he would remember little of his natural parents. His father died, when John was just four years old in 1794 of fever onboard HMS *Vengeance* as the army returned from the capture of the Island of Martinique. His mother, Albinia Jeffereys, soon virtually abandoned her children (John and his three sisters) and eventually remarried but remained estranged. Their Uncle William, now a politician, took on the role of benefactor and it is to him this series of nearly 300 letters are addressed, covering all aspects of John's life, from family news, through interesting military matters, to answering the regular admonishments and well-meant advice of his surrogate father.

At the tender age of nine John entered Harrow School on 26 January 1800 and was taught there until 1803, the fees of £60 per annum* being paid via contributions from all his uncles and aunts who chipped in with whatever they could afford to pay.

---

* This equates to approximately £2,000 per annum today.

A BAPTISM OF MISADVENTURE

Clearly an army career was predestined for John, and he was duly enrolled in the newly formed junior department of the Royal Military College at Great Marlow (the precursor of Sandhurst Royal Military Academy) from 1803 till 1805. John was gifted at languages and spoke French, German and Spanish, and to further both his linguistic and military skills, he went to study in Germany in 1805.

John's early military career is probably summed up most easily by the famous quote by the future Duke of Wellington after his own baptism into war in Holland in 1794: 'I learnt more by seeing our own faults and the defects of our system in the campaign . . . than anywhere else.'[*] He was to be an eyewitness to three ignominious military debacles in his first three years of service, which must have severely damaged his confidence in the British military establishment, although he seems to have retained a high regard personally for all three of his commanders, defending them stoutly when each were maligned in turn.

Family influence[†] would appear to have been at play when John was appointed to join the army; he was gazetted to be an ensign in the prestigious Coldstream Guards, without purchase, on 17 October 1805 when he was just fifteen years of age, saving his uncle the requirement to find the standard purchase price, which stood at fully £900.[‡] John joined the first battalion of the Coldstream Guards at Dover,[§] which then

---

* From *Personal Reminiscences of the Duke of Wellington* by Francis, 1st Earl of Ellesmere, ed. Alice, Countess of Stafford, London, 1904, p. 161.
† The Duke of York was colonel of the Coldstream Guards at this time and it must have been his decision to grant this commission to John Fremantle. The idea that the duke acted as his benefactor would appear to be confirmed by his subsequent appointment to the Staff of General Whitelocke who was himself an appointee of the duke's.
‡ Approximately equivalent to £30,000 in today's terms.
§ There is a little doubt regarding this statement, as his obituary states that he joined the regiment when it arrived in Germany straight from his studies; however, Mackinnon, *Origin and Services of the Coldstream Guards*, quotes a Regimental

promptly sailed from the Downs on 4 November with Lord Cathcart's short-lived expedition to Hanover.* The expedition entered Hanover on 14 December and joined forces with a Russian corps under General Werdereffsky, but following the fall of Vienna and defeat of the Austrian Army and the subsequent signing of an agreement between France and Prussia in January 1806, giving Hanover to Prussia; Cathcart was forced to hastily retire and re-embarked his army on 7 February.

The 1st battalion Coldstream Guards returned to garrison duties at Deal in Kent, but John was not to be left stagnating on the south coast for long. News of the easy capture of Cape Colony from the Dutch by a force commanded by General Sir David Baird and Admiral Sir Home Popham on 18 January 1806 had been received with great joy. But it was closely followed by news that Sir Home Popham had now embarked upon an even greater gamble; taking a force to capture the River Plate area of South America from the Spanish. The fleet sailed from Table Bay on 14 April, arriving off the River Plate on 8 June, although it was 25 June before the fleet moved close to Buenos Aires. Having landed his force under the command of Brigadier General William Carr Beresford, Buenos Aires was captured two days later with seeming ease. However, although things appeared peaceful, the Spanish were planning a counter attack. General Santiago Liniers, a French émigré officer, led an overwhelmingly superior force to retake the city, which fell on 11 August; the 1,400 surviving British troops were forced into a humiliating surrender. News of the capture of Buenos Aires did not reach London until 13 September, one month after the Spanish had actually recaptured the city. The news, however, caused jubilation and great excitement among London's commercial centre, as it opened up South America to British trade. The British government, in their ignorance of subsequent events, determined to reinforce this foothold in South America; they ordered 2,000 troops from Cape Colony under Lieutenant Colonel Backhouse and a force of 3,000 troops already formed under Brigadier General Sir Samuel Auchmuty to sail immediately. By October euphoria had turned heads; this had now grown into a major new campaign for the domination of South America and many hare-brained schemes were proposed. The government appointed Brigadier General Robert Craufurd to command a large expedition to capture Chile, with further

---

Return which shows that John was with the first battalion on 23 October 1805 when they were at Dover. It is therefore more likely that he already returned to England and joined there. This would of course have also allowed him time in London to obtain his uniform and equipment, before joining.

* General William Schaw Cathcart, 1st Earl Cathcart was sent with 14,000 troops to Hanover in an attempt to divert some of the French pressure from Austria.

orders, following his undoubted success, to link up with Beresford and complete the occupation of the area. It was also suggested that 6,000 troops could be sent from England via India, where they would pick up another 5,000 troops, and cross the Pacific to capture Mexico, taking the Philippines on route! There was even a feasibility study undertaken by one General Sir Arthur Wellesley regarding the simultaneous invasion of Venezuela. Thankfully some level of sanity returned and the majority of these madcap schemes were shelved; but the determination to continue with Craufurd's 'Secret' expedition remained. This expedition finally sailed on 12 November 1806, but only twenty days later news arrived in London of the recapture of Buenos Aires. New orders were dispatched after Craufurd in the navy's fastest ship, the *Fly*, ordering the immediate recapture of Buenos Aires; as a precursor, Montevideo was captured by storm on the 3 February 1807 by Auchmuty's force before Craufurd's arrival. Following news of the capture of Montevideo, the government deemed that it was necessary to have a more senior officer to take command of the expedition and on the recommendation of the Duke of York; Lieutenant General John Whitelocke was appointed. Ensign John Fremantle was appointed, undoubtedly by the Duke of York's patronage, as an aide-de-camp* to General Whitelocke, and he sailed with him onboard the frigate, HMS *Thisbe*, at the end of March, arriving off Montevideo on 10 May.

Having formed his troops, Whitelocke disembarked his force of 10,000 men at Ensenada de Barragon on 28 June and marched immediately for Buenos Aires.

General Liniers sensibly decided to defend the city rather than meet the British Army in the open field. On the 5 July, Whitelocke prepared to attack the city with three great columns of infantry driving through the metropolis to the waterfront to capture the heart of the sprawling conurbation.

Presumably with little to do in his role as an aide-de-camp during the storming of a city, John Fremantle volunteered† (or was ordered) to accompany General Craufurd's column, which formed the right wing of the British attack, seemingly attaching himself to the 95th Rifles. Initially the attack succeeded with little apparent opposition; but once deep into the city, the attackers were assailed by cannon sweeping the narrow streets with canister and by infantry stationed on the flat rooftops above.

---

* It is estimated in 1813 that the cost of outfitting an aide-de-camp was some £289 and 11 shillings, including horses, mules and equipment, the equivalent of some £10,000 today. See Burnham and McGuigan, *The British Army Against Napoleon*, Barnsley, 2010.

† His obituary states that he volunteered.

Soon the attack broke down in chaos and small groups broke off to clear the houses, where there was serious hand-to-hand fighting; others drove on and actually arrived at their intended targets near the waterfront, but being continually assailed from all quarters and with coordinated action between the separate columns impossible, the attacks faltered and failed independently. Further resistance became futile and the various columns surrendered at discretion: it was an ignominious defeat. John Fremantle has not left us any information on his movements, but presumably he reached the Convent of Santa Domingo with Craufurd's column and saw with pain their eventual capitulation; a sad baptism into war.

On 6 July Whitelocke was still preparing to renew the attack with his reserve, when General Liniers offered peace terms. If the attack ended immediately, the British troops, including the prisoners from Beresford's attack the previous year, would be allowed to re-embark without molestation. With the obvious impossibility of his force holding Buenos Aires even if he had recaptured it becoming very apparent, Whitelocke eventually reluctantly agreed to Linier's offer. The fleet sailed and even Montevideo was given up two months later, thus ending this sorry tale.

The British public were horrified and General Whitelocke was made the scapegoat, being court-martialled in early 1808 and cashiered for his conduct. John Fremantle was not called to give evidence at Whitelocke's court martial, probably as he was too junior and had not actually been with the commander during the attack.

John rejoined his battalion in England; during his absence it had sailed with the expedition to Copenhagen, which had successfully neutralised the Danish fleet and then returned to Chatham.

However, later in the year John was ordered to Portugal, being appointed (presumably under the patronage of the Duke of York again and Cradock's connections with the Fremantle's in Dublin days) to accompany General Sir John Cradock to Lisbon to serve as his private secretary and extra aide-de-camp. This appointment was made as the first campaign by British forces in Portugal had ended in acute embarrassment.

Following the capture of Lisbon by the French under General Junot on 30 November 1807, General Arthur Wellesley had landed a force at Mondego Bay on 1 August 1808 and swiftly defeated the French at the battles of Roliça and Vimiero; but before Wellesley could order his forces in hot pursuit after the latter battle, he was superseded by the arrival of two more cautious senior officers, Generals Burrard and Dalrymple, and the pursuit was promptly cancelled. Eventually a convention was signed at Cintra and the French were allowed to return to France in British ships with most of their ill-gotten gains. It had achieved a Portugal free from French control, but at what price? The British public were apoplectic with rage over the details of the convention and this clamour led to the recall of all three generals to answer a court of enquiry.

General Cradock was sent out to command the forces remaining at Lisbon, while Sir John Moore led the main British force into Spain to aid the Spanish uprising against the French. Historians are not impressed by General Cradock: they generally state that he was cautious and ineffective. However, it is unclear what could have been expected to have been achieved with only 9,000 British troops and the Portuguese army yet to begin its transformation under Beresford; indeed John Fremantle clearly thought very highly of his new commander. It is at this point, as John Fremantle was in London, awaiting a ship to transport them to Lisbon that his letters to his uncle finally begin.

WITH GENERAL CRADOCK

We join John in London, presumably preparing his uniform and equipment for service abroad, and like all other officers preferring to remain in luxurious comfort in London until news of a ship arrived, rather than reside within the fortress of Portsmouth, where accommodation was reportedly both extortionately expensive and exceedingly poor. John wrote a letter to his uncle informing him of news of a ship having arrived and his immediate departure for Portsmouth on the mail coach, the speediest but probably the least comfortable mode of public transport available.

London, 20 November 1808

My dear uncle,[*]

Colonel Reynell[†] called upon me last night to tell me that General Cradock[‡] was to go today. I shall therefore go by the mail tonight; my baggage is all ready and will be at Portsmouth with myself tomorrow morning.[§] I have not been able to get a soldier recommended to me out of the whole battalion; therefore the only thing that remains for me to do is to make my present man follow me as soon as his wife is able to be moved from her confinement, either to London or Windsor where he has friends. I hope you will make her the same allowance you did last time; I have given him a week, I shall send him tomorrow

---

[*] The Right Honourable Sir William Henry Fremantle MP was a privy counsellor. He also held the office of Treasurer of the Household and Ranger of Windsor Great Park.

[†] Brevet Lieutenant Colonel Thomas Reynell, 71st Foot. He was military secretary to Cradock and then to Wellington from January to May 1809.

[‡] Lieutenant General Sir John Francis Cradock held command of the forces left in Portugal when Sir John Moore led his army into Spain until General Arthur Wellesley retook command in 1809.

[§] At this period the coach journey from London to Portsmouth was normally about ten hours.

to the Green* with my things and from thence he will be able to walk to Wycombe.† I shall thank him to see you the last thing before he comes away, I suppose he can always get a passage over but will you have the goodness to put him in the best way. Captain Warre‡ had been about seven months when he went as ADC to General Ferguson, he is now in Portugal. The person whom General H.§ alluded to is Captain Beresford¶ who had been 10 months at Wycombe when he left to go General Lord Somebody at Brighton when he was recalled. I think this is very clear when one is allowed to go on Foreign Service and the other recalled for leaving the college to go the Home Staff.

With best love, believe me, my dear uncle,
　　　your most dutiful and affectionate nephew

There are some Patagonian mouse skins** among my baggage which I think perhaps might make a muff for Georgiana.

Having arrived at Portsmouth the following morning, he penned another note in expectation of sailing almost immediately.

Portsmouth, Monday evening [21 November]

My dear uncle,
I arrived here this morning, all the baggage belonging to the Staff is on board, the general is expected tomorrow. I have seen Lord W. Stuart†† and everything is arranged for my going on board. I forgot to get the keys of my trunks from my servant when I was coming away, but I have kept one small portmanteau on shore. The general's horses leave town Tuesday and will embark Friday, therefore I may write to Herries‡‡ at Wycombe to urge my servants being here by that time, I shall do the same and desire him to ask for help from Patten, agent for

---

* Englefield Green was the country house of William Fremantle at Windsor.
† This would entail a walk of some twelve miles.
‡ Captain William Warre, 23rd Light Dragoons, aide-de-camp to Major General Ronald Crawfurd Ferguson, whose letters were published as *Letters From the Peninsula 1808–12,* London, 1909.
§ Almost certainly General the Honourable William Harcourt, governor of the Royal Military College.
¶ Captain William Beresford, 8th Garrison Battalion, was a deputy assistant quartermaster general in Portugal.
** The Patagonian chinchilla mouse (*Euneomys chinchilloides*) is a species of rodent found in Argentina and Chile.
†† Captain Lord William Stuart, commanding HMS *Lavinia* of 38 guns.
‡‡ Lieutenant William Lewis Herries, 9th Light Dragoons was then a student of the senior department of the Royal Military College at High Wycombe.

transport, the *Barbara and Anne* is the vessel appointed to take out the horses to sail with the first convoy. Young Wynyard was the first person I met here; he has been two days with General Acland* who is extremely ill. Young Wynyard† has been all the morning giving me a delightful account of Lisbon. General Whetham‡ has asked me to dine with him today. Adieu my dear uncle, always your most dutiful and affectionate nephew,
  John Fremantle

Portsmouth, 22 November 1808

My dear uncle,
Sir John arrived about noon this day and Lord W. Stuart is to come on board by eight o'clock tomorrow if the wind will answer sufficiently for our sailing. I received your letter at 6, and the horses arrived about ½ hour later seven o'clock for which I really cannot sufficiently thank you. General Acland and young Wynyard both look more stout, they were very indifferent at Lisbon. Captain Morris,§ one of the general's ADCs, knew my mother extremely well, as well as the great loss of the family. He has been extremely civil to me and I think I shall like him very much. There will be no difficulty getting the horse on board with the general's which do not arrive until tomorrow (Thursday) and will not embark before Saturday, and the vessel is to wait for convoy. I told my servant Friday positively, if you will tell him to enquire for Mr Allcot¶ storekeeper in the dock, a friend of my Uncle Tom's,** who has been particularly civil to me, he will be sure of being put in the right way. We are to go on board tomorrow if the wind is favourable. With best love, believe me, ever my dear uncle, your dutiful and affectionate nephew,
  John Fremantle

John was lucky not to have to wait at Portsmouth for long before a favourable wind allowed the ship to sail for Lisbon. It would appear that it sailed alone, not waiting to escort the transport ships, including their horse transport.

---

* Brigadier General Wroth Palmer Acland; he commanded a brigade at the battle of Vimiero but ill health forced him home soon after.
† Captain William Clinton Wynyard, Coldstream Guards, was major of brigade to General Acland.
‡ Major General Arthur Whetham, 1st Foot Guards, lieutenant governor of Portsmouth.
§ Captain George Morris, 3rd Foot, was aide-de-camp to Cradock.
¶ The Navy List confirms that John Allcot was a storekeeper at Portsmouth.
** Uncle Tom is Captain Thomas Francis Fremantle, who had captained HMS *Neptune* at the Battle of Trafalgar.

*Lavinia** off Yarmouth, Friday [25 November?]

My dear uncle,

The general with his suite consisting of five, the Spaniards† of four, and the Commissary General Mr Murray‡ of four, all embarked yesterday at ½ past eleven and sailed at one and anchored off Yarmouth [Isle of Wight] at 5. The wind is now directly contrary and we are very much crowded, but Lord W. Stuart is an exceeding pleasant man and has spared no pains to make every one comfortable.

I think there can be no mistake with my servant or the horse, even if he does not arrive at Portsmouth before Tuesday, as the transport will not sail for a week. I have desired your man to remain till my servant relieves him, which I expected would certainly be on Saturday, I have left word for my man to enquire for Mr Allcot, who will give him all the necessary information respecting the embarkation of the general's horses. I will write to you the first opportunity from Lisbon. With best love, believe me always, your dutiful and affectionate nephew,

    John Fremantle

Having called at Corunna to disembark the Spanish deputies and coin for the use of Sir John Moore's army, they sailed on for Lisbon. Presumably the passage was uneventful and the weather calm, as it evokes no comment from John.

Lisbon, 12 December 1808

My dear uncle,

We arrived at Corunna on the 5th of this month, where we left the four Spanish deputies and landed a proportion of the dollars we brought out for the use of the army. We proceeded to Oporto on the 7th where we arrived on the 8th, where I found James Butler,§ he was particularly civil to me. Sir Robert Wilson¶ commanded there, I think from what he said that he had a very indifferent opinion of the Portuguese in general and indeed all the officers with whom I had any conversation seemed to agree in thinking that all energy was lost on their part, and that very

---

* HMS *Lavinia*, was a frigate of 40 guns.
† This refers to four Spanish deputies who had been to England to seek support for the Spanish uprising against Napoleon's troops.
‡ Commissary General Mr John Murray.
§ James Butler was his second cousin via his great aunt, Sarah Fremantle, who was married to Richard Butler, a city merchant. James set up a business in Oporto named Butler Krug & Co., which was dissolved in 1826.
¶ Brigadier General Sir Robert Thomas Wilson was then commanding a brigade of Portuguese infantry. He later became famous commanding the Loyal Lusitanian Legion.

little was to be expected from them. We left the commissary general at Oporto; we proceeded on the 10th and are just arrived. Dispatches were very lately received from Sir John Moore; he was at Salamanca with 22,000 men.* Sir David Baird† cannot join him, and I believe is retreating to Vigo where transports are in readiness, I suppose he will ultimately join us here. Accounts from the neighbourhood of Madrid state that Marshal Bessières‡ had pushed on with 8,000 cavalry 40 leagues, 160 miles in two days and on the 2nd surrounded the town, the answer was most spirited. The Spaniards have cut trenches across the streets and on the 4th the French were still bombarding the town.§ In case Sir John Moore is obliged to retreat of course it will be upon Lisbon. No dispatches from government or any accounts from England have been received here since the 1st of November. We spoke a packet off Corunna with Sir Thomas Dyer¶ on board, I suppose going home with the accounts of the dispersion of Blake's and Castanos's army.** The fighting by all accounts has been most desperate, Blake in particular fought for five days without intermission, no further detail is given. The French must necessarily have lost a number of men. Of course, I cannot tell you what Sir John Cradock's movements are likely to be. He will wait until he receives further instructions from government. Officers seem to think that Portugal will not be defended, in which case we shall come home. Sir John Cradock's horses have not arrived. With best love, believe me always, my dear uncle, your affectionate nephew,

    J. W. F.

---

* In a bold move Moore advanced with his force in an attempt to draw the French away from Madrid; it culminated in the victory of the Battle of Corunna and safe re-embarkation of his army.

† Lieutenant General Sir David Baird commanded a reinforcement for Moore's army. Having marched from Corunna to Astorga, he received orders to retreat, but having retired about 50 miles, the order was countermanded and he advanced again to eventually join Moore.

‡ Marshal Jean Baptiste Bessières commanded the cavalry at the Battle of Somosierra on 30 November, removing the final obstacle to the French advance on Madrid.

§ In fact Madrid surrendered on 4 December.

¶ Lieutenant Colonel Sir Thomas Dyer, Royal York Rangers, was one of three officers fluent in Spanish sent by the government in 1808 to liaise with the Spanish armies; but Canning's reply to Mr Frere dated 10 January indicates that the information regarding the Spanish losses arrived on 9 December with a Mr Mills, who presumably was also onboard.

** General Blake had been defeated heavily and routed at Gamonal on 10 November and Castanos at Tudela on 23 November. The Spanish were often guilty of talking up their martial achievements, even in defeat.

I never upon so short an acquaintance liked any lot of men so much as Sir John and the three people who comprise his Staff. I was quite astonished to find that all ranks approve of the convention.* I think the only blame seems to attach to Burrard for stopping Sir A. after the battle, which however he will be able to justify himself in.†

John quickly settled into his role on the Staff of Sir John Cradock and wrote home of his role and his hopes of a pay rise, along with news of Sir John Moore and the army.

Lisbon, 21 December 1808

My dear uncle,

The night after I wrote to you a dispatch arrived, from Sir John Moore, saying that a junction between him and Sir David Baird was no longer doubtful, and that he was then advancing, we have had frequent communications since, but I believe the accounts in general are by no means favourable, we are sending every man to his army that can possibly be spared. Madrid has capitulated; I understand the people say they were betrayed. The French lost a vast number of men before the town. Had I not been writing for Sir John when our last accounts went home till the latest moment, I should certainly have not failed writing to you.

I think you will be glad to hear that I am acting under Colonel Reynell, the military secretary, for which, if the situation is allowed, I shall receive 10 shillings a day,‡ at all events it will put me in the way of business, and of knowing something of what's going forward, which is at all times gratifying. I assure you it is no sinecure, for I am employed the best part of the day. Mr Villiers§ landed the 17th. Sir John is quartered in a most magnificent palace, there are two rooms

---

* This is an interesting comment. The Convention of Cintra allowed for the French to evacuate Portugal and to be repatriated to France, in British ships, with their belongings. The convention was received with uproar at home, but clearly many in the army approved of it; for despite its critics, it did deliver up all the fortresses of Portugal without having to besiege them and saved Lisbon from a great deal of destruction.

† Having defeated the French at Vimiero, on 21 August 1808, Sir Arthur Wellesley was prevented from pursuing the French army by the arrival of General Sir Harry Burrard, who countermanded the pursuit.

‡ As an ensign in the Foot Guards, John's daily rate of pay was 5 shillings and 10 pence. His pay was therefore hopefully rising quite significantly to 10 shillings per day, the same as an adjutant in the Guards earned. The modern equivalent of these rates of pay equate to £10 and £17 per day.

§ John Charles Villiers, later 3rd Earl of Clarendon, Envoy to Portugal 1807–10.

elegantly furnished on the first floor, all opening into each other.

I have this moment seen Felton* I think he is looking very well, he is all anxiety to go into Spain, but I think it is more than probable that the regiment may not go but remain here. With best love believe me, my dear uncle, your most dutiful and affectionate nephew,

John Fremantle

I heard of Frederick Hervey being quite well a few days ago.

News from Spain was erratic and unreliable and John was to be disappointed in his hopes of more pay.

Lisbon, 4 January 1809

My dear uncle,

I have no news whatever to tell you since I last wrote to you, we have not heard from Sir John Moore nor have we had any instruction of any kind from England, The arrival of the 14th was totally unexpected,† of course it cannot now join Sir John Moore. We heard from Elvas a few days ago that 34 thousand French belonging to the Madrid army had entered Trujillo, levied contributions to a considerable amount and decamped during the night, and took the road to Placentia. We imagine this movement of theirs must either be to assist in attacking Sir J. Moore, or to enter Portugal below the Tras os Montes having in all appearances refused the route by Elvas.

We fully expect that the next account will be of an action between our army and the French, indeed we have just heard from Coimbra that an action had taken place wherein we took 1,000 prisoners,‡ but we hear nothing but reports from morning till night. I will write again the first opportunity. With best love, believe me, your most dutiful and affectionate nephew,

John Fremantle

---

* Felton Hervey was a major in the 14th Light Dragoons. Felton Elwell Hervey, Frederick Hervey and Lionel Charles Hervey were the sons of Selina, John's step-aunt. Selina Elwell had married Felton Lionel Hervey in 1779 and had five children before Felton senior died in 1785, she then married John's uncle Sir William Henry Fremantle in 1797. They both cared for John and his sisters after his father died in 1794, particularly after his mother was re-married to Lieutenant General Sir John Taylor in 1798 and lived at Taylor Castle, County Galway in Ireland. Frederick Hervey was a captain in the 20th Foot, Lionel became a diplomat.

† The 14th Light Dragoons, Felton Hervey's regiment.

‡ This was a false rumour.

I am sorry to inform you that I have no chance of the 10 shillings a day that I mentioned in my last letter.

Lisbon, 7 January 1809

My dear uncle,

On account of the contrary winds the packet with the mail of the 3rd on board, has not been able to get out of the harbour. We have had no direct communication with Sir John Moore since a dispatch was received yesterday from Elvas and one a few hours ago from the commanding officer at Almeida stating officially that some recent skirmishing had taken place on the 20th December between our outposts and the French in which two of our hussar regiments bore the greater part. The French have lost about a thousand men, prisoners,* our loss has been comparatively very trifling, I am not as yet in possession of the details. I hope the corps that appeared near Trujillo as I mentioned in my last and from thence proceeded to Placentia is not with the design of forming in the rear of Sir John Moore's Army, for if a large force is once assembled there perhaps he may find great difficulty in extricating himself. I am quite ashamed of writing to you in this, I fear, almost unintelligible manner, but it is really wonderful how badly off we are for information, not being able to hear from Sir John Moore except by way of Corunna. I am sure there is nothing wanting on the part of Sir J. Cradock, the apathy and indolence that exists among the Portuguese is truly astonishing. I saw a return of the state of their army which was on paper 22,000 men but I do not think there are more than 9 or 10 [thousand] to be calculated upon, and even those I am afraid in a very sorry condition. The vessel with the horses on board parted company with her convoy 4 nights ago in a very heavy gale of wind between this and Vigo, I am afraid when they do arrive they will be in a very bad state, however we are none of us in very great want being each supplied with one from the [Portuguese] Prince Regent's stables. Believe me, ever my dear uncle, your most dutiful and affectionate nephew,

John Fremantle

In late January Lisbon was still unaware of the re-embarkation of the

---

* This refers to the action at Sahagun, on 21 December, when Lord Paget surprised General Debelle's force of cavalry at that town. The 10th and 15th Hussars were involved, although the 15th alone actually charged, overturning the larger French force and driving them from the field with large losses. However, claims of a thousand prisoners are a wild exaggeration; the French cavalry actually lost about 20 killed and 160 wounded and prisoners.

army at Corunna and the death of Sir John Moore.

Lisbon, 21 January 1809

My dear uncle,

We really have never heard from Sir John Moore since I last wrote to you. We heard of his retreat 9 days ago and of his embarkation since and what his future intention is (either of coming into the Tagus or elsewhere) of course we are in total ignorance.* A vessel has been sent both to Vigo and Corunna for intelligence and we are in hourly expectation of its return. I suppose we shall remain here till the last proper moment, before we embark. The 14th were embarked with some other troops to proceed to Vigo to join Sir J. Moore when the above news arrived, and have been on board ever since, ready for a start elsewhere. Admiral Berkeley† arrived here the 15th, by whom we understand that 5,000 infantry were on the point of embarkation when he came away, of which the 2nd Brigade of Guards were to compose a part.‡

The horses arrived here on the 17th in a very tolerable state after their very severe passage, there was only one of them lost which happened to be Sir John's favourite. I have written to James Butler twice recommending him strongly to pack up.§ I have taken the opportunity of writing to you thus far by a friend of mine going home, there will be a vessel sent as soon as we receive accounts from Sir J. Moore, by which I will let you know what are to be our proceedings. With best love, believe me, my dear uncle, your dutiful and affectionate nephew,
John Fremantle

John clearly shows their frustration in receiving no news directly from Sir John Moore's army, learning of the death of Moore and the evacuation of the troops via a copy of a Cornish newspaper! However, he makes it clear that far fewer men were lost in the retreat to Corunna than was stated, as

---

* It seems incredible, but they appear to have heard that the army had re-embarked, but not of the death of Sir John Moore or of the Battle of Corunna.
† Vice-Admiral Sir George Cranfield Berkeley commanded in the Tagus.
‡ The Brigade of Guards at Chatham under Brigadier General Henry Campbell composed of the first battalions of the Coldstream and 3rd Guards; they embarked at Ramsgate and joined other troops forming at Spithead commanded by Major General Sherbrooke. The fleet sailed on 15 January but endured heavy weather, eventually arriving at Cadiz on 25 February, where the Spanish Junta refused permission to land. The fleet sailed on to Lisbon, disembarking on 13 March; the light company of the Coldstream Guards having been wind bound in Ireland did not arrive until 6 April.
§ It is very clear from such statements that the British army under Cradock did not hold any sanguine hopes of holding Portugal long, expecting Napoleon's forces to invade at any time.

some 3,000 men had managed to escape the French pursuit and crossed the mountains into Portugal. He also makes it clear that Cradock was fully expecting to follow suit and was preparing to evacuate the British army from Lisbon.

Lisbon, 14 February 1809

My dear uncle,

I was quite rejoiced to receive your letter of the 6th January. I showed it to Sir John [Cradock] who was also very glad to see such just reasoning, the affairs in Spain have turned out precisely as you foretold. There had been rumours in Lisbon of the death of Sir J. Moore for a length of time, but it was never thoroughly credited until we saw the account in a Truro paper of the 18th of last month, nor did we know of the army having sailed from Corunna till the 9th. At present we know nothing of our loss, nor do I expect we shall until an arrival from England. It will be thought in England no doubt, far greater than it really is, for within this last month stragglers from Sir J. Moore's army have been coming in to the amount of 2,000, and we have heard lately from Oporto of nearly another thousand having turned up there, I also learn from officers who have lately left the interior of the country that we have stragglers and such still remaining to a very great amount. These men at Oporto on account of the hardship of the weather and there being no communication with the shipping for 9 weeks, are now on their march to this place in order to be enabled to embark, whenever such a measure is determined upon. On the above account I expect James Butler from Oporto any hour.

All the British troops in Portugal are concentrated in Lisbon; they will leave it in three or four days to take up a position near Paco de Arcos and Fort St Julian, there to await orders from government. Headquarters will be about five miles from this.

If an embarkation is decided upon here, I have fears for the consequences whenever it takes place, for the Portuguese I have no doubt will endeavour to resist it. The inhabitants are all armed with pikes etc and the government, who have no control whatever over them, are very much afraid of them.

I am sorry to inform you that I have not the slightest chance of getting the pay I mentioned in a former letter, but I am extremely comfortable, very good friends with Sir John, and like the rest of the family extremely.

Felton is still here and going on very moderately, he is very much vexed at the idea of returning to England. I see by a letter from Lionel to him that there is great talk of a regency.*

I have enclosed a letter of my servant's which I believe contains money for his wife; I shall be much obliged to you to forward it. With my best love, believe me, my dear uncle, your dutiful and affectionate nephew,

John Fremantle

We have about 9,000 men here.

By March it is clear that there were hopes that Cradock could defend Lisbon and the army was positioned near Sacavém.

Lisbon, 3 March 1809

My dear uncle,

When Felton was here about an hour ago, I desired him in his letter to say I have so much before me to copy that I despaired of having time to write you a line. However I have but very little to say in point of news, since my last letter. The position which I mentioned of Fort St Julian was not taken up but now there is another one determined upon, I believe principally for the defence of Lisbon. The advance posts are to be at Bucelas and Cabeca de Montachique† the headquarters are to be at Lumiar,‡ about 8 miles from this. I believe the troops will begin their march after tomorrow, and expect the headquarters will be moved in about 6 or 7 days. Our force at present does not amount to 10,000 men, but if General Sherbrooke§ and General McKenzie¶ whom Sir John dispatched with nearly 4,000 men return here (which, on account of not being admitted into Cadiz, I think is very probable), we shall have a very pretty army here.

In an intercepted letter from Soult to Joseph Bonaparte, calling him King of Spain, he represents his army to be in a most deplorable condition, his sick very numerous, and in total want of medical assistance, he begs Joseph to send him *quelque douzaines de Médecins, de Chirurgions* [a few dozen doctors and surgeons] and several thousand pairs of shoes, being totally destitute of that article. He also calculates upon being at Oporto by the 22nd of last month.

I was on a very pleasant excursion a short time ago with Sir John to

---

* With the failing health of King George III, moves were being made to place his son George on the throne as regent, but this did not actually occur until 1811.
† These positions are just in front of Sacavém.
‡ Lumiar is virtually alongside Lisbon Airport today.
§ Major General John Cope Sherbrooke.
¶ Major General John Randoll McKenzie was killed at Talavera soon after.

Cintra, Mafra, Vimeiro and by Torres Vedras & home. I suppose Cintra is the most romantic, beautiful spot that ever was seen. Mafra is only worth seeing on account of the palace which in my opinion is no great thing, and at Vimeiro, where we all turned generals, we agreed with one accord that the French were great fools for attacking us in our very strong position, and well merited the licking they got for so doing. After the battle we were certainly nearer Torres Vedras than the French were and had two brigades that had not been in action. The French marched there that night, and caused the town to be illuminated for their victory, and levied a very heavy contribution. General Beresford* arrived here the day before yesterday, with nine officers to assist him in organising the Portuguese Army. I think he is little aware of the task he has undertaken, for I believe a more despicable, and mistrustful race of beings than the Portuguese in general, never existed.

Sir John Duckworth† was off Cascais Bay before yesterday, and having heard the day before that of the Brest fleet having passed Cape Finisterre in the morning to the amount of 16 sail of the line and four frigates, sent to Admiral Berkeley for the *Norge*, and *Conqueror*, 74s,‡ all of which sailed yesterday, 13 in number, and I hope ere long we shall hear of their being in a British port. We were all *in* grand *terrorem* [in great fear] about two hours ago, Admiral Berkeley came to report that a signal had been made by the look-out frigate for five sail which we thought was the French squadron but has since proved to be an English convoy, where from we do not yet know, or what it contains. With best love, believe me always, my dear uncle, your most dutiful and affectionate nephew, John Fremantle

It is been long reported here that Austria has declared against France, but not hearing anything of it from England, I do not at all credit the report,§ I have only received your letter of the 6th of January.
J. F.

Reports are very various respecting the French army sometimes retreating, at other times advancing towards the frontiers, that I cannot tell you anything for certain, it is however certain that they do not feel themselves at their ease in Galicia. I totally forgot to mention your

---

* General William Carr Beresford, now a marshal in the Portuguese service, commanded a force of nearly 11,000 Portuguese, Tilson's Brigade consisting of 2/87th, 1/88th, and 5 companies of 5/60th with one squadron of the 14th Light Dragoons.
† Admiral Sir John Thomas Duckworth, (1747–1817)
‡ HMS *Norge*, a Danish capture, and HMS *Conqueror* were indeed 74s.
§ It was true, Austria had declared war; the Austrian army had been reorganised and fought very tenaciously, but it was eventually defeated by Napoleon.

speech in the House, for which I am sure you have the thanks of the whole army.

The number of troops at Lisbon increased significantly, including the 1st Battalion Coldstream Guards; however, John betrays little enthusiasm or hope for the future of Spain or Portugal.

Lisbon, 12 March 1809

My dear uncle,
General Sherbrooke with 4,000 men arrived here last evening from Cadiz, and General McKenzie with 3,000 returned this morning, without being allowed to land there. This reinforcement together with 3,000 of Sir J. Moore's army that I mentioned in a former letter brings our forces in Portugal to nearly 17,000 men. The whole will be landed in the course of tomorrow and next day, and I have every reason to think we shall shortly make a forward movement. On account of the augmentation of the army here, Sir John thinks it impossible that he can manage with less than three aides de camp, I am therefore to be put in orders immediately. Lord Ebrington* is appointed extra ADC Felton has been so indisposed for the last week that he has not been able to go with the regiment which is about 20 miles off, he goes tomorrow. The packet sails the day after tomorrow when I will write to you more fully. Believe, my dear uncle, with my best love, believe me, your dutiful and affectionate nephew,
  J. F.

Lumiar, 22 March 1809

My dear uncle,
I have received your letter of the 25th and agree with you most perfectly in all your ideas with respect to this country and Spain, and in proportion as it is nonsense to think of keeping up the farce of fighting for the Spaniards, it is highly ludicrous to continue it for the Portuguese, who if possible are the most unworthy and despicable of the two, and if they ever take any benefit from our assistance, I am confident they will never acknowledge or thank us for it. [General] Bernadine Freire and two of his aides du camp have been massacred by the mob at Braga, from an idea that he had entered into a league with the French not to defend the province, the truth of which I suppose we shall never know, but I think the probability is, that it was to satisfy the envy of some individual, who I should not at all wonder to hear was the Bishop of Oporto. Freire had the chief

---

* Ensign Hugh Ebrington, Viscount, 9th Foot.

command in that part of the country, and I understand the populace had since created Baron Eben Commander in Chief of the Minho, which the Bishop has confirmed; whether Marshal Beresford will approve of it, I think is very dubious, who I should imagine was very little aware of the arduous task he was undertaking when he accepted his present situation as the Portuguese are very well aware that it was mere accident from not being admitted into Cadiz, that General Sherbrooke's reinforcement came here. Headquarters were removed to this place yesterday about 7 miles from Lisbon, and the troops I think are not intended to proceed, but to defend the passes leading to Lisbon, viz. Bucelas, Mafra and Montachique, for which by the by, our force is not sufficient, and still it is too great not to make [a] stand; never was any man, placed in the awkward predicament that Sir John Cradock is, and I think no man in the situation could have done more than he has done.*

The French entered Chaves on the 12th, after having been before it two days, and have since proceeded towards Braga, some distance from which private letters from Oporto state that Baron Eben with the Legion† and the Portuguese peasants have had an affair with them and caused the French a partial check, but of course it never can last. For how is an undisciplined people, particularly Portuguese, to resist a regular force, besides Captain Brotherton of the 14th Dragoons‡ who only left Chaves a few hours before the French entered, states in his official report, that there were a great many Portuguese officers among them, who had gone from this country and returned with the French, and that there were also a considerable proportion of Portuguese troops embodied amongst them. Saragossa has been taken by famine,§ Cuesta has been beaten,¶ Romana is retreating and was on the 14th at Braganza; before Romana retreated the greatest possible animosity existed between his army and the Portuguese, but our officers for intelligence tell us that Romana from their conduct had great reason to be dissatisfied with them. Reinforcements are still expected here by Sir John, but unless they send 5,000 infantry and 10,000 cavalry which England never can spare, what is to become of us at present with 15,000 infantry and 1,000 cavalry, if the French bring

---

* Oman particularly is less understanding and is indeed highly critical of Cradock.

† Colonel Frederick Baron Eben was a British officer in the Portuguese service at this period; the Loyal Lusitanian Legion was led by Sir Robert Wilson.

‡ Captain Thomas William Brotherton, 14th Light Dragoons.

§ The city of Saragossa surrendered on 20 February 1809 following an heroic defence.

¶ The Spanish General Gregorio Garcia de la Cuesta was heavily defeated at the Battle of Medellin on 28 March 1809.

double or treble that number? Cavalry we are however particularly in want of, as well as horses for our guns. Intelligence now becomes every day extremely interesting. However I look upon it that ten days or a fortnight will put an end to our anxiety. I trust it will not end like the Corunna business, but indeed it is difficult to say.

God bless you my dear uncle, with best love, believe me, ever your most affectionate nephew,
John F.

At home, the talk was that Arthur Wellesley was being sent back to take command of the army in Portugal and Uncle William was not slow to write to him to seek an appointment for John on his Staff.

Stanhope Street, 31 March 1809

My dear Wellesley,
I don't ask you whether you are going or not to command in Portugal, but in case you do, you will find John Fremantle acting as an aide-de-camp with Cradock, and if the latter comes away, I should feel myself under the greatest obligation if you would keep this boy with you. The recollection of old friendship & regard towards his father prompted Cradock to take him & perhaps the same feeling may induce you to receive & protect him. He is quick, well behaved, intelligent & a good linguist, but as you will know a complete soldier of fortune.

I can only add, that such a mark of your kindness towards him, would be ever felt by me, with sentiments of the truest gratitude. I don't wish you to answer this letter as I am sure you will keep my request in your remembrance, when you see Cradock & the boy. With best wishes for your success at all times & in every undertaking, believe me, dear Wellesley, ever most sincerely yours,
W. Fremantle

Arthur Wellesley replied by return, very positively.

London, 31 March 1809

My dear Fremantle,
You may depend upon it that I will do everything in my power for John. If he is a captain I will certainly put him on to the Staff, if he is not you will see by an attention of the *new* regulation which has lately appeared that I shall not be able to do so. Ever yours most sincerely,
Arthur Wellesley

John's next letter wrote of the fall of Oporto to French forces under Marshal Soult and the increasing threat to the small British force covering Lisbon. His bland announcement does not portray the horror attending the French sacking of Oporto. The Portuguese troops, militia and populace fought valiantly, but were no match for the seasoned French veterans and once the city was captured, the French began a chaotic pillaging, murdering or raping those that were unfortunate enough to cross their paths. The French lost some 2,000 men killed and wounded in the assault, the Portuguese in excess of 8,000.

Lumiar, 3 April 1809, Monday

My dear uncle,
I have just time to write to you a line by the *Iris*,* which has been ordered off at a moment's notice, nothing extraordinary since my last, except the fall of Oporto, on the 29th, I believe without fighting at all.† The French have about 20,000 men between that and Chaves. Marshal Victor has a corps of 30,000 and is in the direction of Merida and I suppose is only waiting till he hears from Oporto to begin his march in cooperation with the Oporto division for this place. We are altogether 14,000 effective fighting men. Butler is going by the packet on Wednesday when I will write to you more fully. Your most affectionate nephew,
    John Fremantle

News of the shocking Oporto massacres had arrived, but with the arrival of further reinforcements and the Portuguese reorganisation under Beresford starting to take effect, one can detect a glint of hope in John's letters.

Lisbon, 5 April 1809

My dear uncle,
Since my flying letter of the day before yesterday, I have but little to add, in point of intelligence. We have heard of horrid atrocities being committed by the French, since they entered Oporto. There are three hundred French cavalry five leagues on this side of Oporto by the last accounts. The bishop has sailed for England, where I am afraid he will be much better received than he deserves. I do not think from

---

* HMS *Iris* of 44 guns, had been captured at Copenhagen as the *Marie*.
† In the first Battle of Porto (28 March 1809) the French under Marshal Soult completely defeated the Portuguese under Generals Lima Barreto and Parreiras outside the city of Porto. Soult followed up his success by sacking the city; by which in addition to 8,000 military casualties, large numbers of civilians were killed or drowned.

the state of the country where Soult is at present, that out of his army he can spare more than 10,000 men to bring before this place. The division of Salamanca, now at Ciudad Rodrigo (9,000 men) and Victor, after having completely annihilated General Cuesta, has now 25,000 men, the number for which when he summoned Badajoz the day before yesterday, of which we have this instant received information of [that] he demanded rations for. The inhabitants sent out in reply, that they did not think he had that number. I think the French will certainly be enabled to bring before this place 40,000 men. General Hill* is this instant arrived with nearly 5,000 men and 300 artillery horses of which we were badly in need of, but inclusive of this, we shall not be able to bring quite 20,000 into the field. We have at present a very strong position, but yet hardly sufficient force to man it, the Portuguese 10,000 in number, under General Beresford, are to have the right of the position, that being the strongest, and if they are true to themselves, I think we ought to make a tolerable fight of it, but if there remains any fight in the Portuguese, I think with British officers at their heads and a British force by their side we shall get it out of them, but I must confess I still have my doubts. The 14th being the only cavalry we have, except 300 of [the] 20th will have a severe time of it, but ministers have been so deeply engaged with Mrs Clarke's† [affairs] that all consideration, I see by the papers, concerning army matters, are quite secondary.

I am extremely well mounted [having] 2 English horses and two Portuguese, one of them was made me a present and another belongs to the Prince Regent; therefore I am extremely well off. I shall receive pay from the moment of General Sherbrooke's arrival.‡ Whether this letter reaches you with the present of French ribbons at your disposal is quite uncertain, as I have to send it to Butler whom I accompanied down to the beach, and came up immediately to write as I was but just come into town with Sir John from the country, and was occupied from sunrise till sunset in riding over our position yesterday. Pray give my best love to my sisters and let me know about them and let me beseech of you not to wait for private conveyance, Felton gets his letters by every arrival, he has been ill a second time, but again

---

* Major General Sir Rowland Hill, known affectionately as 'daddy' Hill to the army; from his care for the welfare of his men.
† Mrs Mary Anne Clarke, a mistress of the Duke of York, had been guilty of using her influence to sell commissions, which activity temporarily forced the duke to resign as commander-in-chief.
‡ He became an official aide-de-camp, that is officially paid rather than an 'extra' subsidised by the commanding officer as soon as the army was augmented by the troops from Cadiz.

recovered. With best love to all, believe me, ever my dear uncle, your dutiful and affectionate nephew,

John Fremantle

PS The advance of the army this instant determined upon, how it will turn out a short time must show. I own I am not very sanguine as to a forward movement. God bless you, J. F.

Lisbon, 6 April 1809

My dear uncle,

I followed Butler out to sea with a dispatch of Sir John's, till dark, without being able to catch the packet. I believe the contents of his letter, was stating his extreme deficiency in cavalry. We march on Sunday, as I have transferred my packet to a Mr Croft. Best love; believe me, my dear uncle, your dutiful and affectionate nephew,

John Fremantle

Just as Sir John Cradock began to feel confident enough in his numbers to advance from Lisbon towards the enemy, the unexpected news arrived that Sir Arthur Wellesley had been exonerated by the board of enquiry and was heading back to Portugal to take command of the British forces. Cradock was to take command of the garrison at Gibraltar, a not unimportant position. John clearly felt for Cradock and believed that Wellesley was arriving just when a respectable force had been built up with which to advance, hence he would gain the laurels due to Cradock.

However, John makes it clear that he did not intend accompanying Cradock to Gibraltar, but rather his intention was to seek either to join Wellesley's Staff, or to rejoin his battalion which was now with the Army of Portugal.

8 April

My dear uncle,

We were apprised the day before yesterday of Sir A. Wellesley's appointment to the command of the army assembling in Portugal, and of Sir John's appointment at Gibraltar.

I certainly think there can be but one question upon the subject. Sir Arthur, no doubt, is the person whom the country look to, and ministers were perfectly right in so deciding; but you must consider that for the whole of the time Sir John Cradock has been in the country (now going on 4 months) had the enemy approached, which you know we have been in daily expectation of, there was no one decision that Sir John could have made, that he would not have been liable to censure for, perhaps Chelsea* at all events Mr Cobbett,† all of these by the bye, become very unpleasant considerations for officers nowadays. The greatest encomiums (of course) are passed by Lord Castlereagh on Sir John's conduct, when offering him the command of Gibraltar which he has begged leave to resign the first convenient opportunity that may suit Lord Castlereagh's arrangements.

He proceeds thither on the arrival of Sir Arthur, indeed it is a most heart breaking thing for poor Sir John to have been in the state of suspense he has been in for so long a time and the moment a respectable force arrives by which credit and reputation may be acquired, to be taken from the command, but if Sir Arthur does not make great haste, I think everything may be over before he arrives. The French remain nearly as per my last. The last division of our army marched this morning, and we are off tomorrow, the army halts at Leiria. God bless you, believe me, ever your most affectionate,
    John Fremantle

Don't wait for private conveyance of your letters. I shall ask Sir A[rthur] to take me certainly. If he cannot, the Coldstream are here and I do flatter myself not the most disreputable part of the army.

A week later General Wellesley had still not arrived and General Cradock continued to slowly move the army further up country.

Lisbon, 14 April 1809

My dear uncle,
After all I have said to you in my former letters about our departure, you will perhaps be a little surprised at my still dating from Lisbon, but the general set off at eight o'clock this morning to Mafra where he stayed the night on his way to Caldas [da Rainha], where he will arrive the day after tomorrow. The army will be assembled by the 17th between Santarem and Peniche, to which position Caldas is headquarters.

It is very difficult at present to judge of the intentions of the French; their movements are so very partial that it is impossible to decide. They have made no regular change of position since I last wrote to you and

---

* Chelsea had been the location for the recent Court of Inquiry into the Convention of Cintra. John therefore suggests that if the French had advanced then Cradock would have been liable to censure just like Wellesley, Burrard and Dalrymple had been for allowing the French to evacuate Portugal in British ships after being defeated in battle. I must thank Rory Muir for pointing this out.
† William Cobbett was an English pamphleteer and journalist, who strongly criticised progress of the war and called for radical reform of society.

whether we advance beyond our Santarem one, will of course depend on their movements. Sir John was prevented from going yesterday by the arrival of a convoy, which we thought it possible might bring Sir A. Wellesley, but it proved to be the 10th Brigade, I saw Charles Bishop* for five minutes looking extremely well, and quite gay, he says he does not regret having quitted Doctor's Commons.† The regiment are now landing and two squadrons will march on the 20th, and the rest on the 21st to join us. I am extremely glad they are arrived as we were in the greatest want of them. I am now waiting to go with Colonel Donkin‡ our quartermaster general, who goes by the way of Alenquer and has to report officially on the means of that route to Caldas, he asked the general to allow me to accompany him, which I am very glad to have an opportunity of doing.

God bless you my dear uncle, you must not expect to hear from me so regularly for the future. I fully expect I shall in my next letter have to give you an account of an action in which I think there is little doubt that we shall give the French a confounded licking, but the good that is to accrue from it afterwards, I think is very doubtful. With best love, believe me, your most affectionate nephew,

John Fremantle

News of the landing of General Wellesley caused John to contemplate his options, and he was grateful to learn of his uncle's exertions on his behalf with Sir Arthur. His regret at leaving General Cradock is manifest as he genuinely seems to have held him in very high regard, both personally and professionally.

Leiria, 25 April 1809

My dear uncle,§

A thousand thanks for your kind exertions for me with Sir A. Wellesley,

---

* John's cousin, Cornet Charles Twistleton Bishop, 16th Light Dragoons. Charles was John's first cousin. His father was Procurator General in charge of allocating prize money. His mother Marianne (née Fremantle) had helped to bring up John and his sisters.

† Doctors' Commons, also called the College of Civilians, was a society of lawyers practising civil law in London. Like the Inns of Court of the common lawyers, the society had buildings with rooms where its members lived and worked and a big library. Court proceedings of the civil law courts were also held in Doctors' Commons. Bishop's father was a lawyer who adjudicated in cases regarding prize money.

‡ Colonel Rufane Shaw Donkin.

§ John's Uncle William had known Wellington since 1788 when they were both in Dublin Castle as ADCs to the 1st Marquess of Buckingham, and John's father Stephen had been an MP in the Irish parliament with Wellington.

we heard of his arrival about an hour ago. I have just got your letters of 10th and 12th and we all set out in the course of half an hour for Lisbon to meet Sir Arthur. Sir John intended originally to ask him to take Lord Ebrington and myself, this joined to your communication with Sir A. I think will insure it, at all events there can be no chance of my coming home, or could I have gone to Gibraltar, my battalion being here, for I was transferred upon its coming out here. Sir John has resigned Gibraltar, but he must proceed thither according to orders, until he is relieved as requested.

I never was more sorry for anything in my life than for what has happened to Sir John, and he bears it so well, and so much like a gentleman. I really quite adore him, and I assure you however popular Sir A. may be, Sir John is universally respected by the army here.[*]

Nothing can be so complete as the situation in which the army will be delivered up to Sir Arthur; just look at your map, and you will see that Leiria is the prettiest position possible, for a man to start a campaign from, thank God that it has happened so for Sir John, of course it is a most mortifying thing for him, but I think he is well out of the scrape. God bless you my dear uncle, believe me, ever your dutiful and affectionate nephew,

John Fremantle

Having met Sir Arthur Wellesley, John was informed that he could no longer hold a Staff position until he had been a captain for a minimum of one year and so he must return to his regiment at Coimbra.

Lisbon, 28 April 1809

My dear uncle,

I arrived at Lisbon yesterday with Sir John, and have just seen Sir Arthur Wellesley who was extremely civil to me, but he says there is a positive order from the King himself, prohibiting any officer who has not been one year a captain holding any Staff situation whatever, I shall therefore wait here the two or three days Sir John remains previous to his sailing for Gibraltar, and then join my regiment at Coimbra where the whole army will be assembled in six days from the present date, that is the 4th of next month. Captain Burgh[†] is the only one of Sir John's family who has joined Sir Arthur Wellesley; Lord Ebrington goes on to Gibraltar. Sir John has been very unwell

---

[*] This is an interesting statement, as it seems routine for historians to paint Sir John Cradock as a bumbler, seemingly afraid to commit his troops to any action and simply awaiting orders to re-embark.

[†] Captain Ulysses Burgh, 92nd Foot, became an aide-de-camp to Wellington.

for this last week past with a bad cold in his face.

Sir Arthur sets off either this evening or early tomorrow morning, and I suppose will not stop until he arrives at Coimbra, General Mackenzie's Brigade* consisting of three regiments is to be stationed at Abrantes, and I suppose the remainder will proceed towards Oporto, but I know it is Sir John's opinion that there will be great risk in crossing the Douro.

There is the greatest possible want of forage of every sort, for the two last days we were at Leiria, Sir John had nothing but Indian corn, which they do not eat, and the 14th [Light Dragoons] have been for some time on nothing else. And when I left Leiria where they then were, I thought their horses looked very poor, they marched the day after to a place about six miles distant from Leiria, and I suppose must today or tomorrow will be on their route to Coimbra as they generally move first on account of the inability and inconvenience of removing forage into the interior. The 10th [Light] Dragoons have been stopped at Santarem where they can be conveyed to by water. The 3rd and 4th Dragoons will all be landed by tomorrow, but I very much fear our cavalry movements will be sadly cramped, for the further we go, the greater the difficulty will be in providing [for] them. The country affords nothing, positively nothing, and unless our own means can be conveyed to us, which will be attended with a considerable degree of difficulty, I do not see how it is possible for us to make a great movement. I rather think we shall remain at Coimbra until we hear something more decided of Victor's movements.

Felton had a very bad cold, and was looking certainly unwell when last I saw him. I have seen young Fitzgibbon† who I suppose you know is come out aide-de-camp to General Payne.‡

I have just heard there are 100 sail of transports off the river, but we often have such reports which prove to be without foundation. Adieu my dear uncle, with best love, believe me, your most dutiful and affectionate nephew,

John Fremantle

I suppose you are a little surprised at not hearing from Felton, but he has always been out the way of knowing of any useful sailing.

---

* Major General John Randoll Mackenzie commanded 2nd Brigade, actually consisting of 2/24th, 3/27th, 2/31st and 1/45th.

† Ensign the Honourable Richard Hobart Fitzgibbon 1st Foot Guards. Fitzgibbon was a cousin to John via his grandmother Arabella (née Fitzgibbon).

‡ Major General Sir William Payne was in command of the cavalry, he changed his surname to Gallwey in 1814.

John wrote in great detail to his uncle on his future prospects, now that he was a regimental officer again. As the Duke of York had promulgated new minimum periods of service before an officer could advance in rank, the prospect of remaining an ensign for three or four more years in the Guards was causing John to consider transferring to a regiment where he may gain seniority more quickly.

Lisbon, 30 April 1809

My dear uncle,

I only yesterday received your letter of the 6th by Dick Fitzgibbon, and that with your other two of the 10th and 12th which I answered before I left Leiria are the only ones I have received, although I have made the strictest enquiry of all the ships which have lately arrived. I think I mentioned in my last letter my intention of joining my regiment, and as Sir John is still indisposed, I may remain here still another week or more. I am anxious to be at Coimbra by the 4th which I shall but just do, by setting off tomorrow at daylight to Vila Franca [de Xira] by water, where my horse is just gone on to, and riding from thence to Rio Maior which is two stages [further]; General Payne is good enough to allow me to accompany him.

The lively interest you have always shown for my welfare, cannot but in this instance excite in me the highest sense of gratitude. It is your letter of the 6th which mentions the possibility (should it prove advisable) of your being able to procure for me, a company in a West India regiment,* as you may not be aware of the great difficulty there exists, and the great interest required to prevent officers joining these corps when once in them, in order I suppose to deter officers from the idea of these regiments being made stepping stools of. I think it as well to mention that I have just heard so, although as to what regards myself, having once embarked in this service, I am totally indifferent as to what part of the globe I serve in, or where I go to, and I think every consideration should be given way to for promotion. I understand by the new regulations that no officer can hold a majority before he has been seven years in the army, two of which he shall have been a captain and two a major before he can be a lieutenant colonel, which

---

* To help maintain the security of the very lucrative West Indian islands, and in an attempt to stem the horrendous losses suffered by British regiments from malaria and other crippling diseases, eight regiments of native (black) troops were raised but commanded by British officers. Despite various attempts to prevent it, these regiments were often used as stepping stones; officers gained a higher rank in these regiments at lower cost, but never actually joined them in the islands before exchanging to other regiments at their new higher rank.

makes nine.* I have now been three years and a half an ensign with still ten above me, by the last Army List I have seen, and I am afraid you will be a little astonished that I think it will be nearer that same time than two years, before I arrive at a lieutenancy by rotation in the regiment, and that when I get that step, there will be from seven to nine years between it and a company which by the longest calculation makes fourteen. Five years difference by quitting the Guards; but I am by no means sanguine about it, my standing at present being so very low, that the calculation is subject to great error, and at all events there is no loss in remaining one more year in my present situation, which time may give great insight into what it may, at the end of that period, be advisable to do. This is the nearest statement I can give you upon the matter but I think the subject requires a good deal of consideration and at the end of nine months or twelve months during which time I can be at no loss. I shall feel perfectly happy in its being left to your better judgment.

I have no news about the armies to tell you but [the] 16th [Light] Dragoons leave Santarem tomorrow I believe for Coimbra and one of the regiments of heavy [cavalry] supply their place there. With best love, believe me, my dear uncle, your most dutiful and affectionate nephew,

John Fremantle

---

* The Duke of York as commander-in-chief had brought these restrictions in to prevent the abuse of having very young adults being bought high rank by wealthy parents while having gained little or no military knowledge.

WITH THE REGIMENT

The 1st Battalion Coldstream Guards commanded by Lieutenant Colonel Hulse[*] had arrived at Lisbon with General Sherbrooke's force on 13 March 1809, numbering 33 officers, 1,120 rank and file and 17 women.[†] The battalion was originally sent to Belem barracks but were soon sent on to Sacavem, where they remained until April, when they moved to Leiria via Batalha. At this point John left Sir John Cradock and joined his battalion.

With the arrival of Wellesley and large reinforcements, a mood of expectation and great activity seems to have permeated the reinvigorated army. On 1 May the Guards Brigade, consisting of the 1st Coldstream and 1st Battalion 3rd Guards marched into Coimbra, the Oxford of Portugal, to great public joy. Wellesley joined the army at Coimbra the following day and having inspected his 25,000 troops, ordered the march on Oporto on 6 May which Marshal Soult still held. Arriving on the southern bank of the Douro on 12 May Wellesley launched a bold attack across the river at a point hidden from the French and successfully formed a bridgehead threatening the French line of communications with Spain, thereby forcing Soult to abandon the city in haste. John was an eyewitness to the whirlwind campaign.

Oporto, 13 May 1809

My dear uncle,
Since I last wrote to you from Lisbon, circumstances have taken a total change, and I am sure I very little expected so soon to have the satisfaction of giving you such a glorious account of the success of the British Armies, for I think everyone must look upon our entry here as great an achievement as was ever accomplished; it appears to us present, quite like a dream. The cavalry consisting of the 14th, 16th

---

[*] Lieutenant Colonel Richard Hulse.
[†] Mackinnon, *Origin and Services of the Coldstream Guards*, p. 103.

and the 20th [Light Dragoons], 4 battalions of the German Legion,* a
brigade under General Hill,† and one under General Richard Stewart‡
left Coimbra on the 6th and when arrived at the [River] Vouga, Sir
Arthur learnt that the French on the opposite side, chiefly cavalry
were in total ignorance of our movement and in consequence surprised
them in the morning of the 10th, following up the 11th, and yesterday
morning at three o'clock the French crossed the Douro, blew up the
bridges, and then I suppose considered themselves perfectly secure for
the rest of the day; but our brigade which had arrived at the Vila Nova
[de Gaia] about noon, could perfectly distinguish our troops which
had crossed the river in a miraculous manner in the face of the enemy
without losing a man, driving the French before them. We had not more
than 4,000 men engaged which behaved with their usual steadiness.
General Paget§ was wounded early in the action, and I am happy to
say our loss is very trifling and I do not hear of a single officer killed,¶
we have taken eleven guns and about 500 prisoners, and the peasantry
are bringing in more every hour. The French have left 5,000 here, and
I believe their whole force now does not consist of 15,000 men, and
by every account these are in a very bad state. I questioned a French
officer yesterday that was taken who told me that Laborde their best
officer was wounded.**

The Brigade of Guards was formed for three o'clock above
the town of Oporto, and before we left our ground could plainly
distinguish the French straggling very much, and taking up a position
about two leagues distant, I suppose to cover their retreat, but we hear
that General Beresford is at Amarante with the Portuguese, and four
thousand British and that Silveira is not far distant. Our army marches
tomorrow, the Guards are to be in advance, and I hope we shall be up
with them before three days. The troops that were engaged returned
I think about five o'clock so that we have as yet had nothing to do.
Felton has gained the greatest credit, he charged with one squadron of
the 14th (all that happened to be up at the time) through and through
their ranks but was wounded in cutting his passage back again, another
officer of the squadron is also wounded and the other officer had his

---

* The 1st, 2nd, 5th & 7th Line Battalions.
† Major General Sir Rowland Hill commanded the 1st Brigade.
‡ Brevet Colonel Richard Stewart commanded the 6th Brigade.
§ Major General Sir Edward Paget was severely wounded; he went home to recuperate.
¶ According to Oman, one officer was killed on the allied side, a Portuguese ensign
of the 1/16th, but of course John means no British officer.
** General de Division Henri Delaborde is not recorded as having been wounded at
Oporto, but General de Brigade Maximilien Foy was.

knee shot.* Felton never quitted his horse, and I saw him returning with his right arm dreadfully fractured but still in the greatest spirits. He has since lost it high above the elbow [by amputation]; I am told he rose from the operation wonderfully. I have myself seen the surgeon this morning, a very clever man, who tells me he slept for several hours last night, that the fever is very slight, and that he is doing extremely well. I shall see him myself before I go. Everybody gives him the greatest praise for his conduct during the three days. There has not been a single prisoner taken that had not his two watches, and in general a great deal of gold. I am told that within these last two days they have sent away 18 millions of money.† James Butler's house has been greatly damaged by them.

I am a good [deal] fatigued by the march which for the four days has been very severe. I have made 50 guineas by the disposal of my English horses, but was only able to get two month's pay as aide-de-camp. I retain my Portuguese pony for myself to ride on the march and another to carry my baggage.

I have been greatly inconvenienced by the order for all the officers' servants who are soldiers being obliged to join their regiments on the march, the time that one has most need for them and in consequence have been obliged to hire a Portuguese. I am very glad the little mare pleases you; I hope you will keep her. I got the four letters you speak of in your letter of the 10th on the 5th of this month, they must have passed me on my way to Coimbra, Charles Bishop I have not seen since we left Coimbra. But I hear he is quite well.

With best love believe me, my dear uncle, your most dutiful and affectionate nephew,

John Fremantle

Charles Bishop was of course in the affair of the 10th for all the cavalry was engaged that morning and Lincoln Stanhope was wounded in the

---

* The cavalry had been sent to Barca de Avintes to cross the Douro and so arrived on the flank of Soult's force as it hastily retreated from Oporto. It was the perfect moment for the cavalry, but their commander, Murray hesitated. General Charles Stewart rode up and ordered a single squadron of the 14th Light Dragoons to charge their rearguard. Delaborde was unhorsed and nearly captured and Foy was wounded in the arm. Of 110 men in the charge 35 were killed or wounded, but they in turn killed, wounded or captured some 300. Major Felton Hervey who commanded was severely wounded in the arm which was subsequently amputated for which he was granted a pension of £300 per annum. The other officers recorded as wounded were Captain Peter Hawker and Lieutenant Robert Knipe.

† Presumably this would be 18 million escudos, approximately £4 million, worth around £136 million today.

shoulder.* I dine with Sir Arthur today, Fitzroy Stanhope† goes home with the dispatches.

Confidential, 13 May, 9 o'clock

My dear uncle,

In my letter I have given you a plain, and I believe a correct, statement of what has happened to poor Felton, and you of course will break the subject in the best manner to his mother. I am just returned from having been with him for two hours, he is very composed, and doing extremely well, and his spirits have never left him. I understand he was not at all too impetuous, but quite steady, but could not retain his men and it was in the act of calling them off, that he received the wound; he did great execution among them and at last left his sword in a Frenchman. I learnt at Sir Arthur's this evening that the French were burning their gun carriages and magazines and flying in the direction of Braga. We march tomorrow at daybreak.

God bless you my dear uncle, your ever dutiful and affectionate nephew,

John Fremantle

Although the Brigade of Guards were not engaged, they were thanked by Sir Arthur for their steady and soldier-like conduct in passing the river and forming afterwards and it was on their approach that the French gave way to the troops that were engaged.

The army was sent in pursuit of Soult, with the Guards in the van-guard, but an army that flees via mountain tracks, having abandoned all cumbersome equipment will always outrun an army that retains its equipment, and the army eventually returned to Oporto on 24 May.

Oporto, 28 May 1809

My dear uncle,

We marched from hence as I told you in my last was the intention on the 14th, and reached Braga on the 16th, which the French had not quitted more than 12 hours. General Payne with the cavalry was within sight of them the following morning by 10 o'clock; the Brigade of Guards came up by 5 in the evening, and followed them till dark, the light infantry only having been engaged. We halted that night at a place called Salamonde, nearly thirty miles from Braga, the French set on fire everything that was the least likely to afford covering for troops,

---

* Major the Honourable Lincoln Edward Stanhope, 16th Light Dragoons.
† Lieutenant and Captain Fitzroy Henry Richard Stanhope, 1st Foot Guards, aide-de-camp to Wellesley.

and it has never ceased raining from the time we first left Oporto, to this moment, which of course has reduced the troops a good deal. They were also very frequently without spirits and provisions. We proceeded after them two days' march beyond Salamonde in the direction of Montalegre, to a small place called Tradas, where we gave up the pursuit, knowing that they had burnt all their gun carriages, destroyed their tumbrils, baggage, etc., and given up the military chest to plunder (I suppose to prevent desertion) and understanding they had taken the road across the mountains in the direction of Melgaco and Orense, finally I suppose to form junction with Marshal Ney.* General Beresford was at Chaves with his corps as early as the 16th, and had they retreated in that direction, which was imagined he would be obliged to do for want of provisions, he would have been cut to pieces between the two fires, or have surrendered, and as it is, I should think his army must starve before it reaches Ney or any place where he can gets supplies. All the prisoners we took between the 16th and 20th had had nothing to eat but Indian Corn since the day they left Oporto, and they told us the rest of their army was in the same condition, and that in short the soldiers had thrown away their arms and ammunition, and were flying in the greatest consternation. I believe the Portuguese are now in pursuit of them, and are turning the tables on them with redoubled vengeance, for every poor unfortunate tired or wounded Frenchman that falls into their power is sure to lose his life, and even be abused afterwards, but horrid as the reflection is, I do not wonder at it, having seen during our march as many sometimes as three peasants hanging at a single tree by the road side, and the cruelties that were committed by them on coming into this town, are I am told, not to be credited, but by a person who was on the spot to have been an eye witness. Marshal Victor† whose force I understand has accumulated to 40,000 is said to have been at Alcantara some days ago, and there was a report yesterday that he had again retired.

Our army I hear is to be concentrated about Coimbra, in General Orders yesterday it mentioned that it was to be halted; perhaps the idea may be, to wait in position hereabouts until the arrival of reinforcements expected, or till Victor's decided intention is discovered, or to rest the men which is more probable, and very much wanted. You know by my last letter of General Mackenzie's corps at Abrantes, which I dare say is 6,000 men, the present head of our column (that is to say that part of the army which was in the rear

---

* Marshal Michel Ney, Duke of Elchingen, was ordered to subdue the Asturias and Galicia.

† Marshal Claude Victor-Perrin, Duc de Belluno, commanded the I Corps in Spain.

of the Guards on the advance) may have been at Coimbra these two or three days. The Brigade of Guards marches tomorrow, I heard it was to make a halt of some days at Agueda on the way to Coimbra. I don't know of anything else interesting to tell you, Wellesley was monstrous angry at Soult's escape, as you will easily imagine, and indeed we were all very much disappointed, expecting to have had their whole army. The only thing we blame them for, and for which I should think Soult can never show his face to Bonaparte again for, is, not annihilating us while crossing the Douro, which was perfectly in their power, however as it succeeded it tells very well, and the French themselves own that it was as masterly a thing as ever was done, otherwise their retreat once begun wonderfully well conducted, at all events it is a great triumph to us, chasing these fellows, who are the very same that were at the heels of our army through Spain. However they speak in the highest terms, and give every credit to our retreat [with Moore].

I returned here three days ago and have since dined in company with a French captain of dragoons by the name of Argenton,[*] who was deputed by a number of the officers among which were three or four Field officers to make known to us their discontent and disaffection under their present government. He was taken and discovered when returning a second time to ascertain some point that was not clearly understood, and sentenced to be shot the very day we entered the town. Upon their retreat he was carried off but the second day contrived to make good his escape by cutting his way through his escort and making a wonderful leap. Sir A. Wellesley has bought his horse. The man's adventures upon the Vouga before he joined us and escaped altogether would furnish ample materials for a romance, he went off last night to Lisbon, and from thence goes to England with introductory letters to Lord Castlereagh, indeed his mission appears to be of the utmost importance, and I know Sir Arthur thinks so. He says that disaffection is general throughout the army and that Bonaparte is not to be Emperor 6 months longer. I removed Felton out of the town two days ago to a very pleasant country house about a mile off. He was able to walk in his garden the day before yesterday and slept very well the night before last, and yesterday there was the greatest amendment in him, he had scarcely any fever left. I am just now going to see him, and if I have time will send you today's account. I think he seems to expect that Lionel will come over. The cavalry have remained at Braga, I believe for the

---

[*] See Oman's *History of the Peninsular War Volume II*, appendix 2, for Wellesley's personal memorandum regarding Argenton.

convenience of forage I have heard of Charles Bishop he was well. I assure you he is very much liked in the regiment; he takes soundly to his duty. God bless you, my dear uncle, with best love, believe me, ever your dutiful and affectionate nephew,

    John Fremantle

TALAVERA

Although his letter did not indicate it, the army was to march again that very day; this time to attack Marshal Victor in central Spain. They marched through Leiria and Thomar to Abrantes and then into Spain, through Salvatierra to Plasencia, from where John wrote again.

Plasencia, 14 July 1809

My dear uncle,

We marched according as I mentioned to you in my last letter dated Abrantes [not found], from thence the next morning, and arrived at this place the 10th. None of the troops are in the town, but the whole army are halted in the woods in the neighbourhood. The 23rd, 16th, and 14th [Light] Dragoons marched in yesterday. Sir Arthur Wellesley arrived the day before yesterday from Cuesta's army, having remained with him one entire day, his headquarters are at Almaraz, and I understand he has with him some 20 to 30,000 men, of which the officers who accompanied Sir Arthur, make a very good report. Cuesta has taken up a very strong position in the neighbourhood of Almaraz.

A French general of cavalry by the name of Franceschi,* with his two aides-de-camp, who commanded the cavalry last year against us in Spain, and also lately at the affair on the Vouga, has been made prisoner by a Capuchin with a few armed peasants, he was going express from Soult to account to King Joseph for evacuating Portugal, all the papers were taken upon him, and Soult makes out a very good story, but however, we know for certain, that his army is for the present, and will be for a considerable time, completely hors de combat. Franceschi was brought to Sir Arthur at Zarza, when he exclaimed 'Ma foi, c'est grand malheur, un général de la cavalry Française, même général de hussars, d'être pris par un Capuchin, ce n'est pas même la fortune de la guerre'. [Indeed, it is great bad luck for a French general of cavalry, and general

---

* General of Division Jean-Baptiste Franceschi-Delonne died while in Spanish custody 23 October 1810.

of hussars at that, to be captured by a Capuchin. It is not even the luck of war.]

Victor's army I understand does not amount to 25,000 men, they are at present at Talavera and Toledo, some say entrenched at the former place, but I heard yesterday at Sir Arthur's, where I dined, that they were in total ignorance of our approach.

General Craufurd's* force is expected there by the 16th, and I suppose our whole army will be in motion by the 20th. It will be a most glorious thing if we can annihilate Victor's column, we shall then have a little respite at Madrid while the junta is re-establishing.

I was laid up a couple of days at Zarza with a slight fever and have at present got a billet in the town, but I shall be able to join the regiment by the time we march. General Payne has been particularly civil to me. I am to live with him as long as we remain here. God bless you my dear uncle, with best love, believe me, your dutiful and affectionate nephew,
John Fremantle

I suppose Felton has long arrived [in England], but I never heard for certain of his having left Oporto.

The army met with General Cuesta's Spanish army at Talavera, where Wellesley was to be frustrated by Cuesta's indecision, thereby missing a golden opportunity to strike Victor's before reinforcements arrived. Too late the Spanish unilaterally advanced, only to be chased back by Victor's reinforced army. Wellesley agreed to make a determined stand alongside Cuesta along the line of the Alberche streamlet. The Brigade of Guards played a significant part in the subsequent Battle of Talavera on 28 July, at one time losing their discipline in advancing too far. John provides an eye witness account of events but does not mention the Guard's adventures at all.

Camp near Talavera, 30 July 1809

My dear uncle,

Nothing extraordinary occurred on our march from Placencia where I last wrote to you from, till our approach near this place. Our advance was partially engaged on the 20th and 21st. The main body of the army arrived here the 22nd as did also the whole of the Spanish force under Cuesta, amounting to from 30 to 40,000 men.† On the morning of the

---

* The Light Brigade of General Robert Craufurd was not to arrive until 29 July having completed a severe forced march in a vain attempt to reach the army before the Battle of Talavera was fought.
† Cuesta's army numbered approximately 35,000 at Talavera.

23rd our army was formed in column by two o'clock but remained till eight before we were marched off, I understand, waiting for provisions promised to Sir Arthur by Cuesta. The head of our column reached the River Alberche, on the opposite side of which the French were formed, by 12 o'clock, when we were halted, and shortly afterwards, orders came for our return to the ground that we occupied the night before, and to be in the same spot and in the same order by four o'clock on the 24th, which took place, but we found that the French rearguard had decamped four or five hours previous to our arrival. General Sherbrooke followed with a brigade of cavalry, and about 9,000 infantry, and the whole of the Spanish force, about eight leagues, when the French who had received considerable reinforcements, attacked, and drove the Spaniards back, who returned to the town on the 26th and 27th in the greatest possible confusion and disorder, Sherbrooke forming a rear guard to them.*

The French crossed the river on the 27th, our cavalry keeping them in check till the Spaniards took up their position on the right covering the town of Talavera, and the English on their right and left with the extreme left appui'd[†] to some tolerable strong rising ground, which the French made a desperate attack upon between 6 and 7 in the evening, knowing that had they gained those heights we must have surrendered, or have been annihilated, as they enfiladed the whole of our line as far as the town an extent of nearly three miles. They succeeded in getting through our first line, but in the end were totally repulsed, and all was tolerably quiet until about three o'clock, the 28th when a similar desperate push was made by them upon the Spaniards in front of the town where there was a battery manned by the English, and they were there again repulsed with great slaughter. At daybreak a very heavy regular cannonade commenced by them against our left, which we returned. 15,000 men again attempted to gain the heights on our extreme left, but were charged and repelled by General Hill's Division not half their number. We were still very much annoyed by their artillery and the light infantry on both sides were warmly engaged. About noon a grand attack was made against the whole of our line, which ended in their total defeat, and finally their retreat which was covered in a most masterly manner by their sharp shooters, artillery and cavalry, which filed off a little after dark, and we remained in exactly the same position that we first occupied.

---

* Cuesta did take his army in pursuit of Victor and was forced to retreat hurriedly when King Joseph and Soult arrived with more troops; however, no British troops went with Cuesta, nor did they form the rearguard.

† Appui means anchored by.

The whole attack was solely upon the British, I suppose not more than 18,000,[*] and all accounts agree that the French were not a man less than 45,000[†] commanded by King Joseph in person. Sebastiani[‡] is said to be killed, two days' spirits was served out to the French previous to their attack. Their loss of course I cannot tell, but we have suffered very considerably, and bought our victory dearly.[§]

Generals Mackenzie and Langwerth[¶] are killed, Hill and the two General Campbells wounded.[**] The Coldstream have three officers killed, 9 wounded,[††] and 3rd Guards 5 officers killed 6 wounded and about 500 killed and wounded in the brigade.[‡‡] In the company I belong to Sir W. Sheridan and Jenkinson are wounded, the command naturally devolved upon me, two sergeants and 22 men are minus in the company out of 88 that it was complete to before the action. The French are said to be in full retreat, but whether we are to follow them I know not.

To give you an idea, how much we ourselves are beaten, the men scarcely yet feel the victory they have gained. I never was more surprised or glad of anything in my life as when I found they were going off. I suppose there never was a more desperate action fought, with the exception of two hours, we were 28 hours exposed to a constant fire. My account is of course liable to a great many errors, but I have given it you as correct as I could scrape it together. General Craufurd with the Light Brigade came yesterday, if he had been up the day before I think the business would have been put an end to much sooner. Bryan the Adjutant of the Coldstream was wounded very early, since which I have been acting, and as no one senior to me accepts it, most probably I shall get it for a permanency, if so, when I

---

[*] Wellesley's total force actually numbered just over 20,000 men.

[†] Oman calculates the French Army at 46,000 men.

[‡] General Sebastiani was not killed.

[§] Oman calculates British losses at Talavera at 4,521 killed and wounded; the French lost 7,268 killed and wounded.

[¶] Brigadier General Ernest Eberhad Kuon von Langwerth.

[**] Major General Rowland Hill was slightly wounded, as was Brigadier General Alexander Campbell, while Brigadier General Henry Frederick Campbell was severely wounded.

[††] The Coldstream dead were Lieutenant Colonel Ross, Captain Beckett and Ensign Parker; the nine wounded were Lieutenant Colonels Stibbert and Sheridan, Captains Millman, Christie, Collier, Wood, Bouverie (Staff) Bryan and Jenkinson (these last two died of their wounds) and Ensign Sandilands. Losses in 3rd Guards were dead, Captains Walker, Buchanan and Dalrymple, Ensign Ram and Adjutant Irby; wounded were Lieutenant Colonel Gordon, Major Fotheringham, Captain Giels and Ensigns Aitchison, Towers and Scott.

[‡‡] Total losses of the Guards Brigade was 609 killed and wounded.

get to the top of the list of ensigns, whether there is a vacancy or not, I get my lieutenancy for nothing.

Just before the action the news arrived that the Spaniards were 22,000 strong at Toledo therefore as we have paved the way, if Cuesta now only follows up the show with any vigour we ought to have no more trouble. I hope to God it may be so, for I candidly confess I am tired of the campaign, and of the unthankful inhabitants of this wretched country. The army has advanced ever since we left Abrantes; I am only surprised it has kept its health so well.

I saw Charles Bishop last night he was quite well. Pray give my best love to all my friends and believe me, my dear uncle, your dutiful and affectionate nephew,

John Fremantle

I forget to mention that the reason of our returning on the 23rd was on account of Cuesta's begging Sir Arthur to defer the attack till the next morning as he had not quite finished his arrangements for the attack. The French were then not 20,000 strong, and would have fought us all the same. We have taken 19 pieces of cannon.*

John wrote again from Talavera. Cuesta's force had pursued the retreating French while Wellesley was forced to remain. His army, having no provisions, were virtually starving as Spanish promises had come to nought.

Talavera, 1 August 1809

My dear uncle,

Since my letter of the 30th nothing has been done, we are still in our old position, and I have just heard, that the French have moved off the rear guard they left on the heights on the opposite side of the Alberche, and the Spaniards are following them. I think it would be a very difficult matter to decide upon what will be the result of the battle, nor I believe Sir Arthur knows himself; everyone is in total ignorance as to what is now to become of us, but one thing is pretty certain that we cannot remain long in our present station, for if we do, we shall either starve, or be carried away by a pestilential fever, arising from the vapours of the dead bodies, which though every exertion has been used from the first moment to inter, are still in great numbers.

I have just heard that the French within the last two days, moved 300 wagon loads of sick and have taken the direction of Madrid.

Although I am appointed Adjutant to the battalion here, yet my

---

* According to Wellesley's return they captured seventeen guns.

name has never been regularly given as a candidate to the Horse Guards, which is a customary thing to do. I should therefore be much obliged to you to speak to Smyth* or any other of the Coldstream to give in my name officially to guard against any other person doing so before me, which might perhaps displace me.

Great doubts are entertained of Bryan's recovery, and if he does recover, he will never be able to officiate, therefore there is no reason, why, in that case I should not get the appointment.

Charles Bishop is quite well, but I wish you would tell his father when he writes to him to recommend him to pay attention of the advice of his brother officers, who I am convinced are all very well disposed towards him, and Charles who is very young in the world and of course liable sometimes to go astray, cannot bear to have it mentioned to him, he minds me very much, and whenever I am near him I always indulge him with a lecture,† but I will write to you more about him, the first time I am more at leisure. Pray give my best love to my sisters, and believe me, ever my dear uncle, your most dutiful and affectionate nephew,

John Fremantle

The Spaniards expect medals for the battle I suppose though they won't consider the English as deserving of them. I hope Felton is doing well. I have never heard from you.

John's aunt wrote to Uncle William to congratulate him on the survival of his surrogate son.

From Mrs J. Fremantle,‡ 18 August 1809

My dear William,

I rejoice with you most truly at John's safety; he has indeed had a most fortunate escape and it is truly melancholy to see the returns of the killed, and wounded; I shudder for the sufferings of those who are left behind to lament their loss. I leave this place on Monday for your mother's§ as on the 28th I am to be at Stowe. Lady Buckingham wrote me the kindest letter in answer to mine, wherein I said I should bring Mrs Fremantle with me, her reply was, that she would be very happy to see her 'for she is one of those who having been once seen is

---

* Captain and Lieutenant Colonel George Smyth, Coldstream Guards.
† John was actually only one year older than Bishop.
‡ Catherine Henley had married Colonel John Fremantle (another uncle of our John, who had died in 1805) she was therefore sister-in-law to Uncle William Fremantle.
§ Frances Fremantle (née Edwards) was an heiress from a Bristol family.

wished for again'. Her expressions are very flattering and I am sure she deserves them. I positively shall go from Stowe on the 4th September; I should (with you) be sorry for her to relinquish the Ball at Egham or any other pleasure. Therefore if she is at Stowe by the 2nd it will do, although you think it better for me to pick her up at Buckingham on the 4th, only let me know hers, or your destination, before I go to Stowe, for it will look foolish my saying she is to join me there on the 2nd if she does not come. Tom* meets me on Tuesday (with his wife) at your mother's. Therefore I can ask him to forward Georgiana† to Stowe on the 2nd if you like.

God Bless you, my kind love to your wife and Georgiana, and believe me, ever your most affectionate,
Catherine Fremantle

A week later, John wrote from south of the River Tagus; news that Marshal Soult was marching into Wellesley's rear caused the army to march rapidly towards Oropesa with the intention of attacking Soult. However, Wellesley was suddenly undeceived as to the clear superiority of Soult's force:‡ he crossed the Tagus at Arzobispo en route for Badajoz and Elvas. Wellesley had left his numerous wounded under the protection of Cuesta at Talavera, but Cuesta, frightened by shadows, soon retreated, abandoning the wounded to Marmont soon afterwards. Not unlike many in the army at this time, John questioned their incursion into Spain, being less than impressed with the Spanish army. He also appears to be unsure who won the battle; but the British claimed a victory, having held the ground and Wellesley was created Viscount Wellington.

At camp near Merida, 25 August 1809

My dear uncle,
After the action on the 28th we remained at Talavera till the 3rd of this month, when we marched to Oropesa, with the intention of attacking Soult near Plasencia. Sir Arthur having previously agreed with Cuesta, that he should be at Talavera with his army till at least the evening of the 4th, but in the morning at daybreak, when our army was on the point of marching, Cuesta arrived, in consequence of which we crossed the Tagus at the Bridge of Arzobispo that night. The bridge at Almaraz had been previously blown up by the Spaniards, and the French were

---

* Uncle Captain Thomas Fremantle RN who was married to Betsy Wynne (the diarist) and had been a good friend of Lord Nelson.
† Georgiana was John's elder sister whose godmother was Lady Buckingham.
‡ Early reports led Wellesley to believe Soult only had 15,000 men, but in reality he commanded nearly 50,000 troops.

in possession of the town, therefore you will readily conceive our situation was a little unpleasant. The possibility of destroying the bridge at Arzobispo was suggested to Cuesta as soon as his army should have passed it, but Sir Arthur was given the answer that he need be under no apprehension from that as long as there was a soldier in the army the passage of the bridge should be defended. However on the 6th at Deleitosa we understood that the French had crossed the river, and the Spaniards were in retreat. Sir Arthur when arrived at their lines, about four miles from [El Bercial?], out of the 30,000 then they mustered four days before, did not find 10 remaining, and even have since learned for certain, that there were never more than 40 dragoons who crossed the river at a ford, dispersed what they call their army, and took all their cannon. Cuesta thwarted Sir Arthur's plans from the very commencement, I believe they have now found out he is a traitor, at least he is displaced from the command of the army, and I understand the control of it given to Sir Arthur. This I doubt very much.* The Spanish General Venegas[†] has been dispersed near Toledo, who we expected so much from, and Sir Robert Wilson has met with a similar disgrace with his corps near Banos,[‡] and I should think the French must equally laugh at us for our folly. Will the good people of England never find out that their army has no business in this country, or has Sir Arthur entered it, this time, without orders? I look forward with great joy to our return to Portugal for it is really England in comparison to this country, and the Portuguese, bad as they are, are angels compared with the Spaniards; it has not been an unusual thing to have to send as much as 14 miles for a bit of bread the size of a three-penny loaf which we were very glad to give three shillings for. Headquarters were at Jaraicejo the 11th and the army encamped on the banks of the River Almonte until the 20th. They were at Merida the 24th and reached this yesterday and the army is encamped on the Guadiana. They move again the day after tomorrow and reach Elvas on the 30th, and the army to be stationed between that and Alcantara, the Guards are to be at Campo Maior. Our sick and wounded to the amount of 2,500 are prisoners at Talavera.[§] The French entered [on]

---

* This was not true; the Spanish were jealous of control of their armies and it was four years later before Wellesley (then Wellington) gained control of Spanish forces.

† Francisco Javier Venegas de Saavedra, Marqués de la Reunión y de Nueva España was sent in 1810 to protect the Spanish interests in Mexico.

‡ General Robert Wilson and his Loyal Lusitanian Legion troops were defeated near the mountain pass of Puerto de Baños.

§ Mackinnon, who actually commanded the British hospital station at Talavera, marched with some 2,000 wounded to Elvas before the French arrived; but he states in *Origin and Services of the Coldstream Guards*, p. 121, that the French captured the 6th but behaved in the handsomest manner to our people. Captain Christie and Sandilands of our regiment are exchanged; all the other officers are to be sent to Madrid.*

I am sure you will be very much shocked to hear of Henry Neville's death,† he was very ill and much reduced by a violent dysentery some time before the battle but he could not be persuaded to take care of himself, and after it, he continued taking his share of the outpost duty. The fever came on him at Trujillo, and on his way to Elvas, where all the sick are now ordered to, he died at Santa Cruz [de la Sierra], on the 21st then just a day's journey from Trujillo, at nine o'clock in the morning. If it had not been for his brigade passing through, nobody would have known who he was, or anything about him. Most of the officers of the Brigade of Guards attended his burial that night.

Sir Arthur Wellesley sent to me yesterday to say that he had appointed me to his Staff, but he did not want me to quit my regimental duties, I do not know who makes the vacancy, but I am to have pay from today, I have not seen him yet to thank him, but I am going to dine with him today. Believe me ever, my dear uncle, your most dutiful and affectionate nephew,
John Fremantle

The not taking me from the battalion is just what I, at the present moment, could have wished, particularly if we are likely to return to England, as it does not take away from my claim to the adjutancy. You may as well not mention to any of the wives of the regiment my appointment as ADC.‡

The very same day that John wrote this long letter, Arthur Wellesley wrote to his uncle to confirm that John had been taken on as one of

---

six lieutenant colonels, three majors, sixteen captains, thirty two lieutenants and eleven ensigns along with 2,000 rank and file, with one staff surgeon and twenty-one assistant surgeons when they entered Talavera. All witnesses agree that the French took great care of the British sick.

* The Coldstream prisoners were Lieutenant Colonel Sir William Sheridan, Captains Christie, Millman and Bryan, Ensign Sandilands and Assistant Surgeon Whymper. Mackinnon does not mention that Christie and Sandilands were exchanged, but both were severely wounded and left the regiment soon after.

† Captain the Honourable Henry Neville, 14th Light Dragoons. Hall has his death dated as 30 July, whereas Fremantle states 21 August which seems more likely.

‡ Although performing the role of adjutant since Talavera, John was not gazetted in the role until 18 November 1809. The official date of John being appointed to Wellesley's 'family' as aide-de-camp was also November 1809, but he was to continue in his regimental role for the time being.

his aides-de-camp; but he would leave him serving with his regiment as adjutant for the present time, to further his military education.

Merida, 25 August 1809

My dear Fremantle,
I have at last been able to do something for your nephew. I intended to appoint him my aide-de-camp at first, but I understand that the king had declared that he intended his regulation respecting the period of service required for Staff officers, to extend to aides de camp as well as others. Indeed I saw Taylor's letter upon the subject; so that I could not be uninformed. I conclude however that His Majesty has been softened; and I observe that the regulation as originally withheld has not been altered or explained.

In the meantime my family was full, and I had nothing for your nephew, excepting a place at dinner whenever he was hungry; and he has been doing duty with his regiment which I don't think has been injurious to him; and he is now doing the duty of Adjutant instead of major. Besides this my aide-de-camp Stanhope* having gone home; I have appointed Fremantle in his room; insisting however that he shall continue to do his duty as Adjutant of the Guards, which will be a much better thing for him than to be only about headquarters. I hope that you approve of all this. Pray make my best compliments to Mrs Fremantle. I hope that Hervey is quite well, remember me to him & believe me, ever yours most sincerely,
Arthur Wellesley

The Brigade of Guards marched from Merida on 2 September to Talavera la Real, where huts were constructed to shade themselves from the fierce sun.

Camp near Talavera la Real, 21 September 1809

My dear uncle,
Since my letter from the camp near Merida, no material occurrence has taken place. We marched from thence on the 2nd of the month and reached this place on the 4th. Headquarters is at Badajoz three leagues from here. Lord Wellington has been indisposed for some time; and is now confined with an ague. It has been reported here for the last two days that headquarters were likely to be removed to Lisbon, as soon as Wellington was well enough. There are hospitals established at Elvas and Villa Vicosa. The army is encamped by divisions near the

---

* See the editor's *Eyewitness to the Peninsular War and the Battle of Waterloo*, Barnsley, 2010.

villages in the neighbourhood of Badajoz. The division which consists of the Guards, a brigade of Germans, and the brigades of the line is under Sherbrooke. We are all in total ignorance as to what is further to become of us, but I believe there is not a man in the army who is not ready to quit this inhospitable clime. I have never received a letter from you since Lord Wellington's arrival in May, nor can I at all account for it. If you have franked them, they will remain at Falmouth, for I am told that a member [of parliament] has no right to frank a letter out of the kingdom. The letters which are put into the post, with the inland postage paid, never fail to arriving [*sic*] safely. At present it is a most distressing thing to me for mail after mail to arrive, and never to have heard from you since we first began our peregrinations. The directions should be with the army under Lord Wellington. I hope my aunt and the young ladies are quite well. Pray give my best love to them and believe me ever, my dear uncle, your dutiful and affectionate nephew,
John Fremantle

The brigade moved into the fortress of Badajoz on 10 October. Little occurred apart from John almost becoming embroiled in a matter of honour regarding his cousin Charles Bishop.

Badajoz, 12 October 1809
My dear uncle,
I received your letter of the 13th September on the 4th of this month, and that of August 23rd the day before, which was the first I had received since I was first at Coimbra in the beginning of May last. I assure you it afforded me great relief, for I was not entirely without apprehensions respecting you, not having heard of you for such a length of time, besides which I was by no means well myself at that time, having been laid up several days with the dysentery, a common complaint amongst us all, but I am now thank God quite recovered, though a little pulled down still.

It was not until after two days someone thought proper to remove us from our camp at Talavera Real to this place where we have been since the 10th.

Sherbrooke was knighted at this place the 7th, and Lord Wellington set off after the ceremony for Lisbon. What to do? Perhaps you in England are more likely to know than we do. God grant it may be to make arrangements for our army to quit this truly wretched and horrid country, we are not only sick of it, but very many I really believe have died of it. The sickness of the Scheldt army hardly exceeds ours.*

---

* Five companies of the 2nd Battalion Coldstreams embarked with the huge force

Captain Christie of the Coldstream arrived here yesterday from Talavera. Mr Sandilands the other officer who has got his exchange was not sufficiently recovered to undertake the journey when Captain Christie came away. He brings an account of Bryan's death, and also of Colonel Donellan of the 48th Regiment,* they were both buried by the French with military honours on the 2nd September. He speaks in the highest terms of the conduct of the French towards our people on every occasion. The Brigade of Guards is, with very few exceptions, the only one that has not lost any officers by sickness since the battle, the Heavy Brigade of cavalry have at this moment 21 sick officers. Colonel Dalbiac of the 4th Dragoons† was not expected to live four and twenty hours the day before yesterday by the last accounts.

They are quartered at Merida the place where Victor's army suffered so much by sickness last year. Captain Christie brings us no news of the French army; of course what he heard whilst at Talavera would not be correct. I do not know of anything else in the way of news I have to tell you.

Colonel Hulse‡ will write to the Duke of Cambridge§ in my favour about the adjutancy, of course I cannot but agree with you in your opinion, or thank you too much for your advice respecting the appointment with the regiment, and that with Lord Wellington. I cannot think from daily experience that affairs in this country can resume an active turn, but if things should do so, Dawkins¶ will of course take his station as senior adjutant of the regiment with the [First] Battalion, and should I get the appointment, my place will be with the 2nd Battalion in which situation Mr Wynyard,** by getting a person to act for him pro tempore, went abroad, once as an aide-de-camp,

---

sent to Walcheren as a diversion to aid Austria, who had declared war on France. Despite Wellington's demands for more troops, the British government had sent all available reserves, totalling 40,000 men, on this expedition to the River Scheldt, with the aim of capturing or destroying the fleet holed up at Antwerp. However the campaign was poorly led and the troops decimated by disease; forcing an ignominious re-embarkation, having lost over 4,000 men, of which only 106 had died in combat.

* Lieutenant Colonel Charles Donellan died of his wounds on 1 September 1809. (Hall, *History of the Peninsular War*, fails to show his death.)

† Lieutenant Colonel James Charles Dalbiac, 4th Dragoons, did survive to fight another day.

‡ Colonel Hulse commanded 1st Brigade of 1st Division.

§ The Prince Adolphus, Duke of Cambridge (1774–1850), was the tenth child and seventh son of George III and Queen Charlotte. He was colonel of the Coldstream Guards.

¶ Lieutenant and Captain Henry Dawkins, adjutant of the 2nd Battalion.

** Lieutenant and Captain William Clinton Wynyard had been ADC to Major General Acland in the peninsula for the second half of 1808.

and perhaps my being on the spot may give a further claim, in the present instance, and should Lord Wellington as you say, be inclined to renew my appointment with him at any future period, I understand there will be no difficulty made on the part of the regiment. Besides which perhaps you are not aware that the oldest adjutant always looks forwards to the brigade majority, and I am told he succeeds from a lieutenancy to a company. In the same manner, he does go from being the oldest ensign to the lieutenancy, but under any circumstances I shall always feel constant in abiding by your advice.

All the people I have shown your two letters to, were quite delighted by your sentiments about the Scheldt expedition as well as our army and for that, and for what regards myself I really don't sufficiently know how to thank you, including Bryan's vacancy. There still remain five ensigns above me, but I think six months after our arrival in England, whenever that may be, it will bring me to the top of the list. I am quite glad to hear so good an account of Felton's health; but everyone I have mentioned his intention to, of coming out again, is very much astonished.

I saw Charles Bishop yesterday, he has grown so stout you would hardly know him again, he is quartered ten miles from here. Necessity obliged him to parade a gentleman the day after Talavera, who was so great a braggard that no man in the regiment would befriend him. The quarrel originated in words, and from that to blows, and it was so necessary that a meeting should take place, that I was advised to go out with a Mr Penrice* which of course was, for me, the most awkward of situations, and nothing but Charles' character being at stake, should have induced me to have done so; luckily an accident happened, but I think it reflects no credit on the 16th.

I received Georgiana's letter at the same time with yours of the 13th, I don't know, but I should suppose she must have received a letter I wrote to her and another to you in the same envelope from Abrantes the night before the march, which I gave in charge to Dick Fitzgibbon, who tells me he forwarded it. General Payne is here and very civil to me. Dick is heartily tired of him; you will hardly believe he has driven three people out of his Family. Pray give my best love to Mrs F[remantle] and the young ladies, and the rest of my friends, and believe me, my dear uncle, your dutiful and affectionate nephew,

John Fremantle

I have taken the back of your letter to finish this for the country paper is so execrable, it is impossible to get on upon it. I am quite delighted

---

* Lieutenant Thomas Penrice, 16th Light Dragoons.

that the little mare should happen to have suited you; I am capitally well mounted again, I have an English pony and two country horses besides an animal for my baggage, all of which I draw forage for as ADC.

John's pen was still for a month as he was laid up with a severe fever.

Badajoz, 8 November 1809

My dear uncle,
Two days after writing to you from this place I had an attack of fever with a giddiness in my head, a complaint so prevalent in this country, that it confined me to my bed for 13 days and after being up a week, and on the point of returning to my duty, I had a relapse, which confined me for three more days. I am to remove from here in the course of a day or two for a change of air, I believe in the first instance I shall go to Estremoz and if I find I don't gain strength thence, I shall go to Lisbon, which Lord Wellington advised me to do, when he was here last. I fancy he is now at Cadiz, but expected back here every day. There has been a very general report here, for many days past, that the supine Junta at Seville has dissolved itself and published a proclamation saying, that it is entirely owing to the inability of the English general and his king that has forced them to do so; and they are now afraid they will be obliged to submit to the French, it is hardly possible that the whole of the report can be true; if it were only from the circumstance of our remaining in Spain so long after the first rumour.

There has been no mail from England now for four weeks; you can easily imagine what a state of anxiety we must all be in. I will write to you as soon as ever I remove from this place. Pray remember me to all my friends and believe me always, my dear uncle, your dutiful and affectionate nephew,
John Fremantle

His health not improving, he received a route to return to Lisbon to recuperate.

Badajoz, 17 November 1809*

To Ensign Fremantle, Coldstream Guards
Route from Badajoz to Lisbon:

---

* Letter from Add MS 46.5B with the kind permission of the National Library of Scotland.

Elvas
Vila Vicosa
Estremoz
Vimeiro
Arraiolos
Montemor-o-Novo
Vendas Novas
Canha
Aldea Golega
By water to Lisbon
 George Murray Q[uarter] M[aster] General

John reacted quickly to the receipt of his route and was soon ensconced at Lisbon, where he felt his health begin to improve.

Lisbon, 29 November 1809

My dear uncle,

I received your letter dated October 29th as I was on the point of setting off from Badajoz for this place, where I arrived on the 27th. I am happy to say very much the better for my journey and I hope in 10 days or a fortnight to be able again to join the army. The number of sick officers here is quite dreadful, several have returned to England, and there are a great number still to go. I hardly think it possible that the sickness in the islands of Walcheren can be more destructive than it is in our army. Colonel Hawker* is here looking very ill, I believe he is going to England.

I perfectly understand what you mean with respect to the situation I am in with Lord Wellington. I had the entrée of his house before he appointed me, and all the time the Guards were in the neighbourhood of Badajoz, I lived almost entirely at Lord W[ellington]'s, and was considered as much one of the family as any of the rest of them. I assure you he has always been particularly kind and friendly to me. I fancy he was a little surprised at my being able to do the business of an adjutant. Nothing yet has been finally done about the adjutancy, that has reached me, we have not yet, had answers to the accounts of Bryan's death, but I don't suppose my appointment will be delayed a moment after it is known to the Duke of Cambridge, for in his answer to Colonel Hulse's recommendation, he says he is very glad that I happened to be the person, at the same time thinks I am full young [sic], but will not hesitate a moment in backing the recommendation,

---

* Captain Peter Hawker, 14th Light Dragoons, left the Peninsula in April 1810 and resigned from the army in 1813.

however he forgets that I am not so young as Dawkins was, and who never has been out of London. All the officers are much surprised that Dawkins has not joined this battalion, his proper place as eldest adjutant. When he comes it will be a fine opportunity for me to join Lord Wellington, but don't mention that. Bryan died in the latter end of September: I received the pay from the 1st of October till I came away the 18th, but not being appointed the person who acts gets it now, but I shall have it as soon as I join again.

Felton was going to the regiment as I was coming down, I waited a day on the road on purpose to see him but missed him, which I was very sorry for, I am told by everybody he is in very good health and spirits. I think there is very little probability of his being employed on the Staff, both departments are as full I fancy as they can well hold, of course he could only be employed in the Adjutant General's Department, where the chief occupation is writing, but I don't think either desirable, for they meet with nothing but abuse and that from all quarters, I mean the officers employed.

I cannot tell you what a relief your letter was to me. I wish I had anything in the shape of news to tell you in return, of course you will have long heard of the complete overthrow of the Spaniards near Toledo. They lost 63 pieces of cannon out of 70 and 17,000 prisoners, and 5,000 killed, the particulars I think you will agree with me, are somewhat ludicrous, the Spaniards had their cavalry forward in front of their infantry, which when attacked gave way (of course) and the infantry to prevent it breaking their ranks fired upon it, upon which the cavalry charged and routed them. I imagine the French could not have lost a man.* This I heard from General Beresford at table the day before yesterday.

On my way down I bought four Braga shawls at Elvas which are here called Talavera ones, of course you will know the names, notwithstanding they have the Braga arms on them, Lady Emily Berkeley† says they will be quite a prize, they are made out of the Merino wool, and extremely light and warm, I wrote yesterday for some more, I hope I shall be able to succeed in getting them, I will send them over by the first opportunity.

I have received great civility from General Sherbrooke and General

---

* This refers to the Battle of Ocana, which took place on 19 November. The flower of the Spanish army fought here under General Areizaga, but the French under Victor and Sebastiani eventually routed the Spanish who lost 4,000 and had 15,000 captured against French losses of about 2,000.
† Lady Emily Berkeley (née Lennox), wife of Admiral the Honourable Sir George Berkeley, Lord High Admiral of the Portuguese navy.

Payne has been very kind to me, indeed they have all been friendly to me.

I saw Charles Bishop frequently whilst I was at Badajoz; he has been for nearly three months at an out quarter with two other gentlemen like him. Colonel Taylor* is with his regiment at Gibraltar. I should not think staying there was at all the sort of thing he would like, as he never can be sure for how long he may be obliged to remain.

Georgiana must be quite happy visiting about from place to place. She told me in her last letter that Albinia was staying with one of old Allain's daughters who had lately been married. Pray give my remembrance to all my friends, and with best love, believe me, my very dear uncle, your dutiful and affectionate nephew,

John Fremantle

A fortnight later John wrote that he had been appointed adjutant of the 2nd Battalion and that the senior adjutant might be sent out to Spain to replace him. If that happened he would request to remain in the country for the campaigning season with Lord Wellington.

Lisbon, 9 December 1809

My dear uncle,

Since my letter of the 29th no news whatever has arrived here. I am thank God quite recovered and ready to join the army again, but shall wait here the arrival of the next packet, which by a letter from Colonel Hulse two days ago I understand there is a likelihood of Dawkins's coming out by. The Duke of Cambridge must know by letters from here that I am on Lord Wellington's Staff, and may send a peremptory order for my return, as Colonel Hulse tells me that private letters by the last packet mentioned my appointment to the second battalion.

If I have no such order, or indeed if I have, I shall write from here, for the two months' leave I should be entitled to, on my arrival in England, as coming from abroad, and join Lord Wellington; in the mean time perhaps you may be able to get me leave to remain with him, for the remainder of the campaign, as there must be a person acting in my place until my arrival, and I should think there can be no difficulty in his continuing, What might further lead to it, would be offering the pay to [the] person acting, from the date of my leave, till the end of it. I don't know anything else I have to mention to you. I heard of Felton being quite well two days ago. I only knew an hour ago that the convoy which takes home the 23rd Dragoons sails this evening. The shawls are to go with it, but as yet I don't know by whom, I hope and

---

* Lieutenant Colonel John Taylor 88th Foot, John's stepfather, General Taylor of Castle Taylor in Galway.

trust that they will arrive safe. Pray give my best love to all my friends, and believe me, ever my dear uncle, ever your dutiful and affectionate nephew,

John Fremantle

If I get a peremptory order by Dawkins to return, I shall wait here, on the plea of health, till I get an answer to my application for further leave, for my present leave has not yet expired.

During his absence the Brigade of Guards had marched through Portalegre, Abrantes and Coimbra, arriving at Viseu on 30 December. Having recovered his health, John rejoined the battalion here, carrying despatches to the Duke of Wellington by post mule.

Viseu, 17 January 1810

My dear uncle,

I arrived here from Lisbon on the 12th of the month, not the least the worse for a very fatiguing journey, I was obliged to make, having travelled by post mules, day and night, the whole way, with Mr Villiers' dispatches for Lord Wellington I consequently missed seeing Felton, Santarem being out of the direct road.

I have not a word of news of any sort or kind to tell you. This is the headquarters of Lord Wellington, he left it yesterday on a visit to the different posts viz.: Almeida, Guarda, Pinhel etc, and will return in about nine or ten days.

I have found your very affectionate letter of the 29th November, but however, I am, thank God, quite recovered and never was better in my life. My two last letters must have fully explained my circumstances to you with respect to my two situations and I know of nothing further to add except that I just again heard that Dawkins was certainly coming out, but I shall never credit the report until I actually see him, having heard the same thing so often. If he does come, I am afraid it will be thought very unfair, my making application to remain with Lord Wellington. But I suppose I shall know by your next letter whether it will be possible.

I hope the shawls I sent by the 23rd Dragoons have arrived safe. I will write to you more fully by the next packet. Pray give my best remembrance to all my friends, and with best love, believe me, my dear uncle, your most dutiful and affectionate nephew,

John Fremantle

SECOND BATTALION

Two weeks later John was writing to confirm that he had received strict orders to return home and also stated that the talk of the army was that they were expecting orders from home and that the government was sending Wellington back to India to quell the serious mutiny there.

Viseu, 31 January 1810

My dear uncle,

I only yesterday received your letter of December 23rd, and in the same mail I have a positive order from the Orderly Room in London, to repair to England upon the receipt of the communication which I must comply with in the course of three or four days. Colonel Hulse and all the seniors of the regiment think me particularly fortunate in having the appointment; more so as there is but one idea, in the army, of Lord Wellington's reign in this country being now but of a very short duration. He returned four days ago from his tour that I mentioned to you in my last letter, he met with a dreadful misfortune while absent, a fire took place in the stables and burnt three of his horses, two of which were his greatest favourites. He leaves this on the 1st to reconnoitre in the neighbourhood of Torres Vedras, where the army expect very soon to follow him; it is very evident that preparations and or arrangements are making for a move. Accounts have been received here from four days ago, of the French having been beyond the strong pass in the Sierra Morena on their way to Seville, which it is expected by the next accounts we shall hear of their being in possession of.

I do not know how far it may be the truth, but there is a very prevalent report in the army that Lord Wellington is going to India, by the latest English papers we have (of the 16th) there seems very little mention of the India business, perhaps it is intended by government to be as little known as possible, but I happened to be present when Lord Wellington read the dispatches on the subject which mentioned that 18 of the native regiments with all their officers had mutinied, and taken

Seringapatam.* I do not know of anything further to mention to you. I hope the middle of March at latest will bring me to you in England.

I will write to you on my arrival at Lisbon. I fear I shall have very bad weather for my journey, my dear uncle, with my best love your very dutiful and affectionate nephew,
> John Fremantle

His next letter was from Lisbon, waiting patiently for a Royal Navy ship or transport as they could offer free passage home. John fails to mention the fact, but in leaving Portugal he also left his post as aide-de-camp to Wellington.

Lisbon, 10 February 1810

My dear uncle,
I arrived here from Viseu three days ago, but shall wait for next Sunday's packet, for the chance of going in a transport or a vessel of war, which will save me 30 guineas.† I don't imagine any fault can be found, for my so doing, as the officers who are lately come, waited a very considerable time for the same transport. Felton is here in very good spirits, and looking as well as ever I remember him. Lord Wellington left this place for Viseu this morning, he only remained one day; when I left Viseu, there was great talk of a move, but now it is impossible to tell whether it will take place.

Three regiments sailed from hence yesterday, under General Stewart, for Cadiz.‡ Great doubts are entertained of their arriving in time to be of any service. I saw an account in the last papers of the narrow escape, I suppose, of my three sisters. With best love, believe me, my dear uncle, your dutiful and affectionate nephew,
> John Fremantle

---

* This little-known incident involving a mutiny by the British officers commanding native troops in the East India Company caused real concern to the government. The complaints were borne out of inequalities of pay and conditions for those serving in the Bengal and Madras armies. This festering grievance was kept in abeyance during the years of campaigning under Wellesley, but during the ensuing peace it came to the fore again. A number of officer mutinies occurred, leading to suspensions from the service. In the summer of 1809 the officers of Seringapatam mutinied and their native troops blindly followed their officers into resistance. A force was sent to counter this threat but following negotiations Seringapatam surrendered at discretion on the 23 August. Many of the officers involved were court-martialled or allowed to resign the service. See *The Asiatic Annual Register for the year 1809* by E. Samuel, London 1811.
† Equivalent in modern day terms to about £1,070.
‡ General William Stewart was sent with three British Battalions, (79th, 2/87th and 94th) and both battalions of the Portuguese 20th Line Regiment.

Lisbon, 24 February 1810

My dear uncle,

I have this day written to inform Colonel Bayly,* of my having procured a passage in the *Vestal* frigate,† Captain Graham, which is appointed to sail with a convoy on the first of next month. I may therefore calculate upon arriving with you in the course of three weeks. Appearances seem every day more and more against our army remaining in the country. The French have been for some time at Olivenza, in the neighbourhood of Elvas, before Badajoz, and at Albuquerque, their force altogether is estimated at about 20,000 men. I should imagine they are only waiting there for more troops before they continue their march for this country. Letters from Cadiz this day mention our troops having landed, and that the French were bombarding the town. I rode with Felton two leagues the day before yesterday on his way to join the regiment which had marched to Portalegre. He was extremely well, and in excellent spirits.

Young Fitzgibbon arrived here yesterday on his way to England. He is slightly ruptured, owing to excess of exercise at Talavera, I believe we shall go together; we are both at present at Baron Quintella's.‡

I am quite grieved at having again heard of the disgraceful manner in which Charles Bishop is still going on, several people have spoken to me advising his getting an exchange, for his conduct is so ungentlemanlike that it is impossible he can be allowed to continue in the regiment.§ Therefore it would be doing him a kindness to urge his father on the subject. Pray give my best love to my sisters and believe me, my dear uncle, your dutiful and affectionate nephew,

John Fremantle

Approaching England, John took the first opportunity to advise his uncle of his arrival.

HM Ship *Vestal* off Land's End, 23 March 1810

My dear uncle,

I sailed from Lisbon on the 12th and thus far have had a smooth though rather a long passage, I send these few lines by Captain Gordon,¶ who

---

* Captain and Lieutenant Colonel Henry Bayly, Coldstream Guards.
† HMS *Vestal* of 28 guns.
‡ A diamond-trading family who formed part of the *nouveau riche* of Lisbon in the latter part of the eighteenth century.
§ Charles Bishop was accused of drawing his sword on a woman, he remained in the regiment for a number of years, but the scandal continued to rumble on until he left the army in late 1813.
¶ Lieutenant and Captain Alexander Gordon, 3rd Foot Guards was ADC to Lord

has landed on shore in a boat, but however I judge it more prudent, to wait for a change of wind to be landed at Portsmouth or the Downs.[*] Pray give my best love to my sisters. Remember me to the rest of my friends and in best expectation of soon meeting you all. Believe me, my dear uncle, your dutiful and affectionate nephew,

John Fremantle

John was not to settle with the 2nd battalion as within a month he was pleased to announce that his recent replacement had gained advancement and that he was expecting orders to return to the 1st battalion to arrive at any moment.

Chapel Street,[†] 26 April 1810

My dear uncle,

General Harry Campbell[‡] has this day told me that Colonel Rooke[§] of the 3rd Guards who left this, about three months to be the brigade major to the brigade in Portugal has got a Staff appointment, and Captain Dawkins is appointed to succeed him. I therefore imagine my stay in this country will not exceed a week after the arrival of the next packet, although I must confess I regret leaving England and my friends who I have seen so little of, after so long an absence. I assure it is not without a degree of satisfaction that I received the news, as I can't explain to you how painful and irksome my situation has been ever since my arrival with this battalion and as far as business goes I'm sure to be happy with the other. Remember me to Mrs Fremantle and the young ladies, pray write to me quick and tell me when you are likely to leave Englefield Green or to come to town and if I can come and see you. Believe me ever, my dear uncle, your dutiful and affectionate nephew,

John Fremantle

Wellington, but went home between February and October 1810 to sort out his affairs. His own letters, edited by Rory Muir, *At Wellington's Right Hand*, confirm that he sailed home on the *Vestal*.

[*] The Downs was a naval anchorage just off Chatham between North and South Foreland.

[†] Chapel Street in London is first mentioned in 1799 and ran east from Whitecross Street. This is not the modern Chapel Street near the Edgware Road. See *A Dictionary of London*, 1918.

[‡] Brigadier General Sir Henry Frederick Campbell, commanded the 2nd Brigade of Guards but was obliged to return home having been wounded in the face at Talavera. He returned to the peninsula in 1811.

[§] Captain and Lieutenant Colonel John Charles Rooke had been Brigade Major to Major General Stopford and was now Assistant Adjutant General to the 2nd Division.

Three months later, we find John at Portsmouth awaiting passage back to Portugal as his prediction had proven only too correct.

Portsmouth, 27 July

My dear uncle,
I arrived here this morning after having had the good luck to escape the rain every day but this, when we all got a complete soaking. The men were to have embarked as soon as they arrived, but the weather would not permit of it today. If it is more moderate we are to go on board tomorrow at 12 but I understand there is no chance of our sailing for a few days. The *Undaunted*, Captain McKenzie,* who convoys us is painting his ship. I shall be enabled to embark my horse as there is a horse transport going. We are very lucky in having the transport of so large a tonnage as the *Lord Eldon.*† Our party consists of 239 men and eight officers;‡ therefore we might be very well accommodated. God bless you my dear uncle, believe me, your dutiful and affectionate nephew,
            John Fremantle

A further letter from Portsmouth reports that he was sailing with a significant reinforcement for the Guard's Brigade. John was particularly tickled by the ribald songs and choice sayings of the men.

Portsmouth, 29 July 1810

My dear uncle,
My note to you the other day was very short, we had just arrived after a complete soaking which brought on a slight sore throat of which I am now quite recovered. I am just returned from seeing the men on board the transport which is a very fine one named the *Lord Eldon*, we are five of the Coldstream and four of the 3rd Regiment [of Guards] and one doctor. The *Undaunted*, Captain McKenzie, takes the convoy which is very large, he is painting his ship at present, therefore it must be two or three days before we sail. The party which I expected would have been very troublesome on the march, behaved extremely well. There was not a single complaint the whole march, and the men embarked in the greatest order. I never heard such a choice collection of songs and sayings as they have, the only one I can mention to repeat is the meeting, of a Marine on the road with two black eyes, when one fellow observed to him he had been to an Irish

---

* HMS *Undaunted* of 38 guns.
† The *Lord Eldon* was a hired ship fitted out with 16 guns.
‡ This was a reinforcement for the 1st Battalion with Wellington's army.

wedding where they gave black eyes for favours. Three cheers from the party followed and the Marine was very glad to make his escape. I got my aunt's letter yesterday with the enclosure which I shall take care to deliver. She gave me an account of the Monkey Island party;* I lament very much not having been able to make one of it. I hope however I shall not be detained here long. I told you in my last letter that I was certain of taking my horse, but I understand since, it is by no means certain that there is a horse transport to sail with the convoy. Give my love to all at the Green† and believe me as ever, your most affectionate nephew,

John Fremantle

While waiting impatiently at Portsmouth to sail, John was to receive good news; he was gazetted lieutenant and captain on 2 August.

Portsmouth, 5 August 1810

My dear uncle,

I am afraid there is still a probability of my remaining here some days. The *Undaunted* is not to be painted till tomorrow, and I understand orders are come for our sailing not until 36 hours after if the wind is fair. I have had the good luck to dine out three times since I have been here. My horse has been on board these five days, the transport it is on board of is very comfortably fitted up. I find I am gazetted this day. I have not yet seen it but if I am not dated the same day I understand I am promised it will be soon. I have seen Felton's promotion.‡ I am exceedingly sorry poor Talbot§ has been the occasion of it, for I know a better creature never existed. Remember to direct your letters under cover to the Adjutant in Waiting, Coldstream Duty Room. Now Francis Smyth¶ desires his best remembrances to all the party. Your most affectionate nephew,

John Fremantle

Unexpectedly, John was called back to London to give evidence at an investigation but was hopeful that it would not cause him to miss his passage.

---

* Monkey Island (originally Monk's Island) at Bray on the River Thames is now the site of a luxury hotel.
† Englefield Green in Surrey.
‡ Felton Hervey had been promoted to Lieutenant Colonel on 12 July 1810.
§ Lieutenant Colonel Neil Talbot, 14th Light Dragoons, was killed charging a square of infantry at Sexmiro on 11 July. (Challis states that he was serving with the Portuguese army, although he was with the 14th on this day.)
¶ The only Francis Smyth in the army was a major in the Royal Artillery.

Grosvenor Street, 7 August 1810

My dear uncle,

I arrived here this morning at 10 o'clock from Portsmouth, pursuant to an order I received yesterday from the adjutant general's office, desiring my presence at 12 o'clock this day at George Street, Westminster,* to attend at an investigation which took place between Major Tidy† and Major Northey‡ The former accusing the latter of misdemeanours, such as pilfering from his brother officers, or rather marking things, that were not his own. Major Tidy called upon me to know whether I had ever heard such a report in Lisbon, all I had to say was, that I had heard such reports in circulation, but never paid any attention to them. I am desired to attend again tomorrow, when most likely I shall be discharged. There is no danger of my losing my passage if I can get off tomorrow night. I came to town with Mr Robert Browning who goes out passenger in the *Undaunted*. He does not leave town until the wind is fair. If I am discharged early tomorrow I will come down to see you. My expenses will of course be defrayed. This business came out on Saturday and Northey was to have been married yesterday week. I don't think Tidy can positively substantiate his charges, of course Northey will in that case ask for a court martial upon him; everyone blames Tidy for having spoken. With best love to all, believe me, my dear uncle, your most affectionate nephew,
John Fremantle

His next letter announced that he was onboard ship, soon to proceed to Portugal.

On board, Thursday [No date]

My dear uncle,

We have just got underway. I send this by a boat just going ashore. I will write to you as soon as I get to Lisbon with what news I can collect. I don't expect we shall get further tonight than Yarmouth Roads [Isle of Wight]. My Uncle Tom left this morning after he received by a telegraph, orders from the Admiralty, he is not yet returned. It is very

---

* Great George Street Westminster, near to Westminster Bridge, was built in 1757 and much altered in 1806. I can find no record of government buildings being there in the early days, they may have been built during the 1806 phase. Certainly government buildings were there during Victorian times and the great edifice Number One Great George Street was built in 1910–13.
† Major Francis Skelly Tidy, 14th Foot.
‡ Major Lawrence Augustus Northey, permanent assistant quartermaster general.

provoking I should have remained so long and miss you after all. God Bless you my dear uncle, with best love to all at the Green, believe me, your most affectionate nephew,

John Fremantle

PORTUGAL AGAIN

John's next letter announced that he had arrived safely in Portugal and describes how, hearing of an imminent clash of arms, he had rushed to join Wellington's army, which was slowly retreating towards Lisbon in the face of overwhelming French numbers. His efforts were fully rewarded by his arrival at the Sierra de Bussaco in time to witness the battle.

Coimbra, 30 September 1810

My dear uncle,

Since my last letter to you that I wrote in such haste, I proceeded as I told you, on my way to join the army, hearing from everyone I met, that the armies were so near each other, that a battle was inevitable; of course my anxiety was a good deal raised, not being able to travel more than 20 miles a day with my own animals. However, I had the good fortune, a few leagues on the Lisbon side of Leiria to be overtaken by General Otway* who had the order for post mules, and offered to take me up with him. When after riding all night, I arrived at 9 o'clock in the morning at the scene of action, the Sierra de Bussaco.

The battle having partially begun a little after day break, at eight a regular and desperate attack was made by a very strong column on that part on the right of our position where Colonel Mackinnon's Brigade† was stationed. The French walked up the hill in the most gallant style, but to be sure were most handsomely rolled down again, Mackinnon had I think two Field officers killed, and three wounded, and from four to five hundred men. He took a colonel, chef de battalion and some men. At about ten a similar attack was made upon our left in general, and not being able to find my brigade, and nobody at that time caring to tell me, I remained at the point of the mountain where

---

* Colonel Loftus William Otway was on the Portuguese staff at Bussaco and commanded a Portuguese brigade after the battle.

† Brevet Colonel Henry Mackinnon, commanded the 2nd Brigade, 3rd Division.

General Spencer* and his Staff were, a quiet spectator of the scene, exactly as if I had been exalted in a theatre, when after a great deal of firing and charging on both sides the French were driven from all points. I am happy to say chiefly by Portuguese regiments which had English officers. The light infantry brigade also handled some of them very severely. The loss of British is stated at eight hundred, and the Portuguese about the same. The French from five to seven thousand.[†] We have got a general and his aide-de-camp besides the colonel. We know of General Loison being wounded.[‡] The whole extent of our position was a range of mountains and that of the largest size as you will observe by the name sierra. The light was most grand, we could perceive every movement the enemy made and Lord Wellington, his Staff, and Masséna's,[§] and other generals with theirs on the other side. General Spencer's and Hill's Divisions[¶] which compose nearly the half of the army never fired a single shot or were in any way engaged. I suppose the French finding their favourite method of attacking the line in different places by strong columns, failing, is the reason that the action never became general, and that having been so completely beaten in each of their attacks, they desisted from renewing them. The light infantry on our left were engaged the greater part of the day. We others remained on our ground that night. The next day part of their force was observed in motion towards our left, and that night the whole of our army excepting Hill's Division which formed our right, and extended to the Ponte de Murcella marched to our left, and now, 10 o'clock a.m., all our infantry have passed the Mondego, two divisions through Coimbra, and ours (Spencer's) a little to the right and are cantoned about a league down the river. The cavalry are all on the Porte de Coimbra side. I don't know yet whether the army marches tomorrow, if it does, we shall not bring up, till we get to the Lisbon Lines, about Torres Vedras** which have been a great deal

---

* Major General Brent Spencer was second in command and commanded the 1st Division.

† Oman states Allied losses at 1,252, split exactly equally between the British and Portuguese. In comparison the French lost some 4,600 killed and wounded.

‡ General Louis Henri Loison was not wounded, but Generals Maucune, Foy and Merle were.

§ Marshal André Masséna, Prince d'Essling.

¶ The French right engaged Craufurd's Light Division and the left attacked Picton's 3rd Division, few others were engaged.

** The Lines of Torres Vedras were a project instigated by Wellington in secrecy. Using Portuguese labour over the past year, two lines of forts, palisades and escarped ridges were prepared across the Portuguese countryside from the sea to the Tagus, therefore securing the Lisbon peninsula. A third line was constructed around Fort St

improved since I have been away, and that part of them which I passed the other day seemed in a very pretty state. The whole French had marched before we did, although their fires were kept up [on] the 29th. It is expected the force we first observed in motion, was marching for the Coimbra road, but I believe we have no certain account of its having done so; or is it thought that they can have gone back again entirely. If they have given up the idea of Coimbra, for the present, I imagine they will make for Oporto, where there is only Portuguese militia to oppose them but that to the amount of 20,000; but most probably we shall now go down to Lisbon, and if the French come, there will be some very desperate fighting. We were in the field about 30,000 English and 20,000 Portuguese; the French are said to be 60,000 with Masséna,* Ney, Reynier, Laborde, Loison, and (Simon taken), †all the first of France. Since the fall of Almeida we have been going leisurely before them, and it was generally believed down to Lisbon; at Coimbra, the whole baggage of the army was sent in front, as in a regular retreat, but instead of going over the Mondego he marched the army by the right to this position, everybody thought that if he met the French beyond Coimbra, his position would be with his left at the Ponte de Murcella. Our army all the time have never had a forced march and for two days cantoned before they marched to this position, and had provisions of all sorts in abundance on the ground, and luckily spirits; in short the French showed their usual politeness in attacking us. They had no idea of our force being half what it was, but if it had not, the nature of the ground, made it almost impossible for them to force our position. General Simon's aide-de-camp, says that Masséna was in such a state for want of provisions, that the men were either to eat us English, or the mountain.

Felton is quite well, he came to see me on the 27th, he has had a good deal of hard and rough work lately but tell my aunt he does not look in the least the worse for it. He tells me it goes with him capitally, they must not abuse him for not writing, it is only by accident that I am able. My horse and man reached me last night and this morning our division was halted by the side of a road (which I happened to be in) to let another column pass, when I was called to get out of the

---

Julian to protect the point of embarkation for the army if such was necessary. Marshal Masséna, despite his spy network, was completely unaware of these lines until his army arrived in front of them.

* Oman thinks Masséna had 63,000 and Wellington 52,000 at Bussaco.

† Marshal Michel Ney, Duke d'Elchingen; General Jean Louis Reynier, General Henri Delaborde, General Louis Henry Loison and General de Brigade Edouard Francois Simon were all renowned leaders of French troops.

way, and the only means I had of doing so, was putting my horse at a muddy ditch, which he leapt into with me. I luckily got out of the scrape with only being covered with black mud, but the banks being very steep on each side the horse was plunging there for a considerable time and I was at last obliged to have him dug out, and I now have to come to Coimbra where my baggage is to get my horse and myself put to rights again, and therefore am enabled to post my letter in the bag which goes tonight.

There is no officer going home with the dispatch,* but too much praise cannot be bestowed on Lord Wellington. His manner of carrying on business in general, has gained him everyone's good opinion. This last business was a complete chef d'oeuvre [masterpiece]. God bless you my dear uncle, I am now going out to my regiment. I have given you all the news I have been able to collect. Ever your grateful and affectionate nephew,

John Fremantle

What a thing it is for us to know that the Portuguese will fight. Now it will save us if there is any more of it. I have not seen C. Bishop, Felton tells me he is well but as selfish as ever. J. F.

Wellington, despite his victory, was forced to continue his orderly retreat; destroying all provisions in a scorched earth policy as they went. Masséna had followed, but had been brought up in front of the Lines of Torres Vedras on 5 October, unable to attack with any certainty of success and unwilling to retire. The French army simply sat down and starved until they retired to Santarem and Thomar on 14 November in search of fresh supplies. Wellington followed and planned to drive them further; but discovering the strength of their position, let his army go into winter cantonments happy to leave starvation to do the work for him.

Wednesday, 21 November 1810

My dear uncle,

I was prevented writing to you by last Saturday's mail as was my intention, on account of the French to our utter surprise, having decamped from the position in front of us, on the Wednesday 14th proceeding at ten at night. The cavalry and light troops marched in pursuit of them the next day. Sir B. Spencer's and Hill's Divisions marched the day following to Alenquer where we halted on the 17th. Hill crossed the Tagus, I believe with the intention of getting in the rear of their rear guard at Abrantes

---

* Captain Ulysses Burgh, Wellington's aide-de-camp, took the despatch for Bussaco home.

which place he was to reach yesterday. On the 20th headquarters left Alenquer with the intention of proceeding to Santarem as it was expected the French would continue their retreat from thence, which however proved otherwise. The cavalry followed them and picked up nearly 400 men after some skirmishing. Headquarters remained that night at Cartaxo, as did our division. On the 19th we marched with the idea of reaching Santarem, but the enemy's position was found so very strong, that the attack upon it, was given up, which now I have seen it I am heartily rejoiced at, as our brigade was actually at the head of the column, on the march for the attack. We halted that night at a small village one mile off the Santarem road and about four miles from the town but I don't know the name of it.* The road we followed the French upon was strewed with dead men and horses and the villages besides being unroofed and partly burnt were left in a most filthy state. Alenquer one of the prettiest towns I almost ever saw in peaceful times is totally destroyed, and Sobral also. We were stationary here yesterday and I believe are to remain today. There was a report very prevalent yesterday that Masséna with his whole force was returning but it does not appear to be the case. I suppose we shall remain here till it is seen what effect General Hill's movement on the opposite side of the Tagus produces. At present the army is very healthy but I fear if we move much in this rainy season it will soon make an alteration. When we move again, or anything takes place, I will write, at present I believe I have given you all the news relative to our operations. If the campaign ends by the French going off, it certainly is a victory for us, but in general people are still more sanguine. We are extremely well supplied. The prisoners were in a dreadful plight, nearly naked, very badly accoutred, and half starved. They say that discontent prevails throughout all ranks of their army. I saw Felton on the 19th; you may assure my aunt though very thin he was quite well and in very good spirits. Adieu, my dear uncle, pray give my best remembrance, and believe me, your dutiful and affectionate nephew,

John Fremantle

I forgot to mention to you, Colonel Hulse's appointment to command a brigade, and that Colonel Brand[†] has succeeded to the command of our battalion, until Fuller,[‡] whose turn it is, arrives. He is an exceeding pleasant man and I live upon the best possible terms with him.

---

* Probably Povoa da Isenta.
† Captain and Lieutenant Colonel the Honourable Henry Otway Brand, Lord Dacre, Coldstream Guards.
‡ Brevet Colonel Joseph Fuller, Coldstream Guards.

Headquarters, Cartaxo 15 December 1810

My dear uncle,

Since my letter to you of the 21st giving you as good an account as I could collect of our operations since we left the position, nothing has occurred. Spencer with the First Division is in this place about four miles from the advanced post where Craufurd is with the Light Division. The remaining divisions are sufficiently near, for the whole to be assembled in a few hours. We continue to turn out before daylight and remain under arms for an hour. In the few lines I added to Felton's letter to my aunt on the 24th, he pressed me so, that I had not time to mention anything about his illness. Felton tells me by the last letter he got from Selina* she was much better. I trust when we will hear next she will have quite recovered.

Pray assure her that Felton is quite well. His quarter is only two miles from here consequently we live a good deal together, he generally comes here of an evening for his rubber at whist. Colonel Brand, Lord Clinton,† and Smyth mostly form the party.

There is capital sport coursing here, Felton one day started eleven hares, and killed seven of them. Lord W[ellington], Beresford and Romana‡ go out almost every day. Sutton§ I fancy has sailed for England by this time; I am afraid poor fellow he will not last long. Promotion here continues to be very rapid, I am about to have five under me immediately.

I have not heard from you once yet, pray write to me, for the mail from England is the only thing that breaks the sameness of our mode of life.

All the houses in the villages are become no better than ruins. The doors, window frames, tables and chairs, having been made firewood of, from the constant passing and re-passing of French, English, Portuguese and Spaniards, and I am sorry to say we do as much mischief as any army. Pray give my best love and believe me, my dear uncle, your dutiful and affectionate nephew,

John Fremantle

---

* Selina was John's step-aunt, having married his Uncle William in 1797.
† Captain Lord Robert Cotton St John Clinton, 16th Light Dragoons.
‡ General Pedro Caro y Sureda, Marquis de La Romana, who commanded a Spanish army collaborating with Wellington; he was to die of a suspected aneurism only 39 days after the date of this letter.
§ Lieutenant and Captain Francis Manners Sutton, Coldstream Guards, did go home but lived on for many years.

What a disgraceful business my Uncle Jefferyes* has made of it I saw a sort of account of it in the last papers.

They remained in winter quarters and John had gained leave to visit Lisbon accompanied by Felton for a few days.

Headquarters, Cartaxo, 26 January 1811

My dear uncle,
The mail we have been so long expecting arrived yesterday, when I got your letter, which I assure you gave me very great pleasure. In point of news, nothing has occurred here since I last wrote. Both armies have been quite stationary; on or about the 18th the French under Junot made a reconnaissance on the side of Rio Maior with about 3,000 men, and after remaining about there a few hours not finding, as is imagined, the stores they expected, were in the village, again retired, and our picquets that same evening resumed their stations. In the skirmishing, however, it is believed, Junot himself was wounded in the face, by one of our hussars and for the last two days it has been reported he is dead.† I was at Rio Maior the next day about 16 miles from hence and I assure you I should not have thought it possible for double the number of men to have done half the mischief they did during the time they stayed. The officer's house of the 10th Brigade was turned completely topside turvy.

Felton and myself arrived at Cartaxo, from our three days' excursion to Lisbon on the 29th, as I told I believe in my letter of the 29th saying he was quite well, but whether the journey overheated him, or he got into a damp house that night, he was unwell the next day, when I called on him, and not getting better in a week afterwards, went to Lisbon, and returned the day before yesterday after riding very hard to the same house which is a mere shed. For with the door shut and no window, I could read perfectly by the light through the tiling yesterday. I hope I shall succeed in getting him to come to Colonel Brand's house in the town tomorrow where I am, he has promised me he will, if he is not better, but he is a perfect child when there is anything the matter with him.

I only gave you a report, when I last spoke of Charles Bishop, which was when I first joined, and Felton then had not seen him for a long time. I always enquire about him from every officer I meet with,

---

* His mother's brother, George Charles Jefferyes of Blarney Castle; it is unclear what the 'disgraceful business' was.
† Junot was severely wounded in the face, being shot in the nose by Hussar Dröge of the 1st Hussars KGL.

everyone of whom have invariably given me the best accounts. The day I was at Rio Maior the three officers of the regiment who were there, not only spoke of his attention to his business and being much more popular than formerly, and praised him as being an excellent officer in the field, and in a late instance he has particularly distinguished himself, and I dare say will be thanked in General Orders for it, as others have been who have not done so much. He is quartered at Caldas and was patrolling the other morning with six men, when he heard from the peasantry that an officers' party of about 21 men were foraging in a village close to him. He immediately galloped into it and cut off six men and 10 horses who were forwarded to headquarters three days ago, but it is only yesterday I heard it was Charles Bishop who commanded the party. I am delighted at the good account you give of my aunt, I am sincerely sorry for poor Scott, I had not an idea she was so ill. Many thanks to you, for your unremitting kindness to my sisters and myself, I thought when I last went to Mr Watkins* with Jack Butler,† I had arranged what would comprise you to act for me, which you were good enough to undertake to do, but for fear I have not, I shall write to Mr Watkins to send me out the power of attorney to sign. God bless you my dear uncle, I will write when ever anything takes place with best love to you and all, believe me ever, my dear uncle, your dutiful and affectionate nephew,

    John Fremantle

Finally the stalemate was broken and the French army was forced to retire to find supplies.

2 miles from Condeixa [a Nova], 14 March 1811

My dear uncle,

The French left their position at Santarem on the 9th, since which we have been in a full march after them but I am afraid shall make very little of it, as this country is excessively stony and they fight it as well; as yet we have made about 200 prisoners with four or five officers and their loss is calculated at about 2,000. Our Light Division has had eight or ten officers wounded.

    The prisoners say they are going back to Spain. The bridge at Coimbra was blown up by Trant,‡ they have therefore taken the

---

* Mr Watkins was clearly the family solicitor.

† George John Danvers Butler or 'Jack' was not related to James Butler; he eventually married John Fremantle's younger sister Frances in August 1815 and became the 5th Earl of Lanesborough.

‡ General Nicholas Trant, a British officer in the Portuguese service.

direction of Ponte de Murcella, their rear guard is drawn up about three miles from here, and it is now about two o'clock, therefore if we do not take them today, I think we must give up the pursuit. Their position is very strong, but I hope we shall succeed in turning it. For which purpose General Picton's Division* is gone to the right, and the Light Division to the left, and we are waiting the result. The whole force is up and halted. I saw Felton and Charles Bishop yesterday, both well. With best love to all, my dear uncle, most affectionately your nephew,

    John Fremantle

They have respected nothing, everything laid waste in their route, we have bivouacked these last four nights, but the weather is fine. Lord W[ellington] is in the highest favour.

The pursuit continued up to the Spanish border and hopes of taking Almeida and Ciudad Rodrigo were high; but John's letter is only filled with the horrors of the French retreat.

La Alamedilla 13 April 1811

My dear uncle,
I received your letter of the 18th March on the route to this place, where we arrived on the 9th of the present, it is a Spanish village situated five leagues from Ciudad Rodrigo, and the same distance from Almeida, both of which are invested and I should think must be ours in a very short time, as the garrison of the former, report says, does not consist of more than 2,000 men, and the latter still weaker. We have no guns to bring against them, and Lord Wellington does not seem disposed to lose any man. I fancy Almeida has provisions for nearly another week. The whole army with very little exception are on the Spanish side cantoned; I suppose we shall remain until these places fall, then I am sure it will be quite impossible to conjecture what will become of us, but I think it is pretty certain we shall not remain inactive during the season. The army is stronger and more healthy than ever it was. The French have behaved extremely ill during the retreat, you will scarcely think it possible, but I can assure you of the fact. We could trace their march for miles and miles, by the smoke of the different towns and villages they had set fire to. They [murdered?] old women and children, in short respected nothing; from Santarem to this, I am sure upon an average that in every mile there are five dead men or animals in the road, and all stripped naked, therefore you may imagine

---

* Major General Sir Thomas Picton.

we suffered a good deal during our march, indeed I don't think we have ever been worse off. By this time, of course, having seen the dispatches you know more of the particulars than I do, who marched with the division (apropos) under Sir Brent; who I am sorry to say, in the general opinion is very much lowered [from] when first he joined the army. People from his [Staff?] thought that Lord Wellington would find a very good second in him, but there is no doubt now that he stood much higher before this campaign than ever he will again as an officer.

There have been several affairs between our advanced [guard] and the French rear, the last on this side of the Coa near Sabugal was pretty smart, and would have been much more decisive on our part if the Light Division had not been so anxious to repay them for the drubbing they got on the Coa last year. The 43rd Regiment above stood the attack of the whole of Reynier's* corps sometimes with the bayonet, but lost very few men. They went off pell mell in all directions when two other battalions came up. Young Soult's† baggage was all taken, it consisted of 14 mules. He had seven coats, every one of them much more costly than our field dress, and everything else in that proportion, the cook was also taken. They say if we had had any cavalry up, the baggage of the whole corps would have been taken. Colonel Waters‡ of our Staff, a friend of Charles Stewart's and a very active officer, was taken reconnoitring, alone, he refused his parole when it was offered him, and was put into the custody of four gendarmes. He gave his boots to be soled, and desired to have new rowels put to his spurs, and on his march from Ciudad Rodrigo to Salamanca he took his opportunity and galloped into a thick wood where he lost them and has been arrived at headquarters these three days. He says their army is quite entirely disorganised and going off as hard as they can towards Salamanca. There are great dissensions amongst their generals, all defeated with Masséna, and that the army is very glad to find itself again in Spain. Marshal Beresford has a very convincing force [both] English and Portuguese investing Badajoz,§ where Mortier has thrown himself in with 5,000 men. I trust we shall get him. There is a report that the French in that neighbourhood surprised a squadron of the 13th [Light Dragoon] Regiment, I am afraid it will prove too true.

Many thanks and acknowledgements for the kindness your letter

---

* General Jean Louis Ebenezer Reynier.
† General de Brigade Pierre Benoit Soult, the younger brother of Marshal Soult.
‡ Brevet Major John Waters, 1st Foot, Assistant Adjutant General.
§ The first siege of Badajoz was to fail due to lack of proper equipment and hence time before a French relief force arrived.

exhibits. I am sorry you find fault with me for not writing often, but it is quite a chance now when we can send a letter, as they only go when Lord Wellington sends his dispatches, and sometimes we are far from headquarters. The post is not yet re-established through the country. I forget to mention that, by an instruction of Lord Wellington's, that the inhabitants quitted the country as the French advanced. I wrote you a few lines in the field dated the 14th March after the skirmish. I don't know whether they will have reached you.* I have not seen or heard of Felton or Charles since we marched. The cavalry must all go to pieces if they remain here, there is not even a blade of grass for miles around. I have not had more than four days corn since Cartaxo; all the others are the same. Our animals wilt upon the heath; I have sold my horse to Charles Bishop who was riding a trooper. Colonel Brand left this today; he meets Lord Wellington's dispatches at Lisbon. Colonel Fuller is expected to arrive today. I expect soon to have still a few steps. With best remembrances, believe me, my dear uncle, your most affectionate nephew,

J. F.

La Alamedilla, 29 April 1811

My dear uncle,

I received your letter of January 20th which you sent by Colonel Fuller enclosing the power of attorney, three days ago. The baggage not having arrived at the departure of the last mail, he himself joined us on the 16th. I have now enclosed it, having done I believe everything that is necessary to it.

The last time I saw Mr Watkins (with John Butler) I did make a disposition of what belonged to me, viz., to my sisters.

With the exception of a few alerts which we have had during the last three days, we have been very quiet since my last. Lord Wellington left this on the 17th for the neighbourhood of Badajoz, where I understand things had not being going on very pleasantly. Our battalion marched from this place on the 17th to Puebla de Azaba one league distant and to the right. On the morning of the 27th a sudden order came to march; I fancy information had been received that the enemy intended to relieve Almeida, we halted near Nave de Haver, the whole force during the day had been brought up, within reach of Almeida, but no demonstration was made on their part, and in the evening we returned to our cantonments. The Coldstream to this place, where the whole brigade is now. I suppose the idea is not yet given up, we march out every morning at daybreak, in the same direction, and I understand

---

* This refers to the previous published letter.

all the troops do the same. Lord Wellington returned yesterday to the infinite satisfaction of everyone. We have retaken Olivenza. There is another report that Bonaparte has sent to Masséna to say that if he does not relieve Almeida, he is never to appear before him again. It had only 25 days' provisions and the investment was completed on the 12th, it is said that Masséna was to be at Ciudad Rodrigo on the 27th. There was a smart skirmish on the 23rd near Gallegos, we lost six men, the French lost a colonel. A considerable force crossed the Agueda on the same day more to the right and after levying a contribution at El Bodon, retired behind the river. I don't know anything further to mention; we certainly shall have a fight if they think proper to attempt the relief of Almeida.

I have not heard of Felton since my last. I forgot to mention to you that I did not pay Sutton for his map. With best love, believe me, my dear uncle, your dutiful and affectionate nephew,
John Fremantle

CONSTANT MARCHING

Their short-lived rest was shattered by the news that Masséna was advancing with a superior force to relieve the fortress of Almeida. Wellington moved to block the French and battle was offered at Fuentes de Oñoro. On 3 May a serious effort was made by the French on the village which gained little ground but caused huge casualties for both sides. After a lull on the 4th Masséna launched on the following day his greatly superior cavalry upon Wellington's isolated right; forcing this wing to retire in squares while under constant cavalry attack, across an extensive plain into a new position. The pickets of the 1st Brigade were caught by the cavalry and dispersed; Lieutenant Colonel Hill of the 3rd Guards being captured. The costly but ultimately futile contest for control of Fuentes also resumed. With nightfall the French retired, handing victory to Wellington.

Lines near Vilar Formoso, 8 May 1811

My dear uncle,

On the 2nd we marched from Alamedilla and information having been received that the enemy was in motion and had the relief of Almeida in contemplation the whole army was assembled on the present ground on the 4th and on the 5th they made a desperate attempt with their cavalry, in which they were greatly superior to us, to overpower us. After repeated charges on both sides our cavalry and light troops fell back to our line, but the contact with the artillery and light infantry did not cease till dark. There was also some very desperate fighting in a village on our left called Fuentes de Oñoro, the whole day in which we have suffered as well as the enemy. I am however happy to tell you that we are all well. Felton has had a miraculous escape, when they were retiring a canon shot struck the middle of his sabretache entered his chestnut horse and bruised his right leg. The horse carried him 10 yards after this, but the moment he fell four or five men immediately dismounted and offered him theirs. We slept together last night but he

felt his leg so stiff next morning that he went to the village, but Milles*
who was also wounded and is just come from him, says he intended
coming up this evening. For these last three mornings we have been
anxiously expecting their attack, but however, thank God the greater
part of their force had disappeared by daybreak this morning, and the
general idea is, that they are retiring without having been able to effect
their purpose. Our brigade was exposed the whole day to the enemy's
artillery, because this was exactly in the front of us, however there
was only one officer wounded by it. A picket which we had sent out
the night before of five officers and 15 men suffered severely being
charged by a large body of cavalry next morning. Young Harvey† was
knocked down and had a sabre wound on his head but got off. The
captain of the 3rd [Guard] Regiment was wounded and taken,‡ our
ensign I believe is killed and the one of the 3rd [Guard] Regiment was
brought in dead;§ in all the lieutenants of the 3rd [Guard] Regiment
Captain Home¶ is the only one who came back safe and he was prisoner
once and had his epaulettes torn off and hat taken away. What is most
absurd to relate is that for the last three days the two lines have not
been half a mile distant and of course the videttes have pickets in the
intermediate space. Various flags of truce have passed and re-passed
and yesterday afternoon parties from each side went to bury the dead
between the lines. Charles I hear took a colonel himself in the charge.
All our cavalry speak in the highest terms of him. Felton says he misses
his other horse very much. I saw Charles yesterday [who was] quite
well. We have not seen our baggage since the 2nd, it was sent to the
rear, we have been laying on the sand without a single tree to shade
us from the scorching sun. The French are in the neighbourhood of a
wood. With best love, and etc, believe me, my dear uncle, your most
dutiful and affectionate nephew,

John Fremantle

Casualties in the Coldstream at Fuentes de Oñoro were four rank & file
killed, Captain Harvey and 51 rank & file wounded and Ensign Stothert
and 7 rank & file taken. The brigade was expecting orders to march to
Badajoz.

---

* Captain Thomas Potter Milles, 14th Light Dragoons.
† Lieutenant & Captain Edward Harvey, Coldstream Guards.
‡ Captain and Lieutenant Colonel John Wright Guise, 3rd Foot Guards, was
mentioned in Wellington's Fuentes despatch. He was wounded, but I have been
unable to confirm that he was made a prisoner.
§ Ensign William Stothert, Coldstream Guard, was made a prisoner and Ensign
George Parker Cookson, 3rd Foot Guards was killed at Fuentes de Oñoro.
¶ Lieutenant & Captain Francis Home, 3rd Foot Guards.

Puebla de Azaba,* 21 May 1811

My dear uncle,

You will with reason think me most remiss for forgetting to enclose the power of attorney from Alamedilla. We returned to this place on the 11th and have remained undisturbed ever since, but expect daily to be sent for to the Alentejo, where the active operations are now carrying on. Two divisions (Picton's and Hoghton's†) marched from hence to the neighbourhood of Badajoz on the 11th and 12th so that there is now a very considerable force there, in short all that remains in this quarter are the 1st, 6th, and Light Divisions of infantry, and cavalry, of which four regiments are detached. Lord Wellington left this on the 13th, and was to reach Badajoz on the 4th day.

The French force is entirely broken up in our front, and 20,000 men gone towards Badajoz, and it is generally thought will arrive before our reinforcement, in time to raise the siege. The trenches were to be opened before the place on the 10th. On the 9th they made a sortie, and were repulsed by Colonel Kemmis's Brigade,‡ who not content with that partial success, followed them up to their guns, the consequence is we have lost 40 officers and 400 men.§ I suppose they expected to take the town. The business of Almeida has turned out most unfortunately;¶ where the fault is we shall never know, but it is most mortifying to think that the garrison which we lost so many lives to secure should have given us the slip so shamefully.

Lord Wellington exclaimed, 'Oh dear, oh dear!' indeed I pity him; I hear he has taken the blame chiefly on himself.**

The British which were blockading it, were brought up to the line on the 9th and Portuguese troops left there, but when the French

---

* Near Fuenteguinaldo, the site of headquarters for Wellington and his Staff.

† Major General Daniel Hoghton commanded the 2nd Brigade of the 2nd Division, however Major General the Honourable Charles Stewart was absent over the winter and Hoghton commanded the 2nd Division in his absence; he was killed at Albuera.

‡ Brevet Colonel James Kemmis commanded the 1st Brigade of Cole's 4th Division.

§ On 10 May 1811, during the first siege of Badajoz, the French made a sortie, which was effectively stopped by the trench guard; however the British chased the French all the way to the ditch of Fort Cristoval, whose great guns killed and wounded some 400, mostly from the 40th Regiment.

¶ Realising that relief was no longer coming, the garrison of Almeida destroyed the defences and marched away in the dead of night. Due to a combination of unfortunate occurrences and stupid errors the besieging forces did not intercept them and they arrived safely at the French lines largely intact.

** An interesting comment from one who was close to Wellington as he has been implicated in throwing all the blame on Lieutenant Colonel Charles Bevan of the 4th Foot, who ultimately committed suicide. See Archie Hunter's *Wellington's Scapegoat, The Tragedy of Lieutenant Colonel Charles Bevan,* Pen & Sword, Barnsley, 2003.

retired on the 10th, our people were ordered to resume their station which was not done. The explosion took place about 12 o'clock on the night of the 10th, the garrison not now more than 1400 strong having been out two hours and I am sorry to say 800 have made their escape.

The garrison of Ciudad Rodrigo does not consist of more than 1200 men, and about 200 cavalry. I don't hear of anything being intended against it, Masséna is certainly gone to France and Marmont has succeeded him.* Young Harvey returned yesterday quite well, he had a very narrow escape, his hat was entirely cut through and the blow reached the crown of his head. I have not been able to find out whereabouts the 14th are quartered, but I have heard of Felton within these last two days. He is quite well.

Charles Bishop is gone down to Coimbra unwell, he shot the horse I sold him for the farcy† two months afterwards. With best remembrances, believe me, my dear uncle, your dutiful and affectionate nephew,

John Fremantle

I don't know whether you were acquainted with young Wingfield‡ of the Coldstream, he was a great friend of mine. He died at Coimbra of a fever, I fancy from being rather poorly when he got down there.

The news was all from the southern front; where the siege of Badajoz had been lifted and the bloody Battle of Albuera had occurred. The Guards were ordered to march south but having arrived at Penamacor they were ordered to return. Later Wellington learned that Marmont was marching south to join Soult and the Guards Brigade were ordered to march south again. John wrote to his uncle while awaiting this final order to march.

La Alamedilla, 5 June 1811

My dear uncle,
Since my letter to you of the 21st of May nothing of importance has taken place, you will have the Gazette and true account of the Battle

---

* Marshal Auguste Frederic Viesse de Marmont, Duc de Ragusa, proved a skilful adversary for Wellington.
† Glanders (also known as Farcy) is an infectious disease that occurs primarily in horses, mules, and donkeys and is caused by infection with bacterium by ingestion of contaminated food or water. Symptoms of glanders include the formation of lesions in the lungs and ulceration of the mucous membranes in the upper respiratory tract. The acute form results in coughing, fever and the release of an infectious nasal discharge, followed by septicaemia and death within days.
‡ Ensign the Honourable John Wingfield, Coldstream Guards, died at Coimbra on 4 May 1811.

of Albuera long before it will reach us. We understand that Lord
Wellington is very much satisfied with what has been done.*

We had a most harassing march from Puebla de Azava to Penamacor
on the 24th, and returned on the 31st having gone nearly 6 leagues
each day. The whole division was ordered to the Alentejo but when
we reached Penamacor, only one brigade proceeded and the remainder
marched back to their former quarters. In the midst of a grand
entertainment given by our brigade yesterday to Don Julian† and the
gentry at Guinaldo,‡ an order arrived during supper for us to march at
day break this morning, where we are now halted for further orders.
I rather imagine, it is to be more a precautionary manoeuvre, than
any general move, the reason may be that the head of a column was
seen at dusk yesterday evening going into Ciudad Rodrigo, and the
brigade was assembled in consequence. It is generally reported that if
the enemy come on in force we shall retire behind the Coa, which I
hope will soon take place, for we have not had a single quiet day since
we have been in this neighbourhood.

I have received your letter of April 24th with the enclosure, and
have again to express my gratitude for your unremitting kindness. I
hope now your trouble will come to be at an end. The 14th took up
their quarters in front of us three days ago, Felton was quartered about
a mile and a half from Puebla, he was with us last night and dined with
Colonel Fuller. I never saw him looking better, or in greater spirits,
[although] his knee still pains him a little. Hawker§ has returned to

---

* The Battle of Albuera was a very costly affair for the British losing over 4,000
men from an initial force of 10,000. A pyrrhic victory was snatched from the jaws of
defeat and Marshal Soult eventually retired from the field having lost some 6,000 men.
Wellington was undoubtedly dismayed by the casualty list but insisted on a public
display of celebration and a victorious despatch by Beresford to assuage the British
government and public.
† Don Julian Sanchez, a Spanish guerrilla leader nicknamed 'El Charro', literally, 'A
man of Salamanca'. An old Spanish song commemorates him thus:
  Cuando Don Julián Sánchez monta a caballo,
    se dicen los franceses ¡viene el diablo!
  Cuando Don Julián Sánchez monta a caballo
    dicen los españoles ¡vienen los charros!
  When Don Julian Sanchez is horseback riding
    the French say the devil is coming!
  When Don Julian Sanchez is horseback riding
    the Spanish say Charros is coming!'
‡ Fuenteguinaldo.
§ Brevet Colonel Samuel Hawker had commanded the 2nd Cavalry Brigade while
Slade commanded the whole of the cavalry during Cotton's absence at home from
January to April. He returned to command the regiment briefly before being made a

the command of the 14th, and I don't see any probability of Felton's getting it again. I believe he intends to go down and see the siege of Badajoz carried on. With best remembrances believe me, my dear uncle, your dutiful and affectionate nephew,

John Fremantle

Marching through Sabugal and Castelo Branco the Guards crossed the Tagus and marched on through Portalegre to Santa Eulalia, where they arrived on 23 June. Here a draft consisting of Captain the honourable John Walpole, Ensign George Henry Macartney Greville and 101 rank and file arrived from Cadiz and soon after the brigade was reviewed by the Duke of Wellington who was accompanied by the Prince of Orange, then serving on Wellington's Staff.

The French armies finding it necessary to disperse again to find food, Marmont moved back to Salamanca; Wellington therefore ordered the Guards brigade north again. They marched from Santa Eulalia to Portalegre on 22 July, then marched north on 31 July, to Penamacor.

Penamacor, 13 August 1811

My dear uncle,

No doubt you will be surprised at not hearing from me for so considerable a length of time, but with the exception of our camp near Elvas which we reached from this part of the country when the siege of Badajoz was raised, by forced marches, we have been continuously marching, and then we were kept in constant suspense till the French retired, when the whole army as it was thought were to move into cantonments, for which purpose our division marched to Portalegre. We were very comfortable for five days, when to our infinite surprise and discomfiture we received an order to march and were brought up here by marches of three leagues each day, always bivouacking, and I believe I may speak generally for all our people, who are quite tired of the whole scene, and business, nor can one possibly guess where or when it is possible for it to end. I believe however it is very fortunate we moved from the Alentejo, for the army, became very unhealthy during its stay there. Our regiment had never less than four officers sick all the time, but they are all recovered now but two. Poor Major Dalling* who was taken ill at the camp, but who we never supposed in great danger died on his way from Portalegre to the rear, on the day we commenced our march from this on the 31st. He is universally regretted both as a gentleman and officer. I was under great obligations

---

major general on 4 June.

* Brevet Major Edward Dalling, Coldstream Guards, died of fever on 31 July 1811.

to him for his kindness and civility in January when h[
camp to Finch.* It makes a very considerable change in
for Collier† who for some time had stopped the promot[
sum has two seniors not functioning, now is to get Smy[
and there is strong reason for supposing that as low down as Sullivan‡
the lieutenants will in less than six months have their company, Adams
not purchasing,§ but without this I shall have seven lieutenants under
me within the twelve month and I really think in another year I shall
have as many more. Smyth's was quite an elopement for we scarcely
heard of his intention to quit, before he was off. He was quite miserable
all the time he was with us, and nobody at all knew the reason of it.

Lord Wellington's headquarters were at Guinaldo on the 11th with
only a few cavalry in the neighbourhood. The Light Division is at
Gallegos, the 5th at Alfaiates, 1st Penamacor, 4th Pedrogao extending
towards Castelo Branco, the 3rd and 6th are on our left, but I can't
learn where. General Hill's is the only corps left on the other side of the
Tagus. I understand there is a battering train coming up from Lamego.
We have long had an idea that we were to besiege Ciudad Rodrigo; I
hope if we do, it will not fail. I think if Lord W[ellington] undertakes
it, the battering train will be lost rather than relinquish the siege.
Perhaps this late movement may be only to threaten it, and to draw
the French forces from Cadiz or elsewhere, a report is just received
from Guinaldo that 40,000 more French have entered Spain. This is
all the news I am able to give you. The general opinion is that our
next movement will be forward. Our brigade reached this on the 11th
being the fifth time we have passed by it, since the action at Fuentes de
Oñoro. The whole line of the frontier is one of the most mountainous
parts of the country, and the roads are dreadfully bad. Our change
from Smyth and Brand to Fuller,¶ has not been for the best by any
means, there have been several differences since his arrival unknown
before. I did not understand him at first by any means, but we go on
much better now. The next brevet will I suppose take him from the
command of this battalion. The work in this country does not suit him
at all. I have not seen Felton since Elvas; the regiment has changed its

---

* Lieutenant General the Honourable Edward Finch was colonel of the 22nd Foot.
† Lieutenant and Captain George Collier, Coldstream Guards, did become a Captain
and Lieutenant Colonel on 3 October 1811.
‡ Lieutenant and Captain Sir Henry Sullivan, Coldstream Guards, did not gain his
company until 24 September 1812.
§ Lieutenant and Captain Lucius Frederick Adams, Coldstream Guards, gained his
company on 31 January 1812 without purchase.
¶ Brand went home to join the 2nd Battalion in April; Smyth left Portugal in the July
and resigned his commission in the October.

brigade twice, the 16th and it are together now under Anson.* Felton is next to him.† They are stationed between Perdigao and Castelo Branco. Pray make my best remembrances and with best love, believe me ever, my dear uncle, your dutiful and affectionate nephew,

John Fremantle

---

* According to Oman there were three changes to the organisation of the cavalry; On 19 June, the 13th and 14th Light Dragoons were put in Slade's brigade but on 19 July the 13th were moved to Major General George Anson's brigade, joining the 16th; while the 14th moved to Long's Brigade joining the 11th. Finally on the 1 August the 13th and 14th exchanged brigades leaving George Anson commanding the 14th & 16th Light Dragoons. The schedule of the cavalry reorganisations printed by Oman was actually by C. T. Atkinson, a highly respected scholar.

† Major Felton Hervey commanding the 14th Light Dragoons was senior to Major Clement Archer 16th Light Dragoons; hence in Anson's absence he would take command of the brigade.

CIUDAD RODRIGO

On 6 September, Sir Thomas Graham superseded Sir Brent Spencer in command of the First Division and John reported a number of changes at the top in the regiment. The army had moved forward to blockade Ciudad Rodrigo, but there was no sign of Wellington escalating matters into a formal siege.

Nave de Haver, 11 September 1811

My dear uncle,

Enclosed is the power of attorney which I received by Lionel* from Lisbon only yesterday, together with your letter. We reached Penamacor on the 28th, but did not reach this place until the 4th having halted two days. I am not able to tell you what is in any way likely to happen. The battering train about which there has been so much said I believe at this moment is not nearer than Lamego, indeed as far as I can judge the idea of besieging Ciudad Rodrigo seems to be entirely given up. I was at headquarters (Guinaldo) on the 9th and the conversation amongst the Staff was certainly very warlike, but in the course of another week or ten days the rains will have commenced, when of course it will be impossible to commence active operations, added to which the army is very likely chiefly not to want a short stay in the Alentejo, but I am happy to tell you our brigade has not suffered in the least. Colonel Fuller left us when we marched from Penamacor, and is now gone to Lisbon to recover from a bout of fever and ague. I dare say from the great distance he will not join us for six or seven months. Sir G. Stirling† commands *pro tempore*, there is a strong rumour that

---

* Felton's youngest brother Lionel Charles Hervey. He became secretary to the British embassy at Madrid in 1815, and in 1825 he married Frances Mary Wells, daughter of Vice-Admiral Wells.

† Captain and Lieutenant Colonel Sir Gilbert Stirling retired from the service on 1 March 1812.

Colonel Philip* who has been absent from sickness a considerable time is about to quit the regiment, I think it extremely likely. This is the only promotion I know of besides what I mentioned in my last letter from Penamacor. Felton passed through here on the 8th with his regiment on their way to Gallegos [de Arganan] and Martillan, he was looking very well. He told me Charles Bishop was with the regiment. General Graham has joined our division and is at present here; every person who knows him speaks in the highest terms of him. With best love to all, but believe me, my dear uncle, your dutiful and affectionate nephew,

    John Fremantle

Wellington's preparations for besieging Ciudad Rodrigo were already under way but few in the army actually believed it would happen.

Nave de Haver, 18 September 1811

My dear uncle,

You will perceive from my still dating from this place, that no movement has taken place since my last letter, and headquarters remains at Fuenteguinaldo. I was over there, and remained the 15th and Lord Wellington had been out all the morning, and did not return till 7 o'clock with the chief engineer† from reconnoitring Ciudad Rodrigo. There are from 15 to 18,000 men in the place‡ and have only provisions and half allowances to last them to the end of the present month. The heavy guns have reached Pinhel, but I can't hear that they are proceeding from thence; 200 men of the 1st Division were ordered four days ago to be placed under the charge of a captain of the engineers for the purpose of learning to sap and mine, our brigade has provided 80 men towards this number. This whole are at a little village called Batocas, a league from hence and about a mile from Alamedilla. All these manoeuvres look as if the siege was ready to be undertaken, but every person is willing to bet the contrary, I make no doubt our division will have an active part in it if it is.

The last news on the 15th was that a large convoy, escorted, had left Salamanca on the 13th for Rodrigo, but yesterday I heard for certain

---

* Captain and Lieutenant Colonel James Philips actually remained in the peninsula until January 1813, serving at Salamanca and Burgos.

† The Chief Royal Engineer (CRE) was Lieutenant Colonel Sir Richard Fletcher from 1809 until his death at the siege of San Sebastian in 1813.

‡ Marshal Marmont had nearly 20,000 troops in the vicinity of Ciudad Rodrigo at this time, but this was too many for the fortress to hold. When the siege did eventually occur, the garrison of Ciudad Rodrigo numbered just under 2,000.

that it had returned thence. The whole of our force is cantoned very compactly between Robleda (the right) and Gallegos [de Arganan] (the left). The headquarters of the cavalry is at Sexmiro. Felton is at Martillan a mile from thence with a squadron of the 14th. The headquarters of General Hill's Corps is at Portalegre; I believe the army was never more sickly, ague and fever is the chief complaint. Our brigade has increased considerably since the last ten days, but is comparatively very healthy. Colonels Braddyl and Woodford, Bowles, Talbot and Beckford are expected out immediately to supply the late vacancies. Collier and Mildmay* will then go home. I was a good deal surprised the evening before last to meet Lionel; I had nearly passed him without recognising him. He was very hungry and wretched after his journey, having been obliged to leave his servant and horse with a sore back at Castelo Branco. He declared he had nowhere met with such good fare as he did here. I took him yesterday to Sexmiro, where hearing Felton was not at home, I returned. I did not think he was looking by any means well, he complained of having had a slight *bouleversement de l'interior* [confusion of the interior] during his journey which I recommended him to take great care of whilst he was here. Adieu, my dear uncle, with best love to all at Englefield Green, believe me, your most dutiful and affectionate nephew,

John Fremantle

The 4th Division marched through this place yesterday from the neighbourhood of Almeida, where they were very sickly. I did not know at the time that Mr Hutchinson† was with the 7th Regiment. I understand they are not far from here and pray tell Mrs Hervey I will make a point of seeking him out.

In his next letter, John wrote with news of the action of El Bodon which occurred on 25 September 1811, although the Guards were not involved.

---

* Captain and Lieutenant Colonel Thomas Braddyl, Coldstream Guards, arrived with the regiment in October 1811 but had resigned by December 1811. Captain and Lieutenant Colonel Alexander George Woodford, Coldstream Guards, did not arrive in the Peninsula until January 1812, but remained until the war ended. Lieutenant and Captain George Bowles, Coldstream Guards, arrived in the Peninsula in September 1811 and remained until the end of the war. His letters have been published by the editor, *A Guards Officer in the Peninsula and at Waterloo*. Ensign John Talbot, Coldstream Guards. Ensign Francis Love Beckford, Coldstream Guards, arrived in the peninsula in September 1811 and remained until September 1812. Ensign Paulet St John Mildmay, was promoted to lieutenant & captain in October 1811 and went home, but resigned the service in April 1812.
† Lieutenant Joseph Hutchinson, 7th Foot.

Marshal Marmont had sent out strong cavalry patrols to discover Wellington's intentions. One such patrol amounting to 2,500 dragoons under General Montbrun discovered the 3rd Division strung out and unsupported. Attacking immediately, a Portuguese battery was overrun and while the heavily outnumbered allied cavalry valiantly sought to hold the French, Major Henry Ridge led the 5th Foot in an audacious attack against the French cavalry, which he scattered after three volleys and recaptured the guns. Total allied losses were 149 killed, wounded and missing, the latter presumably being captured.

A second strong patrol under General Wathier* proceeded via Carpio towards the 6th Division on the same day. Approaching a wood, the French were ambushed by infantry and charged by squadrons of the 14th and 16th Dragoons, putting them to flight. French losses were 48 killed and wounded, the allied loss was twelve killed and wounded.

Despite these actions, all the talk was of retiring into Portugal for winter quarters as the army was increasingly sick.

Vale de Azares, 8 October 1811

My dear uncle,

I have had no opportunity of writing to you since the action of 25th last, which you will long ago have had an account of; it is an additional proof of the determined policy of the British troops, not to be overcome by the French, when ably conducted, and on the late occasion I understand it was most manfully so. We were quite quiet at Nave de Haver the whole time which was three leagues from hence but could distinctly perceive all the movements. All that happened in our immediate front was an affair of the cavalry between Carpio [De Azaba] and Espeja, in which the 14th and 16th to use the received expression 'covered themselves with glory'.

General Graham spoke in the highest terms of them. We marched for three consecutive nights afterwards, and were considerably rejoiced when past the Coa. The division is now cantoned in the neighbourhood of Celorico [de Beira] and our brigade chiefly in the villages around the sierra, which have not been at all destroyed, and the country is beautiful. Everyone talks of the certainty of our going to Viseu for the winter, I hope it may prove so, as it will in some degree make up for the toils of this most harassing campaign. Operations must cease I should think for the season is entirely broken, and at times very heavy rains. The sickness in the army lately has been quite dreadful. Lord Wellington has been in Celorico this morning visiting the hospital; the establishment of which is very large, but the state of the place is quite

---

* General Pierre Watier (or Wathier), Comte de Saint-Alphonse.

shameful and appears to want any arrangement. Headquarters are at Freineda near Nave de Haver but I imagine are quite temporary, the different divisions are also a good deal scattered. The outposts still keep the line of the Agueda. Lord Clare* and his party left Celorico on the 4th on their way to Lisbon, I fancy quite satisfied with their trip; they were all at the fight. He sent me word he intended coming to see me. I am rejoiced he did not for I am sure I don't know what would have become of him as all our baggage had been sent away some time before to facilitate all movements. With best remembrances, believe me, my dear uncle, your most affectionate nephew,

    John Fremantle

PS I have enclosed a letter to Selina.

News had finally arrived with the army of General Hill's success at Arroyomolinos, where his corps of 10,000 men launched a surprise attack on General Girard's division numbering about 4,000 who were forced to abandon their equipment and flee over the mountains. For the loss of about one hundred allied killed and wounded, the French lost 300 killed, 1,300 were captured with three cannon.

After a short advance the Guards returned to their quarters having heard that a convoy of supplies and a new governor (the previous one having been captured by the Spanish outside the fortress) had successfully entered Ciudad Rodrigo.

Vale de Azares, 5 November 1811

My dear uncle,

We were agreeably surprised on the 1st with the news of General Hill's surprise upon a division of the French near Caceres. He broke up from Portalegre very suddenly and arrived within three miles of Arroyos† without their knowing of his movement, and the morning on which he made his attack, he formed his column within 200 yards of the French sentry, who was detached from a small piquet outside the village, where the Duc d'Aremberg and General Bonet were found in bed and consequently taken prisoners with about a thousand men, another general got off wounded.‡ The loss on our part is said not to exceed 50 men, no further particulars have yet reached us and most likely we shall be obliged to wait their coming from England. The brigade

---

* John FitzGibbon, 2nd Earl of Clare (1792–1851) graduated from Christchurch in 1812, so presumably he had taken some time from his studies for a Grand Tour.

† Arroyomolinos in the province of Caceres.

‡ A small error: Bonet was not present, the officer captured was General Bron.

had marched from Caceres the morning before the attack, and General Hill has detached a corps towards Merida to endeavour to stop it, most probably there will be an addition to his present number of prisoners, as they went off in the greatest confusion. We are all glad it happened to General Hill, besides it will prove he was worthy of the post Lord Wellington has always entrusted to him. Something of this sort was very much wanted to make up for our late ill successes. I am sorry not to be able to give so good an account of our proceedings in this quarter as I could wish. We were back up in our comfortable quarters (comparatively speaking) here at 12 o'clock on the night of the 27th with an order to march the next morning, which we did accordingly, with a view to intercept a new governor, on his way to Ciudad Rodrigo with 200 head of cattle, but we were counter-ordered after a march of two hours. When we returned to our quarters we learnt that the convoy had been put into the place that same night, and the escort had marched back again immediately, it was by all means a large one, and proceeded very rapidly. Lord Wellington understood they were to collect their whole force in these parts for the purpose, in which case I suppose we should have spent another fortnight as we did last time, without being able to prevent its getting in after all. Of course you will have heard of the ridiculous manner in which Don Julian carried off the late governor. Headquarters still remain at Freineda, but I cannot suppose it will be long before we go to Viseu, for as our supplies come from Lamego we have been these last three days without bread, owing to the rains having wrecked the fords.

There is nothing talked of in the regiment but the imminent promotion which is to take place when Cooke and Hamilton* are to have companies and I believe Sullivan will not be long after them.

Smyth has played us a happy trick, Lord Proby† would not allow him to go home until he gave him in his resignation. How he has managed it since his arrival in England we are not able to find out; I dare say it will end by his remaining in the regiment, we are all very much dissatisfied with his whole proceeding and it certainly is not correct of him.‡ Fuller has not yet joined us, from being sick at his home. Colonel Braddyl who arrived a month ago expects to go home very shortly; he is one that goes out. I have not seen Felton this long

---

* Lieutenant and Captain Henry Frederick Cooke gained his company by promotion to captain and lieutenant colonel on 11 November; Hamilton had to wait until 30 January 1812 for his.

† Captain and Lieutenant Colonel Lord John Proby, Coldstream Guards, 2nd Earl of Carysfort, became a brevet colonel on 1 January 1812.

‡ These rumours were unfounded: Smyth did resign from the regiment on 2 October.

time but I have heard of his having returned from his trip to Oporto. With best remembrances believe me, my dear uncle, your dutiful and affectionate nephew,

John Fremantle

I have not received any letter from you since the one by Lionel and only two before.

Vale de Azares, 20 November 1811

My dear uncle,

I received your letter of the 29th September yesterday and am very sorry there should be so great a mistake about the paper you sent me out by Colonel Fuller to sign. It was witnessed by him and I think Sir H Sullivan. I wrote to you on or about the 20th April telling you I had enclosed it, but forgot to do so, it appears as if that letter never reached you, or one from me forwarded after the 5th May; I think I sent it in the latter end of that month, but I am very sorry that I cannot be more accurate. I noted down precisely everything I did about it in my almanac [sic], which I have since had the misfortune to lose, it is possible I may have enclosed it to Mr Watkins. The printed power you sent me out by Lionel, I returned immediately from Nave de Haver, witnessed by Sir G. Stirling and Mr Rose.* I hope there will be no mistake about it. I hope my letter of the 5th has reached you safe. We heard nothing more of General Hill's success than I mentioned at the time. General Reynaud† is still at Lisbon, I hear he is a very mauvais sujet [poor subject].

We are all dreadfully down in the mouth here. We are only paid up to the 24th August, and I am sorry to say there is very little probability of its being made up to us quickly, as the commissariat are in greater distress than the army. One of the chiefs of the militias applied the other day to the chief commissary for eight months' wages due to him for his mules and servants, and was so exasperated at being offered one month that he deserted with all his train. I mention this circumstance, for if the example is followed to any degree I do not know what will become of us, for that is the sole means by which we are provisioned at all. There is no further talk of our going to Viseu. The army is very

---

* Assistant Surgeon John Rose, Coldstream Guards (Drew, no. 2351). Mackinnon, *Origin and Services of the Coldstream Guards*, p. 524, mistakenly states his Christian name to be Thomas.

† General Reynaud, the governor of Ciudad Rodrigo, who was captured by Don Julian Sanchez.

unhealthy; headquarters are still at Freineda and the Light Division at Guinaldo. There was a very strong working party at Almeida for these last three weeks; making of temporary works, perhaps when they are completed we may be brought into more settled quarters for the winter.

Many thanks to you for your wholesome and friendly advice about Fuller. We certainly had some decided differences but these were at an end before he left the battalion, and when I reflected, you may rely upon it they shall not be answered. I expect him up on the 24th. Collier has succeeded the Smyth vacancy, and leaves us in a day or two for England. Everything is settled between Braddyl and Cooke; I expect the promotion will continue very rapid for the next six or even twelve months. Felton I heard of the other day hunting at headquarters. They have hunted up a great many hares there. Charles Bishop is with the regiment but I have not heard of him. Our only amusement here, for those who don't shoot, is walking up to view the perfect scenery above the mountain. I hope my Uncle Tom* likes his new station; perhaps he may have further opportunities of distinguishing himself. Adieu my dear uncle, with best love and remembrances, believe me, your most dutiful and affectionate nephew,

    J. Fremantle

John continued to write of preparations for a siege, including the arrival of the siege artillery at Almeida, but without any real belief that a siege was to be undertaken.

Freineda, 11 December 1811

My dear uncle,
I received your letter of October 20 on the 22nd of last month, and on the following day marched at an hour's notice from our comfortable quarters at Vale de Azares without intermission till we reached Nave de Haver, where we were still on the alert, and on the 3rd of this month reached Pinhel, which is to be our stationary quarter, it was formerly a very nice place, but suffered extremely by the French, and the passage of the different troops since. Our officers have been very hard at work ever since they came, getting up doors, windows and some fireplaces, for at first houses were mere skeletons. There is one of the most curious Moorish castles here we have ever seen, and the only one in

---

* Rear-Admiral Thomas Fremantle had joined the Mediterranean Fleet under Admiral Cotton, then Pellew, where he supported operations in eastern Spain from his base in Minorca, before going to Sicily, the Adriatic to counter Murat and then to defeat the French in Dalmatia.

which there were any guns and these I suppose were the first ever cast.

The cause of our late movement was, it is said, upon false information of the French being in motion, and it certainly appears so, there is a dreadful hoax in consequence of it. The French say, they only have to assemble 30 cars at any time to make us collect our army. The information was that they were again getting ready some supplies to put into Rodrigo. I suppose Lord W[ellington] was anxious to be beforehand with them in case they attempted it, having escaped his vigilance once before, whatever it was, we have had a very discomfiting march here, changing our quarters from good to very bad ones. The people who have always been his staunchest friends begin I fear to change very much. The working party at Almeida is not yet discontinued; the heavy train of artillery so much talked of, is all in there, seventy pieces all 24 pounders. I am sure I cannot guess what is the reason of it, of course it would oblige us to fight whenever the French show any head towards it and I should think prevent our leaving this part of the country as long as it remains. Besides the transport of it is tremendous, it occupies several hundred bullocks and cannot travel more than a league each day. I am very sorry I cannot comply with your wish of knowing our numbers [of] sick here, for I don't happen to know any of the Adjutant General's Staff, and if I did I daresay I should not succeed for they are so very particular about their returns that none of the people at headquarters will ask for me.

I came over from Pinhel to Lionel yesterday and do not return until tomorrow. In general there is excellent sport, they rarely go out without finding two or three foxes, the worst of it is to work up their horses upon this bad forage, besides the country is very heavy. Felton generally comes once a week and is expected tomorrow. I have not seen him now for a long time, but I hear he is quite well, Charles Bishop is at Gallegos.

General Graham is remarkably civil, we all like him very much, he says he knew my Uncle Tom very well. Perhaps you may have heard that Bayly and my successor have had a dreadful and serious disagreement. The next brevet will include him in the major generals.* A report has prevailed here lately that all our major generals' company were to be given up. If it takes place it will be a grand thing for the younger part of the brigade. The Coldstream would get five or six steps by it and the regiment nearly double as many, but I don't suppose they would all be allowed to go in the regiment. I have now eight lieutenants under me. I don't know of any more for the present. With

---

* Brevet Colonel Henry Bayly, Coldstream Guards, was made a major general on 1 January 1812.

best love and remembrance, believe me, my dear uncle, your dutiful and affectionate nephew,

John Fremantle

Pinhel, 31 December 1811

My dear uncle,
I hope my letter of the 11th from Freineda has reached you, I have no news, or anything interesting to tell you since then, our sick is [*sic*] very numerous, and I heard from very good authority yesterday that the deaths in a late week amounted to 250. The hospital at Celorico, which is by no means a large establishment, had 15 deaths in one night and a great number of the mates and nurses had been taken ill, thank goodness we have in the whole only eight men in our brigade there, and we are fairly healthy here. The working party at Almeida still continues and a proportion of every brigade have been making fascines and gabions ever since my last letter. Our people have already filled a whole field with the latter and there is no order yet for them to discontinue.

We all suppose they are meant for Ciudad Rodrigo as soon as ever the season permits, for my own part I should prefer that, to such a marching campaign as last was. General Anson has left the army to go to England for a couple of months and Felton is now in the command of that brigade of light dragoons. I heard of him by a person who saw him yesterday quite well. They march tomorrow from their outpost on the Agueda to the neighbourhood of Viseu for forage I hear their horses have suffered very severely since they have been on that duty and I was told by a person who saw the heavy brigade on their march to relieve them that they were looking wretchedly. Lord Wellington said lately that the country people were to be forced to make hay by next year. My steed is in a wretched state, but I have been much more lucky than half my neighbours, never having lost a single beast. They never think of offering corn to the infantry officers, all we get is rye straw, which the animals go four or five leagues to fetch. Felton is expected here tomorrow and I believe will remain a day or two.

Hamilton of the Coldstream has left Cadiz with the idea of getting his company as soon as he gets to England, we none of us know who goes out. Pray give my best love to my aunt and all at Englefield Green. I have enclosed you a long letter for Selina. Believe me, my dear uncle your most dutiful and affectionate nephew,

John Fremantle

PS Pray tell Selina not to send me an almanac as I have got one already for 1812.

Finally, despite the poor weather, John was able to write home to inform his uncle that they had advanced to besiege Ciudad Rodrigo, while the French forces were dispersed collecting supplies.

Naves, 7 January 1812

My dear uncle,

I received your letter of the 9th December the day I sent my last from Pinhel. I was considerably surprised on the arrival of Felton the following day, he brought news from headquarters that we were likely to march at a moment's notice to lay siege of Ciudad Rodrigo, which everyone disregarded whom I told it to, but however to their dismay the order reached us in the middle of the night of the 3rd January for our march on the 4th which as ill luck could have it was as bad a day as ever remembered, and to add to our comfort when we reached this, an order which had been dispatched to Pinhel forbidding our march we learnt had taken a wrong direction, and we halted here in consequence. I went on tour to Freineda on the 5th where they talked of nothing but battle and the trenches. I saw his lordship who asked several times about the weather, and upon the strength of the two last days past went yesterday to take up his quarters at Gallegos. We expect to march hourly; our brigade goes to Carpio and Espeja. The Light Division to Tenebron on the right bank of the Agueda. The 3rd and 4th to San Felice [Saelices?] and El Bodon [respectively]. The five divisions are to relieve each other every 24 hours [in the trenches]. I am very glad we happen to be cantoned so handy to the place as some of the regiments will have to go and return three leagues. The 26th and 79th Regiments were sent to Viseu previous to our march on account of their very sickly state. They belong to our division* which suffers unluckily at this moment.

An order has just arrived for the march to our station tomorrow morning. I will write to you a line from thence by the first mail. Pray abuse all the 'Blind man buff party' for their hateful message and should any doubts remain with respect to my smiles on that subject pray dispel them. And with best love, believe me, my dear uncle, your dutiful affectionate,

John Fremantle

The siege of Ciudad Rodrigo commenced in earnest on 8 January 1812 and the Guards went into the trenches for the first time on that day; having to march from Espeja at dawn and not returning until the evening

---

* The 1/26th and 1/79th formed part of the 2nd Brigade of 1st Division with the 2/24th, 2/42nd and 1 company of the 5/60th.

of the following day, a distance of fifteen miles each way. Wellington needed to prosecute the siege rapidly, before Marshal Marmont had time to collect his forces and intervene.

Gallegos, 15 January 1812

My dear uncle,

We left Naves the morning after I wrote to you and marched to Espeja. The next day the whole division relieved General Craufurd's in the trenches before Ciudad Rodrigo. They had previously stormed in the most gallant manner a small work outside the town.* Our brigade went to work at sunset on the 8th and did not cease till after daylight next morning; the ground was all fresh, but our battalion happily lost but one killed and four wounded. The 3rd [Guard] Regiment was less fortunate, it came to our turn again on the night of the 13th from 6 till 1 when the ground was also new, but a great deal of the fire from the place was directed to a convent which had been carried by assault about 10, and the whole brigade had only three wounded; those belonged to us. The other two brigades in the division suffered considerably. As we were marching home yesterday morning we had a beautiful sight of a skirmish which took place on account of their jealousy at our possessing this convent. They were driven back in great style by the 24th and 42nd Regiments and our battalion. Our batteries opened yesterday evening and have been hard at work ever since. Another convent close to the town, in which there were guns, was taken possession of soon after our fire opened. So that now there remains nothing to them outside the place. I trust it will not come to our turn again more than once as it is bitter cold work. The first night we have [*sic*] not a bit of wood, and I assure [you] the outside of my cloak was quite glazed over. We were better off last time, for we brought wood with us. I went into the trenches last time because Fuller commanded there but only for a short time. *Grace à Dieu* [by the grace of God] I am not obliged to remain constantly. I doubt very much having served my credit, whether I shall appear again. It is a full 15 miles from Espeja to the works, and we are obliged to start before daylight to arrive there by 11 o'clock. It is nearly three before our return on the following day.

Marmont is expected at Salamanca on the 17th and that is four days' march from hence, but I understand he cannot possibly collect more than 20,000 men which will not at all incommode us in our operations

---

* Colonel Colborne led a successful storming party against the San Francisco redoubt on the night of 8 January, which probably accelerated the siege by some five days.

if the place does not fall before, which they seem to think it must. Part of General Hill's corps is moving this way, and the 7th and 6th Division's cavalry that were in the rear are all moving up. I am not certain whether I told you that the troops employed in the siege are the Light Division, 1st, 3rd and 4th. I make no doubt we shall have an action before all this ends.

Felton is just gone through here from the rear with his brigade; I fancy they will be cantoned in the immediate neighbourhood. He goes on to look at Ciudad Rodrigo, and so to dine and sleep here as I do. Charles Bishop is quite well. I make no doubt if there is anything to be done Lord Wellington will still continue Felton in his command during it, although he has several cavalry officers here senior to him.

The mail arrived last night with letters to the 1st. The brevet has taken Braddyl* in amongst the major generals and Fuller will go home to what is called command the regiment, though in reality he only has the junior battalion of the two. This will either bring us Lord Aylmer[†] or Brand.[‡] The former is fighting very hard not to come and I fancy the latter is not over-willing.

Lord Wellington and all the people are just returned, he says he thinks the town in a bad way. Felton says he would write if his fingers were not so very cold. Pray make my best remembrances and with much love, believe me, my dear uncle, your dutiful and affectionate nephew,

John Fremantle

The next letter home announced the capture of the fortress on the 19th after the storming of two breaches, with the loss of 568 killed and wounded. General Barrie was captured with 1,300 unwounded men of the garrison and the remaining 650 were killed or wounded. The Guards were not involved in the storming.

Gallegos, 21 January 1812

My dear uncle,
I have only time to tell you of the fall of Ciudad Rodrigo the night before last by assault. Our brigade had nothing to do in the business; the only troops employed were the 3rd and Light Division. I am afraid

---

* Braddyl was not given a major generalship but retired from the service, Cooke purchasing his company. He became a Groom of the Bedchamber to the king in March 1812.

† Brevet Colonel Matthew Lord Aylmer, Coldstream Guards, arrived in the peninsula in November 1812 as assistant adjutant general.

‡ Fuller remained in Spain until May and Brand joined to take command in June.

our loss is considerable, General Mackinnon was blown up on the breach, Craufurd is dangerously wounded[*] and General Vandeleur[†] slightly. I fancy our people did great harm after they were in the place.[‡] The governor and all the principal officers are saved. He dined with Lord Wellington yesterday and behaved so ill that he was obliged to silence him. Adams and White[§] get their promotion by Mackinnon's death. Report says that Marshal Marmont is in the neighbourhood of Salamanca with 50,000 men, but I should hardly imagine he will attempt to incommode us with that force.

Felton leaves this tomorrow for his brigade. The whole of the troops which were in the rear viz. the 7th, 6th and 5th Divisions have all joined us here and are ready at a moment's call. Pray make my best remembrances, and believe me, my dear uncle, your most dutiful and affectionate,

John Fremantle

John wrote again a few days later, having witnessed the consequent devastation at Ciudad Rodrigo and the urgent repairs undertaken to ensure that Marmont would be unable to regain it by a coup de main. Otherwise all the intrigues of regimental life went on without intermission.

Espeja, 29 January 1812

My dear uncle,

I hope my letter of the 21st will have reached you. Gordon[¶] is making so much fuss about everybody loading him with their letters the day before he started that I did not like to offer him mine, however Fitzroy Somerset[**] was good enough to put it for me under the paper which contained General Charles Stewart's letters; which I conceived would be forwarded to you. Nothing particular has arrived since the fall of the place, the small body which was sent from Salamanca never came further than within 10 leagues of us, and has since returned. All our works are entirely levelled, and the breaches are nearly repaired. The

---

[*] Craufurd was mortally wounded and succumbed on 24th; he was buried in the breach.

[†] Major General John Ormsby Vandeleur, was only slightly wounded.

[‡] The troops sacked the place, but it proved a mere shadow of the awful scenes to come at later sieges.

[§] Adams gained promotion to captain and lieutenant colonel and Ensign Charles White became a lieutenant and captain.

[¶] Alexander Gordon, Wellington's aide-de-camp, was sent home with the despatch announcing the fall of Ciudad Rodrigo and was made a brevet lieutenant colonel in the army although his regimental rank remained unchanged.

[**] Brevet Major Fitzroy Somerset, 43rd Foot, was military secretary to Wellington.

provisioning of it is also in a state of forwardness.

I went to the town the day after it fell, and everybody agreed that there never was such a scene witnessed. English and French dead and dying in the streets and burning ruins, and what little furniture had been in the houses was turned out of doors. Our men who got into the place behaved like absolute monsters and savages, in the shape of human creatures, but still I think the people all say that the garrison was let off too easily, several French officers told us that it was almost unlawful of the governor to stand the assault, with so weak a garrison, and behave so defensively. However it is some satisfaction to us to know that we took the place in 11 days, which the French were six weeks before, with a very powerful army. Our batteries opened five days sooner than theirs. The people at Lord Wellington's are in the highest spirits and indeed it has revived the whole army, some coup of this nature had been long wanted to put us in good humour. Poor General Craufurd died in Ciudad and was buried at the foot of the breach where the Light Division entered. Lord Wellington and the whole of the Staff attended the funeral. He certainly is a great loss to the army, as an officer, and very much regretted. General Clinton* who has not yet joined, is talked of as his successor.

We have been under orders these two days to hold ourselves in readiness to march at a moment's notice. I fancy we are first of all to go to Pinhel and all our old quarters. If Marmont takes such another walk as his last, we are to go down to Abrantes for our clothing where it all is, and afterwards we shall be handy to Badajoz, which will certainly be the next aim, although we are certain not to get that without a general action.

The Spaniards are to be put into Ciudad as soon as it is finished and I almost hope they will be able to keep this part of the country against any minor incursion, while we arrange matters elsewhere.

I believe I have now given you nearly all the news I am with. No change has taken place in the regiment; it is still doubtful whether Lord Aylmer or Bland will come out to succeed Fuller. The Duke of C[ambridge] has written very strongly to remonstrate against the former being on the Staff which I think can be of no avail. Fuller asked me some days ago if I wished to get to England, as he thought there might be no difficulty in arranging an exchange between someone and myself when he went home. I know Burroughs† is very anxious to

---

* Major General Henry Clinton arrived in the peninsula in February 1812 and was given command of the 6th Division.

† Lieutenant and Captain William Burroughs, Coldstream Guards, did join the Peninsular army in July 1812 and served with it until succumbing to his wounds in

come out, and altogether I am afraid of Fuller as I know he is a very deep schemer. I made him no decision however, and appeared very indifferent about the matter. I am senior adjutant of the two here, and I should not think it at all unlikely that Dawkins was advanced on the Staff here, when his uncle General Clinton joins. And then I should certainly not wish to give up my claim for the brigade majorship; but I confess that if this does not take place, I do not know how I could hesitate between England and being pushed about in this horrid country as a regimental officer, seeing ones' animals starve before one; at all events there can be no hurry about it and I shall be glad to have your opinion before I give Fuller my answer. Him and I have got on famously lately and he told me the other day that if I did not go home he should take care that no adjutant in the London brigade should get promotion who was junior to me.

I am anxiously expecting to hear from you, it is now a considerable time since I have had that full advice. And as for Selina I begin to think she has given it up, although I am sure I have not been remiss. Pray give my best love and remembrance to all and believe me, my dear uncle, your dutiful and affectionate nephew,

John Fremantle

The army retired to their previous quarters to rest as the weather was exceedingly wet. John forwarded a return on the Guards with his letter, which he urged his uncle not to publish. Wellington had complained bitterly that intelligence from the army was being published in the newspapers and thus directly informing Napoleon, who was known to read the English papers.

Espeja, 5 February 1812

My dear uncle,

I have very little to say to you since last week, all the divisions have moved back, nearly to their old cantonments, except ours, and we are in constant expectation of it. We are in great luck not to have stirred as yet, for within the last four or five days it has been raining torrents and the whole country is a sheet of water. Lord Wellington moved back to Freineda two days ago, where I think he is likely to remain during the bad months. He has a pack of foxhounds and General Stewart a pack of harriers, there, and all the Staff have built fireplaces and made themselves quite comfortable, apropos I forgot always to tell you, that I furnished the former with a huntsman, who was my batman.* He had

---

the final action of the war at Bayonne.

* General Graham records that this man was Tom Crane, a private in the Coldstream,

been brought up with hounds, in his younger days, and they are very well pleased with his performances, and I was not very sorry to get rid of him, besides I can always have one of my animals there feeding on corn, which he takes care of, this latter article is become a serious grievance. They never think of serving out any to regimental officers, everything is monopolised by the Staff, and our beasts left to starve, however it affords us something to grumble about in the market place. Changes still continue in the regiment, and I have no doubt will be kept up as long as we remain abroad. Fuller will go home the moment somebody comes out to replace him, and that most likely will be Colonel Brand as Lord Aylmer has been given out in orders here as Deputy Adjutant General appointed from England which I think very possibly will give a step to the regiment, as the Duke of Cambridge is exceedingly angry at his accepting the situation, and of course he would prefer leaving the regiment, rather than give it up. We expect his arrival here very shortly. General Howard[*] is a very likely person to get a regiment very soon.

Enclosed are two states, which may give you an idea of what the wear and tear is, of a regiment on service; that of the 3rd [Guards] Regiment is very correct, but I believe there has been some little difficulty in making up the one of the Coldstream, owing to some of the papers being lost, but the grand totals are correct. If you have any curiosity to have the returns in a different shape I will get them made up, but I am afraid I cannot procure you any more general [ones]. There are daily states of the whole army, but it will be impossible for me to get one. I am by no means sure that it is right sending them but of course you will not publish them. Felton is gone back towards Seia and Gouveia[†] with the brigade. I hear he is quite well. With best love, believe me, my dear uncle, your dutiful and affectionate nephew,
John Fremantle

The details John provided are set out in tables on the pages following.

---

who had been huntsman to a Border pack. See *General Graham, Lord Lynedoch* by Antony Brett-James, Macmillan, London, 1959, p. 240.
[*] Major General Kenneth Alexander Howard; he later became the 1st Earl of Effingham.
[†] These villages are in the Estrella mountains.

Average of loss and gain of His Majesty's 2nd Brigade of Foot Guards commanded by Major General Campbell from embarkation in 1808 to 31 December 1811

	Coldstream			3rd Regiment			Total		
	Sergeants	Drummers	Rank & file	Sergeants	Drummers	Rank & file	Sergeants	Drummers	Rank & file
Strength on embarkation	73	22	1,198	71	20	1,217	144	42	2,415
Joined since	27	7	402	27	4	400	54	11	802
Total	100	29	1,600	98	24	1,617	198	53	3,217

	Coldstream			3rd Regiment			Total		
	Sergeants	Drummers	Rank & file	Sergeants	Drummers	Rank & file	Sergeants	Drummers	Rank & file
Killed in action	–	–	32	4	–	46	4	–	78
Died of wounds	–	–	46	4	–	59	4	–	105
Died of sickness	21	7	378	14	5	326	35	12	704
Sent to England	4	–	117	3	3	169	7	3	286
Prisoner of war	3	–	83	3	–	78	6	–	161
Total loss	28	7	656	28	8	678	56	15	1,334
Strength, December 1811	72	22	944	20	16	939	142	38	1,803

Return of the non-commissioned officers and privates wounded since the embarkation*

Regiments	Sergeants	Drummers	Rank & file
1st Battalion Coldstream	13	1	293
1st Battalion 3rd Guards	15	1	299
Total	[28]	2	592

List of officers dead of 2nd Brigade of Guards since the embarkation in 1808

1st Battalion Coldstream		1st Battalion 3rd Guards	
Lieutenant Colonel Ross	*Killed in action*	Captain Walker	*Killed in action*
Captain Beckett Balls†	"	Captain Buchanan	"
Captain Bryan Adjutant	"	Captain Dalrymple	"
Captain Jenkinson	"	Ensign Adjutant Saby	"
Ensign Parker	"	Ensign Ram	"
		Ensign Cookson	"
Major Dalling	*Died*	Captain Harnage	*Died*
Ensign Wingfield	"		
Ensign Long	*Drowned*		
Ensign Ashburnham	*Died*		

Officers	*Coldstream*	*3rd Foot Guards*
Killed in action	5	6
Died of wounds	2	1
Drowned	2	–

---

* The total of wounded sergeants (28) is omitted in the report but clearly should be included.

† He is normally referred to as Lieutenant and Captain Richard Beckett, but Fremantle adds 'Balls' to his surname.

First Battalion Coldstream Guards Average of Loss from Embarkation on 31 December 1808, to 31 December 1811

	Captains	Lieutenants	Ensigns	Adjutant	Qtrmaster	Surgeons	Assistant Surgeons	Sergeants	Drummers	Rank & file
Strength on embarkation	9	14	13	1	1	1	2	73	22	1,198
Received from 2nd Battalion	7	12	20	2	–	–	1	12	6	402
Promoted from ensign on the Staff	–	–	–	1	–	–	–	–	–	–
Promoted in the battalion	–	1	–	–	–	–	–	–	–	–
Promoted from corporal	–	–	–	–	–	–	–	35	–	–
Reduced from sergeant	–	–	–	–	–	–	–	–	–	17
Received from drummers	–	–	–	–	–	–	–	–	–	1
Received from supernumerary drummer	–	–	–	–	–	–	–	–	1	–
Total gained	7	13	20	3	–	–	1	47	7	420
Service to Staff Employ	1	1	–	1	–	–	–	–	–	–
Retired	3	2	–	–	–	–	–	–	–	–
Dead	1	3	4	1	–	–	–	21	7	456
Transferred to 2nd Battalion	3	5	–	1	–	–	1	5	–	170
Promoted to Sergeants	–	–	–	–	–	–	–	–	–	35
Promoted in 2nd Battalion	–	3	16	–	–	–	–	–	–	–
Reduced to private	–	–	–	–	–	–	–	17	–	–
Discharged to drummer	–	–	–	–	–	–	–	–	–	2
Deserted	–	–	–	–	–	–	–	–	–	5
Doing duty with 2nd Battalion	1	2	1	–	–	–	–	–	–	–
Prisoners of war	–	–	1	–	–	–	–	–	–	–
Discharged on promotion	–	–	–	–	–	–	–	2	–	–
Prisoners of war discharged	–	–	–	–	–	–	–	3	–	6
Absent with leave	–	3	1	–	–	–	–	–	–	–
Absent without Leave	–	1	–	–	–	–	–	–	–	–
Total lost	16	29	23	3	–	–	1	48	7	674
State of battalion 31 December 1811	4	7	12	1	1	1	2	72	22	944

BADAJOZ

There is a gap in the letters here of well over a month, possibly because the army was constantly on the move; but the failure to mention their march south would indicate that John had written in between, these letters now being lost. Having repaired the defences of Ciudad Rodrigo, Wellington had marched the army south to besiege Badajoz with all possible speed. The Coldstream Guards had marched for Abrantes on 9 February, ostensibly to get new clothing, marching via Aldea de Ponte, Sabugal, Caria, Alpedrinha, Castelo Branco, Sarnadas, Nisa and Govao, arriving at Abrantes on 20 February.* Having received their new clothing, they rested until 3 March, when orders were given to march for Estremoz. They marched through Fronteira to Monforte and arrived at Elvas on 15 March. Here the 1st Division was placed under the command of Sir Thomas Graham with the 6th and 7th Divisions with two brigades of cavalry and two brigades of artillery. This force was to advance on the road to Seville, to cover the siege operations. They marched from Elvas at 5 a.m. on 16 March passing over the battlefield of Albuera, which still exhibited the carcases of many of the fallen, and on to Santa Martha. The following day, they marched to La Parra, where John's letters resume.

[Campo de] La Parra 4 leagues from Zafra, 18 March 1812

My dear uncle,

I have only just time to tell you we marched in here this day, and proceed five leagues tomorrow I believe to Villafranca [de los Barros]. The 1st, 6th, and 7th Divisions and all the heavy cavalry from Graham's Corps are to be a covering army during the siege. The Light, 3rd and 4th Divisions moved forward last night. Hill's Corps was to be at Merida yesterday and is to cooperate with ours. General Drouet's headquarters I understand are now at Llerena, and if our movement of tomorrow does not move him, I suppose we shall have an action,

---

* This route comes from the diary of John Mills, edited by Ian Fletcher, *For King and Country*, Spellmount, Staplehurst 1995.

but everyone seems to think they are not strong enough. We have had doubtful weather today and yesterday, but not enough as yet to affect the men. I received your letter before yesterday and one from Selina this day, I will answer them whenever we halt. God bless you my dear uncle, with best to all, believe me, your most dutiful and affectionate nephew,

John Fremantle

Promotion still goes on rapidly.

Constant marching meant that John did not write home again for another seven weeks. During this period, Badajoz had fallen on 6 April after a short but extremely bloody siege. The defending governor, General Philippon and his 5,000 men had devised intricate defences which defeated the storming parties with horrendous losses, but two diversionary attacks, turned into real escalades, succeeded against all odds and the town fell to uncontrolled pillage and rape by the enraged soldiery. Wellington's force lost 4,670 killed and wounded during the whole siege operation; losing no less than 3,713 of these during those few nightmarish hours of the storming.

During the army's absence at Badajoz, Marmont had led his forces on an incursion into northern Portugal, therefore much of the army marched rapidly north again and he immediately retired into Spain. With the frontier fortresses in Wellington's hands, all the talk was of marching on into Spain.

John also refers to the action at Villagarcia, where on the evening of 10 April, General Cotton knew that the French were occupying Llerena in force but discovered that there were a considerable number of French cavalry five miles closer to him near the village of Villagarcia. Cotton decided that he should attempt to trap the French cavalry with his superior forces. During the night he despatched Ponsonby* with the 12th and 14th Light Dragoons to probe the Villagarcia area, while Le Marchant's Brigade was sent on a circuitous march to get on the French left flank and, it was hoped, cut off their retreat.

Two squadrons of the British light cavalry forced the French videttes out of the village of Villagarcia but, around dawn, ran into the full force of the French cavalry and were then chased back. Ponsonby subsequently found his two regiments faced by the three strong regiments under Lallemand and had to make a controlled withdrawal while skirmishing against heavy odds.

---

* Lieutenant Colonel Frederick Cavendish Ponsonby 12th Light Dragoons, who is perhaps most famous for his account of his severe wounding at Waterloo and subsequent trials until he was eventually saved after the battle.

Following his orders, Le Marchant* had moved his brigade though the night over tortuous terrain for a considerable distance and he and the 5th Dragoon Guards had pulled considerably ahead of the other two regiments of the brigade. Le Marchant noticed, looking through the trees of the wood his men were moving through, that French cavalry, drawn up in two deep columns of squadrons, were pushing the six squadrons of light dragoons back towards a narrow ravine flanked by stone walls. Le Marchant realised that an immediate charge was needed before Ponsonby's squadrons were forced into the congested and broken ground to their rear.

At this point the advantage that the French had enjoyed in the action was suddenly reversed. Le Marchant led his dragoon guards out of the woods and they formed their ranks while accelerating into the charge. Simultaneously with Le Marchant's charge the 16th Light Dragoons, led by Cotton, appeared to Ponsonby's right rear; they jumped a stone wall in line, and also charged. The French cavalry were thrown into instant confusion and were swiftly broken. The British pursuit, continuing to inflict casualties and take prisoners, was conducted all the way back to the walls of Llerena.

The French lost 53 killed and wounded and 136 prisoners, compared with the British losses of 14 killed and 37 men wounded.

Nisa, 6 May 1812

My dear uncle,

I assure you it has caused me much uneasiness not having written to you for such a length of time, particularly since the receipt of your kind letter of February 20th, but from the 3rd of that month [actually 3 March], the day on which we marched from Abrantes, until the 1st of the present when we arrived here, we have been daily on the move, and some of them I am sorry to say were not only unnecessary, but we learnt afterwards unintentional. During the siege we formed part of Sir Thomas Graham's corps, who occupied us with marching and counter marching the whole time two nights in particular to surprise a French corps, at Llerena which failed completely, *faute de* . . . [Blank in letter – *mieux*? For want of something better]. They were but 2,000, all of which might properly to have belonged to us. They only had half an hour's start of us, but the town and country was quite flat except one side, and if the cavalry of which we had abundance, had been sent beyond, or even a division or part of one of the three, not a man could have escaped. The force that morning certainly exceeded 12,000 men, it made us all call loudly for the peer, indeed I believe he is the only

---

* General John Gaspard Le Marchant.

one. There was a similar trial made three days afterwards with the 6th Division alone, in our front under General Clinton which succeeded no better. He made the men reverse their caps, having the plate behind, in order that the enemy might not think they were attacking, and the most odd, that the knapsacks were ordered to be put on the stomachs, and an officer put under an arrest for riding with his face towards the horse's tail. He [Clinton] is lately come out, and is dreadfully disliked. From thence we retreated to Albuera where we remained three days on the position expecting Soult. But the place falling [Badajoz] we marched immediately for the north and proceeded as far as Sabugal passing by Badajoz, Portalegre, and Castelo Branco to punish Marmont for his incursion. They have burnt Castelo Penamacor, and several other places, and levied heavy contributions upon Covilha, and all that rich country. We returned here immediately from Sabugal, having been constantly marched with a good deal of rainy weather. It was a mistake our ever having travelled so far, but our order miscarried, although I don't suppose even a French army ever made such marches I don't find the men have at all suffered, it generally shows itself after five or six days halt.

Lord Wellington's headquarters still remain at Fuenteguinaldo, the Light Division 3rd, 4th, 5th and 7th are there in the north. The 1st and 6th are about here. We expect to move now immediately direct into Spain, I imagine a combined movement from the north will be made with ours. Magazines are forming at Albuquerque, and orders have been agreed to the purpose of motion. General Hill's corps went up to Almendralejo when we left that neighbourhood, and still remain there. They are always in luck, to get good and stationary quarters, whilst we are in perpetual motion. They were 10 months in Olivenza and only moved out for three days to bring back General Girard's Corps.[*]

I must not omit to mention the affair in which our Felton of the cavalry, met with such brilliant success at Llerena[†] after we retired, and were on our position, I have not seen Felton since, but it is talked of as being as fine a thing as ever was done, and I am very glad Sir Stapleton[‡] was there.

I agree with you perfectly as to your idea about Fuller's proposal to me respecting an exchange. I only mentioned it to you as having taken place; I did not intend it should cause you so much alarm as it appears to have done. I am well aware Fuller is very apt (in his greatness) to promise in a small way more than he can perform, I thought it very

---

[*] This refers to the action at Arroyomolinos.

[†] The cavalry action referred to is commonly referred to as Villagarcia.

[‡] Lieutenant General Sir Stapleton Cotton.

probable that General Clinton, Dawkins's uncle might have applied for him but I don't think it likely to happen now. The place of brigade major is what I, as adjutant always look forward to, and as that is likely to be distant for some time, I think the letter for Lord Wellington that you speak of can do no harm, for if we are to have to leave the country soon, I dare say it would not be long before he was employed elsewhere, and here it is certainly the finest situation an army man can wish for.

I am happy to tell you the promotion is continuing and likely to do so very rapidly; they talk even as largely as five or six steps immediately. Fuller has had another attack of ague, he has been away with it for three weeks but we expect him up in a few days from Abrantes. He has been long longing [*sic*] for Lord Aylmer to come out to relieve him in the command of the battalion, he is heartily sick of it. I very much doubt his lordship's arriving before he is a major general by brevet. Fuller too is getting very high, since the last return I sent you, 200 men have joined us from England and we expect 94 more tomorrow. Adieu my dear uncle, pray make my best remembrances and believe me, your dutiful and affectionate nephew,

John Fremantle

John's next letter was largely concerned with the slow rate of the repairs to the two recently captured fortresses, but also false rumours of the release of prisoners from Verdun.

Nisa, 14 May 1812

My dear uncle,

Since my letters of this day week we have all (thank goodness) been quite stationary excepting the 6th Division which has moved from Castelo de Vide towards General Hill. By a letter from Guinaldo, I received this morning I am informed, that Marmont is still at Salamanca with two divisions, the rest of his force is thrown back on Avila and Zamora, and our advance is on the Tormes, about five leagues in front of Ciudad Rodrigo.

The works there go on very slowly, the want of money is so great that hands cannot be procured, and the garrison are little employed, it is however in a state to prevent an assault, and there are even redoubts nearly finished. We are giving to them in a magazine of 500,000 rations, to be under the charge of a British commissary which is to be preserved in the event of the enemy blockading the place.

The Bridge of Alcantara is ordered to be repaired which will materially shorten the march of the troops in the north, in the event of their moving southward, which it is supposed will be their direction as soon as the provisions are arrived at Ciudad. The sick and wounded of the army are improving daily. The new men lately arrived from England have about made the army the same strength it was at before the siege of Badajoz. The Spaniards here have however been very dilatory; they don't get on with the repairs at all. General Graham went from hence by a horse from Lisbon three days ago to set them to rights.

Fuller joined us three days ago from Abrantes where he had been ill with the ague, and has since been attacked with it again; I imagine he will go to England as soon as he is strong enough. Sullivan I believe has purchased his company by this time, and Raikes* who is next to him (now in England) for three months, is expected to get his before the expiration of that time. There is a report here that Sir W. Sheridan and Milman,† are about to be exchanged from Verdun. The arrival of the former will cause considerable alterations as he is senior to Brand. I should think the duke will never consent to his commanding either battalion. This is all the news I can collect. Felton with his regiment is at Frandina near Estremoz, I have not seen him for a long time. With best love, believe me, my dear uncle, your dutiful and affectionate nephew,

  John Fremantle

Two weeks later, John was reporting the stunning success by General Hill at the bridge of Almaraz. This bridge, being the only practicable crossing over the Tagus available to the French in central Spain and thus a vital link between the two main French armies, was captured by General Hill on 18 May. With infantry alone Hill launched a surprise dawn attack and the French garrison fled, abandoning the forts which commanded the crossing and the bridge of boats. Allied losses were 189 killed and wounded; the French lost 400 including prisoners. This effectively ended any possibility of coordinated movements by the French armies to the north and south of the Tagus.

Other news was the anticipated advance on Salamanca and the assassination of the prime minister.

---

* Lieutenant and Captain William Raikes.

† Brevet Colonel Sir William Sheridan and Lieutenant and Captain Francis Miles Milman, Coldstream Guards, were both severely wounded at Talavera and captured by the French. They were held at Verdun as prisoners of war and were only released with the end of the war in April 1814. The exchange of prisoners of equal rank was very rare during the Napoleonic wars as Napoleon actively discouraged it and he encouraged French officers to break their parole; for example, see the case of Lefebvre-Desnouettes.

Nisa, 28 May 1812

My dear uncle,

We were disturbed on the 20th by a sudden order for march, it was thought at first we were going decidedly into Spain, but it turned out only to be a movement in favour of General Hill in case he should have wanted any assistance, but on our second day's progress we heard of his successful operation against the forts at Almaraz thrown up by the French, and we returned immediately to the Castelo de Vide. The report was then that he had taken 600 prisoners, but it now proves only to be between one and two [hundred], a great many were drowned in the Tagus and others bayoneted, our loss is not to be spoken of, and the whole business was achieved in the most masterly manner. We are just marched in here from Castelo, but we can't at all guess what occasioned the move. I don't think our stay will be long. The advance into Spain is very much talked of, the idea of headquarters coming down in this direction is entirely put aside, and they say are soon to proceed towards Salamanca. General Hill has fallen back to Merida, and the 6th Division is at Castelo de Vide. Sir Thomas Graham returned here this morning. The divisions in the north are all stationary.

Fuller left us when we marched from hence and intends going to England on the recommendations of a medical board. Colonel Philips commands in the meantime. I should think it will not be long before Brand comes out, as Lord Aylmer was very ill by the last accounts.

I do not hear of any more changes likely to take place. Felton is at Frandina with his regiment but I have not seen him for a long time. An English mail arrived last night, by which we hear the report of Mr Perceval's death. What a disgraceful act, if it be true, that he was shot by a Liverpool merchant.*

Adieu my dear uncle, with best love, believe me, your dutiful and affectionate,

John Fremantle

---

* Spencer Perceval has the dubious honour of being the only British prime minister ever to have been assassinated. The assassin was John Bellingham, a Liverpool merchant who had incurred business debts in Russia. He had tried to recover compensation for his losses, but was refused and sought revenge on a representative of the government. Bellingham was tried for murder and hanged.

SALAMANCA

Three weeks later we find John and the regiment at Salamanca, having marched from Nisa on 31 May and marching via Castelo Branco, Caria, Castelheiro and Sabugal, arriving at Malhada Sorda on 8 June. Here they waited for the order for the army to advance deep into Spain, which came on 11 June. As they advanced the French retired, abandoning the city of Salamanca except for three convents which had been converted into mutually supporting fortresses, San Vincente, La Merced and San Cayetano. A regular siege was begun on 18 June by the 6th Division, the rest of the army covering the siege.

Headquarters, Salamanca, 18 June 1812

My dear uncle,

Since my letter from Nisa we marched from thence over Castelo Branco by Sabugal to a camp near Ciudad Rodrigo where we halted one day and then proceeded within a day of this place where the advance fell in with that of the enemy, commanded by Felton with the 14th and part of the 1st Hussars, and drove them for five miles within one mile of this place, which was continued yesterday by the 6th Division, the French force having retired leaving 600 men in a fort which our batteries open against tomorrow morning. Marmont retired this morning by the road to Toro. The Light and 3rd Divisions are in advance of this place, the 5th and 4th are posted near a ford on the left of the town and the 1st and 7th Divisions are in a wood on this side of the river. The army expects to advance immediately, that is as soon as the commissariat can be got ready. Felton's regiment in the advance was attached to Graham's corps comprised of the 1st, 6th and 7th Divisions, but this morning joined his brigade and is a league in advance. I dined with him yesterday when I did not think he was as well as I could have wished. I have seen Charles Bishop this day, I cannot say his conduct is what one can approve of, I believe at this moment he is in a scrape about duty. Thank goodness I am quite well.

Felton said yesterday he should write but I doubt his having done so, owing to his march this morning. His regiment is in a beautiful condition though weak, Lord Wellington is most fond of him. Brand is coming out immediately. Burroughs has given up the adjutancy and is also expected to join. Forgive my writing as it is quite dark, with best remembrance, believe me, dear uncle, your most dutiful and affectionate nephew,
    John Fremantle

The forts of Salamanca proved a tougher nut to crack than anticipated and an attempt to storm on the night of 23/24 June failed with heavy losses. Siege operations were then delayed by the reappearance of a reinforced Marshal Marmont and his army. On 21 June the two armies faced each other and everyone expected a great battle; but both commanders were cautious, fearing making a rash error, and the two armies marched and countermarched for days in close proximity of each other without battle being formed. However, the letter ends with a postscript mentioning that the forts had finally succumbed on 27 June.

Camp near Salamanca, 29 June 1812

My dear uncle,
Two days after my last letter from Salamanca the army was assembled on a very pretty position in advance of the town, to meet Marmont who on returning with his reinforcements to endeavour to bring away the garrisons left in the three forts as instruments for the purpose of preventing or at least retarding our progress over the border. There was little idea at that period of their holding out many hours nor do I suppose the calculation would have been amiss, had the proper measures been adopted, but they were looked upon in so trivial a point of view, as not to require greater means. The two armies looked at one another for two days, the main bodies not being two and a half miles asunder. The French retired the third night to a position about a league distant, to the great regret of the army that they were not obliged sooner, as they certainly were inferior to us in numbers and their flanks '*en l'air*'. The three forts were eventually assaulted that same night the 23rd, but I am sorry to say without the smallest success. The 24th was entirely spent in manoeuvring. The French crossed the river with a sufficient time to oblige Graham's corps to cross also, and three times in that way, in order to keep opposite to them, it was a dreadful harassing day, all our halts were in the scorching sun, and we were under arms from before daylight till after dark. They abrogated again the night of the 27th, and we have been on march after them since.

I cannot venture even of a thought where it will end. Our column near the centre is nearly in a line with the San Cristobal [de la Cuesta] road, but today were marched straight across the country over the cornfields. I mentioned to you that Felton was a little squeamish in my last, but he took care of himself for a couple of days and was perfectly recovered. I saw Charles Bishop yesterday, not looking very well I thought. He met with a wonderful piece of business, the final morning after the French retired. He was flanking with a single dragoon, when he discerned a car with an escort of 11 men, and when he was joined by six guerrillas charged the party, and took them prisoners. There was a lady with the party on her road to join her spouse which he has since protected, and wrote to the officer to give an account of her, a very polite answer has been returned to him and Lord Wellington has given him leave to take her in as soon as the regiments gets near enough to them. I saw Hutchinson today he is quite well. Pray give my best love and remembrances and believe me, my dear uncle, your dutiful and affectionate nephew,

John Fremantle

PS The forts fell on the 27th.

The army advanced to the Douro, but Marmont having received substantial reinforcements soon felt strong enough to resume the offensive. Counter-marching resumed, with Marmont determined to turn Wellington's flank and threaten his communications, while Marmont also awaited the arrival of further reinforcements from the Army of the Centre.

Villaverde [de Medina], 13 July 1812

My dear uncle,
Our march from Salamanca here was uninterrupted. Headquarters were at this place on the 2nd when the right column moved to Medina del Campo, and our advance was pushed up to the Douro, they proceeded on the 4th to Rueda, with the Light Division where they still remain though always very unsettled, the troops moving into the town and villages by day, for the sake of shelter and turning out at night to bivouac, which you will readily conceive becomes extremely harassing and disagreeable, being obliged to pack up one's all twice a day, and always under arms by ½ past 3 o'clock, and it was not till seven this morning that we turned in. The country is quite open which I suppose renders such precautions necessary.

There was a slight movement of our troops yesterday owing to the French having crossed a corps over the river, but I do not know to what amount. Our division came here from Medina del Campo which is a little more to the left, in which direction the others have likewise moved; we being on the right of the line. We are all waiting most anxiously the result of the next movement. I fancy the first bridge we attempted to construct by the assistance of the spring wagon failed, and they are now going on with another.

A letter of Marmont's is said to have been intercepted in which he says he is not now sufficiently strong to attack us, although joined by Bonet's Division,* without that of Caffarellis'† which I believe is in Navarre. Consequently we may look at each other for many more tense days. I should think soon there must be a great want of money, which will affect our supplies for the Spaniards get very crusty if their demands are not attended to immediately; as to the army it will be four months in arrears on this 24th. I believe there is some on the road, but most likely it will all be required for the commissariat. I dined at headquarters on the 5th they were all in high feather; Felton's regiment is there, he is quite well. I suppose he has told you of his change from the 12th and 16th to that of the hussars, which he does not at all like.‡ Ponsonby of the 12th and him were inseparable. I expect Brand will arrive in the course of 10 days. There was a report by the last mail that Lord Aylmer had some thoughts of getting the regiment. With best remembrances, believe me, my dear uncle, your dutiful and affectionate nephew,

John Fremantle

In his next letter John was able to report that all the countermarching was over. Wellington had finally shown his offensive abilities and roundly defeated Marmont's army while over stretched on the march. The Battle of Salamanca on 22 July was one of Wellington's most accomplished victories, but it was dearly bought. Unfortunately for John and the Guards, they were merely spectators, losing 7 men killed and 31 wounded or missing, almost all in the light company which formed a skirmish line. Allied losses numbered 896 killed and 3,865 wounded or missing; French losses totalled some 14,000 killed and wounded, including some 7,000 prisoners and 20 cannon captured.

---

* General Jean Pierre Francois Bonet.
† General Marie Francois Auguste de Caffarelli du Falga.
‡ On 1 July the 14th Light Dragoons were exchanged with the 11th Light Dragoons; the 14th were then in Von Alten's Brigade with the 1st Hussars KGL.

Cantaracillio, near Penaranda [de Bracamonte], 24 July

My dear uncle,

Since my letter of 12th from Villaverde we have experienced the most horrifying time I yet remember, nothing but marches and counter marches attended with every privation, but thank goodness we are at last repaid for our toils and *amply so*, when least expected, by a most signal victory gained over Marshal Marmont, on the heights two leagues from Salamanca on the 22nd.

Our army remained two days on, and about, a position near *Canizal* after the French crossed the Douro, offering them battle, and as they moved by their left, we marched parallel by our right, till arrived on the forenoon of the 22nd, when Marshal Marmont presuming upon his manoeuvring, committed himself, which our Noble Peer has turned to so good an account. The report of the French loss is 20,000, but I think it must be greater and ours is certainly about 5,000, they have certainly lost 19 pieces of artillery. Our cavalry has positively covered itself with glory. All the people in the road agree the account of Marmont having lost his arm,* and that two other generals are wounded, one was killed, and another found nearly so in a village yesterday.† General Le Marchant was killed,‡ Beresford, Cole, and Leith wounded. Sir Stapleton Cotton was hit in the arm, the night before last, returning from posting the pickets, by one of the Portuguese sentries. Felton gave me the account yesterday. He was riding with him at the moment the two shots were fired, and the other wounded his Staff orderly.

Our division and the light were not engaged at all, there was a tragedy of one brigade, which has suffered very severely. We had a beautiful view the whole time and followed them till the moment after they retired. I believe the pursuit is now given up by the infantry, and I suppose will, tomorrow, by the cavalry, for they also require a little organisation.

Every arrangement was made by Lord W[ellington] on the 22nd for our retreat at 10 a.m. which was put off till night, owing to some intelligence of a reinforcement to the enemy's cavalry which might have harassed us too much in the daytime, when the fortunate attempt of theirs to halt so completely turned the scale. Never was defeat more complete and I think the good consequences owing to us from it,

---

* Marmont was severely wounded in the arm but did not lose it.

† Generals Ferey and Thomieres were killed, Bonet was severely wounded and Clausel slightly. Generals Desgraviers was mortally wounded and Menne severely wounded.

‡ Major General John Gaspard Le Marchant was killed while leading a devastating attack upon the French infantry with his heavy cavalry.

will be most material. I have no time to give you any further details. King Joseph is said to be on his way from Madrid to join their army but not with any creditable body. Adieu my dear uncle, pray make my best love and remembrance, and believe me, your most truly and affectionate nephew,

John Fremantle

PS Charles Bishop is sick at Salamanca.

Three weeks later John was writing with news of the capture of Madrid and the surrender of the Retiro, which housed huge stockpiles of arms and powder; he also reported how Wellington received a hero's welcome.

After the battle the Guards had marched through Arevalo, Olmedo, and Valladolid then turned to take the capital, marching through Los Huerjos, Segovia, St Raphael and El Escorial to Madrid.

Madrid, 15 August 1812

My dear uncle,

Now our last year's labours and privation was amply repaid by the entrance of our army into the neighbourhood of, and this city on the 13th and 14th. Headquarters were to have been established here on the 12th had not a mishap befallen our Portuguese cavalry which was in advance; however that is entirely forgotten by the good fortune of the unconditional surrender of the Retiro, strongly fortified by the French. The garrison marched out yesterday evening, 1,800 men, 180 pieces of cannon are in the place, and a great quantity of stores of every description. I have heard the garrison of Guadalajara is also expected to entreat terms. Our work since the action you will perceive has not been trifling; we did not march straight to Valladolid, but made attacks, and then came from thence to Segovia. I saw both these places in the evenings after the march and was extremely gratified. The latter most particularly, the town is very curious, we were shown the room in which Gil Blas was confined.* Our camp on that day was in the park belonging to the Palace of Riofrío† a magnificent building, but I believe was never lived in by any of the royal family. I regret much not having seen that of Ildefonso,‡ it was so far off, and I so tired that I could not,

---

* The eighteenth-century novel *The Adventures of Gil Blas of Santillane* by Alaine-René le Sage, first translated into English in 1730 by Tobias Smollet, became a huge success. The hero is confined for a period in the tower of Segovia.

† Actually the Palacio Real [Royal Palace] Riofrío near Segovia which was used for hunting expeditions.

‡ The Royal Palace of La Granja de San Ildefonso, near Segovia.

but they say it was beautiful. On the 11th our camp was in the park of the Escorial, which I had a fine opportunity of examining as we halted the following day. It did not take me less than four hours to walk over and through it. It is reckoned the largest building in Europe, and indeed it gave one the idea of a world, the splendour and magnificence is not well to be described.

Nothing can equal the joy with which Lord Wellington was received, he can't venture out of the palace, without being mobbed, the city is beautiful, some even go so far as to say that London does not deserve to be compared to it but I can't say that I agree with those. The Light Division marched this morning I believe for cantonments and they say our division is here tomorrow for the same purpose.

Felton is just gone from here, I don't think he is looking well. He has been living here (headquarters) for some days past. Brand has recovered, but we have eight others absent. I have been unwell myself for a few days with a sore throat, but it has now quite left me. With best love, believe me, my dear uncle, your dutiful and affectionate nephew,
John Fremantle

The next letter finds the First Division living at El Escorial,* John had spent much of his time at headquarters while at Madrid and was now hoping finally to be taken upon Wellington's Staff.

El Escorial, 22 August 1812

My dear uncle,
Your letter of July 23rd I received the day after I gave mine to Burgh for you from Madrid. I thought it very probable that the second, which was Albinia's enclosure, might have been the one you talked of some time ago for Lord Wellington.

I am extremely obliged to you for yours; as usual it was full of news, I am always very glad of them. Albinia's too, from Sunbury, was a very pretty, interesting epistle, and a better one I assure you I never read. She is full of gratitude for the kindness she has received, from all our relatives, and speaks most properly so of yourself. The least mark of your goodness was not forgotten, and I am sure I feel it the more, as I well recollect now, the conversation which you had with me, on those matters one Sunday at Englefield Green in 1804; to be sure what you then said about the expenses of the lawsuit, was quite different, consequently I feel it was the more kind of you. You may depend upon mine being made the proper use of.

The operations in this country do indeed as you say, begin to look

---

* The royal seat of San Lorenzo de El Escorial about 28 miles north-west of Madrid.

flourishing, since my last, I understand the French have returned to Valladolid, and that General Clinton who has about 10,000 men has retired to Almeida. The idea is that if they advance further after him, that a movement from hence will place us in his rear.

Report says that Suchet has marched against General Maitland who has landed at Alicante, his force I fancy is much inferior to Suchet and I suppose our force will remain, until we hear the result of those movements.* King Joseph is gone to Cuenca. Our advanced posts are established on the Tagus, Lord Wellington will be at Madrid with the 3rd and part of the Light Division. Ours marched from the camp in the walks close to the city on the 18th and in here on the 19th where is also the 4th, 5th and 7th Divisions, I may say almost in the same building, the most uncomfortable situation that troops can be put in. I suppose it was meant to be agreeable to us, but for my own part I prefer a bad Portuguese village. All but 10 or 12 of the officers of our brigade are in the garden and bivouacked in the walks. We were all very sorry to leave Madrid, indeed it was a treat after what we had undergone, and I think hardly fair not to let us enjoy it for a time, but they had the opinion at headquarters to tell us that they were afraid of a second Capua business.† I dined at headquarters three of the four days I was there, and his Lordship did me the honour to converse a long time with me at the ball given by the municipality on the 16th, and got me a couple of partners, indeed he is always extremely kind, and on this last occasion he might easily have discovered my partiality for headquarters, and if I had had an opportunity I am not at all sure that I might not have mentioned the subject of your former letter, for at present all the English with him are Fitzroy Somerset, military secretary, Colonel Campbell, Major Burgh, and Gordon, Lord Worcester, and Canning, aides-de-camp. This latter is an idiot and suffered by Lord W[ellington], Lord March was Fitzroy's fag and assistant who I dare say will be prevented coming out again by the duke. Clinton I dare say will not return and he has lost Lord Charles Manners who has joined the regiment he has lately been appointed to.‡

---

* An Anglo-Spanish force commanded by Lieutenant General Frederick Maitland landed on the east coast of Spain in an attempt to prevent Marshal Suchet joining the French forces facing Wellington. It achieved little of note but did succeed in keeping Suchet occupied.

† In 1799 the Austrian General Mack had been cornered at Capua and forced to surrender his whole army, causing the king of Naples to abandon the mainland and defend only Sicily.

‡ Brevet Lieutenant Colonel Colin Campbell was assistant quartermaster general. Lieutenant Henry Somerset, Marquess of Worcester, was an ADC to Wellington. Captain Charles Fox Canning remained as an ADC to Wellington throughout the

I know of no young persons here, except Reynell who are at all likely to be appointed and he is a dreadful bad scribe. I believe it is a matter of great indifference to Lord W[ellington] himself who he has with him. Therefore I think the letter you spoke of some time ago would be of great service now.

I was writing in Lord Fitzroy's room the other evening when he observed he must have somebody, and upon another person offering me, he replied that I was adjutant; this was all in a light manner. I remained silent but as he is a very good friend of mine, I think I shall go over in a day or two, and speak to him seriously upon the subject, and in case that he succeeds for me, before your letter may arrive, it may be as well to let you know now, that whenever it may arrive to the point of my resigning the adjutancy, which I suppose you would wish me to do, as I see no prospect of Dawkins's advancement.

I shall have no difficulty in putting it on the plea of my health for although I have never been a day absent, I do not find I am quite so strong as I have been. My throat was inflamed for two or three days but Madrid entirely cured it before I came away. Burgh generally did a great deal of business for Fitzroy, but March was his regular assistant. I can't tell you what a favourite Felton is of Lord W[ellington]. I think indeed he is one of the first in the army; he is quartered out of Madrid but lives chiefly at headquarters. I am sure he was there for a whole week or more lately. I think he had revelled too much there, for he was a little pulled down when I saw him.

Charles Bishop is still at Ciudad Rodrigo I hear dreadfully diseased. With best love my dear uncle, believe me, your dutiful and affectionate nephew,

John Fremantle

PS Brand is entirely recovered and joined us from having had a severe attack of ague, Raikes too has joined, he was dangerously ill for some time with a fever. We have now 10 sick absent officers. We never have been so unlucky.

---

remainder of the war and was killed at Waterloo. Captain Charles Lennox, the Earl of March, was an extra ADC to Wellington. Lieutenant Colonel Lord Charles Somerset Manners was ADC to Wellington until July when he joined the 3rd Dragoons.

BURGOS

Wellington wished to secure his position in central Spain by capturing the fortress of Burgos, which was not expected to put up a serious resistance. This was to be a serious and costly miscalculation by Wellington.

The Guards moved on 30 August towards Valladolid on route for Burgos.

Camp near Hornillos [de Eresma], 5 September 1812

My dear uncle,

We marched from the Escorial on the 30th and reached Arevalo on the 3rd. Headquarters were there on the 3rd and moved to Olmedo yesterday, they halt today. The troops now employed on this movement, are Anson's light brigade of cavalry and Colonel Ponsonby's heavy [cavalry]. The 1st, 5th, 6th, and 7th Divisions with Pack's and Bradford's Brigades* of Portuguese. I suppose tomorrow we shall reach very near Valladolid, and as General Clausel has decamped from thence in the direction of Burgos, we shall not halt very short of the Ebro, Alten's cavalry, 3rd, and Light Divisions, are at Madrid. The heavy brigade of Germans are near San Ildefonso [o La Granja].

General Wheatley† of the 1st Guards died at the Escorial, after a severe attack of fever on the 1st, and General Hulse's life was despaired of for some days at Arevalo, but he is now better. I don't think the army generally speaking, sickly. It is the astonishment of everyone how it's kept in such constant motion, I am happy to say they have contrived to give us a fortnight's pay lately, and the paymaster is expected up tomorrow with another if we don't march very far. I have no other news to tell you. I expect soon to have a letter from you; a mail arrived

---

* Brevet Colonel Thomas Bradford commanded the 10th Portuguese Brigade. Colonel Denis Pack commanded an independent Portuguese brigade.
† Major General William Wheatley, 1st Foot Guards, died of typhus at El Escorial on 1 September 1812.

today by which we learn Lord Wellington is a marquis.* I am heartily glad of it he surely must deserve it. Adieu my dear uncle, I will write again whenever we come to a halt. With best love, believe me always, your dutiful and affectionate nephew,

      John Fremantle

The march continued to Burgos and John renewed his efforts to gain a place on Wellington's Staff, but the great chief only had unpaid positions for 'extra' aide-de-camps.

Torquemada, 13 September 1812

My dear uncle,

Since my last short letter to you from Hornillos, we have continued our march without interruption, save two days at Valladolid where I believe Messieurs would have stood had we attacked them. Ours and the 6th Division moved forward for that purpose but it was put off in the evening, owing to the 5th Division not having reached its destination in time, however I am just as well contented that it turned out so, for their hill in our front was a very ugly one. Headquarters were yesterday at Magaz [de Pisuerga], and today are here. Our advance came up with their rear towards evening yesterday, where a few shots were exchanged. We expect to be at Burgos in three days, they say there are works there. General Castanos with 12,000 men joined us yesterday.

I received yours of August 17th yesterday and am much obliged to you for it. It is very gratifying for us to see that our labours have not been thrown away, at last the good people in England do seem to give every due credit to the exertions.

I am sorry to tell you the army has been deprived of one of its ablest officers by the death of poor General Hulse at Arevalo† a few days since, regretted by everyone who knew him, Lord Wellington is very much concerned for he reckoned upon him as his greatest support. I believe if it were possible he never had an enemy.

His appointment to our brigade arrived last March which makes the loss greater to us as we have been commanded for some time by a most worthy man, but a complete old woman, Thomas Fermor,‡ who now I fear will be continued in it. Colonel Rooke the [Assistant] Adjutant General is now dangerously ill at Valladolid, and Rose, our surgeon, has not been able to proceed further than Arevalo. Most of our other absent sick officers have returned to us. It rained very heavily yesterday

---

* He became Marquess of Wellington 18 August 1812.
† Hulse died on 7 September 1812.
‡ Brevet Colonel the Honourable Thomas William Fermor.

and the day before, which has concerned our sick a little. Thank God I remain the same.

I can hear nothing of Hutchinson who is at Salamanca. Charles Bishop has not left Ciudad Rodrigo, but I have not been able to hear otherwise of him since I last mentioned him.*

I am most anxious for your letters [addressed?] to me about Lord Wellington, for [these four days ?] the only British with him have been Fitzroy, Canning and Colonel Campbell, in fact [he has] only one aide-de-camp, [as?] Gordon is despatched to Hill and Worcester [somewhere else?]

I dine here today and [circumstances are?] such that if I can find a good opportunity I certainly shall broach the matter to him. With best love and remembrance, believe me, my very dear uncle, your dutiful and affectionate nephew,

John Fremantle

I have spoken to Lord Wellington who was extremely good natured, and acknowledged that I had a very good claim, but said there was no vacancy nor is there upon pay, but acting there is nobody. However I look forward with great hopes for your letter, J. F. I believe we halt tomorrow.

A short note from Burgos announced the commencement of siege operations and a promising early success, with the detached horn work of St Michael falling to a surprise attack.

Villatoro [near Burgos], 21 September 1812

My dear uncle,

I have only a moment to tell you I'm all alive and well. The castle of Burgos was invested the day before yesterday by the 1st Division, and General Pack's Brigade of Portuguese. The outwork was carried the same night by the 42nd Regiment. We are still proceeding with the work, but I believe it will take us 10 or a dozen days to reduce it entirely. It looks a stiff place, but as it is quite given to the 1st Division I trust we shall do it well, when it comes to the end. I received a letter from Georgiana today, by which mail we heard of the arrival of Burgh in England, with Lord Wellington's dispatches from Madrid; I see he has got his lieutenant colonelcy by brevet.†

---

* This letter has an ink stain across it at this point, making it difficult to read. The words encased in square brackets are therefore a best guess.

† It was customary that the bearer of dispatches announcing a victory was granted brevet promotion in rank by a grateful king.

Poor Brand is now very ill again having had another attack of ague. I do not think we shall see much of his services for some time, which is a great loss for me to have to do business with old Philips instead, as there has been great doubts entertained of him for a long time. With best remembrances, believe me, my dear uncle, your dutiful and affectionate nephew,

John Fremantle

John was now truly immersed in the horrors of war in the trenches of Burgos. On one occasion during a short truce he helped to recover the fallen from a failed assault. It is clear that he like many others had little taste for the brutality of siege warfare.

Camp near Burgos, 27 September 1812

My dear uncle,

I trust you received my letter, or rather note of last week. I scribbled it [in] a hurry in Fitzroy Somerset's room which I happened to go into just before the mail was going to be despatched, as I judged even a single line might be acceptable to tell you what I was doing. I assure you we have had a very busy time ever since, but I had no idea that it would ever come to my turn to be in the trenches, which however I was for 24 hours from daylight on the 23rd last, attending on the officer commanding there for that time. Luckily this happened to be Major Cocks late of the 16th Dragoons, a most able officer. I hardly know what would have become of me had not an order come from Lord Wellington to Cocks to send a flag of truce to ask permission to bury the dead, and carry away the bodies of the officers who fell on the preceding evening in an attack made on the outwork of the castle, which failed completely. I was deputed by Cocks to go with the message which was readily agreed to, and I was with them three hours within 30 yards of their wall, which later we both agreed was far more sociably spent, than the time to come was likely to be. We found the bodies of Major Lawrie 79th Regiment* who commanded the party, and two officers of the German Legion close under the wall and 22 other bodies which we buried. They likewise sent out from the place five wounded men who had later been carefully dressed, and attended to. The spot where they were buried was close opposite to that part of the wall that a party of our men attacked, two of the ladders were still remaining, I believe the only ones which were long enough. I confess the place did not appear very tremendous, and I have no doubt the attempt would have succeeded had the opposite attack been made with

---

* Major Andrew Lawrie, 79th Foot, was killed at Burgos on 22 September.

as much spirit as ours was. The party was furnished by detail from the division, McKenzie Fraser* of our regiment is badly wounded in the knee, and young Talbot our other officer, my particular friend, has escaped unhurt. The French officers observed to me that it was an enterprise tardi, which I acknowledged, but told them as it had succeeded so well on the evening before, there was every reason to hope this would have done so as well. They were exceedingly polite, and I think seemed very respectful. Our artillery and engineers have had a great difference of opinion. We have erected a battery which has not opened owing as it is said, to its being enfiladed. I don't expect the place will be ours yet for some days.

The 5th and 7th Divisions are encamped two leagues from here in a very strong position, where I shall be much happier to meet the French, who are about seven leagues off, than to have this business.

A reinforcement has joined them, but they do not seem inclined to come on. The Marquis is in very good spirits, I have had no further communication with him since I wrote to you, I dined there on that day. Brand continues very unwell and very low and talks most seriously of going home, if he does not soon get rid of his complaint. However I don't suppose Philips will ever be allowed to keep the command of the battalion, I am sure I hope not. Sir H. Sullivan who succeeds to poor Hulse's vacancy, will leave us as soon as ever the Gazettes reach us. Young Bradshaw† resigns as soon as this business is over, and I believe Mr Mills‡ will soon follow him. Therefore Shirley§ may prepare for his embarkation immediately. Everyone who comes from England gives the best of character of him as a person; therefore he will not want friends on his arrival. No news of Felton, Charles Bishop, or Hutchinson. With best love and remembrance, believe me, my dear uncle, your dutiful and affectionate nephew,

    John Fremantle

---

* Lieutenant and Captain Charles MacKenzie Fraser, Coldstream Guards, subsequently lost his leg.
† Ensign James Bradshaw resigned on 16 December that year.
‡ Ensign John Mills, Coldstream Guards, actually saw out the war but resigned on 31 August 1814.
§ Ensign Charles Shirley, Coldstream Guards.

ON THE STAFF

Wellington was forced to retreat as superior French forces massed and the paucity of his means to capture Burgos became all too obvious. The siege was finally abandoned on 21 October, the Coldstream Guards having lost no less than 3 officers and 54 men killed and 3 officers and 130 men wounded or missing.

The army retreated through Hornillos, Torquemada and Palencia to Tordesillas, where they offered battle to the French as they attempted to cross at the bridge here, which had not been destroyed. Both armies drew breath facing each other across the Douro when John found time to write.

John's letter was a bitter-sweet one, announcing the abandonment of the siege of Burgos and the commencement of an arduous retreat back to the Portuguese border, but also announcing that Wellington, on the back of a letter from his uncle, had invited John into his 'family', which he had joined immediately, taking leave of the regiment that very morning. His life was now to change radically.

Headquarters, Rueda, 31 October 1812

My dear uncle,

I received your letter at Torquemada four days ago, at which moment I was completely worn out with fatigue and anxiety having experienced more distress for the month previous, than ever I remember. Our retrograde movement had only been begun two days and a half, but they were dreadful ones. I did not forward your enclosure till the 28th when I was sent for an hour after, and saw this 'Man of Men', who after a little preamble, told me he would appoint me the next day, and it appeared in orders this forenoon, I arrived here an hour ago accordingly. Fitzroy Somerset tells me I am to be immediately under him, what can be more desirable? Judge then what my feelings of gratitude must be for this additional piece of kind interference for my welfare and future prospects. I left the camp this morning the envy of everyone who wished me goodbyes.

[Barrow?],* Bowles, Burroughs, Lascelles and Sandilands,† all, in this battalion are candidates for the adjutancy and send in their applications this mail.

Nothing can equal the kindness of Philips upon this occasion instead of humming and hawing about my going, he, in a moment, wished me joy. I trust now no impediment will be thrown in my way by His Royal Highness the Duke of C[ambridge]. No great difficulty has been made and none recalled from the Staff, but at present there is not a single one in this whole battalion save myself. It would be doing me a great piece of service if you would have the goodness to see HRH yourself.

I judge I have most to fear from Fuller's insincerity, he has always affected great kindness for me, and I really believe wishes me as well as he can anybody else.

I shall write to him a resignation of my adjutancy and a copy of my appointment as extra ADC and tell him how much I shall regret your taking me out of the regiment in case I am not permitted to remain with Lord Wellington, which surely the duke will scarcely have the incivility to refuse him.

All here is hurry-scurry getting the mail off which has been detained for these last nine or ten days. The troops halted today opposite Tordesillas, the bridge is destroyed and I trust we shall go no further than our present line of the Douro. You must not be surprised at my not having written lately, for during the siege we had a cruel time. Walpole will not lose his arm as was expected, Crofton's wound was very slight; poor Wentworth Burgess‡ lost his life on the top of the forward parapet of the enemy works. He commanded the advance party and behaved most nobly. Adieu my dear uncle with best love to all, believe me, your most dutiful and affectionate nephew,

John Fremantle

---

* The writing is very unclear here but the only other captain with the battalion with a name starting with a 'B' is Captain Thomas Barrow.

† Lieutenants and Captains Edward Lascelles and Patrick Sandilands, Coldstream Guards. Sandilands was severely wounded at Talavera and became a prisoner of war, but was released in November 1809.

‡ Lieutenants and Captains the Honourable John Walpole and the Honourable William George Crofton, Coldstream Guards; Walpole was recorded as severely wounded at Burgos and received an annual pension of £100. Crofton is also recorded as having been severely wounded at Burgos, despite Fremantle's comments. He was killed on 14 April 1814 during the sortie from Bayonne. Ensign Wentworth Noel Burgess, Coldstream Guards, was killed at Burgos on 18 October.

A short note revealed that John's position was no sinecure, being placed as a deputy to Fitzroy Somerset in his role as Military secretary to the duke.

Headquarters, Rueda, 3 November 1812

My dear Uncle

During these last forty eight hours I have filled nearly 11 sheets of paper. I never wrote so much before in my life, but believe me I am heartily content to do it. I have no doubt I shall be able to satisfy Fitzroy Somerset. General Hill is to be at Maello tomorrow, but I think we are more likely to move towards him, than he to us. I expect Felton here tomorrow to see his friend Ponsonby, who is going on very well.

With best love to all and in great haste, believe me, my dear uncle, your dutiful and affectionate nephew,

J. Fremantle

Another hurried note told of the army's continued retreat upon Salamanca, where Hill's and Wellington's forces would join. It is clear that John was revelling in his new role running messages.

Headquarters, Pitiegua, 7 November 1812

My dear uncle,

You will think it very extraordinary me writing you these scraps; but I know that is better than not writing at all. I was dispatched in a jiffy yesterday by the Lord, from Catrejon [de Trabancos] to General Hill at Cantaracillo, which I was very proud of, and made a very good though a difficult journey to him, and succeeded in making as good a one from General Hill to Lord Wellington this morning. General Hill's corps marched over the Tormes this day, by Alba de Tormes and this corps crosses tomorrow, and headquarters are to be in Salamanca. We expect to remain three days, I suppose we shall then get over the Agueda. His lordship is in wonderful spirits and I trust all will go well yet. General Hill has not been pressed, nor have we since we broke up from the Douro. It was late in the evening when I arrived at General Hill's yesterday therefore could not go and see Felton, but Tweedale* told me he was quite well, however we shall all meet tomorrow. I am as happy as the day is long and as content.

Pray tell Selina I received her letter and the tooth-brushes the day before yesterday, I will find time to answer it when I have a leisure opportunity. Adieu my dear uncle, with best love and remembrance. Believe me, your most dutiful and affectionate nephew,

John Fremantle

---

* Major George Hay, Marquis of Tweedale, 41st Foot, assistant quartermaster general.

The army retired and Wellington even offered battle on the battleground of Salamanca once again, but the French declined. On 15 November his disgruntled army commenced marching for the Portuguese frontier in appalling weather and with no food and hence suffered immensely, the French however eventually ceased the pursuit and both armies moved into winter quarters. John wrote from the warmth of his room at headquarters within the fortress of Ciudad Rodrigo, but still thought of the regiment he had left behind.

Headquarters, Ciudad Rodrigo, 20 November 1812

My dear uncle,
We arrived here the day before yesterday after the most distressing time that the army has ever yet experienced during any period of the campaign. I am sure if I had been with my regiment these last three weeks it would have been too much for me. Felton is here and thank God quite well. He intends asking Lord Wellington this evening to let him go to England, in which case he will start in a day or two. His journey to Lisbon will be as quick as possible; therefore you may expect him very soon. He desires his best love to you all.

Where we are to go for the winter is not yet decided upon but I dare say it will be Viseu or somewhere thereabouts. We all look forward to this movement with the greatest anxiety. I have been so busy that I have not time to write any more. Charles Bishop has joined his regiment after a very long absence, he is nearly quite recovered. With best love and remembrances to all. Believe me, my dear uncle, your dutiful and affectionate nephew,
John Fremantle

Headquarters, Freineda, 9 December 1812

My dear uncle,
I would have sent you a line last week on the receipt of your letter immediately, enclosing one for Lord Wellington, had I not been sent off in a jiffy to the other side of Alcantara. I did not return until the 3rd after a very unpleasant journey. However I am glad of it in as much that it shows that he can employ me, and I am quite satisfied and happy, though very anxious to know whether any difficulty will be made by the Duke of Cambridge to my remaining on the Staff. Lord Wellington was extremely angry the other day, when Colonel Jackson* forwarded to him an order he had received from the 2nd Battalion to join the battalion here and said the Duke of Cambridge had better come and

---

* Lieutenant Colonel Richard Downes Jackson Coldstream Guards, assistant quartermaster general, serving on the Staff in Spain.

command the army, but I imagine it is less his doing than Fuller's,* as he always likes to make himself of consequence if he can. Jackson is at the head of the Quarter Master General's Department with Hill's Corps, and Lord W[ellington] has no intention from that intimation to remove him. It was done on account of Brand's illness in order that the command might not remain with Philips, but by the latest accounts from England Brand had profited considerably by the sea passage, but I think it will be much more indecent if they attempt to interfere with me being on his personal Staff, indeed if they do I shall be very happy that you should judge me fit for my exchanging, much as I should regret leaving the Guards, particularly the Coldstream, because I must look on being in Lord Wellington's family and the good will he appears to show me as paramount to every other consideration in the army, and shall be happy to know your further opinion on the subject, but I do seriously hope this may not be necessary. General Hill is at Coria, and the [2nd Division?], 1st Division near Viseu, 3rd Division Leiria, 4th and 6th at Guarda, 7th Celorico and Light Division hereabouts. Lord Wellington expects to take the field by April next year, and talks very big upon the prospect of his operations. He goes to Cadiz in two days and arrives there in 7 more. I suppose he will make all his arrangements about his Spanish command.† I fear he will find it a difficult task to render them at all effective. Felton left this place on the 3rd and was to go to [Lisbon?] as quick as possible, but I fear he must have been delayed a little on his road by the stupidity of a Portuguese boy of mine who was left on the road with his horse, with orders to bring back mine which Felton was riding, but not arriving for four hours after the supposed time I told the boy, he brought back Felton's little brown horse here. I hope no accident has happened to him, but I have not heard from him.

I parted with one of my mules lately, and purchased two horses, which makes my establishment now consist of 4 [horses] and the mule, and if I have luck with them during the winter, I shall be very well mounted when the campaign opens. Charles Bishop is with his regiment, but when I saw him last he was uneasy about getting an exchange out of the 16th. The regiment was very clamorous about him before I saw him in Salamanca, and persuaded him to join. He was then in a convalescent state. Pray make my best remembrances at Englefield Green, and with best love, believe me, my dear uncle, your most dutiful and affectionate nephew,

John Fremantle

---

* Brevet Colonel Joseph Fuller, Coldstream Guards.
† Wellington had finally been given command of the Spanish troops.

With Wellington away at Cadiz, John and the Prince of Orange took a few days out to travel to Oporto; they were to become good friends during this sojourn.

Oporto, 19 January 1813

My dear uncle

I have not written to you since my arrival here, as I really have nothing to say. I accompanied the prince* here from Freineda, and made it out very well with him, ever since his arrival, before I was appointed he had always been very civil, and now I may say we are quite friends, nobody else came down with him, and he brought nothing but a pair of saddle bags on his dragoon's horse. We had no idea of remaining more than 10 days, only the Lord's stay at Cadiz, was so much longer than he at first intended, that the prince agreed there was no occasion for our hurrying back much before him. I suppose we shall leave this, therefore, in four or five days, so as to reach Freineda a day or two before [the duke].

By the arrival of the last mail I saw Lascelles's appointment in the Gazette to succeed me,† which delighted me more than I will express to you, as I always was very much afraid there might be a difficulty made by the Duke of Cambridge, to my remaining in this regiment, on the Staff. I therefore request as I feel awkwardness in writing myself to His Royal Highness that you will make known to him the high sense of gratitude I feel for this additional mark of his kindness.

I also received a letter from Fuller three days ago, which came by the mail full of good nature upon the occasion, and I really believe he made no attempt to throw a difficulty in my remaining. I have written to him to thank him for his goodwill, and to make up more completely the little differences that had subsisted between us. I mentioned to him the regret it would have occasioned me, to have been obliged to quit the regiment, a battalion of which I have been so closely connected with ever since I had served. Which, soldier of fortune as he knew I was, must have been the case, rather than have relinquished Lord Wellington's patronage.

I have not yet received your letter, but I cannot imagine this could have been accomplished so easily, without your interference, of which I am not unmindful. I am sure it is what you highly approve, and I assure you when I saw it (by chance) I don't remember when to have been so happy. I trust my endeavours will give satisfaction to Lord

---

* His Serene Highness Colonel William the Prince of Orange was an aide-de-camp to Wellington.
† Lascelles became adjutant.

Wellington for the time to come, and meet your approbation, which believe me, my dear uncle, to be always the sincere and steady wish of your affectionate nephew,
    John Fremantle

PS I fear I am in disgrace with Selina, but I have delayed writing so long that I am now almost afraid. Pray make my best remembrances to all at Englefield Green. Pray tell Felton that his little horse was placed in storing here, but is now quite well. He has not answered my last letter, he is a much worse correspondent than I am. I hope Fanny got the little present I sent her by Mr Sydenham to be left in Stanhope Street. Adieu once more, my dear uncle, John Fremantle.

The next few letters from John, while they lay in winter quarters, deal mostly with accounts of his new role and the army's preparations for the forthcoming campaign.

Mangualde, 25 January 1813

My dear uncle,
I received your letter of November 22nd the day after I sent mine from Oporto. I thought very likely it would prove that you had sent it under cover to Lord Wellington but how could you imagine I should consider your style as preaching, far from it I assure you. It is always wholesome, and believe me, welcome. I hope as long as I live I never shall think myself so wise as not to be able to improve, and if I attend to what you say I am sure I cannot be a loser. I am as well aware as you can wish me to be of the importance it may prove my gaining Lord Wellington's good opinion and promise you I will use my best endeavours to do so. The task I consider by no means difficult, for by attending fairly to my business, and by a readiness to execute what I am ordered, I think it is to be accomplished. This surely is not difficult after what I have gone through, besides liking him as I do, and feeling a pleasure in serving him. Since Burgh's arrival I have not had so much employment with Fitzroy but I am always ready to do what may be required of me by him. I believe Worcester is before me to go home, but his stay is altogether very uncertain. I understand from you, and nearly so from himself, that I am to have the first vacancy.* You urge most that of assistant military secretary, but there is no difference, the employments being just the same, those who can write only do. Many

---

* That is, the first available position as an official aide-de-camp on official pay, rather than as an 'extra' aide-de-camp paid by the general.

thanks for your kind offers about any clothes.* I wrote to my tailor and to our sergeant major (Childs) to give the former such and such orders, the moment another adjutant was gazetted. Therefore I am sure as little time will be lost as possible on my receiving them. [Lord] March has given me a full dress coat that was too little for him. In short the only thing I want is my cocked hat, which Mr Cater† with his accustomed inattention I fear will delay, notwithstanding I paid him his £19 before I left England. I arrived here with the prince yesterday, and reach Freineda the day after tomorrow when I expect our lord will have arrived. Give my best love and remembrances and believe me, my dear uncle, your dutiful and affectionate nephew,

    John Fremantle

Headquarters, Freineda, 18 February 1813

My dear uncle,

I had not time to send you a line last week, and have not much more time now. I have been hard at work writing the whole fortnight, but there will not be so much after a little while when all the papers are got through that were waiting while they were at Cadiz.

The army has not yet begun to improve in health, and the deaths have been quite dreadful. Amazing preparations are making against the opening of the campaign. Lord Wellington is soon to visit the cantonments of the troops. Tell Felton he need not be in a great hurry to come out, for I think in two months he will find us here. Believe me, my dear uncle, your most dutiful and affectionate nephew,

    John Fremantle

John refers in his next letter to the high sickness rate in the army, which thankfully was now beginning to decline; however the Guards were suffering badly, particularly the 1st Brigade of Guards, now consisting of the 1st and 3rd Battalions 1st Foot Guards, which remained so sickly as to be sent to the rear to Oporto to recuperate and thus missed much of the campaign of 1813.

Freineda, 24 February 1813

My dear uncle,

You may depend upon it I will attend to the injunctions contained in your last letter which I received on the 18th. Nothing can be more pleasant and agreeable than my occupation here. I have just enough

---

* John was now required to get himself kitted out in the finery of an aide-de-camp, not an easy task while on campaign.
† Of F. & J. Cater of Pall Mall, a famous military hat- and cap-maker of the time.

to do to make the time pass quickly. I attend about noon, and if Lord Wellington does not go out riding I write from then till near dinner if Fitzroy has employment for me so long. We were always great friends, I mean he rather patronised me, and I trust he will continue it, he is an excellent good creature and liked by everyone who knows him, and gives universal satisfaction by his mode of doing business. Lord W[ellington] is quite well; he got ducked overhead in the water out hunting the other day.

The French attacked our post at Bejar in the sierra the other day, but were beaten back; I imagine they only came for plunder. Another division is to move up there (the 4th) for fear they should offer to engage it again, our loss was about 12 men. The sickness in the army is not quite to so great an extent as it was, but still very great. The 1st Regiment of Guards has dropped off by hundreds, and our brigade has suffered very materially. I know of no other news to give you. Pray remember me to Felton and tell him his paymaster brought my pony up in a dreadful state and my saddle totally spoilt. His little horse is in beautiful order and so I have two others. My cocked hat that I was so anxious about had arrived at Lisbon, and I hope soon to have it up, and I believe a box of clothes and so I shall soon be ready for a start, which by the by I don't think there is much chance of for at least three or four weeks. Make my best remembrances to my aunt, Selina and Eliza Frederick Lionel and believe me, my dear uncle, your dutiful and affectionate nephew,
John Fremantle

John's next letter spoke of a major disagreement between the new divisional commander, General Stewart, and the Guards over privileges. Wellington was severely irritated having to correspond on such matters during his campaign preparations.

Freineda, 10 March 1813

My dear uncle,
I received an hour ago your letter of February 18th from Stowe. I sincerely regret for your sake Lord Buckingham's death.* Lord Wellington heard of it two days ago by a later mail, which arrived before the present one, which we were afraid was lost. Lord W[ellington] was also very much concerned at his loss. I fancy Mr Stewart will come

---

* George Nugent-Temple-Grenville, 1st Marquess of Buckingham, had been sponsoring the Fremantle family for many years. They were his neighbours in Buckinghamshire at Aston Abbots, and then Swanbourne. He died on 11 February 1813.

up from Lisbon to invest him with the blue ribbon.* We are to have a grand fete at Ciudad on the 13th for the purpose of investing General Cole with the Order of the Bath.

I have been employed ever since morning copying seven sheets of long paper concerning the privileges of the corps of Guards, which General W. Stewart who now commands the 1st Division has been endeavouring to infringe by wishing to inspect the accounts of the men; a right exclusively belonging to officers belonging to the brigade. The whole is sent to the Duke of York for his decision, which I have no doubt will be in our favour. Lord Wellington was very angry at being troubled with such a long correspondence upon such an occasion, and when he has so much to occupy him of a more worthy nature. I hope Felton will have arrived at Lisbon by the 1st of April, his name however has never been mentioned. I don't expect we shall move much before the month of May. I think his lordship will have under his command including Spaniards, 100,000 bayonets.

Badcock† of the 14th was here a few days ago for the purpose of writing a march to Talbot's memory and he told me the regiment had improved considerably. Felton's horse is in high condition. Pray make my best remembrances and with best love, believe me, believe me, your dutiful and affectionate nephew,

John Fremantle

John's latest letter brought news of the arrival of his new uniform, disagreements within 'the family' and scandal.

Freineda, 14 April 1813

My dear uncle,

I received your letter of March 22nd last week and am very much obliged to you for the interest you have taken about the things I expected from England. I was very anxious about them I confess, on account of their being so much longer on their way than they ought to have been owing to the inattention of Sergeant Major Childs to my directions respecting them. They are all arrived except my saddle which is immaterial as I would have disposed of it on its arrival, not being at all what I directed Childs to get me, and having had what I wanted given to me here viz. a common trooper's hussar type with the appendages. My box of clothes I am happy to say is also at Lisbon and I expect the contents up daily. In short before the end of the month

* This actually refers to Charles Stuart, British ambassador at Lisbon, who was to present the Order of the Garter to Wellington.
† Captain Benjamin Lovell Badcock, 14th Light Dragoons.

I hope to be quite completed, and I don't think we shall have moved before that time. James Butler's partner at Lisbon has been of the very greatest service to me in getting me up my things. Albinia's shirts arrived the other day most opportunely. In your letter you say you were at a loss to know what to send me out by Felton, and as people here will only dispose of animals when they have been battered by work, and mine are in that way, I really shall be exceedingly obliged to you to send me one. If young Jones would part with his pony, it's that sort of thing that would suit me better than any other, for though not young it has never been ill used.

Colonel Brand and Mr Rose will not be long before they return to this country and either of them I am sure would bring it out to me. The latter is my particular and intimate friend and *camarade* [comrade] and I think you would be gratified by his acquaintance, and it would oblige me very much. He bears a very high character in this army as a professional man, and is a great favourite of Lord Wellington, and is universally esteemed by everyone who knows him. There has been the devil to pay here lately. No less than three boils in the family with Lord March, which were nigh ending seriously. He has been generally made so much of that he is quite spoiled, and is never rosy except when putting his jokes into practice or amusing himself at the expense of his neighbours. We were and are now very good friends, but it happened to me to be obliged, the first, to have an understanding with him on that point. Gordon, (the second) who I believe is as little disposed to be quarrelsome as myself was more unpleasant, as the sparring with words took place at table and ended most grossly, before Lord W[ellington], who was exceedingly vexed at it. Lord G. Lennox* has been appointed to us, and I believe is very little better. Lord Worcester has been playing the fool considerably at Lisbon, intriguing with half a dozen men's wives and I hear he is to join his regiment the 10th.

I have now given you all the scandal, which pray don't open your mouth about. I am well alive of course to the object of promotion, I hope it will arrive in due time, I understand March is the first for dispatches, but to tell you the truth I think the second is likely to be of most importance. I don't see any prospect with the Prince of Orange, when he goes, which however he knows no more of than any of us.

I expect soon to find some changes in the regiment. I understand they are very busy at Cambridge Terrace† endeavouring to give old Philips a share at least so Rose told me, and that Gore, who is coming

---

* Lieutenant Lord George Lennox, 9th Light Dragoons, became an aide-de-camp to Wellington in 1813.
† This reference is odd, because Cambridge Terrace was not built until 1824.

out here, is in a bad way, it's an ill wind that blows nobody good. There was a duel a fortnight ago at Mesquitella between Collier and Dawkins, which had nearly cost the latter his life. The quarrel was brought on by a practical joke. I suppose campaigning sours people's temper, there has been a great deal of quarrelling in the regiment for this long time past.

I had a letter ready for Felton against his arrival in Lisbon to tell him I had sent his order of [KTS*] care of Mr Steed that he might have the satisfaction of sporting it, before Madame Lugo his French love there. He did not know of it till he got my note, and I think he was so gratified by it, he said he was to leave Lisbon this day for this place. They are all anxious to see him. Thank Eliza for her ring I like it very much, it fits me very well too. I pay my devoir to Lord Fitzroy every morning after breakfast, and write as long as he has employment for me. I get on famously; make my best love and remembrance. Adieu my dear uncle, your dutiful and affectionate nephew,

  John Fremantle

Hurried notes brought news of major preparations for the new campaigning season.

Freineda, 28 April 1813

My dear uncle,

I have only time to tell you, that I think in all probability we shall be off from here in the course of another week. Some of the cavalry are already crossing the Douro into the Tras os Montes.

Felton left this yesterday in the middle of the rains for his regiment, which he reached today. I never saw him looking better. He brought me a seal from Selina, which I am very much obliged to him for. I have not a word of news. Ever my dear uncle your dutiful and affectionate nephew,

  John Fremantle

Wellington had rested his army over the winter in the certain knowledge that Napoleon had been draining Spain of his best troops, to replace the horrendous losses the Grand Army had sustained in the Russian snows. His army was well rested and provisioned and he prepared to advance

---

* He was wearing the award of Knight of the Tower and Sword, a Portuguese award. Felton Hervey is not listed in any British publication I can find as having received this award, but he was awarded it on 12 October 1812 and it was duly published in the *Gazeta de Lisboa*, no. 26, 1 February 1813. I must thank my colleagues of the Napoleon Series Website for resolving this query for me.

against the French who had prepared strong defensive positions upon the successive river lines.

Wellington remained with the centre of the army facing Salamanca while General Graham marched a large corps through difficult country to the north which effectively turned the French defensive lines, which they were obliged to abandon without a fight, to prevent their position being encircled.

Once the turning movement was well under way, Wellington and Hill advanced upon Salamanca, then turned north to join Graham and drive the French back towards the Pyrenees.

Confidence was extremely high within the army and there was much talk of driving the French completely out of Spain; but the French were not to go so meekly.

Freineda, 10 May 1813

My dear uncle,

I have not written to you for these last three posts, in the first place because I've always been waiting till the last moment, and I should otherwise have had little or nothing to say.

The scene has considerably changed since my last letter. Lord Wellington has been to see some of the divisions, which were most at hand previous to their marching, and I have been indulged with some decent rides. We returned yesterday from seeing the hussars, which was a real treat. They turned out exactly as if from barracks in England. The brigade marched this morning and proceed to Miranda [do Douro], to form a part of the column on the left, under Sir Thomas Graham who left us this morning to join his command. Lord Wellington has nothing here but the Light Division, German Hussars and 14th [Light Dragoon] Regiment, which of course will proceed to Salamanca, and I imagine we shall march in a couple of days or so. General Hill is to be the length of Salamanca by the 24th. I do not expect to have any check before we reach the Douro, or indeed, Burgos. The army is quite new again, and has been for some time anxious for the move. There has been quite as much rain as is necessary for the harvest, and the weather, is quite settled and beautifully fine.

We have had some little changes in the family. Lord George Lennox has joined as extra ADC and Worcester is going the day after tomorrow to join the 10th [Light Dragoons]. He fell in with the regiment yesterday, which makes me one nearer going home with dispatches. I did think, and must still, that he was the only one before me, for March has certainly had a turn, but Fitzroy said the other day that he was first, however be it as it will, I shall never speak of it one way or the other. I see no prospect of my receiving pay [as an official ADC], for those on the establishment of it are Fitzroy, Burgh, Canning and Gordon. The two first together with March receive 10 pounds a day as secretaries, but I shall not be surprised if one of these three resigns in my favour. Promotion I understand is likely to continue in the Coldstream. Felton has been staying here for two days; he went away this morning looking very well, and in high spirits. I saw Hutchison last week at the review, he said he was quite stout but I think he was looking poorly. With best love and remembrances, believe me, my dear uncle, your dutiful and affectionate nephew,

    John Fremantle

The advance proceeded to plan and having taken Salamanca, Wellington swung his forces northward to join Graham.

Carbajales [de Alba], 31 May 1813

My dear uncle,
Our troops passed the Tormes and entered Salamanca on the 26th. The French had only one division, but they suffered severely, for their bravado in waiting too long. Our artillery having overtaken them and played upon them, for the distance of three miles, we destroyed them, about 300 men.

    The River Esla was forded this morning, and tomorrow I expect headquarters will be in Zamora. The French evacuated it this morning. General Hill will also join us there. We have had a very decent week's work. The Grande Lord passed in one day from Salamanca to Miranda.* Lord Worcester joined his regiment this morning, and Lord George Lennox joins the 15th tomorrow.† Adieu my dear uncle, in great haste believe me, your most dutiful and affectionate nephew,

    John Fremantle

PS I saw Hutchinson yesterday quite well he has got an order for six months' pay for Frederick‡ which he offered to me to send, but I desired him to write himself. I expect Charles Bishop will join his regiment in a few days.

---

* On the morning of 29 May, Wellington rode at speed the 50 miles from Salamanca to the banks of the Douro opposite Miranda do Douro, where there was no bridge over the rapids. He had to be winched over the river in a wicker basket on a rope!
† This is an error as Lord George Lennox did not leave his role as aide-de-camp and remained in the 9th Light Dragoons.
‡ Captain Frederick Hervey, 20th Foot was Felton's younger brother and eventually succeeded to the baronetcy, he was not in Spain again after serving in the Corunna campaign.

DESPATCHES

We suddenly find a gap of more than two months in John's correspondence, but this can be easily explained.

The army continued to advance rapidly, driving the French back beyond Burgos, which was destroyed by them in their retreat. King Joseph and his generals brought their various corps together at Vitoria, and here they awaited Wellington's approach, confident of success.

Wellington arrived to find the valley before Vitoria defended by the French army, deployed behind the River Zadora. The allied army numbered some 75,000 against 57,000 French, but the French had over 150 cannon against the allied total of only 90 cannon and they had the advantage of a strong defensive line along the river.

However, discovering that the French had neglected to destroy the bridges over the Zadora, Wellington launched a determined attack on 21 June 1813 against the French left and centre, while General Graham led two divisions in a great flanking movement which threatened to cut the French lines of retreat.

The French fought stubbornly until Graham's force cut the road to Bilbao and sought to cut the only remaining line of retreat via Pamplona. Eventually, although Graham was prevented from closing this final escape route by fierce resistance, the French army, fearing for its safety, began to retreat in haste.

The French managed to retreat in some order, but the great plunder they had accumulated over years of occupation was abandoned. The British army was guilty of being drawn to the plunder and the French army was allowed to escape without vigorous pursuit.

Wellington ordered John home with the despatch announcing the victory of Vitoria, carrying Marshal Jourdan's baton and a colour of 100th Ligne Regiment; he left for England on 22 June, giving him no time to write before he arrived in London himself.

John arrived home and had the honour of presenting the despatch to the Prince Regent, who presided as regent on behalf of his 'mad' father,

George III. The despatch was duly placed in the Gazette on 3 July, which by coincidence was the very same day that the Gazette published the announcement of John's promotion to the rank of major.

Uncle William wrote to Lord Grenville.

Stanhope Street, 3 July 1813[*]

My dear Lord,

. . . I was most agreably [*sic*] roused this morning by the arrival of my nephew John Fremantle who has brought dispatches from Lord Wellington. The contents of them will be better learned from the Gazette, as I have literally only seen him for ten minutes but as I am sure you would participate in any happiness of mine, I can't help informing you of this event which is really a most gratifying thing to me. He says the French army fought extremely ill . . . This is a son of my brother Stephen, who I have always since his death, had in charge, & who Lord Wellington very kindly made his A. du Camp [*sic*] at my request. This gives him at the age of 28 the rank of Major.

This caused a problem for John, because the government were not prepared to sanction a brevet promotion for bearing the victory despatch on top of his newly announced promotion, which would appear as a 'double step'. This led to series of letters between his uncle and the government regarding the matter and it finally seemed that a way round the dilemma had been found.

Thursday 8 July 1813

My dear Fremantle,

I did not fail to bring Major[†] Fremantle yesterday before the Prince Regent, who entered into it with every kindness, and commissioned me to see the Duke of York upon it. I have accordingly done so this morning, and find he dreads the double step may be drawn on with precedent, for he will not allow the case of Lord Clinton[‡] to be any, but he has suggested a mode of which it may be done and avoid being a precedent, namely to send back Major Fremantle with the duplicate of the Regent's letter and the thanks of both houses to Lord Wellington

---

[*] National Archives Add. MS 58967 ff52-3

[†] He had been promoted brevet major on 21 June 1813, but the Gazette announcing it was not published until 3 July.

[‡] Captain Lord Robert Cotton St John Clinton was aide-de-camp to Wellington in 1812 and was sent home with the Salamanca despatch; he became a brevet major in the 41st Foot on 18 August without purchase. Having delivered the despatch on 16 August, he was promoted to lieutenant colonel on 25 August.

and the army apprising His Lordship that on the delivery of those dispatches, by way of special distinction, he is to have the rank of lieutenant colonel.

Follow this up immediately by some civil communication with the Duke of York, and the thing is done.* Most sincerely yours,
    J. McMahon†

        To His Royal Highness, The Duke of York, Stanhope Street, 8 July 1813
Sir,
Colonel McMahon has this moment communicated to me Your Royal Highness's most gracious and kind intentions respecting my nephew, Major Fremantle. I can only assure Your Royal Highness that I wanted no new proof of your unbounded kindness to add to my gratitude and devotion, but allow me, Sir, to say that as long as I have life, so long shall I remember this instance of Your Royal Highness's goodness, than which nothing on earth could have gratified me so much.

I have the honour to be sir with the most profound respect and devotion, Your Royal Highness's most obedient and respectful humble servant,
    W. H. Fremantle

Dear Fremantle,
I gave the letter to Lord Bathurst,‡ and accompanied the delivery of it with all that it was in my power to say. The House was in a great bustle, and Lord Bathurst could only say that he would pay every possible attention to your letter. What can be done I guess not; but truly glad shall I be if the object can be attained. Lord Bathurst does not intend to speak to Major Fremantle today upon the subject. In haste yours,
    Hubbard

                      Stanhope Street, 8 July 1813
Private
My dear McMahon,
No words can express the real sense I entertain of the kind intentions of the Duke of York regarding my nephew but indeed I feel that I owe this event so gratifying to all my wishes to the gracious and kind disposition of the Prince Regent. I know not how I am to throw

---

* This did not happen.

† Colonel Sir John McMahon was the Prince Regent's Keeper of the Privy Purse and private secretary.

‡ Earl Bathurst was Secretary of State for War and the Colonies.

1 *John Fremantle's wife Agnes Lyon,*
1829

2 *His sister Albinia Fremantle*

3 *Louisa Caton, who married*
Felton Hervey

4 *Uncle William Fremantle*

5 *John Fremantle,*
'bearer of the despatches'

6 *Miniature of John Fremantle*

7 *John Fremantle by M. Carpenter*

8 *John Fremantle 1829*

9   *General Alava*

10   *Arthur, Duke of Wellington*

11   *The Duc d'Angoulême*

12   *Field Marshal Blücher*

13   An aide-de-camp, 1815   14   *Wellington and his Staff at the Battle of Vitoria,*
1813

15   *The Duke of Wellington and his Staff at the Battle of Waterloo*

16   Fitzroy Somerset

17   Lord Arthur Hill

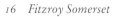

18   Colonel John Fremantle

*19   Colonel John Fremantle, aide-de-
camp to King George IV, 1832, by
A. Dubois Drahonet
(Courtesy of the Royal Collection)*

Field Marshal The Duke of Wellington, K.G. &c.&c.

TO HIS MOST EXCELLENT MAJESTY GEORGE THE FOURTH KING OF GREAT BRITAIN &c.&c.

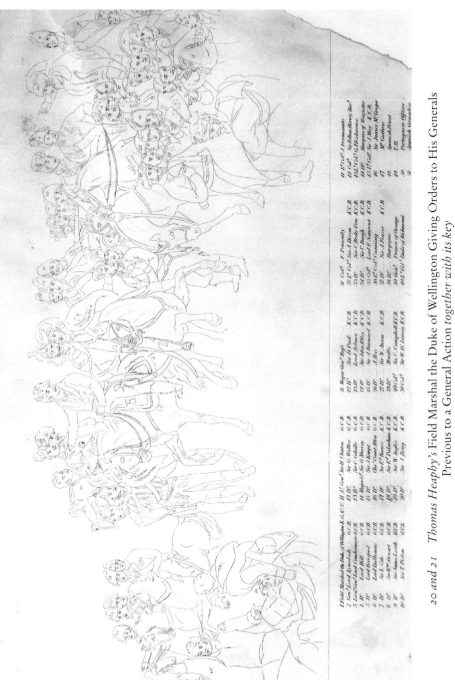

1 Field Marshal the Duke of Wellington K.G. &c	G.C.B.		11 Lieut Genl Sir H. Clinton	G.C.B.	21 Major Genl Bns		Sir D. Pack	K.C.B.	31 Col.	F. Ponsonby		41 Col. J. Fremantle	
2 Gen.l Lord Lynedoch	G.C.B.	12 D.o	Sir G. Walker	G.C.B.	22 D.o		Lord Aylmer	K.C.B.	32 Lt Col.	Sir J. Dixon	K.C.B.	42 Col.	Sir John Henry Bns.
3 Lieut Genl Lord Combermere	G.C.B.	13 D.o	Sir C. Colville	G.C.B.	23 D.o		Sir John Elley	K.C.B.	33 D.o	Sir C. Broke Vere	K.C.B.	43 Lt Col.	G. Fitzclarence
4 D.o		G.C.B.	14 Major Genl Sir G. Murray	G.C.B.	24 D.o		Sir J. Barnard	K.C.B.	34 D.o	Sir T. Burgh	K.C.B.	44 D.o	Marquis of Worcester
5 D.o Lord Hill	G.C.B.	15 D.o	Sir J. Kempt	G.C.B.	25 D.o		J. Bell		35 Col.	Lord F. Somerset	K.C.B.	45 Lt Col. Sir J. May	K.C.B.
6 D.o Lord Dalhousie	G.C.B.	16 D.o	One Count Alten	G.C.B.	26 D.o		Sir W. Anson	K.C.B.	36 Lt Col. Canning		46		Sir James M.Gregor
7 D.o Sir L. Cole	G.C.B.	17 D.o	Sir E.o Barnes	K.C.B.	27 D.o		Sir J. Fraser	K.C.B.	37 D.o	Sir J. Fraser	K.C.B.	47		M.r Guthrie
8 D.o Sir W.m Stewart	G.C.B.	18 D.o	Sir E.o Pakenham	K.C.B.	28 D.o		Merville		38 D.o	Burgoyne		48		Spanish Priest
9 D.o Sir James Leith	G.C.B.	19 D.o	Sir W. Inglis	K.C.B.	29 Lt Col.		Sir C. Campbell K.C.B.	39 Genl	Prince of Orange		49		T.H.
10 D.o Sir T. Picton	G.C.B.	20 D.o	Sir J. Bng	K.C.B.	30 Col.		Sir H. D. Laures K.C.B.	40 Lt Col Duke of Richmond		50		Portuguese Officer
												51		Spanish Grenadier

20 and 21   *Thomas Heaphy's* Field Marshal the Duke of Wellington Giving Orders to His Generals Previous to a General Action *together with its key*

22 The Duke of Wellington visiting the outposts at Soignies *by Hippolyte Lecomte*
(By kind permission of Apsley House & English Heritage)

23 John Fremantle *by Comte d'Orsay, 1818*

myself at his feet, how I can ever sufficiently mark my gratitude. Truly have I always been sensible to the real kindness of the Royal Family to me and hope my public and private conduct have never disclosed an insensibility to it, but this instance of His Royal Highness' goodness is one that of all others I shall ever look upon with sentiments of gratitude and thanks. The boy has been adopted by me from his earliest youth and there is nothing on earth that would have gratified me so much as the favour which has been shown him.

As to saying anything of your individual friendship I only wish you could look into my heart and you would there see how I value it.

I have endeavoured to lay my feelings before His Royal Highness in a letter, if you think it right you will deliver it.

If I could presume to ask an interview to offer my personal thanks I should be happy to have the opportunity, but do pray advise me what is best. To that advice I shall strictly adhere. Believe me ever, dear McMahon, most sincerely yours,

W. H. F.

I have done what you advised.

But problems did occur, and John was to be denied his promotion to lieutenant colonel.

Duke Street, Thursday 8 July 1813

Dear Sir,

You will I hope do me the justice to believe that on every account it would have given me the sincerest pleasure to have proceeded the wishes you have expressed that Major Fremantle should have a second promotion.

But after what passed on Lord Clinton's promotion, I feel that I should not be able to succeed, and I think therefore that it is much fairer by all parties not to attempt it.

Lord Clinton has been long promised a majority by the duke; this promise was on the point of being fulfilled, and Lord Clinton had received an intimation of it when he arrived with his dispatches. Had his lordship obtained only a brevet majority in consequence of the news he brought, he would in fact have obtained nothing, for he would have had the rank otherwise. The Duke of York however expressed at the time the utmost reluctance to grant this second promotion even under these circumstances from the apprehension that it might be drawn in precedent in cases which were not precisely similar and it was my open and full understanding that no such conclusion was to be drawn from this instance of favour, that his Royal Highness at last thought he might consult his own wishes, without prejudice to the service.

Having stated this, you will I am sure excuse me from not bringing forward an application the answer to which I must be so well prepared to receive. I have the honour ever your servant,
>   Bathurst.

>   To the Prince Regent, Stanhope Street,* 9 July 1813

Sir,
It is quite impossible for me to convey to Your Royal Highness the sense I entertain of your gracious favour conferred on my nephew Major Fremantle. I wanted no new motive to bind me in gratitude and devotion to the royal family, but this instance of marked distinction to my nephew I owe personally to Your Royal Highness and personally shall I ever feel myself in gratitude called upon to acknowledge it. I throw myself at Your Royal Highness's feet to accept my real, my sincere, my heartfelt thanks and to implore that Your Royal Highness would do more justice to my feelings than I can convey by any language expressed on paper

I have the honour to be Sir, with the most profound respect of duty and submission, Your Royal Highness's obedient and dutiful subject,
>   William H. Fremantle

>   Carlton House, Friday 9 July 1813

Most Secret and Confidential
My dear Fremantle,
I am truly concerned to find that in a cabinet of [the] commander-in-chief, the Irish Lord of the Treasury and the War Secretary, there has arisen a diversity of opinion with respect to the giving of Major Fremantle the second step that at present it will be both politic and prudent to push it no further. The outline I gave you in confidence yesterday, was precisely what the Duke of York had himself stated as the mode to do it, and I was sure the Prince Regent would have cheerfully acceded to it. But I find this morning, that in bringing Lord Vesey† and Lord Bathurst into the consultation upon the measure that it cannot now take place, yet still I am persuaded that by being

---

* William Fremantle lived at 6 Stanhope Street, Mayfair; this is now known as Stanhope Gate. Later the notorious Mrs Fitzherbert lived there before her death in 1837.
† William Vesey Fitzgerald, Baron Fitzgerald and Vesey (1783–1843) was Irish Lord of the Treasury until its amalgamation with the British office in 1817.

perfectly quiet, the major will soon attain it. Ever with sincere regard faithfully yours,

J. McMahon

PS The Prince Regent has been highly pleased with your letter.

To the Prince Regent, Englefield Green, 12 July 1813

Sir,

Although your Royal Highness's benevolent intention towards Major Fremantle has been from public motives for a while suspended, I cannot but humbly approach you sir and acknowledge with most unfeigned sincerity my heartfelt gratitude and thanks.

The value your Royal Highness has so justly annexed to the splendid victory of Vitoria and the popularity you have acquired throughout England by the well judged rewards you have been graciously pleased to bestow, must ever stand as a record to Your Royal Highness's military judgement and capacity. I have only once more to beg to be permitted to assure Your Royal Highness of the personal respect and gratitude I owe you, which will live in my remembrance to the latest hour of my life. I have the honour to be, sir, with the most profound respect,

W. H. Fremantle

Carlton House, Monday evening

Private

My dear Fremantle,

I certainly know it would be quite proper and pleasing to His Royal Highness, to deliver your letter, which I have accordingly done. In haste with sincere regards, ever yours,

J. McMahon.

John remained in England for a few weeks waiting to return with despatches for the Duke of Wellington and noticeably does not mention the 'double step' issue.

47 South Street, 18 July 1813

My dear uncle,

I am engaged tomorrow and the next day, consequently cannot come down till Friday. I dined at W. Pole's* yesterday; he tells me he has

---

* William Wellesley Pole was a brother of the Duke of Wellington; he was MP for Queen's County and held a series of major political positions. He eventually became 3rd Earl Mornington.

written to you about being one of the stewards for the fete on Tuesday next at Vauxhall. I hope you will. I have now my horse, but I am to Butler, where I shall be tomorrow or next day. My other animal has arrived safe at Portsmouth. I think I had better not send the amount of my bills before I come down; ever your most affectionate nephew,

John Fremantle

47 South Street,* ½ o'clock, Thursday 22 July 1813

My dear uncle,

I had some conversation last night with Lord Bathurst at the ball, who said he would give me a letter for Lord Wellington before the next post day, which is on Wednesday next, on which day I will be with you on my way. I have not heard from Torrens.† I dine with Lord Bathurst today.

I wrote last night to the army saying I should come out in the next packet. I made every enquiry at the admiralty, but I could not hear of any ship of war sailing from any of the other ports.

Heaphy‡ has finished my picture, he has this moment told me that he never made a better in his life. I will get it from him today and send it down to you before I come, if you like. I explained to him about meeting him en chemise.

There is no hurry about the horses embarking, ever my dear uncle your most dutiful and affectionate nephew,

John Fremantle

I called on J. Butler on my way from Dorking yesterday morning.

47 South Street, Saturday 22 July 1813

My dear uncle,

I received your letter this morning and I suppose you had one from me which I sent by the Englefield Green coach the evening before.

I received a note from Torrens last evening, desiring me to call at the Horse Guards by 3 o'clock to see the Duke of York, but he had left the office to go into the country by 2 o'clock when I called. The duke is at

---

* South Street runs off Park Lane and is next to Hyde Park.

† Colonel Henry Torrens, 3rd Foot Guards, was military secretary to the commander-in-chief.

‡ Thomas Heaphy did a series of life sketches of the major military figures in Wellington's headquarters in 1813/14, many of which now reside in the National Portrait Gallery. These were used for his painting *Field Marshal the Duke of Wellington giving orders to his generals previous to a General Action* (see plates 20 and 21).

Windsor, he returns tomorrow. Torrens does not return till Monday. I have written to him to know whether I had better wait on the duke before his return or not. I shall leave my name at York House today.

The Duke of Cambridge and seven other men dined at Lord Bathurst's yesterday. Lord Bathurst mentioned again that he shall have something for me to take to Lord Wellington before I go. I had a good deal of conversation with him. Ever my dear uncle, your dutiful and affectionate nephew,
> John Fremantle

47 South Street, 27 July 1813

My dear uncle,

I saw the Duke of York yesterday, and he desired me to call tomorrow at 4 o'clock for his letters to Lord Wellington. I have been with Lord Bathurst this morning who NOW says he has nothing to send, but if he should have, he will send them to me. I shall be in time if I go on Thursday night for the Sunday packet. Therefore I shall wait and see you here, as you are to be up that morning. I have heard nothing from Colonel McMahon. My horses started yesterday, one of Lord Brooke's for his brother Colonel Greville.* I fear they will be detained some time at Portsmouth.

Ever my dear uncle, your dutiful and affectionate nephew,
> John Fremantle

William Fremantle still sought a brevet for his nephew, but was rebuffed once again.

Stanhope Street, 1 August 1813

My dear McMahon

My nephew left town yesterday on his return to Lord Wellington deeply impressed with a sense of obligation to the Prince Regent for the kind intention manifested by HRH towards him. He informed me there was a general belief of an intended brevet promotion on HRH's birthday. At present he stands the single instance of an officer bringing home dispatches from a commander in chief recounting a great victory, not being exclusively promoted.

I well know the kindness, the liberality and the princely conduct of the regent on all matters, and his proper feeling on military subjects. I have already had a proof by your kind communication of his personal

---

* Henry Richard Greville, 3rd Lord Brooke, was a Tory politician. His brother was brevet colonel the Honourable Charles John Greville, 38th Foot, who commanded a brigade in the 5th Division.

favour to me on this question, only be assured my dear McMahon that if by his gracious command Major Fremantle should be included in the next brevet I shall consider it as a personal obligation from His Royal Highness which I shall be bound to express to the end of my life. Ever my dear Mc Mahon, most truly yours,

 William H. Fremantle

Carlton House, Sunday 2 August

Private

My dear Fremantle,

I have this moment shown your letter to the Prince Regent who has read it with every kind disposition towards your nephew, but His Royal Highness says 'There will be no brevet on his birthday'. He was in such a hurry going to Windsor that I had not the power to touch upon the other subject. In haste, believe me, sincerely yours

 J. McMahon

I do not think any brevet will come out, at any time, which will not include Major Fremantle.

SPAIN AGAIN

John sailed with the fleet for Spain from Portsmouth on 9 August, eager to return to Wellington's family. During his absence he had missed a failed attempt to storm San Sebastian and Soult's bold assault on the allies in the passes of the Pyrenees and his ultimate defeat by Wellington at the three day battle of Sorauren.

On board the *President*[*] off Cawsand Bay, 1 o'clock 9 August

My dear uncle,

We are just under weigh with the whole of our convoy, consisting of about 40 sail to join Lord Wellington.

The *Sparrow*[†] came in this morning, having left the Spanish coast nine days ago, the captain is badly wounded. He told me how the guns which were used in the siege of St Sebastian had been once embarked and re-landed. The garrison made a successful sortie, and we an unsuccessful assault upon the place, but they had no idea the siege would be eventually raised. They also say we had the worst of it in an action which took place 7 leagues from Pamplona and 9 from San Sebastian.[‡]

Adieu my dear uncle with best love. Believe me, ever your dutiful and affectionate nephew,

John Fremantle

---

[*] There was a gunboat of this name carrying 14 guns in a squadron of small vessels employed at the siege of San Sebastian in 1813.

[†] HMS *Sparrow* of 16 guns, commanded by Captain Tayler, had led a squadron of gunboats employed at the siege of San Sebastian. Tayler was apparently injured while attending a shore battery consisting of guns landed from his ship by a shell actually landing on him. Presumably it did not explode!

[‡] This refers to the combat at the Pass of Maya on 25 July, which was actually the start of Marshal Soult's offensive to drive Wellington from the Pyrenees and to relieve Pamplona which ended in his own defeat at Sorauren.

PS The *Jaseur** returned to Portsmouth just as the *President* with her convoy put in here.

William Fremantle received a letter from the Duke of Wellington regarding his nephew. He had clearly appealed to the duke regarding the 'double step'.

Lesaca, 19 August 1813

My dear Fremantle,
I have received your letter regarding your nephew's promotion of which I had heard before. The fact is that the aides de camp and general officers who were promoted were very improperly recommended to me by the general officers who availed themselves of my permission that they should recommend officers for promotion, to put forward their own Staff.

It appears to me however that it would have been impossible to give two steps for bringing the account of one victory, and that the precedent could have been a dangerous one, Clinton's case cannot be deemed a precedent; and if it is deemed one, that alone would be a sufficient reason for taking advantage of such an action as that of Vitoria to revert to the old style of one step of promotion for the bringer of the news of a victory. I'll take care that your nephew shall not want the other step.

I had heard of the separation which you mention in your postscript; but I never think of home politics or politicians. Ever yours most sincerely,
    Wellington

In a hurried note John announced his arrival at headquarters after a passage of only ten days.

19 August 1813, 4 o'clock

My dear uncle,
I have only time to tell you that I have this instant arrived, and have received your letter, but can tell you nothing. I gave our Lord your letter, but he has not spoken to me.

I saw my dear aunts,† I will write to you whenever there is an

---

* The cruiser HMS *Jaseur*, was brand new, having been launched at Ipswich in 1813; it proceeded to Canada to partake in the Lakes campaign.
† His Aunt Marianne Bishop lived at Sunbury, and his widowed Aunt Catherine was a frequent visitor there, both aunts had helped to bring him up. He probably saw them en route to Portsmouth.

opportunity, and will let you know what I hear. We took a rich American prize from Nantes on our passage, and I have got a great quantity of gloves and ribbons, which I think I will send by the first safe opportunity. Your most dutifully and affectionately,

  John Fremantle

John wrote more fully, with news of 'family' intrigues and of the duke's lumbago; he also wrote of renewed efforts to take San Sebastian. Meanwhile news of the disastrous retreat of Sir John Murray's army in Eastern Spain, abandoning his guns, had filtered through.

Lesaca, 24 August 1813

My dear uncle,

I hope you received my note the other day to tell you just of my arrival. I had not time to say more, but have the satisfaction now to mention to you the very gracious reception I met with here, not only from my Lord, but from all hands. I believe I may venture to say, they were all content with the manner in which I executed my mission. My Lord asked considerable questions, as did the rest of the household, he particularly was delighted, and grinned much. I rode close with him the other day when he also questioned a great deal. I gave him your letter amongst others, but he has taken no notice of it to me, nor have I referred to it, thinking that he knows best concerning the business; but I wish to assure you that I will not be at all disappointed if it does not take place notwithstanding you were so sanguine about it, but if it does, as we settled before, *tout mieux* [so much the better]. I cannot be without hopes, now that fortune has begun to smile upon me, that I shall soon have another 'Fall'; events appear very big and the land at present lies thus; if it had been anybody else's turn but Canning's, (who is so damned an ass) the prince would not have gone, but the matter is settled, and he content to get his promotion and the £500,* consequently it is a 'job' for him and I do not know whose turn it is now; March can't profit by a trip, he is rather unwell; Worcester has joined us; Gordon has bitched himself, he was huffed at Lord Wellington for not mentioning him in his dispatch for being wounded, and wrote to him about it, of all things. I always thought before this that his headpiece was a little awry. I never was so astonished when I heard it in my life. He is at the seaside at present with Beresford.† The

---

* This comment is obscure, as neither Canning nor William the Prince of Orange gained promotion at this period.

† Gordon was struck in the left arm by a musket ball at the first Battle of Sorauren, 28 July, which came out six inches below at the elbow, luckily without damaging the

wound is a flesh one, but I dare say he will go to England; so much for the 'family', but my Lord has got a touch of the lumbago, but he managed to give me a twist after him for 9 hours up and down the mountains here, and he is going a gasper [exhausted] tomorrow.

I have been riding my brother's horses, my own not having joined from Vitoria which I am rather uneasy about, and shall look very blue if they don't arrive tomorrow.

The fifty pieces that came with me open tomorrow morning,* and if we don't succeed at the breach they will make, I think it will be a bad job, and everybody concurs in the idea of its being a very surly place, by George it looks so to me, they saluted my ship as it came in. I had a beautiful view of Bayonne yesterday at the distance of 5 leagues, and St Jean de Luz. The country further on looks very inviting, much more so than these mountains. Our position is as strong as the one at Lisbon, and theirs about the same distance as it was down there. Suchet advanced upon Lord W. Bentinck, made him notice, blew up Tarragona,† retreated, and Lord Wellington advanced again, so far so good. Pamplona has still a month's provision in it. I received a letter from you when I arrived, pray don't be uneasy about my matters, I shall send home some money to pay for everything I owe immediately without fail. I am put upon the establishment of aides de camp. I will write, and have written as yet, like a house afire. We took a prize coming out and I made some French gloves out of her, which I will send home by the first safe opportunity. I have not seen Felton or Charles Bishop, but hear they are well. I have seen Hutchinson who is very well, I hope you or somebody will write us a good account of the

---

bone or the arteries. He went to Zarautz near Getaria to recuperate where Marshal Beresford was residing for his health.

* An additional battering train was delivered consisting of twenty-eight cannon to help break down the fortifications. Soon after a second convoy of guns originally destined for the defence of Cuxhaven arrived with a further fifteen 24-pounders, eight 18-pounders and four 10-inch mortars.

† General Sir John Murray took command of the Anglo-Sicilian force which had landed to besiege Tarragona. Despite some success with his siege guns, allowing for the possibility of gaining the city by storm; Murray was continually frightened for his rear and exaggerated rumours of Suchet's advance led him to abandon the siege, leaving his siege guns on the beach. Lord William Bentinck, commander in chief of the British force in Sicily, arrived during this operation, took command and returned with the troops to that island. Murray was eventually court-martialled for this ignominious failure but he continued his military career.

ceremony. Burrard* and Allix,† friends of Knightley's‡ have made very great enquiries after him.

Pray give my best love to all the people and believe me, ever my dear uncle, your dutiful and affectionate nephew,
John Fremantle

PS I landed Heaphy at Bilbao, under Taylor's charge, I hope he will join in a day or two. The Lord grinned a good deal and will be delighted to sit.

His next letter told of the capture of the town of San Sebastian by storm which occurred simultaneously with a Spanish victory at San Marcial, when Soult attempted to relieve the fortress. The French defenders of San Sebastian still held out in the castle on Monte Urgull overlooking the town.

Lesaca, 2 September 1813

My dear uncle,

We have had a constant series of operations since I wrote to you last. Always out from day light till 9 or 10 o'clock at night which ended in a slight affair on the 31st, in which the French got a severe beating even by the Spaniards, when the French attacked them. It was an attempt on the part of Soult to relieve San Sebastian, but it was very poor indeed. They all retired across the Bidassoa in the course of the night, and we resumed our former positions. I omitted to mention in my letter last week, as you desired, how I succeeded with all my parcels. They all arrived quite safe I am happy to say. My horses from England arrived here five days ago and in very fair condition, but those I left at Vitoria arrived with nothing but their bones, not a morsel of flesh upon them. I don't suppose the man I left with them was ever sober since I went away, at least if I may judge from his appearance.

San Sebastian was assaulted the day the French made their attack upon our position, and after two hours of extreme hard fighting, we took the town from them, and still hold it. They still have possession of the castle but it is so high they cannot fire a shot upon our people, and I imagine we shall shell them out of it in 48 hours. We lost about

---

* Ensign William Burrard, 1st Foot Guards, who was soon to be fatally wounded during the storming of San Sebastian and died on 2 September.
† Lieutenant and Captain Charles Allix, 1st Foot Guards, Brigade Major.
‡ Sir Charles Knightly, 2nd Baronet, who was married to Selina Mary Hervey, Felton's younger sister.

1600 people in the attack.* Graham's Hare† carries home the dispatch. I think when it falls we shall proceed into the French territory. Felton went from hence this morning. Heaphy has not been able as yet to get Lord Wellington to sit to him, but I dare say he will tomorrow. It is wonderful how he has stood the last week's work. With best remembrances believe me, my dear uncle, your most dutiful and affectionate nephew,

> John Fremantle

Lesaca, 20 September 1813

My dear uncle,

It is very provoking that you did not get my letter at the same time as Lord Wellington's, as by the receipt of your last, I find I had anticipated all your enquiries, as to my horses, parcels, packages but thank goodness I have not had a single accident.

There has been no news since the surrender of the castle of San Sebastian. I hope in another two or three weeks we shall have Pamplona, but I am afraid it may be too late by that time for any advance. John Wells‡ left this, this morning to go and visit the position. Hutchinson is quite well and safe after all his perils and dangers.§

Pallet¶ has been very successful in all his undertakings, and I believe it will answer to him even beyond his expectations. He is a great bore though, and I wish him away with all my heart.

Success to Selina, pray remember me when you write to her. I have sent the French gloves by one Captain Tyler,** ADC to General Picton, and I sent some a mail ago by a messenger. Adieu my dear uncle, with best love, believe me, ever your most dutiful and affectionate nephew,

> John Fremantle

Another note told of the imminent capture of Pamplona and the continued failure of east-coast operations.

---

* Allied casualties were 47 officers and 809 men killed and 100 officers and 1,316 men wounded, a total of 2,332 killed and wounded.

† Major Richard Goddard Hare, 12th Foot, was assistant adjutant general to Graham's corps.

‡ 2nd Captain John Neave Wells, Royal Engineers.

§ Joseph Hutchinson, 7th Foot led the stormers of the 4th Division at San Sebastian.

¶ From references in later letters 'Pallet' would appear to be a sobriquet for Heaphy.

** Lieutenant John Tyler 45th Foot served in the Peninsula throughout the war and also served as aide-de-camp to General Picton from June 1811 virtually uninterrupted until Waterloo. It is odd that Fremantle refers to him as 'captain' as he did not gain this rank until February 1814 when he exchanged into the 93rd Foot.

Headquarters, Lesaca, 27 September 1813

My dear uncle,
I have nothing to tell you since my last note; we have been quite quiet since the fall of San Sebastian, but we are all alive with expectation of a move across the river whenever the weather clears up a little. Pamplona has still in it provisions for a week for the garrison.

I suppose you will have heard of the deroute on the other side as we call it here, they certainly are very unlucky there, or Suchet is too much for them.

I have sent you by the messenger a pair of fur boots, which belonged to the governor of San Sebastian; I think they will do to wear in a carriage very well. Adieu my dear uncle with best love, believe me, ever your most dutiful and affectionate nephew,
    John Fremantle

Another week on and Pamplona remained defiant; John also announced he was now assistant military secretary at the wish of Fitzroy Somerset.

Lesaca, 4 October 1813

My dear uncle,
Nothing new has occurred since this day week. Lord Wellington made a small excursion to the right at Roncesvalles and returned two days ago. Pamplona has yet the same quantity of provisions as when I last wrote, and it is likely to hold out as long. I still imagine we will march soon.

I dare say you will be glad to hear that I am to bear the title of assistant military secretary instead of March who is to bear that of ADC. It makes no sort of difference in any way to either of us; the change is quite unofficial on my part. Fitzroy chose to have it altered; all goes famously. Lord W[ellington] is rather husky after his journey.

When the gloves arrive which I sent by Captain Tyler, will you distribute them to my sisters. I am sorry I could get no stockings or lace. I wish you would send me some pairs of worsted gloves in parcels of two each which will come by the post through our orderly room.

I don't think Pallet will return for some weeks yet, he has been hard at work ever since his arrival. Bishop has sat to him; he has been very successful in all his undertakings. I should think the fellow must be making a fortune.

I have had my bad luck with Frederick's mare, never having been able to get on her once. I must attribute it to roguery, him liking to keep one sick, for she feeds well.

For goodness sake write to me, with best love, believe me, ever my dear uncle, your dutiful and affectionate nephew,
John Fremantle

PS Lady Caher* has sent me a beautiful shell bridle by Sir James Leith[†]

Finally the monotony had been broken and the army had advanced, crossing the River Bidassoa which occurred on 7 October with relative ease with little fighting. Marshal Soult was led to expect an attack on the left of his line in the Pyrenees mountains, but while a force attacked the mountainous area in the centre of Soult's line where the light troops incurred a number of casualties driving the French from a series of redoubts; the overwhelming majority of Wellington's army made a crossing at a ford near to the mouth of the Bidassoa on Soult's extreme right, where they captured the French redoubts with relative ease and formed a secure bridgehead, forcing Soult to retire to the line of the Nivelle.

Vera, 10 October 1813

My dear uncle,
We completed yesterday evening one of the prettiest operations that I suppose ever took place in military history, crossing the river Bidassoa in 9 or 10 different places, attacking and carrying all the strong positions in the Pyrenees, which the enemy occupied. The duty was performed by the troops which occupied our left and centre of the old position; our left now occupies half way between St Jean de Luz and Andaye. Our loss is nothing, for the French behaved most dastardly, abandoning the strongest ground almost without waiting for the attack. March you will learn carries home the dispatches, it was decided upon this morning to the astonishment of us all, for the dispatch was finished last night, and it was to have gone in the same ship with Sir Thomas Graham, without an ADC; March had started with a letter to the left to Sir John Hope.[‡]

I received your letter the other day, and am much obliged to you for it. I am very anxious to know whether you received my first letter; you acknowledge the one of the 2nd. My establishment, which it is good of you to enquire after, is in pretty good order, and my horses are in tolerable good condition, thanks to the English hay, which we have lately received. My servant is a very decent fellow, but indeed he is more expensive than I imagined, and I could do very well without

---

* John's aunt, Lady Emily Caher (née Jeffreys of Blarney Castle).
† Lieutenant General Sir James Leith had been wounded at the siege of San Sebastian.
‡ Lieutenant General Sir John Hope commanded the 1st Division.

him. My boy Thomas is also very unhealthy. Crooke, the other man, does I think, upon the whole, justice to my horses. I still continue to work very fair in the office and think all will continue well.

It is too great an undertaking to write to Sir Charles Knightly, but I will to Selina the first post that business does not press my hand as she desired me. Pray let me know when the gloves arrive, and what they think of them. Pray give my love to Eliza and my sisters, and believe me, my dear uncle your dutiful and affectionate nephew,

John Fremantle

His next note informed his uncle of the enforced resignation of Charles Bishop to avoid a huge scandal.

Vera, 18 October 1813

My dear uncle,

I received the enclosed from Hay,* the commanding officer of the 16th [Light] Dragoons the other day, and I understand that Charles Bishop has given in his resignation, in order to avoid the disgraceful issue of a court martial. He has never written to me himself, nor have I the smallest idea of what is best, or what can be done for him, and shall wait until I hear from you.

I am afraid to write to my Aunt Bishop myself upon the subject, for the story is, that Charles drew his sword upon a woman; and you are now in possession of everything I am acquainted with, about the matter, and God knows what will become of him. You may depend upon it he will never do in an infantry regiment.

We have had a small affair since last week, our chain extended too far in its centre, towards the French position, and they attacked and carried a hill, which the Spaniards occupied, that was connected with their line.

We are only waiting for the fall of Pamplona to make another advance, and I hope to tie up our winter war. I trust it will not hold out another week. There is no other news. Bonaparte was at Berowska on the 28th,† if you don't already know it.

Heaphy went over to Felton's the day before yesterday. The fellow amuses himself by telling lies all over the country wherever he goes. I hear he gave out at Sir Stapleton's [Cotton] that I brought him out upon condition of being put into his large picture.‡ I have a mind to

---

* Lieutenant Colonel James Hay 16th Light Dragoons.

† Presumably 28 September, when Napoleon was at Berowska just outside Moscow.

‡ Heaphy's great picture was published in 1822; entitled *Field Marshal the Duke of Wellington Giving Orders to his Generals Previous to a General Action'*. Fremantle is depicted in the picture.

take his head off when I next catch him. Adieu my dear uncle with best love and remembrances, believe me, always your dutiful and affectionate nephew,

John Fremantle

After a short defence against his uncle's complaint of infrequent correspondence John followed it with jubilation at the news of Napoleon's troubles in Russia and more about Charles Bishop's predicament.

Vera, 25 October 1813

My dear uncle,
I received your welcome letter of the 4th since I wrote to you last week, indeed I feel exceedingly grateful for your general good correspondence and feel equally your reproach, which is however quite unmerited, for upon my word, I have missed [writing] but one week since my return. This is particularly unfortunate, as I never have been guilty of writing so regularly before. I have generally put the letters under cover to Torrens, which however I shall not do any more.

The Lord, and of course that means all of us here, are quite cock-a-hoop, about the affairs in the North,* from the sole circumstance of the silence upon that head in our front, for they generally let us know anything that is favourable to themselves.

I can't hear from Charles Bishop, or do I know anything more of him than I told you last week. His resignation has certainly gone in, but it has never reached here. I believe the history about the woman a fabrication.

We have not a word of news here. We expect to hear of the fall of Pamplona every hour. Sir George Collier† they say, is going home, resigned, which we are very glad of, for he does not do at all. I dare say he will be succeeded by an admiral.

I greatly fear that the glanders has got into my stable, my little mare has always been ailing and I am much afraid sentence of death will be pronounced upon her, however I found a Portuguese today who pronounced stoutly in her favour, which has delayed it, the rest are only in a middling state. Thanks for your enquiries;

I assure you I am highly flattered by the enquiries that royalty have

---

* He refers to Napoleon's campaign in Russia, which had yet to turn into a disaster for the French.

† Commodore Sir George Collier worked with Wellington to control the coast of northern Spain and south-western France during the operations in the Pyrenees and beyond. Wellington was very critical of the navy's inability to stop the French resupplying San Sebastian. Collier was sent to fight the Americans in 1814.

been graciously pleased to make after me, and I beg you will express the same.

Heaphy has not returned from Felton, I believe he intended to go from thence to Sir Rowland Hill. Felton is expected here tomorrow. Adieu my dear uncle and remembrances. Believe me, your dutiful and affectionate nephew,

John Fremantle

Heaphy has drawn all the great officers of this army. I think Charles Bishop's is as like as any I ever saw.

John's next announced the surrender of Pamplona, which effectively denoted the end of French influence in Spain. Charles Bishop was not resigning until he had attained his captaincy.

Vera, 1 November 1813

My dear uncle,

By the mail which reached us yesterday I received your letter of the 21st from Fawsley,* I am glad that you have received my letters, as I hope I am now excused from the blame you were pleased to attach to my laziness. I saw Lord Wellington read your letter at last; I think it was written on note paper, he said nothing to me about it, and put it aside from the ones he tears [up]. Felton arrived and dined here yesterday, Lord W[ellington] told him he had heard from you, and he asked what he said, Lord W[ellington] told him politics. Pamplona has fallen, the report reached us an hour ago, I understand Worcester was to go home, but I overheard him just now, say he would wait for another opportunity, it is a thousand pities if no one goes, for it loses a step to some person.

I heard from Charles Bishop since my last. He is waiting he says till his father gets him his company which Hay will not prevent. We have had dreadful weather this week, such torrents of rain, and the troops in bivouac must suffer dreadfully, however I hope it will now soon be at an end. Adieu my dear uncle, believe me, your most dutiful and affectionate nephew,

John Fremantle

A note announced that his mare had to be destroyed.

---

* Fawsley Hall near Daventry was the seat of the Knightly family.

Vera, 2 November 1813

Dear uncle,

Since writing yesterday I have taken the opportunity of Lord Arthur Hill's* going home to send you a few lines. He did not intend to have gone home till next week, but I believe it was some scheme of the office here; but at all events Lord Wellington did not intend to send an aide-de-camp. I think it is a thousand pities, and I fear Worcester will have the next, which will dish me for this year. I shot my mare last night, Felton proclaimed her incurable. Adieu my dear uncle your dutiful and affectionate nephew,

John Fremantle

In his next, an unhappy John wrote of his frustration that Worcester had declined to take the despatch home and that the duke had not then considered sending him.

Vera, 8 November 1813

My dear uncle,

I have been dreadfully down in the mouth since my note last week, sent by Lord A. Hill; as soon as I had written it which was just before Lord Arthur started, I accompanied Felton on his road back, who told me that Fitzroy had spoken to him, about letting me go with the account of Pamplona, as they decided it was not of sufficient importance for my Lord Worcester to take home, but they decided, why I cannot tell, that I was not. Worcester expects to go with the next, which we all think extremely unfair, his turn having naturally passed. Gordon therefore intends to apply next time, in the hopes of being made colonel. The Prince of Orange is to be made major general,† on the prince's birthday, and Fitzroy expects to be made Prince's ADC in his room. Had Fitzroy done me the favour to address me instead of Felton on what so particularly concerned myself, I should unquestionably have gone, as I should have spoken to Lord Wellington, who I cannot conceive would have refused it. You may imagine I am very angry at this want of confidence, and have taken care to show my disapprobation of such proceedings.

I intend to speak to him quietly about it the first opportunity, as it will never answer to be made a tool of, made to scribble, all at his pleasure, and then put to the wall. I feel every proper deference towards him, but he is neither in age or service much my senior, for

---

* Captain Lord Arthur Moyses William Hill, 10th Hussars.
† William Prince of Orange was indeed made a major general on 13 December 1813. The prince's birth date was 6 December; he was only twenty-one this birthday!

me to allow this. I shall not quarrel with him, therefore be perfectly easy, and I think he feels awkward at my distance and shyness towards him, but I think the 'doers will be done'. Our attack was fixed for yesterday, but put off on account of the bad weather and I begin to fear we shall not be able to have another operation this season. You are well aware of the essential difference this makes to me, as I should certainly have got my rank in this year had I gone, and as Worcester would not go, surely it was the 'dog in the manger' preventing another person from going, therefore you must allow there is a reason for the feeling I express, but I would not for the world have you communicate with Lord Wellington on the subject. I think it very odd he did not think of me himself, as your letter which he received only the day before was fresh in his memory.

It was not kind of Felton not to speak to me upon such a subject, when he knew the intrigue which was going on, but I am sorry to say I think he has been jealous of me ever since I joined Lord Wellington. I may be wrong, but it strikes me very forcibly, and you will say, I know, that it is very unlike Felton. I have now told you all my ails and aches, which however I think you must approve of. I have no news to tell you. If we don't attack them after tomorrow at the latest I think we must go back for winter quarters. Pallet has got 25 private portraits and is universally observed to be the most impudent dog alive. Adieu my dear uncle, your most dutiful and affectionate nephew,

John Fremantle

A week letter John was writing to inform his uncle of the action on the Nivelle. Wellington launched his army of 82,000 men against Soult's forces numbering 62,000, but with the French well entrenched along the river line in very strong defensive positions. While General Hope made a feint on Soult's right near St Jean de Luz, a major assault was made upon Soult's centre around the Great and Lesser Rhune and his left was assailed by Hill's troops. The French, after some determined resistance were driven out of their lines of redoubts and retreated on Bayonne. The French lost 4,300 men killed and wounded and a further 1,400 prisoners; the allies losing only 2,500 despite being the assailants. From discussions with the French officers, it was clear that the French army was losing its taste for this war.

St Pe, 14 November 1813

My dear uncle,
We are fortunate enough since my last letter to have four very fine days without any rain, which had before rendered the roads quite

impracticable; our attack was consequently determined upon and put into execution on the morning of the 10th, and succeeded most admirably. The position which the French occupied was most imposing, and I do not think they could ever have driven us from such a one, but they behaved unlike Frenchmen or soldiers. It is quite impossible to enter into the detail of it, as I am so busy I am even writing this by stealth, we have however taken 51 pieces of cannon and 1,400 prisoners.* Worcester is going home with the dispatches, and has promised me to take this. I suppose we have now done for the winter, but the army is not yet cantoned, nor do I think there is cover yet for them in the country we have come over, and the enemy still remain in an entrenched position, on this side of the Adour which seems to me to be our natural line, and I believe it to be what everybody wishes, how feasible it is I suppose My Lord knows best. We have received all the news from the north, and a colonel whom we took on the 10th, when asked where the headquarters of the enemy was, answered, '*Il n'y a pas de HQ, il n'y a plus d'Armée,*' [There is no HQ, there is no army any more], and he was so rash a Frenchman that he told us making war with them, was making it against ourselves. I mention this to show you how badly they thought of the business among themselves. Indeed it does appear that they are quite unsettled, and I hope this crown, or rather dynasty, will soon be at an end. If there is ever a chance of it I think it must be now.

I have not yet spoken to Fitzroy, but I fully intend it. I saw Felton the day before yesterday he is quite well. Adieu my dear uncle in great haste, believe me, ever your most dutiful and affectionate nephew,
  John Fremantle

You may assure Sir Charles that Barnard† is in no sort of danger. He was wounded in his right breast but we had a letter from him this morning.

Now in winter quarters, John informed his uncle of Charles Bishop's return home and makes it clear that his failure to gain his lieutenant colonelcy by carrying home the despatch for Pamplona still rankled with him.

---

* Oman states 1,200 prisoners and 59 cannon were captured in the redoubts, but John's figures must be considered more accurate, as he prepared the official returns with Fitzroy Somerset, and they agree with Wellington's despatch of 13 November.
† Lieutenant Colonel Andrew Barnard, 95th Foot was struck in the breast at the Nivelle on 10 November, but survived to fight at Waterloo.

St Jean de Luz, 5 December 1813

My dear uncle,
I received your letter of the 11th a few days ago and I am very glad to find you do not think me so very idle about writing. In general one has but little to say, but as you say a single line is better than no line at all. I had not a moment to spare for half a one last week, for I was occupied until the very last moment. I am glad you like the boots, I sent some ribbons by Pallet who sailed last week, if they are liked I can get plenty more, and have ordered some shoes from Bayonne,

Charles Bishop sailed last week, or the week before, but he has never come near me, or wrote to me. His resignation is forwarded by this packet, addressed to Torrens.

I am very glad that my uncle and aunt are sensible of Hay's kindness towards Charles.* You may assure them from me that he put up with more than two thirds of the officers of the army would have done from him. It has just struck me that it will do no harm my writing to Torrens to beg him to delay presenting the resignation, for three or four days or a week until Bishop or yourself shall have communicated with him upon the subject. If he is inclined to oblige me he can do this very easily, and perhaps it will give you more time to breathe, and he has no right to be offended at such a request.

Upon the subject of rank it is quite no hope with me for this year. I must be content until fortune smiles again, however I am by no means miserable about the matter. I can't conceive there would have been the slightest difficulty made about giving me the rank, had I gone for Pamplona.

We have not a word of news here. The French fired a grand salute of an hour long at 8 o'clock this morning in honour of Bonaparte's coronation, it is supposed.

I rather think Heaphy has an idea that I have given him an order for a copy of Lord W[ellington's] picture (50") he said something confusedly to me about it, but I beg you will undeceive him if you find he still thinks so. His trip answered wonderfully to him, but he is allowed to be the most impudent fellow alive. Adieu my dear uncle, believe me, your most dutiful and affectionate nephew,
John Fremantle

Presumably John's next letter was lost, as following this letter, on 9–12 December, Wellington ordered an advance to force a crossing over the

---

* Charles Bishop resigned and apparently spent a short sentence in Exeter gaol, but he re-joined the army as a cornet in the 21st Dragoons and sailed with them to the Cape of Good Hope, where he died in 1815.

River Nive. General Hill successfully crossed the Nive despite bad weather, Soult led a counter attack on Wellington's left the following day; and after the temporary bridge was broken by the floodwaters on the 12th, against Hill's isolated corps that day, utilising his ability to move his troops to either bank via the bridge at Bayonne. Soult was successfully held and Wellington maintained his hold of both banks of the Nive, both sides losing around 1,600 men. The exhausted armies then retired into winter quarters.

This is confirmed by a letter from William to Lord Grenville.*

Englefield Green, 31 December, 1813
... I had a note from John Fremantle from [the] Head Quarters of Lord Wellington dated 16 [December] in which he speaks of the desperate attack and the gallant resistance, I wish it had been with less loss on our side & with more advantage in our position ...

---

* National Archives Add. MS 58967 ff 56–7.

A NEW CAMPAIGN

The army remained in winter quarters, but remained vigilant; however, the French army did not appear to have much fight left in them and the local populace appeared to be heartily sick of Napoleon's demands.

St Jean de Luz, 5 January 1814

My dear uncle,
There is nothing new from this side of the water since you heard from me last. We are all anxiety to hear from England, our last accounts being of the 10th last. I think therefore we must have lost a packet, or two, at sea.

The people are just come in from hunting who say that My Lord saw some signals towards Hasparren, and went to sleep at Marshal Beresford's in consequence of [the] lateness. A report has since arrived from Sir S. Cotton from Hasparren dated 6 o'clock to say that the enemy were coming on, but he did not know, whether in earnest, or for a reconnaissance. I am inclined to think the latter, for they have not much attack left in them.

Those of his family who did not go and join him this evening, are instead going over early tomorrow morning, but I am afraid I shall not be able to go as I have been unwell for the last week, with a violent cold and sore throat which I caught on a late expedition to Hasparren with my Lord. He, thank goodness, continues as usual.

We are in anxious expectation of Grammont's* return to this country, and to know how the object of his mission has turned out. Every day convinces us more and more of the detestation of the people of this country to Bonaparte's yoke, and to have a new order of things

---

* Captain de Grammont of the 10th Hussars was sent by Wellington to King Louis who was in exile in England, as a Monsieur de Mailhos had arrived at headquarters stating that a significant proportion of the French people wanted a French prince to join the army and for the army to declare for Louis XVIII and to raise the white standard of the Bourbons.

established in France, and they universally wish us success. We have had several people come to us from the interior, who tell us that the same feeling everywhere prevails. We are all of us most sanguine as to future events.

You will oblige me much if you will tell my sisters that their friend Signore Ottana of the Portuguese service who was wounded and taken prisoner on the 10th September has been exchanged, and is now here, and doing very well. I desired him to bring me some silk stockings from Bayonne, which he did, for them, but I do not like them, and am not sure that I shall send them.

I hope you have seen Pallet since his return. He promised me he would let you see his performances before anybody. I believe the letter I wrote to you expressing my fears that he thought I had bespoken a portrait of Lord Wellington for 50 guineas was lost in the packet that was taken. If so, pray explain to him, that I had no such idea.

I had a letter from Felton dated the 1st wishing me the compliments of the season, which I pass. He says the town and neighbourhood of Urcuit [or Urketa] is very good and invites me to go over and see him.

I have never heard anything more of Lionel's intention of his coming out here being put into execution, but pray assure him that if the most delightful of climates, the use of my horses, and of course Felton can be an inducement to him, I recommend him by all means to come. It is almost spring weather now. Adieu my dear uncle with best love and remembrances, believe me, ever your most dutiful and affectionate nephew,

John Fremantle

Writing goes on swimmingly. Only make a few mistakes in copying every now and then, which puts my Lord in a passion, I hope you have a leaf.

The weather remained very bad, restricting the movement of the armies, so John had time to consider other things.

St Jean de Luz, 9 January 1814[*]

My dear uncle,

I received yours of the 18th two days ago, and that of the 31st this morning, for which I really am very much obliged to you. Your watchful eye to my interest is more than I know how to thank you for, but as I told you in my letter which you received by Hill, I am perfectly satisfied, particularly as my name was brought into question,

---

[*] Fremantle writes 1813 in a number of letters here, but he clearly means 1814.

which I think will without doubt ensure my being the next bearer of a dispatch, at least I shall be disappointed after all that has passed, if I am not.

We have been very busy since last Monday until yesterday. The French disturbed us on our right and gave us a great deal of trouble, but however it ended in our establishing ourselves just as we were before and I hope everything will now remain quite quiet for some time, indeed the rain has now set in again, which renders the roads quite impracticable.

With regard to Bayonne, it never was provisioned by land, and at this season the sands are above the cart wheels, which makes it quite out of the question, provisioning the town by that means, besides the country on that side affords nothing.

The answer is arrived to Charles Bishop's resignation, which is that a Special Reply will be sent, which appears as if Torrens was inclined to do anything for him that is in his power, but I am glad to find from your letter that all intention of keeping him in the army is given up. I really feel for my aunt and his father. It is shocking to think that such parents should be cursed with such a reprobate, and there certainly never was a youngster started from a family under such good prospects as Charles was. What will now become of him I am anxious to know.

I am glad my Uncle Tom has determined to remain in the Mediterranean.* I hope he will have an opportunity of doing something more. Everything seems to be going on very well, I only hope we shall not make peace with Boney, and have him down now, or never. Our politics here are that peace is not at all likely.

Will you send me an almanac, nobody has sent me one for this year yet.

With best love and remembrances. Believe me, my dear uncle your dutiful and affectionate nephew,

John Fremantle

Boredom had clearly set in, but news of the French public railing against Napoleon's conscription laws abounded.

St Jean de Luz, 22 January 1814

My dear uncle,

I did not write to you last week, having no news to tell you, nor

---

* Rear-Admiral Thomas Fremantle was officer in command of the Adriatic station under Admiral Pellew. He was based at Lissa (now Vis) off the coast of Croatia, from where he recaptured Trieste and the Dalmatian coast, and was eventually made a baron of the Austrian Empire.

have I much to say now, they talk of nothing but insurrections at Bordeaux and its neighbourhood, in consequence of their putting the conscription laws in force. It is certain that they have marched away two if not three divisions of their army,* and the people say here, it is to quell these insurrections, but there are such a variety of reports, as you may believe, that one does not know how to give credit to any of them.

I had a very civil note from Torrens respecting Charles Bishop by this mail. I have not heard from you by the two last.

Felton has been here these last 5 days, and desires to be remembered to you, he is quite well, he wishes you to put Lionel in mind to send him out the whole of [capinifa leaf?†], fitted up as he directed. It should be sent to Lord Bathurst's, requesting him to forward it, under cover to him & Fitzroy Somerset. Adieu my dear uncle, believe me, ever your most dutiful and affectionate nephew,
John Fremantle

The rains continued, preventing any movements; but the big news was that the Louis Antoine, Duc d'Angoulême, the nephew of Louis XVIII had arrived with the army under a pseudonym to judge the French public's reaction to a return of the king. After his triumphal entry into Bordeaux on 12 March 1814, the allies were convinced to support a return to the throne by the Bourbons.

St Jean de Luz, 4 February 1814

My dear uncle,

I have the pleasure to inform you that I yesterday had the opportunity of becoming acquainted with the Duc d'Angoulême, who is here under the name of Comte de Pradel. I was sent to Oiartzun‡ with a letter for him from Lord Wellington and he has since expressed himself in the most gracious manner to me, and thanks for my exertions. Both himself and the Comte Damas§ asked particularly after you and my Uncle Tom. I don't expect they will declare themselves until we are masters of a greater extent of country, and consequently can have a

---

* The divisions of Leval, Boyer and Treilhard were removed from Soult's army during January and were sent to boost Napoleon's badly depleted army fighting on the eastern front.
† This may be copaiba or copaiva, a balsam derived from the copaifera tree of South America. It was used in medicine as an antiseptic and as a diuretic.
‡ Now Elizalde near Pasajes.
§ Joseph Élisabeth Roger, Comte de Damas d'Antigny, (1765–1823), who escorted the Duc d'Angoulême to France in 1814. His memoirs were published at Paris in 1912.

greater scope for ascertaining the sentiments of the French people. You will easily conceive how anxious we all are for such an event taking place, but I fear our want of money will be a considerable impediment, and if the weather was to clear tomorrow, it would require a fortnight at least before the country would be sufficiently dried to permit the passage of our army.

The latest news here from Paris is of the 22nd [January]. Boney had quitted Paris and was to repair to Epernay, bad luck to him. Adieu my dear uncle believe me, ever your dutiful and affectionate nephew,
  John Fremantle

To show how little the arrival of these people has been possible to be kept secret, a muleteer challenged me yesterday as I was going out of Oiartzun with the words '*Va y viene el Rey de Francia*'. [The king of France comes and goes]

There is unfortunately a gap of some two months in the correspondence here; it is unlikely, given all the great events that occurred at this period, that John did not write even once to his uncle, but it is possible that pressure of work prevented him from doing so, but he does not mention this in later correspondence; if he did write, the letters appear to have been lost.

Following a week of dry weather, Wellington launched his advance on 12 February, whereby Hill led a turning movement around Soult's left flank which caused him to pull his whole army back from three successive defensive river lines to avoid them being taken in flank and rear.

On 23 February General Hope's troops crossed the mouth of the River Adour by boat to form a bridgehead and under cover of his troops the navy was able to form a bridge of boats across the mouth of the river by the 26th, securing his communications and Bayonne was invested the next day.

The next day Wellington also launched an attack, again based upon a turning movement by Hill to push Soult away from Bayonne, thus isolating the garrison. Soult was forced to retire on Orthes, where he resolved to fight.

The hard-fought Battle of Orthes, on 27 February cost the French another 4,000 men, including 1,300 prisoners, which Soult could ill afford to lose. The allies suffered around 2,600 casualties and were lucky not to lose Wellington, who was slightly injured when a ball drove his sword sheath into his thigh.

Wellington continued to drive Soult's forces, but also received a deputation from Bordeaux, and Beresford was dispatched with two divisions to receive the city. On arrival Beresford found that unbeknown to Wellington the Duc d'Angoulême had also arrived independently and was received with great acclamation and the city declared for King Louis XVIII.

Meanwhile Wellington continued to drive Soult eastwards, fighting an action at Tarbes on 20 March and arriving before the great city of Toulouse on 26 March.

But at this point John was no longer with the army, having been sent home with the despatch announcing the victory at Orthes, for which he finally became a brevet lieutenant colonel dated 21 March 1814.

John's next note announced his arrival at Plymouth on 31 March on his return journey to the south of France, having delivered the despatch at the War Office on 20 March.*

Kings Arms Inn, Plymouth Dock,† 1 April 1814

My dear uncle,

We arrived here after a most prosperous journey late last night; Lord Keith‡ had been remarkably civil to us. We are to sail as soon as the wind is fair in the *Fancy* Cutter.§ I sincerely hope you are recovering from your indisposition.

Pray remember me to my aunt and Eliza and believe me, always your very dutiful and affectionate nephew,
    John Fremantle

All my traps [personal belongings] are arrived safely.

John arrived at Bordeaux on 14 April only to discover that peace had finally been proclaimed, following Napoleon's abdication on 6 April. Unfortunately news of this event was slow to reach the front and the Battle of Toulouse was fought on 10 April and although Wellington was successful, the city was gained with the loss of 4,500 allied troops and 3,200 French defenders. A sortie at Bayonne on 14 April had also cost 850 allied and 950 French casualties. It is shocking to think that some 9,500 men had been killed or wounded despite peace having been declared at Paris more than a week before.

---

* Extraordinary London Gazette, number 16872, dated Sunday 20 March 1814.
† The King's Arms still exists on the quay at Oreston in Plymouth.
‡ Admiral George Keith Elphinstone, 1st Viscount Keith, was in command of the English Channel station.
§ The *Fancy* of 10 guns was a hired cutter, Mr Hallands was master.

Bordeaux, 15 April 1814

My dear uncle,

We only arrived here yesterday, when the first thing that met us was the bloody Battle of Toulouse after hostilities ought to have ceased; it really is shocking to think of, and our loss is near 4,000, however it is a pleasant thing that we licked them so confoundedly as I understand we did.

The ferment here is beyond anything, and I think before long they will be cutting each other's throats, and that it will be ended by the knife. The constitution was burnt last night at the theatre, with such acclamation, as I cannot suppose was ever before exhibited, and the cries of '*À bas le Senat*' [Down with the Senate!] unbounded; in short, from what I can collect, they certainly prefer Bonaparte to what is at present proposed, and here they are most determinedly determined.

The Duc d'Angoulême was particularly gracious to me, as ever all his people are just standing, having been kept a considerable time waiting to get Worcester under weigh.* He is pretty well considering.

Lord W[ellington] is expected here hourly, but heaven knows what will be his movements. I think eventually Paris must be, and very likely we shall meet him on the way either here or there.

God bless you my dear uncle, I will write to you again by the first opportunity and I trust I shall not be long before I have accounts from you, and trust that you will be conveniently set up again. With best love to my aunt and Eliza. Believe me, ever your most dutiful and affectionate nephew,
John Fremantle

John hastened to Toulouse in two days and found Wellington and his family still there and found lots of work to do with formal treaties suspending hostilities being prepared.

Toulouse, 19 April 1814

My dear uncle,

I write you a few lines to acquaint you of my arrival here on the 17th after a very tiresome and fatiguing journey from Bordeaux, although I passed through a most beautiful country.

I found Lord Wellington as well as ever, and in very high feather. Count Gazan† arrived two minutes after me to conclude the treaty for

---

* It is unclear what Worcester was waiting to carry as Major Lord William Russell took home the Toulouse despatch which arrived in London on 25 April.
† General Honoré Théodore Maxime, Comte de Gazan de la Peyrière (1765–1845) was Marshal Soult's chief of staff.

the suspension of hostilities with Soult's Army, which this day has also been concluded with that of Suchet's. We are all at a loss here to know where our steps will next be best. People about Lord W[ellington] say my Lord is going to Madrid, but as for myself I doubt that part of the story, and am sure I hope it may not prove so. You may depend on it however, that I will accompany him wherever he goes provided he does not disapprove of it.

What a horrid slaughter there has been in the Coldstream at Bayonne. Poor Crofton was a very particular friend of mine.

I think there will be row here yet, the Bordelais scream against the new constitution, and the cry of '*À bas le Senat*' was, when I was there, as strong as ever it was of '*À bas le Tyran*' [Down with the Tyrant]. It is also very unpopular with the armies, at least as far as we can understand.

Felton is here looking very well. I hope I shall soon hear from you, and that you are quite set up again. I will take the earliest opportunity of sending you the horse I spoke of. I have ordered him to Bordeaux from St Jean de Luz for that purpose. Give my best love to my aunt and Eliza, and believe me, my dear uncle, your dutiful and affectionate nephew,

    John Fremantle

I have not had the pen out of my hand since I arrived.

PEACE

John wrote again from Toulouse, informing his uncle of the secret of Wellington's new appointment: with war at an end he was to be ambassador to France at Paris, perhaps not the most subtle of appointments.

Toulouse, 30 April 1814

My dear uncle,

We are all busy and rattled; my Lord starts for Paris in half an hour, only with Fitzroy. Worcester and Felton start tonight on their own score; if any letters come for him, I hope I will steal a trip. He intends to be back in a fortnight, but I don't believe him for three weeks.

Suchet arrived yesterday, the Duc d'Angoulême goes with him after tomorrow to review his army. Nothing but fetes here since my arrival. My Lord [is] appointed Ambassador at Paris, but will go to England first, *A Great Secret*. Ever your most dutiful and affectionate nephew,
John Fremantle

As he had hoped, John was required to follow Wellington to Paris with mail that had arrived only hours after the party had left Toulouse. Wellington was to return to the army before going on to Madrid and then Paris and London. John hoped to follow Wellington to London soon as he was already tired of Parisian society.

Paris, 10 May 1814, 5 a.m.

My dear uncle,

I received your last letter as I was on the point of starting from Toulouse with a mail which arrived a few hours after [the] D[uke] of W[ellington] had left the place. I dined with Lord Cathcart* the

---

* General William Schaw Cathcart, 1st Earl Cathcart (1755–1843) was ambassador and military commissioner to Russia. John's Aunt Frances (née Fremantle) was married to Lord Cathcart's brother, Reverend the Honourable Archibald Hamilton Cathcart.

following day where I met everybody save the Emperors and the King of Prussia; viz. Schwartzenberg, the Prince Royal, Blücher, Vorontzov,* etc., with 30 other people, and I was exceedingly gratified. Felton will tell you better than I can, how Lord Wellington is spoken of here, and how he was received. He starts this morning for Toulouse, where he stays 4 or five days, to send the army home, and then goes to Madrid, from thence he returns here, and then goes to England. I am left here to bring any dispatches after him which may arrive. I have not spoken to him about coming with him, when he returns to reside, but Fitzroy says he will, and I shall be very much disappointed if he does not take me. Nothing on earth would gratify me so much, but I think that you had better not write to him on the subject before he arrives in England. I am quite out of conceit with Paris already, and don't care how soon I leave it, having the same acquaintance one had of the army is too much, and there is no society except of that sort.

I received Eliza's letter this morning for which I am much obliged to her. Adieu my dear uncle, believe me, ever your most dutiful and affectionate nephew,

John Fremantle

I had anticipated your wishes with respect to Lord Buckingham.†

Two days later, John was on route to Toulouse and Bordeaux and hopefully England after that.

Paris, 12 May 1814

My dear uncle,

I start in an hour for Toulouse with dispatches from Lord Cathcart for [the] D[uke] of W[ellington]. I shall stay there a few days, go to Bordeaux, settle my affairs and get off as soon as I can. I trust I shall be with you in a fortnight or three weeks at furthest. Adieu my dear uncle, your dutiful and affectionate nephew,

John Fremantle

---

* Field Marshal Karl Philip, Prince Schwarzenberg, of the Austrian army had commanded the Grand Army of Bohemia against Napoleon in 1813–14. Bernadotte was the Prince Royal and heir to the throne of Sweden. Field Marshal Gebhard Leberecht von Blücher, Fürst von Wahlstatt, was the most prominent Prussian commander and led the Prussian army during the Waterloo Campaign. General Mikhail Semenovich Vorontsov commanded the Russian occupation forces.
† Richard Temple Grenville Marquess of Buckingham, MP and later 1st Duke. He was present with the army at this time as commanding officer of the 1st Provisional Battalion of Militia which arrived in southern France just as the war ended.

John arrived at Toulouse, to find that the duke had just left on his way to Madrid and he was forced to chase after him. He then settled at Toulouse to await Wellington's return.

Toulouse, 19 May 1814

My dear uncle,
I left Paris on the 13th and arrived here with dispatches for Lord Wellington on the 17th at 8¼ o'clock, when I found that he had left the town a quarter of an hour on his way to Madrid. I consequently had a gallop after him. I had an opportunity of speaking to him respecting the stay with him in Paris, but I think it is as well as it is until he comes back.

Headquarters remain here until the French garrisons leave Tortosa and the other places,* which will be in about a week, we then move to Bordeaux and there wait Lord Wellington's arrival which will be in about three weeks. He returns to England by Paris, but whether he will take all of us with him we shall not know until he comes back, but I shall certainly try. Tell Felton I will write a line whenever the day of embarkation of the regiment is fixed. Adieu my dear uncle, believe me, ever your most dutiful and affectionate nephew,
    John Fremantle

Toulouse, 26 May 1814

My dear uncle,
We are still here in status quo, and the idea is we shall not break up for a week from hence. As my horses have at last arrived at Bordeaux, from St Jean de Luz, I shall go down there in a day or two to look after them.

I have shot a mare for the glanders and intend to send a horse I have here, with Lord Wellington when they go to Paris, and dispose of any I can at Bordeaux. There will only remain two [mules?] and a horse when I have embarked the black horse for you. Felton said he thought it would suit you, and I hope it will.

Matters are going on swimmingly in Spain, Cadiz is the only point in the country now where the king's government is not popular.

The duke's carriage broke down at Mondragon which will delay him a day. You may depend upon it, when Fitzroy comes back I will move heaven and earth to get Hutchinson an ensigncy,† but I have

---

* The east coast of Spain was still under French control when the war ended, but was eventually handed over to Spanish forces.
† Presumably this ensigncy was for a younger brother of Ensign George Hely Hutchinson, 14th Light Dragoons, nephew of General Hutchinson, 2nd Earl Donoughmore. John, 3rd Earl Donoughmore, and Henry both eventually served in the army.

great fears of my success now; for the last year, I had only to ask the question, and it was done, but now I don't think there will be any more recommendations. With best love believe me, my dear uncle your very dutiful and affectionate nephew,

    John Fremantle

PS Felton, the American expedition;* all just at Bordeaux waiting for transport. Lord Wellington never thought it would sail, or land at least. J. F.

John wrote again on the eve of his moving to Bordeaux, where he was to await the duke who had been severely delayed by carriage break downs.

Toulouse, 28 May 1814

My dear uncle,

I wrote to you a few lines two days ago by a person who was going to Paris to let you know a little how the land laid here. It is very odd, we have no accounts from the other side of the evacuation of the fortresses.

The French in the first instance wanted to carry everything away belonging to the Spaniards, which of course was inadmissible, but there has been nearly time since that, to put such misunderstanding to rights.

We have heard of the arrival of his grace at Mondragon, a day and a half after he expected, the carriage wheels having twice failed him. He will also be detained a day at Vitoria to get new ones. I calculate he could not have arrived at Madrid before yesterday, and his business there will take him ten days; he therefore cannot possibly arrive at Bordeaux before the 13th June, so that I shall not have the pleasure of being with you until long after I expected, as I believe it is your wish I should accompany him to the last.

Otherwise there is no reason why I should not embark from Bordeaux. I shall start from hence on the 1st and establish myself at Bordeaux as Lord Buckingham has invited me until our establishment reaches there.

By accounts from Bordeaux today, they say no transports are arrived but that there was an Admiralty Report stating that the Americans were treating for peace.† Of course you will know much more than we can.

---

* Many of Wellington's troops were ordered directly to North America in an attempt to tip the balance in that war with the fledgling United States of America.

† Peace negotiations did begin in Belgium in August between the United States and British governments, but peace was not declared until December of that year.

We have been very gay here and if we stay much longer it will become I am sure quite the capital of the British Army. I send you a ticket for a party, which it has been considered necessary to give, very much against my inclination as it costs me £20. Pray direct to me at Bordeaux, and believe me, my dear uncle, your dutiful and affectionate nephew,
John Fremantle

The duke had returned and was soon off to Paris, but there had been no room in the carriages for John.

Bordeaux, 11 June 1814, 9 o'clock

My dear uncle,
I received your last letter in answer to mine of the 19th from Toulouse, yesterday, which gave me great pleasure in as much as in some degree I had anticipated your wishes respecting my residence at Paris with His Grace whenever he returns thither to take up his abode. He returned here late last night from Madrid, but up to this moment I am as much in the dark as when I last wrote to you and am in the agonies of the damned in consequence of it. When I spoke to Fitzroy about it last night, he returned me for answer, that he had spoken to the duke about it, but that he had given no positive answer, but said he would speak again this day; this may be true or not. He may have some other person in his eye, God knows.

I cannot go to Paris on the 14th with His Grace, *faute de conveyance* [lack of transport], but Lord Buckingham having offered me a passage in his carriage to start on the 13th, I shall make up my mind and ask the question myself in the course of tomorrow.

I am happy to say Hutchinson will be recommended next packet for a vacancy there is in the 7th Fusiliers.* But if he is not taken away from Marlow,† his commission will be annulled even after he is gazetted. It is a rule which has been made this year past and fifty from this office have been annulled in the same way, but remember he risks being reduced just at this moment.

That regiment will be in England in a week or 10 days, as they embark in a day or two on board men of war, now waiting in the narrows. They land at Plymouth.

In haste for I have been writing all day, believe me ever, my dear uncle, your most dutiful and affectionate nephew,
John Fremantle

---

* No Hutchinson joined the 7th Fusiliers, nor any other regiment this year.
† The junior department of the Royal Military College at Great Marlow actually moved to Sandhurst in 1812.

Postscript: Shirley,* who sails tomorrow, has got three gowns for my girls [sisters], directed to you. Two, as far as I am a judge, are quite beautiful. I think they had better toss up for choice.

The duke did not stay long in Paris as he was in England on 23 June, where he was met with cheering crowds all the way home to London. John presumably accompanied the duke, but we next find him back with the Coldstream Guards one month later.

The duke had requested his assistance again in his new role as Ambassador to France at Paris, which was now official.

Coldstream Orderly Room, 25 July 1814, 5 o'clock p.m.

My dear uncle,

I was in the duchess's† room this morning, when the duke came up, and told me briefly to ask the Duke of York's leave to go with him (I suppose of course to Paris). I have this instant asked the Duke of York who says he has no sort of objection if the regiment can spare me, therefore I consider it as settled. I shall call on the Duke of Cambridge. I am ever my dear uncle your dutiful and affectionate nephew,

> John Fremantle.

A fortnight later John was on the eve of travelling to Paris.

[London], 11 August 1814

My dear uncle,

I am surprised Lionel is not yet come to town, will you have the goodness to tell him that I shall have an order on him tomorrow from the Comte de Chartres‡ to release two equipages on the other side of the water.

Hume§ and I start on Saturday morning and go by way of Calais. I wish he could make it convenient to come with us as perhaps it may be awkward and unpleasant his going alone. I am not certain whether Percy¶ is of our party, or not.

Ever my dear uncle, your dutiful and affectionate nephew,

> John Fremantle.

---

* Lieutenant and Captain Charles Shirley, Coldstream Guards.

† Catherine Pakenham, the wife of the Duke of Wellington. It was by now a largely loveless marriage on Wellington's side but Kitty remained loyal and seems to have continued loving him.

‡ More commonly known by the title granted on his return to France as Louis Philippe Duc d'Orleans,

§ Deputy Inspector of Hospitals John Robert Hume (Drew, no. 1988).

¶ Major the Honourable Henry Percy, 14th Light Dragoons, was an extra aide-de-camp to Wellington at Waterloo and carried the Waterloo despatch to London.

Undated but dated on the reverse 12 August 1814

My dear uncle,

I have been since yesterday morning trying to get my accounts paid me before I set off, which is really out of the question, as Mr Booth, our Commissary of Accounts, tells me they have not even given him an office yet.

My travelling expenses amount to £264 and a standard form £36 or 7. I have besides 100 at my agent's and 150 at our Paymaster General's. This however will not be sufficient to clear me as I should like before my departure and as you were good enough to offer to lend me any in case I should want, I should be obliged to you for £100 or £150 if you think I had better not touch that at the bank. I have besides 85 guineas, which Mr Davis tells me is good. I have drawn upon my friend accordingly. Mr Booth has offered to lodge the money for me, where I direct.

Lionel has settled to go with us on Sunday, they, the whole four will start together, remaining four weeks. Your dutiful and affectionate nephew,

    John Fremantle

     264
      36
     100
     150
      <u>85</u>
     <u>635</u>

I saw Torrens the day before yesterday, he is very kind, told me to call today, but had not the answer he should like, that is to say decisive; but told me to call tomorrow. J. F.

PARIS

John began the journey to Paris to set up the duke's embassy, but he was acutely short of money and needed a loan from his uncle to cover his travelling expenses. The Duchess of Wellington would be attending her husband at Paris and would be taking a few ladies in waiting with her, his older sister Frances Arabella was in the running.

Dover, 17 August 1814

My dear uncle,

I arrived here this morning with Lionel from Ramsgate, where we remained two nights as the rest of our party had not left town in time, indeed Percy is not come down yet, however we are to sail tomorrow morning early. I am sorry to say we have been obliged to pay the duty on our horses, as we neglected getting an order to the contrary before we left town; or rather Campbell neglected putting our names down in the order for the duke's equipage.

I was so bothered before I left town that I had not a moment to write to you, paying my bills, etc., but believe me I am not the less grateful to you for your good nature. I am now completely white washed, having paid all my bills except the tailor's, and I have now £150 to start with on my road to Paris.

I had a long conversation with the duchess the night before I came away, and I really think from what she said, she will take Fanny, if she does not take Caroline Fitzroy,[*] whom she is afraid of, as being too much for her; but she fears giving offence to Lady Anne.[†]

I have not seen Watkins again, I called upon him but he was not within. If upon my arrival at Paris, I find there is no wages coming to me, I am afraid I shall be obliged to sink my money, but I will write to you as soon as that is decided. I have desired Mr Booth the

---

[*] Carolina Anne Fitzroy daughter of Sir Francis Charles Fitzroy.
[†] Lady Anna Maria (née Fitzroy) who had married the Duke of Newcastle.

Commissary* to bring my money to Paris at Greenwoods as soon as he can get it for me, and have acquainted Davis to that effect. Ever my dear uncle, believe me, your most dutiful and affectionate nephew,
    John Fremantle

I have not mentioned to Fanny anything about the duchess.

He arrived in Paris on 21 August and was given the duty of issuing passports to travellers. John was clearly irritated that there were problems with the issue of gold medals to senior officers for the last twelve months campaigning, for which the duke's Staff were normally eligible.

Paris, 26 August 1814

My dear uncle,
Lionel and myself arrived here on the 21st after a very prosperous journey, I got very smart the first day as I posted in my buggy. Our horses came yesterday, not having met with any accident. The duke arrived the day after us, but I don't think he is very well; he was prevented travelling one day on account of a severe cold.

We were at court all day yesterday and today. We went in the king's carriages; Percy and I had one to ourselves drawn by eight horses with running footmen. We bowed condescendingly to all the people who pulled off their hats, excepting an old bitch who put out her tongue at us, and I did the same. *Tout va grand train* [Everything is going at full speed]. I don't hear anything about wages.

What I alluded to in my last letter from town was the medals. Torrens told me the last thing that we were to have them, but the duke won't sign the list until he gets a written authority. I have written to Torrens to tell him so, and enclosed at the same time an unsigned list in order that no time may be lost.

I have taken the department of the passports. Ever my dear uncle your dutiful and affectionate nephew,
    John Fremantle

The cost of maintaining himself at Paris concerned John and much of his writing concerns the delay in getting paid. He did, however, get to sit next to Marshal Ney at dinner.

Paris, 7 September 1814

My dear uncle,
I received your letter of the 30th which delighted me exceedingly, in

---

* Assistant Commissary General William Booth.

answer to my first scrawl, but I was terribly hurried, yours was a most comfortable long one, and I will endeavour to adopt the same mode. To begin as you did with my finances, as yet I have no sort of expense, except my three horses, and 2 servants, but I much fear that Lionel and myself will be obliged to buy one more in order to have a pair for a carriage, that is, if we cannot establish one of the duke's, which at present is not quite perfect, for he frequently takes the Berlin that we intend he should have nothing to say to, and here, it is quite out of the question going on foot at night; however I hope it will be arranged otherwise. Quite 300 a year, I cannot judge yet, whether it will keep me, but I have 80 now of the money I brought over, which when I am at the bottom of I shall be able to make my calculation better. I assure you I am not inclined to be greedy, and if I can hold my present ground it is all I covet and am gaining getting about of an evening. As to pay, I hear nothing about it, and argue very badly in consequence. I cannot sufficiently thank you for your good nature, about getting me the annuity in case of necessity, which I hope will not be the case.

I am bored to death about the medals. When I left England, I thought the business was settled, but there is yet a hitch. I included myself for Vitoria, Nive, Nivelle and Orthes.

As yet there is little or no society, some dinner parties; I sat next to Ney the other day at Berthier's grand dinner to the duke. Lady Aldborough tells me I have made a conquest of La Princesse Neufchatel,* but however she is too ugly I am afraid.

We are generally able to shut up shop by two o'clock and take our ride, which is very fair. Talleyrand's is the latest house, the people seldom go before midnight, and it breaks up in an hour; a very stiff circle. The duke's house has not been opened yet; all Paris is impatient. He is waiting for his liveries. He is quite recovered from his cold.

I hear Austria and the French are likely to come to loggerheads about the division of the Italian states, everything else seems perfectly peaceable. Pray give my best love to my aunt and sisters and Peepy and believe me, my dear uncle, your dutiful and affectionate nephew,
John Fremantle

I see you have not given up thoughts of Miss Giles, though I have.

John continued to discuss money matters, but he also mentions that the

---

* Marshal Michel Ney, Duc de Elchingen; Louis Alexandre Berthier, 1st Prince de Wagram, 1st Prince de Neuchâtel; Lady Elizabeth Aldborough (née Hamilton), wife of John Stratford, 3rd Earl of Aldborough and Berthier's wife, Princess Maria Elisabeth Franziska Pfalz-Zweibrücken, only daughter of Duke Wilhelm of Bavaria.

great politicians were now leaving for the great congress called at Vienna to agree the borders of the new Europe, which was required be laid out following Napoleon's destruction of the Ancient Order.

Paris, 15 September 1814

My dear uncle,
I received your last letter too late to answer it by the messenger of Monday. I cannot thank you sufficiently for the constant interest and perseverance you show to my welfare in this; as on many other occasions since my first outset. I have written to Mr Watkins who I think has always shown the greatest goodwill as far as my observation goes, in all that he was concerned in with respect to my sisters and myself, to tell him that I should wish an annuity were purchased with the two the £2,000, in order that I may have the remaining £659 at my own disposal in case of necessity, provided it met with your approbation. But at all events, I shall be too happy if you will alter it, if you should think proper, for truly I am in the greatest ignorance of everything concerning money matters and shall be perfectly content with any final arrangement you may make with Watkins on the subject.

I have nothing in the way of news to tell you since I last wrote. We all go on here in the same way. Burgh is chief in the office and Percy, Lionel and myself are scouts. Fitzroy I expect will be here in a fortnight. The Duchess will be here next week.

Talleyrand left this for the congress yesterday, the only mischief I hear of likely to be, is the dethroning [of] Murat.* I suppose Mr Bull† will have a finger in the pie if it comes to blows. Ever my dear uncle, your most dutiful and affectionate nephew,
John Fremantle

The office was now functioning well and the duchess was due shortly. Clearly Miss Giles had been close to John and a betrothal may have been hinted at, much to John's horror. The arrival of a Mr Giles in Paris made him very uneasy in case it was her father or brother, but he could rest easy, it was not *that* Mr Giles. The medal distribution was still being delayed, to his great chagrin.

---

* Charles Maurice de Talleyrand Périgord, 1st Prince de Bénévente, who worked skilfully as a politician for both Napoleon and Louis XVIII, and Joachim Napoleon Murat, installed as king of Naples by Napoleon. He survived as king until he sided with Napoleon once again during the Hundred Days.
† John Bull.

Paris, 19 September 1814

(*Marked no. 4*)
My dear uncle,
It is a sad thing to begin to complain already of the stupidity of Paris, but I assure you at present it affords very little scope for even a steady and good correspondent, which however I do not or ever did profess to be. We go on here very steadily, it is precisely what our office used to be when with the army, and the duke himself is exactly the same person.

The more the people here see, and know of him, the more they like, and admire him. The Duchess will be here next week, but however I don't suppose her appearance will add to our gaiety. We had a party here last week, which the French people liked exceedingly. All theirs are dull and stupid to the greatest degree.

I don't know what to make of Lionel, here, whether he likes his *séjour* [stay] or not. I am happy to say we had given up all idea of having horses to the carriages. If the duke does not find a conveyance of that sort, one of the gigs which the *garçons* [lads] use here, with treads of a servant behind, we agree will do admirably, and answers every purpose.

I was terribly alarmed the other day on receiving a slip of paper with Mr Giles's name upon it; however, two days afterwards I found it was Lady Salisbury's Mr Giles and therefore my troubles eased. I hope you are not still alarmed.

I have still considerable fears about our medals. No answer from Torrens to my letter or the return. I am afraid it is 'out of sight out of mind' with him, and I own I am very much annoyed, because I understood when last I saw him that no kind of difficulty any longer existed; and that nothing remained to be done after his receiving the return, but to order the medals to be struck. It is possible he may have acted upon the return that was sent to him but it is odd that he did not send word. Ever my dear uncle, your dutiful and affectionate nephew,
John Fremantle

John found that the work load was increasing and he was not amused that his delayed lieutenant colonelcy was also the cause of his failure to be awarded any of the gold medals he had expected.

Paris, 29 September 1814

(*Marked no. 5*)
My dear uncle,
I hope you have received my letters regularly. I have only had two

from you. I have very little news to tell you. As for real business, that would all be got over very easily, but there are numberless requests and applications, passports and invitations, which bore us in a way that is not to be told and really take up nearly our whole day. It will be worse in that respect when Fitzroy Somerset comes, who of course, will do less of such dirty work than Burgh, who is a capital slave.

It annoys Lionel and Percy as much as it does me, and I am determined to speak. Sir Charles Stewart passed by here the other day on his way to Vienna. He had with him a secretary of legation and another one (During*) an army man, who is to receive a salary, and it really is too absurd that with an embassy like this, there should not be even a clerk allowed besides the chief secretary and I think can only require explanation.

I am very much annoyed that after all that has passed, I am cut out by a few days from receiving any medal, by an official letter from Torrens. Only those of the commander in chief's aide-de-camps having the rank of lieutenant colonel are entitled to them, and as I was only made after Orthes and was not present at the Battle of Toulouse it appears I have no claim. I should not be disappointed, if I had not been told to suppose I should have them before I left England. Believe me, my very dear uncle, your dutiful and affectionate nephew,
      John Fremantle

There was a delay in John's correspondence as the workload had increased significantly while Percy had been ill, but they were all still bored with Paris society.

Monday, 17 October 1814

My dear uncle,

I have missed two or three mails now, without letting you hear from me, but since poor Percy has been so dangerously ill we have been seriously employed. He is now however very much better, but I fear it will be some time before he will be able to resume his functions here. I mean for his sake business goes on *rondement* [promptly], meaning our office, but the French are going to loggerheads with themselves and their neighbours *au grand galop* [at a great gallop], and I think Bull is their bitterest pill.

London seems fairly transported. Lady Hamilton† who is a particular friend of mine has taken a hotel for six months and gave a

---

* Major George Baron During 1st Line Battalion, KGL.
† Lady Susan Hamilton (née Beckford), was married to Archibald Hamilton, 10th Duke of Hamilton in 1819, on 26 April 1810.

soiree charmante a few days ago which is to be repeated constantly.

Lady Harrowby, Heathcote, Darnley, Hardwicke, [Michelha?], Aylesbury, and all England seem to be here. The Popkin and *filles* [daughters] arrived about ten days ago.* I invited them to our weekly party, but am too much engaged to be able to visit them. I beg you will not be alarmed on that score.

Paris is dreadfully stupid in point of society French I know of none worth speaking of. They tell us it is to be very gay in the winter, but I am inclined to doubt it.

We have been out several times with the royal hunt, which is the greatest burlesque that ever was witnessed. The hounds are to go out next week, which will afford us something to look forward to.

I think the duke is bored with the employ here, but if he wished ever to give it up, I don't imagine it could be feasible for some time. The duchess is very much liked by all the French people. The Bishops† have been upon the fringe quietly, ever since they set their foot in Paris. They intend to leave after our party on Thursday to the great regret of all the party (save Billy) who has been bored to extinction since the second day. Fitzroy Somerset will not be here for a fortnight or three weeks to come; his wife has been poorly, which has obliged him to defer his departure.‡ I hope you will not defer your trip here, until late in the spring. With best love, believe me, my very dear uncle your ever dutiful and affectionate nephew,

John Fremantle

Paris, 7 November 1814

My dear uncle,

You may possibly think I have been very idle of late, but I can assure you I never in my life have been less so, I have not written to you, but have so, very considerably for our gentleman with the long nose.§

---

* These ladies were: Lady Susan Harrowby (née Leveson-Gower), wife of Dudley Ryder, 1st Earl of Harrowby, a politician; Lady Frances Heathcote (née Thorpe), wife of Sir William Heathcote, 3rd baronet; Lady Elizabeth Bligh (née Brownlow), wife of 4th Earl Darnley and Lady Elizabeth Hardwicke (née Lindsay), wife of Philip, 3rd Earl of Hardwicke. It has proved impossible to identify 'Michela' despite exhaustive research. Aylesbury is actually Lady Henrietta Ailesbury (née Hill), daughter of 1st Baron Berwick) and wife of Charles Brudenell Bruce, Earl of Ailesbury. It is likely from later comments that 'Popkin' refers to either Aunt Frances or Marrianne.

† His cousins, see footntoe p. 152.

‡ On 6 August 1814 Fitzroy Somerset had married Lady Emily Harriet Wellesley-Pole, daughter of the 3rd Earl of Mornington, the Duke of Wellington's niece.

§ He refers to the Duke of Wellington, of course.

Lionel* and myself are determined not to continue in the same strain much longer without striking for wages. I dogged Mr Hamilton about it, when he was here, and I live in hopes of succeeding. The public mind has been in a terrible state for some time past, and I see not the slightest probability of its mending, and I foresee the duke's stay here is not of a long duration. I can't go into particulars but I think Europe will soon be by the ears worse than ever Boney had it.

I enclose you the papers, which were in question before I left England, signed, and if you will let Stag† receive the money, and remit me £97 after taking 100 which I borrowed from yourself and pay one hundred to my tailor, I shall be very much obliged to you. Not having had occasion to draw since I came here, you will perceive by this, my finances are at least in a flourishing state, having been able to lose 15 louis at play and back four horses.

Watkins sent me the return state of the annuity purchased last week. I have returned him for answer this day that I approve entirely of the whole arrangement and beg that on the 4th April he will remit me the half of the £170 that is to say if I am at Paris which is really uncertain. I dare not tell you any more news.

I am never able to get out between breakfast and dinner *au force de écrire* [because of the need to write]. I never thought I should be able to reconcile myself to it, even as much as I have done. *Mais je trouve que cela gagne* [But I am finding that it's winning me over], and in time I suppose I may make what is termed *un homme d'état. Il y a de quoi à fournir aujourd'hui* [a statesman. There are plenty of them today]. I always go out of an evening, but the French *cuite* [boozing] is terribly stupid.

Popkin is here with her *filles*, but they have quite left me alone. Lady Hamilton, my particular friend has offered me her daughter,‡ if I will wait, and change my name. But I depend upon your secrecy on this point (joking apart). Believe me, ever my dear uncle your truly dutiful and affectionate nephew,

John Fremantle

John's letter regarding Lady Hamilton must have caused his uncle to send a letter of admonishment and he spends much of his next letter reassuring his uncle that he had no intention of coming between husband and wife.

---

* It would seem that Lionel Hervey's visit had turned into an official role.

† Presumably Stag was a banker or financier to Fremantle.

‡ Lady Hamilton's second child, but her first daughter, Susan, was born on 9 June 1814, hence John joked regarding waiting to marry her.

Paris, 28 November 1814

My dear uncle,

I am sorry you considered as gospel what was contained in my last letter. I find I must write to you in a more serious strain, and not that of a merry mood. I beg your fears will entirely cease as to the subject in question, for I am not so inclined to quarrel with my bread and butter, as you seem disposed to think me.

I was entirely in joke and I wonder how you could think the hint necessary, except from your watchful anxiety for my well being. I have every hope however that we shall have an allowance granted, I made Mrs Hamilton speak to the duke on the subject when he was here, but with or without it I shall lament excessively when it is at an end. I see you are entirely for my following him when this takes place, and I believe, however I may wish to remain, it will be the best thing I can do.

You may also dissipate your fears respecting my interference between the man and wife, I never was less inclined than in the instance before me.

The miss* in our family has been making fierce play at one of our society but it won't do; and I think her sickness which has taken her to bed tonight, instead of going to Mother Paton's Ball is in consequence of it. Her sister's love to her husband was quite a joke to what she has done here, we all detest her.

I see by a letter which Lionel got today that my grandmother† is much better, and that you had returned. We had a dance the other night in Popkin's, at which all the great people attended. Adieu my dear uncle, believe me, ever your dutiful and affectionate nephew,
    John Fremantle

PS Pray send me the money I begged you to have got for me, and if there should be any delay at the commissary general's office, let me know.

There were great changes in the French government and rumours of conspiracies to kill the king.

Paris, 5 December 1814

My dear uncle,
There has been a considerable change in affairs since you last heard

---

* Frances was due to marry George Butler, 5th Earl of Lanesborough, presumably therefore he hints at Albinia, who did not marry until 1827.
† Old Mrs Fremantle (née Frances Edwards), of a wealthy Bristol family, had been staying with her sister Lady Cave.

from me. Marshal Soult has replaced Dupont as Ministre de la Guerre.*
Monsieur Angles has replaced Comte Buignon as Ministre de la
Police.† All Paris was in an uproar the other night on a report having
been circulated that there was a conspiracy against the king, to be put
in execution as he was going to the theatre, a considerable body of
troops were put under arms in consequence, but I imagine there never
was any foundation for the report.

We go on much in the old way. Burgh goes off this night. Percy,
Lionel, and myself keep office, and as yet Fitzroy has only come in
for an hour or so in the day to look at us. He seems to have nearly a
sinecure of it.

Miss Fitzroy has been seriously indisposed for this last fortnight, and
is now suffering under all the horrors and anxiety of disappointment.
I never saw such a horrible, abominable, nasty little cat in my life as
it is. The duke's children‡ are coming out here to spend their holy
days. With best love, believe me, my dear uncle, your very dutiful and
affectionate nephew,

    John Fremantle

Paris, 15 December 1814

My dear uncle,
I have very little time except just to tell you that I continue affairs
which I am sure will please you, particularly as there is a degree of
responsibility attached. I feel more interested, and less bored, although
more confined, and more to do. I find him as ever a man as any in the
world to do business with.

It was very unlucky you sent me a bank post bill, for I lost more
by that than I should have done in any other way, but it was my fault
for not telling you so. I should not have been in such a hurry only I
have no credit at Paris, and I desired Davis to send me an abstract of
my account before I left England, which he has never done, nor will he
ever, unless you will send Stag or somebody to him.

I believe peace is very likely to be made with America.§ They are
going on much better at Congress.¶

---

* General Pierre Antoine, Comte Dupont de l'Étang was superseded as minister of
war by Soult on 3 December 1814.
† All evidence I can discover states that Minister of Police Savary, the Duc de Rovigo
was superseded by Jules Angles in April 1814, however John seems to indicate that
Comte Buignon was in post from April to December 1814.
‡ The duke had two boys, Arthur Richard and Charles Wellesley.
§ Peace was signed between Britain and the Unites States of America at Ghent on 24
December 1814.
¶ The Congress of Vienna was sitting in an attempt to come to an agreement to sort

With best love, believe me, my dear uncle, your dutiful and affectionate nephew,
John Fremantle

Paris, 29 December 1814

My dear uncle,

I could not possibly write to you by the last two posts, we were so dreadfully busy; and I have been very unwell for the last three days with a violent cold, which I did not take sufficient care of at first but I hope now am all right again.

I continue to be delighted with the proceedings of my master. I have never had a cross word with him since the first morning, when I proved to him without a remark there was no blame necessary.

It is rather a nice situation as both Percy and Lionel are older than me in point of years, but we have gone on most amicably as yet. I enclose you a note for Watkins, desiring him not to send me my quarterly annuity, till he receives further directions from me. Adieu my dear uncle, believe me, your very dutiful and affectionate nephew,
John Fremantle

In January John wrote to say that he was going with the duke to Vienna, where his influence was required to help protect British interests.

Paris, 23 January 1815

My dear uncle,

I have been so overwhelmed these last three weeks, I have not liked to write to you for fear of committing myself. I expected to have seen you in England 'ere this, but I am off to Vienna tomorrow with the duke which I feel will gratify you, as he takes nobody else with him, but William Lennox.[*]

There are various surmises respecting his departure, but the reason is that ministers don't think they can wade through their mire without Lord Castlereagh, *et de plus* [and moreover], if I may judge, will not even feel very strong with his assistance. Therefore now's your time, if ever, I will write to you from Vienna. With best love, believe me, ever your very dutiful and affectionate nephew,
John Fremantle

John now found himself in a position of some importance at the congress,

---

out the mess resulting from twenty-three years of war in Europe and to reinstate various rightful rulers.

[*] Lieutenant Lord William Pitt Lennox, Royal Horse Guards.

finding that his knowledge of the German language was of great benefit, something the duke lacked.

Vienna, 6 February 1815

My dear uncle,

I had only a moment to write to you previous to my leaving Paris, our departure was so very sudden, I was over head and ears in business.

We arrived here on the 2nd after a most prosperous journey. I found the duke an excellent *compagnon de voyage* [travel companion]; he has been unwell however ever since his arrival, and today he only got up for an hour or two, having had a good deal of fever all the forenoon, but he was much better at 10 this evening and I trust a day or two's quiet will entirely set him up.

Lord Castlereagh leaves this on the 13th. I shall then be established as the Mr Planta* having Mess[ieurs] Merry, Ward, Antrobus, and Temple† remaining with me. It is a great bore not being better acquainted with them than I am, but I trust our business will go on smoothly. I don't think intentionally I am inclined to accompany any lady. These gentlemen must be rather jealous at seeing a military person among them, but that is no fault of mine.

During the whole of the journey, and since our arrival, I have found my German of the greatest service to me. Of course I cannot think a moment about that, without feeling again, and again, my duty of gratitude to yourself. I never of course thought it would be put to such good purpose as the late.‡ I trust my dear uncle I shall continue to deserve by application in my new career, (as I look upon this to be) your good opinion.

I never during the whole of my career have had that idea absent from my thoughts. I understand our stay here is likely to be of much longer than I ever had any idea. I now hear three months talked of as likely, before the machine is wound up. I shall be sorry I confess to remain so long, I don't suppose it will be near so pleasant as Paris, *mais c'est égal* [but it is equal]. I am in a much higher station here, and am induced to feel very flattered and gratified by it. Believe me ever, my dear uncle, your ever very dutiful and affectionate nephew,

John Fremantle

---

* The diplomat Joseph Planta (1787–1847) was secretary to Lord Castlereagh.
† John William Ward, later the 1st Earl of Dudley. Sir Edmund Antrobus, 1st baronet, and Henry John Temple, 3rd Lord Palmerston.
‡ His Uncle William had sent John to learn French and German in Hamburg in May 1805, where he was offered protection by Marshal Bernadotte.

John's next letter was clearly written in haste and in some anxiety; for his uncle had clearly admonished him severely in a letter for his gambling and subsequent drawing money to cover his losses.

Vienna, 14 February 1815, 12 p.m.

My dear uncle.

I received your letter half an hour ago, and am enabled to answer it by a messenger who leaves this in half an hour. I assure you however that nothing has caused me so much uneasiness for a long time. I read it before the whole chancellery, and was nearly overcome by it; how could you think of using such a language, although kindness itself, it made me cry like a fool. Don't you know there are few besides yourself and my sisters, that life is worth keeping for, after that, *je n'ai pour maître que le tambour* [I have only the drum as master] in the shape of the duke, who I have a right to believe is satisfied with me; for Gerald Wellesley* told me he expressed himself so at Paris, and I certainly stand now in a prouder light than your most sanguine expectations ever led you. I consider myself now, after the ministers, as one of the first personages. I am asked I suppose by virtue of my rank to all the great ministerial dinners, which I don't perceive by any other embassy, and they are quite astonished to see in the lieutenant colonel so young a person, however I hope I shall hold way with them.

My last letter from Paris and from hence of the 6th or 7th I hope will open your eyes. I never was more mortified in my life than today. Pray tell that nothing has affronted you in any way or occurred between the duke and you which would make me miserable, and indeed having your best interests at heart, which I need not tell you, it is always a source of real pleasure to hear you. Uncle my conscience thank God answers for me in a very few words. I told you the other day that my first study was to deserve your approbation. I hope to God I shall never forfeit it. You think I have some mystery which I don't like mentioning. I have no disguise, I did play latterly at Paris, and coming away in a hurry I borrowed £100 of James Butler but that does not distress me, it annoyed me I confess for three weeks while it was going on. I have no other secret in the world and I never will have for you. Confidence is the greatest comfort in the world, and I should not consider you a friend to me, and not unburden everything.

I received a letter from my Uncle Tom today. I will settle his business

---

* Reverend the Honourable Gerald Wellesley was the younger brother of the Duke of Wellington.

for him *à l'instant* [instantly] with respect to forwarding his patent of Maria Theresa.*

It is in Chevalier Gentz, who is Metternich's secretary,† and he is the Chancellier de l'Ordre [Chancellor of the Order]. I have begged the duke to speak to him, which he has promised me. With best love, believe me, ever your most dutiful and affectionate nephew,

John Fremantle

Lord Castlereagh leaves this tomorrow and will be in London in about three weeks.

---

* He was to receive the Order of Maria Theresa for his services in the Adriatic.
† Friedrich von Gentz was secretary to the Congress, Prince Clemens Wenzel von Metternich being minister of state for Austria.

NAPOLEON RETURNS

During the night of the 6/7 March 1815 an urgent message arrived at Vienna which set the world alight. Napoleon had gambled all and landed with his Guard of 1,000 men on the coast of France on 1 March and began a march to Paris to regain the throne. Unfortunately for Napoleon, all the great heads of Europe were still at Vienna and agreement was rapidly gained to stop him at all costs. On 13 March the congress declared that Napoleon was an outlaw and a great pan-European army was ordered to be mobilised to march upon France to rid the continent of Napoleon forever.

After a fatiguing day of preparing despatches John penned a short note to his uncle to give him the latest news. He ordered his uniforms forwarded to Paris where he expected to return with the duke, little realising that Napoleon would take France again so easily and would enter Paris in triumph on 20 March.

Vienna, 13 March, 2 a.m.

My dearest uncle,

I have been working like a drag horse all day and am almost done up. The duke has done wonders today.

The emperors of Russia and Austria and the king of Prussia have sent officers to the king of France with full powers to move their armies, as he judges necessary against the common enemy, the eight powers are all unanimous upon the subject and are determined to *écraser* [crush] the monster. The duke thinks however that Louis won't require assistance. The duke will certainly bear a forward game in the breeze if it comes to that. He has offered to go anywhere.

Affairs are very much hurried in congress by this late event, and a treaty will be signed in a fortnight certainly. I must beg of you to send to our orderly room for a Sergeant McRea, Fitzroy's clerk, who was left in charge of papers two years ago in Portugal; he has two or three uniform coats of mine which I beg may be sent to the Foreign Office

to be forwarded to Paris without loss of time. The duke will certainly
not remain here longer than a message can return from England with
answers to this day's dispatches.

I received your letter of the 21st and trust you are contented with
me. If you are I am happy. I have never had a single word, good, bad,
or indifferent, with the duke further than business requires. We go
on famously. Ever, my dear uncle, your most dutiful and affectionate
nephew,

     John Fremantle

PS My Uncle Tom's business is not yet settled. They are such slow
people these Austrians.

This letter arrived in London twelve days later and William wrote to
Lord Grenville:[*]

                              Stanhope St, 25 March, 1815

'*Private*'

. . . I have got a letter from my nephew dated Vienna 13th March
in which he says 'The emperors of Russia & Austria & the k[ing] of
Prussia have sent officers to the king of France with full powers to
move their armies as he judges necessary against the common enemy:
The 8 powers are all unanimous upon the subject and as determined to
écraser [crush] the monster. Affairs are very much hurried at Congress
by the late events & our treaty will be signed in a fortnight certainly.
The duke will certainly not remain here longer than a messenger can
return from England with answers to this days dispatches' . . .

John hurried a note off to his uncle with news of a new military role for
the duke.

                                       19 March 1815

. . . The armies are to be put in motion immediately. We set off for
Brussels in a day or two, the duke will have a command of at least
120,000 men and I dare say we shall have the first run at Boney . . .[†]

A week later John wrote that he still expected to leave Vienna any day
with the duke and that their destination was Brussels. He was confident
of his high standing with the duke and handled all of his business.

Vienna, 23 March, 1 a.m.

My dear uncle,

I was delighted by the receipt of your letter of the 6th enclosing my Uncle Tom's. I am very sorry all his plans are frustrated for the present. I beg of you to tell him that Nugent* left this, to take possession of the Island of Elba in the name of the Congress a day or two ago, and left the business to be begun yesterday, in the hands of an agent, who I have seen; he assures me it will take at least four weeks. Nugent always undertakes more than he can perform, but in this case he has done worse; he told me a month ago the business was on the point of being settled.

The duke will speak to Prince Metternich about it again, and I will do everything that is in my power as long as I remain, but there is no chance of my being able to get it done before I go, as I expect to be off in two or three days. My horses and servant will have arrived in London long ere you may receive this, therefore I request you will pack them off again to Brussels post haste with all my baggage, etc etc and whatever my man may think necessary, that he has not got already.

I have drawn for no money since I left England, consequently must have eight months' pay at Greenwoods, and half a year's annuity in Watkin's hands. This I must beg of you to get for me, and send me what my servant does not require.

There is a man named Hanell (late whipper-in), who[m] the duke has dismissed, of my regiment, who might come with my horses to help my man who is not very au fait; but if this man is not to be had, or the huntsman either, *Crane* I must have another, *coûte que coûte* [at all costs], as Webster cannot take care of three [horses], and I must have that number. What baggage Webster cannot bring with him, may be left to come out with the duke's. I trust the exigency of the times will be sufficient apology to you for begging all this of you, for what can I do, when my things are at sixes and sevens in such a way, you know it is not my fault.

I am happy to tell you in answer to your enquiry, that I am chief here in every way. The duke only does business with me, and I have no reason to think he is not satisfied, and hope he will never be otherwise, though I have the management of the house expenditure I fear I shall not leave Vienna any the richer, though I must think I have a very fair claim. Lord Castlereagh's secretary (Planta) has a very large salary but I know my situation is different. If the duke would say the word I am confident nothing would be refused him, but I don't like to ask him, as

---

* Austrian Major General Lavall Nugent was a plenipotentiary at the Congress; he was sent to Italy and defeated Murat in Tuscany.

it would not be worth the while, if it annoyed him.

I am amply repaid for the confidence I made you respecting my late follies by your nobleness and generosity; all I can say is, I am truly grateful for it, and I hope I shall never abuse it.

I believe James Butler is the best creature that ever existed. I have a true love and regard for him, and I think he has the same for me. I shall not be able to repay him, until this breeze is over, as I never can know *à la guerre* [at war] what my expenses are likely to be, but when quiet again I can always have a hundred pounds, but am equally sensible to the kindness of your generous offer, as of your genuine good nature. It is the best lesson I could ever have, and I hope you will never hear of a repetition of the same thing.

A messenger has just arrived who left town 9 days ago, but as I gave the duke his dispatches in bed I do not know what the instructions may be. The messenger tells me that Lille was in possession of the town people, the Imperial Guards having quitted it. He also says he heard there that the country had risen against Boney.

Suchet is in Strasbourg, and all is good there. It is very important for our army if we make to have Lille secured to us. With my best love and remembrances, believe me ever, my dear uncle, your ever truly dutiful and affectionate nephew,
    John Fremantle

Five days later, having received news of Napoleon's triumphal entrance into Paris, they were off to Belgium.

28 [March], 1.00 a.m.

My dear uncle,
We start tomorrow for Brussels. News as bad as can be. Yours most affectionately,
    John Fremantle

Only one week later they were in Brussels and John was back to being a simple member of Wellington's large 'family' again.

Brussels, 6 April 1815

My dear uncle,
I received your letters of the 1st and 2nd today and yesterday. We arrived here yesterday. I found Webster and one horse and the portmanteau, everything else having been left behind. I cannot conceive how Lionel could have managed so ill. I just heard from Percy that he has another at

Ghent, and has left a mare with Sebastiani* without getting the money. Can you conceive anything half so stupid, as the whole arrangement, they must have been finely bothered.

Fitzroy and Burgh join the duke therefore it will be a clubbed concern amongst us. I am very well satisfied. I could not expect to have been chief, neither do I think I am fit for it.

Perhaps I may get 10 shillings as ADC and 10 as assistant military secretary per diem, and then I shall be very well off, perhaps be enabled to save something.

If you could get me such an animal as I bought from Frederick I should be very much obliged to you, and also a saddle and bridle from Cuffs, and forward to me the remainder of what money may belong to me.

I heard a few hours before your letter the news of poor Charles Bishop's death.† I can easily conceive what my good dear Aunt must suffer on the occasion. I will write to you more fully next time. Ever my dear uncle, your most dutiful and affectionate nephew,
    John Fremantle

PS I should be glad to have all Sergeant McRea's things sent to me here.

It would seem that there were a number of petty squabbles as each member of the 'family' arrived and settled into their individual role and established their seniority.

Brussels, 15 April, 1.00 a.m.

My dear uncle,
I have just received your letter of the 10th and the one by Stanhope‡ I received the day before yesterday. It a source of sincere pleasure to me, to find that in some instances I anticipate your wishes, before I received your letter recommending the course you wished me to pursue, the arrangement had already been made, Fitzroy is installed as military secretary, and Burgh, myself and Percy are assistants. Burgh and myself receiving an additional 9s 6d to our pay as aides-de-camp. This was all I desired, and what I intended to have applied for, but the

---

* This presumably is the French General Horace François Bastien Sébastiani de La Porta, who actually went back to Napoleon during the Hundred Days.
† Charles Bishop died 5 January1815 at the Cape of Good Hope after joining the 21st Dragoons.
‡ Lieutenant Colonel the honourable James Stanhope, 1st Foot Guards. His letters and journal have been published by the editor as *Eyewitness to the Peninsular War and the Battle of Waterloo*.

duke arranged it without a word being necessary on my part, though Fitzroy candidly told me he made an objection to it in favour of Percy, who in the duke's first arrangement was not to have any pay, and then Fitzroy recommended there should be three assistants, which gives an allowance to Percy; therefore nothing can be pleasanter, and all is very gratifying to me, but I do think I perceive a little jealousy among my colleagues, *mais je me moque de tout cela* [but I make laugh at all that]. Fitzroy I do not think so friendly to me as he used to be, but I am sure I can't imagine why, as I never have done anything that could in the least tend to disoblige him. Burgh I thought rather sneering at first, but I in a moment showed him that I had no other intention than to play second fiddle to him, and therefore no jealousy shall exist there.

Fitzroy is very fond of Lionel, and has procured him the situation *aupres de* [close to] Louis 18, with all his expenses paid him, which is as much as Lionel could wish for, I should think, particularly as the duke wrote this night to Lord Castlereagh to secure him a footing in the office, which cannot be refused. Fitzroy is also very attentive to Percy, but do not be afraid of my taking offence at anything of this nature. I shall steer my course as usual, and I hope keep clear with them all.

I see there is a terrible breeze respecting Lord Castlereagh's accounts. Thank God, I have receipts for every farthing that I drew, and do not fear an investigation to a farthing. The accounts are not gone home yet. I do not like to send them until some person is going home, to whom I could entrust to witness their examination, without which, my being of another cloth, they might at the office endeavour to puzzle, for I had a specimen, at Vienna, of the extreme jealousy on this head. The young diplomats fancy it is eating of their bread, a redcoat coming among them.

I hope the account I have given you will be satisfactory, but pray let me know at all times your wishes, nothing ever is so gratifying or so salutary to me as your advice, and I always feel myself stronger by it. I have been in a terrible fuss respecting my equipment until now, but everything by your goodness is perfectly *appliqué* [applied], and thanks to you I am now in want of nothing.

The tailor has sent me a couple of coats. I have bought a cheap little horse and am perfectly set up. I fear my things, chattels etc are all gone to the bottom with the duke's papers in the Tagus* (but if so it can't be helped), that were under the charge of Sergeant McRea. It is just what I should wish for my annuity to be paid into Greenwoods by Watkins.

You will perceive I have now a beautiful income, which I hope will

---

* I have been unable to identify a shipwreck in the vicinity of Lisbon at this time.

not be thrown away idly, I fear however the war will not last for me to enjoy it long, do not be under any anxiety respecting the other nations coming forward. I tell you nothing can be better together or more unanimous- all are as one, whether they will continue so, is another consideration, but of this I do not doubt.

With my hope to continue to deserve your good opinion, always my first object, believe me, my dear uncle, your most dutiful and affectionate nephew,

John Fremantle

The duke toured tirelessly, inspecting the troops of his army of many nations and reviewed the work in progress to secure the safety of the frontier fortresses. Felton Hervey had arrived and was clearly a particular favourite with the duke.

Brussels, 21 April 1815

My dear uncle,

Since you last heard from me, I have been making a tour of the frontier with the duke, inspecting the works of the different places, and reviewing the troops, which was altogether very interesting, and I think he was very well satisfied with what he saw. We receive constant accounts from France which vary much in different points, but in one they all agree, that great discontent prevails, and in my opinion, whether by his enemies, or otherwise, Boney's reign will be of short duration. Since the duke has returned from Vienna, he is quite alive again, in short I have never known him in such good health and spirits. We are all most anxious to be on the wing, but our legs are necessarily tied until the others can act with us.

On returning home through Ghent yesterday evening, Felton met us at the inn, and the duke bought him here. He was exceedingly glad to see him, and conversed all the way home with him. I do not know yet what he will make of him, but you may depend upon it, he will do whatever he can, that Felton wishes. He is a very great favourite, and I know the duke has the highest opinion of him. The mare you sent me arrived this afternoon, and in my life I never saw a prettier creature, and Felton tells me it is a delightful mover. I cannot tell how grateful I am for such a present, at such a moment.

Lionel tells me that by a letter he received from my aunt this morning that you have some intention of coming here. I hope it may be so, you will find it a delightful place, but you must come immediately, and I shall be overjoyed at being of use to you. The duke enquired of Felton last night particularly how you and yours were respecting war or peace, and seemed I thought pleased with Felton's account.

With best love, believe me, my dear uncle, your most dutiful and affectionate nephew,

John Fremantle

A note penned the same day as the previous letter told of the scandal surrounding Lieutenant Colonel Baron Ernst Otto Trip van Zoutland, 60th Foot, who was a Dutchman and principal aide-de-camp to the Prince of Orange and as such had been welcomed into the Capel household at Brussels. A clandestine affair had begun with Miss Harriett Capel, which Mr Capel had discovered, so he demanded a duel which took place on 17 April. Capel fired and just missed. Trip did, apparently, fire also but missed on purpose.

Brussels, 21 April 1815

My dear uncle,

We all forgot today to let you know of an affair that has lately taken place here. An amour as I understand had been for some time kindling between Trip, and the eldest Miss Capel, who[m] I believe was very much in love with him, and Capel found his picture in her possession. An explanation had previously taken place between the male parties, and Capel on making the discovery, returned Trip the picture *en lui traitant de scoundrel* [and treating him as a scoundrel], upon which Trip challenged him, and some time afterwards when C[apel] could find a second, who turned out to be the Duke of Richmond, a meeting took place, but no blood was spilt. Trip did not fire at Capel, but swears Capel's ball went very near to his ear. I am just returned from Lady Charlotte Greville's,* where I saw Capel, his two younger daughters, and Trip. Ever my dear uncle your very affectionate nephew,

John Fremantle

The petty 'family' jealousies continued unabated and John voiced the generally held concern regarding the loyalty of the Dutch and Belgian troops.

Brussels, 28 April 1815

My dear uncle,

I received your letter four days ago, which gratified me very much, but as yet I cannot say I think there is any change in our cabinet, with respect to myself. Your hints are most useful. Everything rests just as it

---

* Lady Charlotte Greville (née Cavendish Bentinck) was wife of Mr Charles Greville.

did, which I am very sorry for, as a coolness exists with my colleagues which I can in no manner account for. I cannot charge myself with having slighted any of them, and I cannot understand the reason of it, but I will steer as clear as I can.

Gordon is well acquainted with Major Forster,* and says he is a very gentlemanlike good sort of man, and I hope Albinia will be happy with him, but I am excessively anxious to hear more of it, Albinia has never thought proper to make me the smallest communication on the subject. I have been on another tour with the duke since you heard from me, round the frontier, reviewing the Dutch and Belgian troops, of the latter there are considerable doubts, all the officers have served in the French armies and dislike being kept in any order or discipline.

But the duke's arrival in the country has made a great sensation in the king's favour. With best love, believe me, my dear uncle, your dutiful and affectionate nephew,
John Fremantle

PS Lionel is just arrived from Ghent to assist at the duke's fete in commemoration of the investment of the several Knights of the Bath.

Lionel Hervey wrote a short note to Uncle William to defend himself from John's complaints.

Ghent, 3 May 1815

My dear Fremantle,
I send you two letters which I will thank you to frank, we are in a state of *dreadful* preparation here and hostilities must and will soon commence unless some unforeseen event should occur. Do you still persist in coming out? If you do come in ten days from Ostend to this place you can come by the canal posting dreadfully slow and tedious, let me know and I could make arrangements for sending horses from hence to meet you between this and Bruges. I congratulate on Albinia's marriage.† Yours ever, most sincerely,
Lionel Hervey

PS I hear that John accuses me of negligence. I can only say that he left only one servant. I got away or sold all his horses and received all his things except a saddle. His servant might have brought them all but

---

* There were four Major Forsters in the army at this time, but it is impossible to identify which was romantically attached to his sister. It came to nothing, however.
† She did not marry until 1827.

preferred saving his own. Jack* is the best off amongst off us all, and there is not a word of truth about his horse having been sold without obtaining the mon[ey].

Brussels, 5 May 1815

My dear uncle,
I received your letter of the 3rd this morning, and am glad you are so far satisfied, but I have been living upon the idea and hopes of seeing you out here, as both Felton and Lionel also thought it was likely that you would make the trip. I am sure you would like the country, and this place very much, and I think you would find a great deal to interest you at this moment, but what I most fear is, that you will put it off until I can be of no use to you; for we can't last many days in the present state of things.

I am very sorry for poor Albinia, but I am of the opinion it is better to suffer disappointment for a little, than beggary in the end, which 500 a year certainly is, and I am sure her good sense will get the better of the former idea.† Do not be afraid of my falling over head. I was in a bad way once, and I do not think desperation ever takes place in reality a second time on the score of love.

The little mare has met with two accidents since she arrived. It ran a nail up its nostril the second night, and the third a Cossack pony got loose in the stable and bit her terribly on the neck, so that I have only mounted her once, and she is in beautiful condition and will be fit to ride now in a few days. I shall hope to have a nice one for you to ride in case you come. Felton I think will be appointed assistant quartermaster general of the cavalry,‡ which is the greatest thing he could have desired.

When I last saw Lionel he was suffering from a fall from a horse of mine which hurt his knee. I hear he is very comfortable at Ghent. With best love, believe me ever, my dear uncle, your most dutiful and affectionate nephew,
John Fremantle

Alarms were frequent but proved to be mere scaremongering, but whether they were simply symptomatic of the nervous anticipation of

---

* John was frequently known as Jack or Jolly Jack.
† Clearly Major Forster's dowry of £500 per year was deemed totally inadequate for Albinia to live upon and the marriage proposal was therefore rejected.
‡ Felton Hervey did gain this position as suggested; and served in this capacity in the Waterloo campaign.

the populace or caused by design was impossible to judge.

Brussels, 10 May 1815

My dear uncle,

I think we shall have a breeze here in a day or two, they are moving opposite to us, but however I think we are stout enough, not to have any occasion to fear them. If we don't go I will write to you in a day or two. Ever your most affectionate nephew,

John Fremantle

John finally cleared the air with his fellow 'family' members; preparations continued for war, but John judged Wellington's army a 'motley bunch'.

Brussels, 19 May 1815

My dear uncle,

I am very much obliged to you for your letter of the 11th. I was indisposed and in bed when it reached me, but am again tolerably hearty.

Since I last wrote to you, I have been to Ghent with the duke, and in a conversation there with Lionel, I found that an idea had existed among my colleagues that I had given myself airs, from having been with the duke to Vienna. Fitzroy desired Lionel to speak to me about it, at least so he told me then, but this he did not do at the time, which I wonder very much at; but to tell you the truth, great regard as I have for Lionel, I think even himself has been more backward toward me than I can account for. However upon learning this from him, I immediately upon my return spoke to Fitzroy fully on the matter and had a most satisfactory explanation with him on the subject, and everything is understood in the light I most desire. Burgh is going home tomorrow to be married,* therefore I shall be nearly what I was before. Lady Fitzroy was brought to bed two days ago of a girl, this is all the news of the family.

When I last wrote to you it was under the idea that we were to commence operations immediately. The French were moving, as we thought to attack us, but it was in consequence of fearing an attack from us, all is quite quiet again. Murat they say is at Paris, and will probably command the cavalry of Bonaparte's army.†

---

* Captain and Lieutenant Colonel Ulysses Burgh married Maria Bagenal on 20 June 1815 and thus missed the Waterloo campaign.

† Murat was actually in his kingdom of Naples and was soon to march his army against the Austrians in northern Italy. His move was premature and he was defeated heavily at the Battle of Tolentino (2–3 May). He fled his throne but was eventually caught and executed on 13 October 1815.

Your calculation of the force from hence to the Rhine is very just, but remember although we have (I mean the duke) near 80,000 men they are a motley race, and will require a great deal of looking after, if ever we take the field, but my decided opinion is, that B[oney] will be overthrown before the armies of the other powers reach the Rhine which they cannot do before the first of next month.

Felton is newly disgusted with his sejour here. He is just as much advanced as when he first came in his negotiation, and I confess I have almost my doubts, of what the duke will be able to do for him. Sometimes he talks of going home again. He is now at Ghent with Lionel.

I am delighted with the idea of little Fanny's prospect of getting a husband, and that my Uncle Tom should be afloat again. John Wells* passed a couple of days here. I think he was looking poorly.

The whole of the duke's baggage is arrived in Hamilton's place from Paris. Tesson, the maître d' hotel, has 100 Napoleons of mine in payment for a horse he sold previous to his coming away. I will write to him this evening to deliver it to any person coming from you, and the whole of my baggage I wish to come with the duke's. This will go very far to pay James Butler, which perhaps you will have the goodness to arrange for me.

I am afraid I have no chance of ever getting in the cavalry as you suggest. I should be too happy if I could. With best love, believe me, my dear uncle, your most dutiful and affectionate nephew,

John Fremantle

The 'family' was still not settled and petty jealousies continued to flare up. John had received a few cuts and bruises following a crash in his gig, but there was no major damage.

Brussels, 30 May 1815

My dear uncle,

I received your letter of the 24th late last night on my return from a Grand Review of all the cavalry,† which Old Blücher was invited to come and see, and left us again this morning. I am very happy you are satisfied with what I have arranged about my private concerns, and I think everything will go square now. Burgh said when he left us that

---

* 2nd Captain John Neave Wells, Royal Engineers, his brother Henry Wells eventually married his sister Albinia in 1827.

† Six thousand British cavalry and artillery were reviewed by the Duke of Wellington and Field Marshal Blücher at Schendelbeke on 29 May 1815. Blücher was extremely complimentary regarding the British horses particularly.

he intended to return in a couple of months with his wife. But I learned a piece of news yesterday which has put us all a little in a fuss. It is that Apsley* is coming out here as a civil secretary to the duke. He did not mention it to any of us when he was here for a day or two about ten days ago, on his return from Vienna, but young Dawkins whom he mentioned it to, told me of it, and was very much surprised that Apsley had not communicated it to us, as well as himself. It is quite out of the question that Fitzroy can act under him, and very doubtful whether I will. I am perfectly certain that in justice to myself I ought not, but I think very likely he will only come out as a looker-on, with as large a salary as all three of ours put together. From what I know of him, I should say he was anything but a man of business and one that I am sure dislikes it very much.

Nothing can be more gratifying than the account you give me of Fanny's intended.† I knew the father in Portugal, and saw a good deal of him with Felton and Colonel Brand. I should be glad to know when it is to take place.

Felton was appointed this evening in orders as an Assistant Q[uarter] M[aster] General, and will be attached for the present to headquarters.

I had a terrible fall from my gig yesterday, and have damaged both knees, and both elbows, unluckily my head did not come to the ground till last.

I am not very much disappointed at hearing of the loss of my things that were with Sergeant McRea, but I think I have a right to make a charge for them. I am very much obliged to you for the trouble you have taken about my things at the duke's. With best love, believe me, my dear uncle your dutiful and affectionate nephew,
    John Fremantle

John's next note was merely a letter of introduction to his uncle, for the French royalist, General Donnadieu, who was travelling to London. John predicted that the fighting would start within a fortnight.

---

* Henry George Bathurst, first son of 3rd Earl Bathurst was known by the courtesy title of Lord Apsley. He was Commissioner of the India Board and an MP at the time. He did not actually join Wellington's 'family'.
† Fanny's intended was George John Danvers, who became 5th Earl of Lanesborough in 1820. His father was Augustus Richard Butler Danvers, brother of the 3rd Earl. George's half brother Henry married John's half sister Cecilia Taylor.

Brussels, 2 June 1815

My dear uncle,

This letter will be presented to you by General Donnadieu,[*] a royalist, who, as he is not going to remain long in England, but is to accompany the Duchess of Angoulême[†] to the west, it is worth your while to invite him to dinner. Though a savage looking bird, he is perfectly au fait at all military matters, passed, and passing now, and will amuse you. He enjoys also the duke's confidence; as I don't like to write news, and he asked me if he could do anything for me, I thought it a very good way of employing him, and at all events there can be no harm done, if you don't like it. I think another fortnight cannot elapse without a beginning, ever my dear uncle your most dutiful and affectionate nephew,

John Fremantle

---

[*] Lieutenant General Gabriel Donnadieu had also served the Duc d'Angoulême in the south of France in 1814.

[†] Marie Therese of France, 'Madame Royale' the daughter of Louis XVI, who married the Duc d'Angoulême.

WATERLOO AND BEYOND

Fourteen days to the day after John's last letter, on 16 June, Wellington's outnumbered forces fought with stubborn determination to prevent Marshal Ney from capturing the strategic crossroads at Quatre Bras, while the rest of the duke's scattered troops hurriedly marched up to support them. Having received reinforcements, Wellington managed to retain the crossroads that day, but having learnt of Blücher's defeat by Napoleon at the Battle of Ligny fought at the same time, he was forced to order a retreat on 17 June.

Having successfully retreated to the area of Mont St Jean, Wellington's army took position that night across the road to Brussels to offer battle on 18 June. Wellington was slightly outnumbered as he stood that day on what was to become the most famous battlefield in history, Waterloo; but he had been promised support by Marshal Blücher, who was marching to join him.

The Battle of Waterloo, fought on 18 June, was one of the most intensely destructive battles fought in history to that date and it has rarely been surpassed in terms of the numbers of killed and wounded in a single day ever since, nor in such a small area of ground.

Napoleon threw everything he could at Wellington's defensive line, but the allied line held precariously, until the arrival of Blücher and the Prussian army tipped the scales firmly against Napoleon. Rout ensued and the French army disintegrated; Paris fell to the allies on 7 July. Napoleon abdicated and attempted to flee to the United States of America, but realising that flight was impossible, he eventually surrendered to the Royal Navy on 15 July. Napoleon was transported to St Helena and the Great War* finally ended, bringing relative peace to Europe for four decades.

The Duke of Wellington bore a charmed life that day; always in the heat of battle and never touched. A number of his 'family' were not so

---

* The wars against Napoleon were referred to as the 'Great War' until the phrase was applied to the First World War.

lucky: Fitzroy Somerset lost his right arm; both Canning and Gordon were killed although others such as Percy, who carried the despatch home and Cathcart survived unscathed along with John Fremantle.

Harry Smith of the 95th records that after the battle Wellington slowly rode back to headquarters to find 'The table was laid for the usual number, while none appeared of the many of his staff but Alava and Fremantle'. Smith however was not an eye witness and was told this by Alava two years later; as many other members of his Staff survived is this a bit of poetic license?

Like everyone else who could write, John penned a letter immediately after the Battle of Waterloo, to announce his survival and to give a hurried account of such a glorious victory, yet ghastly day. He was unwounded, but had had a horse shot beneath him when riding it at Quatre Bras.

Brussels, 19 June 1815

My dear uncle,

We returned here this morning after three days [of] as severe operation as ever were known I suppose in the annals of military history. I don't pretend to enter into the details of the two days action, viz. the 16th and 18th for if once begun, there is no knowing where to end, indeed the dispatch itself is very concise, for such an operation.*

Bonaparte was like a hard run fox, and at the last attack just before dark, headed his Imperial Guard in person, and when that attack *manqué* [missed] they all went *à la debandade* [helter-skelter], followed by us, and the Prussians, who had arrived quite fresh,† and the former are after them now, *l'épeee dans les reins* [with a sword in the kidneys]. The French have left upwards of 100 pieces of cannon, and all their baggage. Two of Bonaparte's carriages have been taken, and their soldiers are all throwing away their arms, in short there never was such a business from beginning to end, ever known. The duke did wonders and earned well his victory, we were near losing the day four times, and I assure you that nothing but his countenance kept the matter going; you will see that great havoc has been made among our Staff. Percy had a horse killed, Cathcart two, and myself one on the 16th. Felton's horse was wounded 3 times, and how the duke escaped we are at a loss to know, for he was in the thick of it from morning till night.

I received a deed from Mr Watkins this day which I will sign, and send as soon as I get it ready.

---

* Wellington's Waterloo despatch has been heavily criticised for its brevity and failure to praise individual actions enough.

† 'Quite fresh' is probably a little over the top, many Prussians having marched throughout the day before arriving at the battle.

Felton has taken charge of our department by the duke's desire. He is quite well. Ever my dear uncle your most dutiful and affectionate nephew,

John Fremantle

I rode the little mare the whole of yesterday, and was carried to perfection. I like her very much indeed. We start this night, or tomorrow, when the whole of our army will be put in motion after them.

John wrote little of his own exploits during the Battle of Waterloo, but he does appear in the accounts written by others. Like all of Wellington's aides, he would have spent the day weaving across the battlefield, through the thick smoke continually on the lookout to avoid the pockets of enemy cavalry that milled around the infantry squares to convey the duke's orders to various commanders.

He also performed one very important role towards the end of the day, in guiding the Prussian advance in the most beneficial way to relieve the pressure on Wellington's forces as the crisis of the battle loomed. John wrote a reply to William Siborne explaining this role in a letter dated 20 November 1842[*]

I am very glad to state to you the occurrence which took place with the Prussian Army on the 18th June.

Many officers were sent in the morning in search of the Army. Towards six o'clock Sir Horace Seymour came and reported to the Duke of Wellington that he had seen the Prussian column.

The duke called upon me to go to the head of their column, and ask for the 3,000 men to supply our losses. Blücher had not arrived, but Generals Ziethen and Bülow were at the head of the column, who gave me for answer – that the whole Army was coming up, and that they could not make a detachment. I said I could [would?] return to the duke with such a message. On my way back I found a Prussian battery of eight guns firing between our first and second lines, and desired the officer to cease firing. I returned to the knoll so well described in your model, and begged the generals to send orders for the battery to cease fire.

The last attack was now in full force, and when the dense smoke cleared off, we saw that the French were in full retreat.

Blücher, who had arrived, met in the village of Belle Alliance the Duke of Wellington, when it was agreed that he should follow them during the night; he did so. Believe me, &c.

John Fremantle

---

[*] See *The Waterloo Letters* by H. T. Siborne, letter no. 11.

John wrote again from the village of Gonesse, only ten miles from the centre of Paris, where they halted while they continued detailed negotiations in an effort to prevent the need to storm Paris, with its inherent heavy loss of life and inevitable destruction.

Gonesse, 2 July 1815

My dear uncle,

You must not be surprised at not hearing from me, for I really have been so busy, that I have not been able to write to you, when the last couriers were going away, but however I should not have been able to tell you much. We are now in a very unpleasant state for military people 'treating, and marching'. They are very anxious to save Paris, and as they are very strongly fortified, and it will cost a number of lives, I think it is better we should treat. The commissioners have been with us these three days, but Blücher will not [agree] as yet. I received your letter the other day, our boutique goes on very well, Felton and myself of course can have no difference. I am to him as I was to Fitzroy, and I cannot be affronted at his being put there.* The French general is this instant arrived, who says he is come from the army to the king, if so everything is up.

I will write to you as soon as we get to Paris. Ever my dear uncle your most dutiful and affectionate nephew,

John Fremantle

The Convention of Paris had been signed on 3 July and the allies marched into Paris on 7 July; King Louis XVIII entering his capital once again the following day. However, John still spent a great deal of time talking about the machinations of 'the family'.

Paris, 10 July 1815

My dear uncle,

I was '*en cours*' [in progress] when our last accounts went away from Gonesse, and before that I think, Liancourt.† I have suffered a little from our journey not being quite set up before I started, but I trust in a short time to be all right again. Felton has been ailing for some days, but he is much better now.

I thought very likely when he was first appointed that the duke might have been angry with me, although I was at a loss to attribute

---

* Felton Hervey became an aide-de-camp to Wellington after Waterloo and took on the role of military secretary as Fitzroy Somerset was wounded, despite having only one arm!

† Liancourt is a small village 3 miles south-east of Clermont.

any cause for it, but I am quite *réparer* [mended], by Burgh's arrival, to find that he still goes on at the head of the boutique; if Burgh had been here when such an appointment took place I should have been very much surprised, as he had been so much longer at the business than myself, but as far as I can perceive, Burgh appears very well satisfied.

I dare say you are astonished, at Felton being at the head of so great a concern, as he certainly never had any schooling for such a thing, but he does admirably well, besides which, he is such a very popular man with the army. He was of wonderful assistance to the duke on the 18th.

I am afraid there is no chance for me respecting the Bath that you are so anxious about, they intend to let the number die away very much and to diminish it eventually to half the number, none but general officers are to have the 2nd Class. I shall be very angry though, if I don't get the 3rd, which I understand is to come out.* I wrote to Colonel Torrens from Brussels putting home about getting a medal for Orthes; a good opportunity offered as a list of other recommendations was going home; I spoke to the duke about it, and he allowed me to write, and to mention his name, but I have not received an answer from Torrens.

The king made his entry amidst the acclamations of the populace on the 8th, all the people were dancing for joy in the streets till a late hour, *quelle canaille* [what scoundrels]. The town is quite quiet, but the Prussians are doing themselves a great deal of mischief, by allowing their army to commit every excess on the country. However it raises our character in proportion; as our people are in the most perfect order, and just as quiet as if in England. If you wish to see sights and great people, I wish you could come now, for a short time. You will never have such another opportunity, and I do think you will afterwards be sorry to have missed it.

The sovereigns† are just arrived, and I suppose congress will be opened forthwith. Adieu, my dear uncle, believe me, your most dutiful and affectionate nephew,

John Fremantle

---

* The 1st Order of the Bath was Knight Grand Cross, to which only Major General James Kempt was invested on 22 June 1815; the 2nd Order, Knight Commander, was inaugurated in January 1815 with large numbers added on 2 January, in recognition of service throughout the Napoleonic wars; only a further three were added after Waterloo, Major Generals George Cooke, Peregrine Maitland and Frederick Adam. The 3rd Class, of Companion of the Bath was inaugurated with another large issue on the King's birthday, 4 June. A great number were further admitted on a list issued on 22 June following Waterloo, one of which was Lieutenant Colonel John Fremantle. See Burnham and McGuigan, *The British Army against Napoleon*.

† The emperors of Russia and Austria and king of Prussia arrived in Paris together.

A week later John wrote of the true aversion to the Bourbons and of Prussian reparations.

Paris, 17 July 1815

My dear uncle,
I have received yours of the 8th. Nothing can be more just than your ideas of the situation of affairs here. I never could have believed there had existed such a rooted aversion to the Bourbons, as I now find reigns, and in my opinion it is the only point in which the people show any sense; they are to be sure so despicable a race. The French army has submitted unconditionally to the king and his government, therefore there only remains to settle the terms upon which peace is likely to be rendered permanent; a difficult job to be sure, and likely to last a considerable time. It is the old history of last year, conferences and little done.

You need be under no apprehension of the country not being made to suffer, I can promise you it is bleeding famously; though not so much by our means as I could wish, however we have not paid a farthing for anything since we came in, nor do ever intend; the Prussians have levied a contribution of 5 million sterling* besides clothing complete for 110,000 men, to enforce which they have imprisoned all the chief bankers in the city.

In my letter the other day I endeavoured to persuade you to come over. I am sure it would amuse you and you never can have so good an opportunity. If you don't come, I shall certainly go over to Fanny's wedding.

I cannot give you any hopes that your wishes for my advancement will be fulfilled to the amount you propose in your note. I shall however get a medal for Waterloo.†

Believe me ever, my dear uncle, your most dutiful and affectionate nephew,
John Fremantle

A short note spoke of a trip home.

Paris, 27 July 1815

My dear uncle,
I received your letter of the 23rd. I cannot send you Watkins's paper as

---

* This would equate to approximately £180 million today.
† At this time it had not been settled that the Waterloo medal would be universal to all ranks. Previously only commanding officers and Staff officers of the rank of lieutenant colonel and above could expect a medal.

the deed is made out for Brussels, which will not do. There are several treaties of subsidy concluded which I intend to ask him (the donkey) to take over for ratification and return, and will bring the deed with me. Lionel starts on the 1st and I think I shall come with him. Ever, my dear uncle, your most affectionate nephew,

John Fremantle

I am getting quite well.

A few weeks later he was back in London.

Coldstream Orderly Room, 16 August 1815

My dear uncle,
I have not seen Watkins myself but young Danvers was there the day before yesterday and was altogether very well satisfied with the progress that was making. His father I suppose was very much averse to the arrangement of what Watkins mentioned at your last interview of £350 for younger children, for I understand some words took place between him and Fanny upon his saying that you were unfair. What more I see of him, I cannot say impresses me with a more favourable opinion of him, little Fanny I thought very much out of spirits last night.

I saw the young lady at the opera the other night but they were all gone to Wanstead when I called the day after. There is a party there on Friday, and I am to call there today with Lady Emily Fielding who is a relation of theirs,* and asked me some questions about her before she told me so, therefore on the whole I think I had better not come down. I shall be able to tell you more positively in a day or two, but I think Lady E[mily] F[ielding] has taken me by the hand for this purpose. She told me yesterday that she had [£]40,000 only.† You probably know more of her than I do, and I should be glad to know whether you thought my surmise just. I have just heard from Percy of the 10th and all is well. Adieu my dear uncle, your most dutiful and affectionate nephew,

John Fremantle

From White's Club, John wrote of partying and match-making; but whomever he was being lined up for, it did not ultimately end in matrimony.

---

* Lady Emily Fielding was an unmarried daughter of Major General William Fielding, Viscount Fielding.
† £40,000 would equate to £1.4 million today.

Whites,* 19 August 1815

My dear uncle,

I am happy to tell you matters have been quite restored between the young parties. He returned yesterday from Brighton, where he went the day before, to secure an abode. I have not seen Watkins since you last heard from me but I will go on Monday.

My love is still in its childhood, and I should think there cannot be time for it. I went to their Ball last night and was courteously received by the old lady, and I thought very well by the young one. It strikes me, (but it may be fancy) that it is in their heads in the same way that it is in mine. I told them both that I understood from Campbell that she was married or going to be, which seemed to amuse them very much. Adieu, my dear uncle, I will write to you whenever there is anything worth reporting, ever your most dutiful and affectionate nephew,

    John Fremantle

Can you lend me a seal containing my arms to have one made by J. F. The last time I saw Torrens I settled with him that I was to have the medal for Orthes, the 3rd class is to come out very soon.†

John wrote that the Reverend Gerald Wellesley was prepared to lead the ceremony of marriage of his sister Frances to George Danvers Butler at St George's, Hanover Square, on 29 August 1815.

Whites, 23 August 1815, Thursday

My dear uncle,

I have had two letters from Gerald Wellesley, saying that he will not fail to attend whenever we will send to him to say that a day is fixed.

I was unwell for two days last week from a pain in my stomach, and not eating, but I have recovered my appetite, and my stomach has again resumed its proper functions. I am to see Torrens again about the 3rd Class. They are so decidedly puzzled, they do not know what to do. I should not be surprised if it was not to come out at all. Ever my dear uncle your most affectionate nephew,

    John Fremantle

---

* White's is a London gentlemen's club on St James's Street. From 1783 it was the unofficial headquarters of the Tory party.

† He refers to the issue of the 3rd grade of the Order of the Bath, which he did receive as a CB dated 22 June 1815.

Chapel St,* Monday [28 August]

My dear uncle,
I settled with the clerk of St George's yesterday respecting Gerald Wellesley's permission to perform the ceremony. Both of them say the hour must be called half past nine, for if the ceremony does not begin by ten, it will not be over by half after, when the doors are opened.

I received letters from Percy last night. The Russian Orders are distributed, but I am not included. The same persons of the duke's family get them who received the Austrian ones. Ever my dear uncle, your very affectionate nephew,
  John Fremantle

The newlyweds were honeymooning in Europe and John travelled with them to Paris. He seems to have taken a shine to his new brother-in-law.

Brighton, 2 Saturday September

My dear uncle,
We are arrived here yesterday at 7 ¼ o'clock, Danvers' horse had been taken on, so we went post, tandem, the post boy riding the fore horse, and went very fast. Fanny arrived half an hour after us. Danvers was not determined about going today, however we got all his things on board in the forenoon, and we are going on board ourselves in half an hour. His horses embark on Monday, and his coachman waits till then for his harness & portmanteau. If they do not arrive before that time, Bradshaw will take care of them. Watkins is going over with us, he says he will write to you from the other side. Ever my dear uncle your most dutiful and affectionate nephew,
  John Fremantle

PS That Danvers seems a very accommodating fellow indeed.

It would seem that within a few days John was at Valenciennes, as Thomas Creevey recounts in his diary on 9 September:

> ... The Duchess of Kent, had an old, ugly German female companion with her, and the Duke of Wellington was going about amongst his Staff before dinner, saying 'Who the devil is to take out the maid of honour?' and at last said 'Damn, Fremantle, find out the mayor and let him do it.' So the Mayor of Valenciennes was brought up for the purpose ... †

---

*   Chapel Street is found near Hyde Park Corner, off Belgrave Square.
†   The Creevey Papers, p. 184.

Two months pass before another letter and presumably some are missing; it would seem that Uncle William had crossed the English Channel and might be on route to Paris.

John was very despondent for the new French government as the country railed against the enforced detention, trial and exile of Napoleon's supporters and the increasing tax burden.

Paris, 8 November 1815

My dear uncle,

Your courier Fassola paid us a formal visit the other morning and announced your safe arrival on this side of the water, as far as he attended you, as being without let or hindrance, therefore as we are here for a long time, I hope you will be tempted again during our stay.

I think even you and yours will be satisfied with the terms of the peace which are on the eve of being signed, but it is quite of the question in my mind that the state of things can remain thus.

In their present position in France. I speak with respect to the French themselves, the government of which is committing *bêtise* [stupidity] upon *bêtise* every hour. Since the law has passed *arrestations* [detentions] have taken place beyond any beliefs & exile is generally the consequence without any trial. The contributions which are levied by the government to pay the armies cause general dissatisfaction on account of the mode in which they proceed; viz. no proportionate scale is fixed by which a person can be taxed according to the amount of his income, but it is totally arbitrary with the government to send to any person and say he shall pay so much for the exigency of the times, and they all swear they will not come down, until a law has passed the chambers fixing the mode by which the taxes are to be levied.

I saw my Austrian friend last evening who I have been in a degree of correspondence with ever since, who told me he had spoken to Metternich, who said he would see to my affair as soon as he got to Milan and I believe what he said. I am sure if Metternich likes, he can do it for me. I will take an opportunity of speaking to him before he goes, which will be in a few days. Mr Floret also mentioned to me that the duke had told Metternich that he intended to go to Milan during the winter; if so I shall certainly be glad to go with him.

Poor little Fanny has been very ill ever since you went away, but is now a great deal better. Albinia was run away with the other day on the race course on Felton's Achmet.

Ney's trial commenced this morning. I dare say he will be let off.

With best love to my aunt and Eliza, believe me, my dear uncle, your most dutiful and affectionate nephew,
John Fremantle

John had taken a major tumble while hunting but came off with little more than cuts and bruises and a sore wrist. The attitude of the French people to the British presence concerned John as it was changing for the worse.

Paris, 15 November 1815

My dear uncle,
On my arrival from the country on the 12th, I found your letter. I had been there on a wild boar chase & had a terrible fall which I feel the effects of still in my right hand. I have also been attacked with a violent rheumatism in my arm, which has pained me dreadfully, but is better within the last day or two. I am delighted to hear you were so content with your journey by the north, home. I was afraid it would not repay you.

We are here certainly for the winter, if the French do not oblige us to quit by their insolence, for even already there is no insult they do not practise upon us. I mean in petty ways, but which, multiplied, aggravate exceedingly.

Lady Caher succeeded to gain apartments which we procured a billet upon, but she is obliged to turn out, but I have provided a Prussian to replace us, as the conduct of the host has been most unworthy. Felton & I were both obliged to quit upon the duchess's arrival; we are however to occupy the Élysée Bourbon* on Saturday next, where there will be room for us all.

With respect to society, there is none as yet. Lady Castlereagh's suppers have always continued. The peace treaty will be signed tomorrow, & I understand Monday is fixed for the day of their [the sovereigns] departure.

The Duchess of Wellington will have her two evenings a week to receive, as soon as we get into our new house. I understand Westmeath & his wife† are coming here immediately.

You may depend upon it when Lord Buckingham‡ arrives nothing

---

* King Louis XVIII offered Wellington the use of this palace during his stay in Paris; which he did with his 'family'.

† George Thomas John Nugent, 1st and last Marquess of Westmeath and his wife Lady Emily (née Cecil); George was a first cousin to John.

‡ Richard Temple Nugent Brydges Chandos Grenville, 1st Duke of Buckingham and Chandos. Lord Buckingham was the Fremantle family's 'friend in high places'.

on my part will be wanting to show him every proper attention & civility that lies in my power.

Little Fanny is quite stout again and I think the party continues going on very well. With best love to my Aunt and Eliza, believe me, my dear uncle your most dutiful and affectionate nephew,

John Fremantle

Marshal Ney's trial for treason had ended in his being found guilty. Despite heartfelt pleas to the duke by Ney's wife, he did not feel able to interfere in the trial, which was purely a French affair. News of John's grandmother's death had also arrived.

Paris, 20 November 1815

My dear uncle,
I received a letter from Watkins this morning; I have sent him eight pounds which I received as his expenses of travelling from hence to Brussels which I think is pretty fair.

Peace is signed this night, and I suppose you will hear of it as soon as you will receive this. What occupies us all now is the breeze about Ney, who wrote to the duke as a *dernier rapport* [last request] to claim his protection according to the 22nd Article of the Convention of July 9th. Madame Ney also had an interview with and published a false statement of the conference. Some English have also published a paper against the measure of his being tried supposed to be between Kinnaird, young Bruce, & others, to which the duke I believe intends publishing a note he has written as a sort of reply.

I heard from my Uncle Tom the day before yesterday, he is very comfortable at Milan.* The girls are quite well.

We have just heard the melancholy tidings of my Grandmother Grove's death,† which has placed the whole family Caher, Bradshaw, etc. in the deepest distress. Pray gave my best love to my aunt and

---

* Rear-Admiral Sir Thomas Fremantle KCB was touring Italy with his family who had many Italian relations. He had been appointed vice-admiral and commander-in-chief in the Mediterranean.

† This was the announcement of the death of Arabella Fitzgibbon in Dublin on 9 November 1815. Arabella had taken the family name of Grove in 1811 in compliance to the will of her first cousin, the wife of the 1st Earl Annesley. She was the eldest daughter of John Fitzgibbon and sister to the 1st Earl Clare and had been married to James St John Jeffreys of Blarney Castle and had one son and four daughters. Her son was George Jeffereys and the four daughters were John Fremantle's mother Albinia, Lady Caher, the honourable Mrs Cavendish-Bradshaw and Anne who had died young. She was therefore one of John's grandmothers on the maternal side. She was also a second cousin to the Duke of Wellington.

Eliza, and believe me, my dear uncle, your most dutiful and affectionate nephew,

    John Fremantle

They had now changed their abode to the Élysée Bourbon, but it was a damp, cold building and they all suffered the consequences.

Paris, 30 November 1815

My dear uncle,

I expected to have heard from you by the last two mails. I wrote to Watkins by the same post, sending him his money for the journey to Brussels to which I have also received no answer. I also gave him directions respecting my half year's annuity which he informed me he had received, but have had no answer, therefore conceive some mishap must have been occasioned though I do not hear of any mail having been lost.

We are going on here in the good old way, having changed our abode to the Élysée Bourbon, where, by the by, we are not near so comfortable as we were at the Hotel de la Rivière,* it is so very cold, without any means of warming the house sufficiently.

Lady Caher left the rue de Mondour when we changed, but I have taken especial care to put a Prussian in the house, on account of the bad *mien* [look] he made us whilst we were there.

Felton I do not think is altogether as he ought to be, sitting up does not certainly agree with him, he is always very well when he keeps quiet. Percy is very far from well. The duke is much better, but has been very much discomposed by a violent cold.

Fanny has changed her house, they found mine too cold for them. With best love to my aunt & Eliza. Believe me, my dear uncle, your most dutiful and affectionate nephew,

    John Fremantle

John announced the execution of Marshal Ney and explained the domestic arrangements of the duke and duchess at the Élysée Bourbon, the duke was apparently in a constant bad humour. The army was due to take up quarters on the border around Cambrai, an unattractive proposition to John.

---

* The Hotel de la Rivière is still on the Place de Vosges.

Paris, 6ᵉ December 1815

My dear uncle,

I have received your last letter which I was uneasy about. I am very much obliged to you for your enquiries, both my hand and arm are perfectly recovered. We do not know here what disturbance is, we only read of it occasionally in the English journals.

Ney was executed this morning without the least fuss at 10 o'clock near the Observatoire.† He would not allow his eyes to be bound, and gave the word to 'fire' himself, he acknowledged himself a traitor before his death. I hear Lavallette‡ is to be banished.

The distribution of the apartments within the palace is as follows. The duchess occupies the whole of the upstairs, & the duke occupies the state room on the *rez-de-chaussée* [ground floor], our office is the large blue room near the *petits apartements* [small suites] opening on the garden. We all sleep above the duchess except Felton who lives at Bonard's. The duchess is going to England on the 12th or 13th and our head quarters will remove by the end of the month, it is supposed to Cambrai, which will be a dreadful bore. However I do not suppose the duke will be quite a fixture there, as soon as the army is installed in its new quarters I believe he intends paying his respects to the [prince] regent for a few days, he has been invited twice by him.

Lord Buckingham is here, but I have only had one good long *entretien* [interview] with him. We have been tolerably busy since the peace§ with the new army arrangements. The duke has been in a dreadful humour, & I cannot conceive what has crossed him so, nothing pleases him, & he seems always dissatisfied. I do not think it can be the duchess for poor soul she never sees him except across the table at dinner.

---

* This must be an error of dating by John as he speaks of Ney's execution that morning. Ney was actually shot on 7 December 1815.

† The French Observatory was established in 1667, pre-dating the Royal Observatory at Greenwich by eight years.

‡ Antoine Marie Chamans, Comte de Lavallette, escaped with the help of British officers, having exchanged clothing with his wife during a visit, shortly before his planned execution. There was a huge diplomatic scandal.

§ The Peace of Paris was signed by John Fremantle on behalf of the duke, on 20 November 1815, by which France agreed to indemnify the allied powers the sum of 700 million francs and was reduced to its 1790 borders. The allies were also to maintain an army of up to 150,000 men on French soil for five years, at French expense, while the French government secured their hold on the country and to guarantee the reparations. The pound sterling was then worth 25 French francs, therefore the French government had agreed to a reparation of £28 million, which would be worth approximately £950 million today.

Lady Caher is established in the rue de la Ville l'Evêque & has millions of the French about her, and she seems quite happy. Fanny's house is near the rue de la Paix, poor little thing she is very unwell with pain in her head and has had a sore throat for a long time.

I did not lose sight of my friend Mr Floret,* he promised faithfully I should hear from him from Milan, and spoke confidently of my getting the order. He promised to call on my Uncle Tom. I have never heard a word respecting Mrs Jeffery's will,† I do not suppose she could have had a shilling. I always understood she was very much embarrassed in her circumstances, and surrounded by a lot of female sharks, nieces of hers named O'Connell,

Felton was attacked with a fit of the lumbago yesterday, and was obliged to go to bed, but he is better today; however it is always the case with him, the moment he is the least better, he takes liberties with himself, consequently never allows himself to get thoroughly well. I will write to you about him on Monday again, with best love to my aunt and Pussy,‡ believe me, my dear uncle, your most dutiful and affectionate nephew,

John Fremantle

The army was preparing to move to Cambrai as soon as the contingents of the other armies had marched clear. However, John was more sanguine as the establishment at Paris was to be retained.

Paris, 11 December 1815

My dear uncle,

I received your letter with Lord Buckingham's enclosed this morning, and as he expressed great anxiety respecting the one I now enclose, I have put it under my covers. The army is to move as soon as ever the road is clear from the passage of the other foreign troops, which will be between the 16th and 20th, & I imagine the duke will move in his own person as soon as ever the army has reached its new destination, which will be before the end of the month. Headquarters are to be at Cambrai, but I understand we are to have an establishment here, which will make it very comfortable as I feel sure he will be backwards & forwards constantly.

I mentioned most of the queries you made me in your letter the other day. The duchess is off tomorrow. The duke will make a tour

---

* This would appear to be one Peter von Floret, who had previously been in Paris in 1809 discussing the marriage of the Austrian Princess Marie Louise to Napoleon.
† Arabella Jeffreys, Grandmother Grove.
‡ Presumably is a nickname for Felton's youngest sister, Elizabeth Hervey-Bathurst.

round the fortified places the first thing, and I think as soon as things are all in their right place, he will go & pay his respects to the regent. Do you advise me to come with him if I can? Fanny continues much the same.

With best love to my aunt & Eliza, believe me, my dear uncle, your most dutiful and affectionate nephew,
    John Fremantle

John and the army celebrated Christmas in Paris, the march north being delayed; however boredom had set in and all seemed to be eager for the change of scenery. John noted that the duke's humour had improved recently: was it due to the fact that the duchess had already left?

His hopes for the French were not very high and he thought that the allies might have to dethrone the king and install their own government. Lavallette's escape had deepened the crisis and was highly embarrassing to the French government.

Paris, 25 December 1815

My dear uncle,

I did not write to you last post, for as usual my stock of news would not furnish wherewithal I thought, to turn the corner. It is very odd, but almost all the army people are bored with the *séjour* here, and I confess I am at best one of that number, and look forward to our departure with pleasure, rather than the contrary. The Duke of Richelieu* has long been wishing to get rid of us, & I understand there was a considerable dispute between him & the king the other day upon the question of our going or staying in which the king overruled him, it is however again since the last two days talked of very much, and some of the troops are leaving this neighbourhood for the Departement du Nord, but I expect we shall be here ourselves till the middle of January. The duke is quite himself again. It was not bad him shovelling the duchess off on the first chance, when he never could have had any idea of stirring. Cambrai will be a very nice place for her, while of course his business will lay very much this way.

Mrs Bradshaw† has been dangerously ill, but is recovered again considerably, Lady Caher has *affiched* [made a show of] herself very much with the French, who I am not certain as yet whether they laugh at, or not. She, however is very much amused, which of course is the main point.

---

* Armand Emmanuel Sophie Septimanie de Vignerot du Plessis, 5th Duke of Richelieu had superseded Talleyrand as prime minister.
† His aunt, Mrs Marianne Cavendish-Bradshaw, formerly Lady Westmeath.

Lavallette is clean off, and Madame is still in confinement.* Barbe Marbois† they say is to be tried for not executing him the day he went off.

The deputies of the chamber were occupied the whole of yesterday debating whether there should be a general *deuil* [mourning] throughout the kingdom for Louis 16th. All classes, *pour ainsi dire* [as one may say] are dissatisfied with the present order of things, nothing seems to go on in any department. I should not be in the least surprised if the allies were obliged to appoint a regency, for it appears they are quite incapable of governing themselves. It is not to be described to you the honour in which we are held, and our nation.

Little Fanny is still very poorly, they talk of proceeding to Italy in the spring, but I can't conceive what he will ever do with himself outside Paris, he will certainly die of *ennui* [boredom], or destroy Fanny with his temper. I am told he is very brutal, but have never seen it.‡

Adieu my dear uncle, pray write to me, and believe me, your very dutiful and affectionate nephew,

John Fremantle

PS I do not think the duke saw more of Lord Buckingham than he does of any other traveller that passes through Paris.

The Lavallette business rumbled on into the New year as a number of British officers had been implicated in his escape and had been imprisoned. The case of Hutchinson, a serving officer, was seen as a dangerous precedent and John criticised the duke for not having challenged its legality, especially as he had not been given prior warning of his intended arrest.

Paris, 18 January 1816

My dear uncle,

As you will no doubt hear a thousand contradictory reports respecting the imprisonment of Sir Robert Wilson, Bruce and Captain Hutchinson.§ I am anxious to give you the correct detail.

---

* Following his daring escape, his wife was imprisoned, but eventually released to join her husband in exile in Germany.

† The attorney general, Monsieur Barbe Marbois was implicated as he had delayed sending the order of execution for two days, during which time Lavallette escaped.

‡ It would appear that his brother-in-law may have been guilty of intimidation rather than physically striking his wife.

§ Sir Robert Wilson, Mr Crawford Bruce and Lieutenant and Captain John Hely Hutchinson of the Grenadier Guards were implicated in the escape of Lavallette.

On the 13th they were all taken from their different beds, and conveyed to the Prefecture; the government having got possession of a letter to Lord Grey giving the whole account of the escape of Lavallette with himself (Sir R[obert Wilson]). They did not leave this until the 9th. They went with their own horses the 1st post, and then took post horses. Young Hutchinson went with the horses near the carriage, in order to avoid the possibility of their being detained, for a considerable distance. The Post Master detained them at the 2nd post, but upon Wilson's talking a little with the officers, suspicion on his part ceased, and they proceeded. At Cambrai he also met with difficulty, but however he saw him safe across the frontier and returned after an absence of only 60 hours. His letter he sent to Sir Charles Stuart by his *larquecy de place* [lackey?] who being in pay took it direct to the police, amongst his papers.

I am told there are some very bad prosecutions. He would not answer a single question that was put to him, and he has since been conducted to the Abbaye* the other two remain at the prefecture. The duke has protested against the mode of Captain Hutchinson's arrest viz. without his being informed of it, but has not claimed him, which I as a military man am exceedingly hurt at, for they of course have the same right to arrest the duke himself as one of his officers, he belonged to the G[renadier] Guards. One of the two brigades which formed the garrison of Paris marches tomorrow, but not far. I expect we shall be off certainly before the end of the week.

With best love and in great haste believe me, my dear uncle, your most dutiful and affectionate nephew,
John Fremantle

PS The not claiming Captain Hutchinson is quite *entre nous* [between ourselves].

The 'family' continued in poor health and the only news was the continuing saga of Lavallette.

Paris, 19 January 1816

My dear uncle,
I avail myself of the opportunity of an extra messenger to send you a few lines. R[ussell] & I were very busy yesterday on account of Felton

---

They were found guilty and sentenced to three months in prison, the most lenient sentence available. It should be noted that the Prince Regent had renamed the 1st Foot Guards the Grenadier Guards in July 1815.
* The prison de l'Abbaye was in use from 1522 until 1854.

& Percy being unwell, however they are both down again; but I cannot think that Felton will be ever quite right till he gets something like a run at grass, for these attacks are constantly coming upon him.

Nothing worth mentioning has occurred here since the arrest of the three persons. They are now in the Prison de la Force* Newgate; I fancy their trial is to come on immediately. Lord Buckingham leaves this on the 24th, neither him or Arundell† seems to admire the sejour of Paris at all. Little Fanny‡ I am happy to say is recovering very fast, and is again in tolerable good spirits.

Little William Lennox§ is never away from Albinia's side, and she is *entourer* [surrounded] besides by two or three youngsters, who all seem to like our chick very much. There is young Gore,¶ Stewart, Barnard** etc. but I am afraid nothing substantial offering itself.

We have a masked Ball at this house on this day week, I imagine with respect to our departure, we shall never know till the very day before, and it may be in a day or a month.

I understand there is a great deal of very curious matter in Lord Grey's & Wilson's correspondence.†† What a thousand pities he could not have been quiet after taking Lavallette safe off. Pray give my best love to my aunt and Eliza, and believe me, your very dutiful and affectionate nephew,

John Fremantle

---

* La Force Prison was located in the rue du Roi de Sicile, in what is now the 4th arrondissement of Paris. He compares it to Newgate Prison in London where the executions took place.

† James Everard Arundell, 10th Baron Arundell of Wardour, was married to Mary Anne Nugent-Temple-Grenville, the Duke of Buckingham's sister.

‡ Fanny had miscarried.

§ Lord William Pitt Lennox.

¶ Captain the Honourable Charles Gore, 85th Foot, aide-de-camp to Sir James Kempt.

** Probably Ensign William Henry Barnard, Grenadier Guards.

†† Wilson and his co-conspirators were convicted largely on the evidence of his correspondence with Earl Grey, which was intercepted, where he had given full details of the operation.

THE ARMY OF OCCUPATION

The British contingent of the Army of Occupation, whose supreme commander was to be the Duke of Wellington, was to number 30,000 men, as equally were the forces of Prussia, Russia and Austria; Bavaria, Denmark, Saxony, Hanover and Württemburg supplied a further 30,000 men between them, giving a grand total of 150,000 men.

The Army of Occupation was to occupy a corridor along the north eastern border of France and the British contingent was allocated the portion nearest the English Channel, centred around Cambrai. All of the national contingents had marched from Paris to their assigned zone by the end of January 1816.

The duke and his 'family' remained for a while longer, but after finally removing to Cambrai, still regularly returned to Paris on business. The web of social intrigues continued unabated.

Paris, 29 January 1816

My dear uncle,

Here we are still in status quo; all the troops have left the capital on Saturday last, and we were two days at the Élysée, without a single *factionnaire* [sentry], we have now the post of the Garde Royale.*
I confess I do not understand our footing at all in this way; all our heads of departments remain, which does appear to be the most extraordinary thing in the world. It cannot however last long, for my own part, my *malle* [trunk] is made [up], as we may start at any hour. In the first instance, we shall make the tour of the frontier, and then perhaps stretch over to England, if not come [back] here, as the houses & establishments still remain. Campbell and Hill are off to England for Webster's trial.† William Russell is also gone, so that our family you

---

* That is, the French Royal Guard now performed protection duty for the duke.
† Lieutenant Sir James Webster-Wedderburn, 9th Light Dragoons, was married to Lady Frances Caroline Annesley. He accused Wellington of having an affair with his wife and considered demanding £50,000 from Wellington as a 'crim con' case

see, is very much diminished. I suppose one officer will be left here in charge of the house. I shall not stir myself one way or the other, but go with the tide, exactly as I am told.

Your ideas about Albinia are perfectly just, you have no idea what a universal favourite she is, but it would have been very hard to have prevented her going out with Mrs Astor* during Fanny's confinement. Fanny did not like it at the time, but thank goodness the little woman is herself again and able to go about. I wish as you say the scene could have ended, by getting Albinia well off, and this I should not despair of, had we time. I do not believe anything of the story of Barnes's engagement with Miss Capel.† On the contrary with Mrs J. Astor's help and a little more time, I think he might be hooked.

The bay mare you speak of, is very much improved, and I think is quite your cut of an animal, and you may depend upon it, I will keep her for you, she will be far better next year. I can spare her at any time you chance to write for her, for I have three other riding horses.

Lady Burgh has miscarried,‡ Lady Caher is indisposed with a sore throat. Her ma[de]moiselle is very much admired.

I hear there is great consternation in the court circles about the marriage of young Sade Csabray§ at Vienna, but that is a younger brother whose marriage was settled when I was at Vienna, with best love to my aunt & Eliza. Believe me, my dear uncle, your most dutiful and affectionate nephew,

John Fremantle

(criminal conversation) as they were then called. The duke, however, managed to persuade him that there had not been an affair and the case was dropped. However the *Morning Chronicle* published numerous articles regarding the alleged affair and he took them to court for libel. He eventually won and was awarded £2,000 in compensation (approximately £70,000 in modern terms).

* Mrs Sarah Astor (née Todd), wife of John Jacob Astor.

† Major General Edward Barnes had proposed to Maria Capel but was rebuffed. He then turned his attentions upon the older sister Harriet, whom Baron Trip had spurned. Clearly John had hopes that Barnes might marry Albinia, but it was not to be.

‡ This would appear to be Lady Anna Louisa Burgh (née Hely-Hutchinson) who had married the Reverend Thomas John Burgh. She was fertile at this period, having already had eight children and was to have another four, but perhaps tellingly there is a gap of six years from 1814 until 1820 with no offspring.

§ This actually refers to the marriage of Princess Maria Kohary de Csábrág et Szitnya to Prince Ferdinand Georg August of Saxe-Coburg-Saafeld in Vienna on 30 November 1815. This would have caused consternation in the British royal family who were trying to arrange a marriage with this house. The younger brother Leopold did eventually marry Princess Charlotte of Wales who unfortunately died in childbirth in 1817.

PS I am afraid you will not be able to make this out, for there have been a dozen people talking all the time.

The duke was unwell again but in good spirits; the trial of the Lavallette conspirators was still delayed and the scheming to gain a husband for Albinia continued full tilt.

Paris, 12 February 1816

My dear uncle,

Still in status quo, but it cannot last another week. The duke though rather suffering from a cold these last few days, has been in great good humour lately.

I hear the traitors (as they are facetiously termed here), are not to be tried for a fortnight to come, which their friends are outrageous at, and exceedingly angry with Stewart for not managing better for them.

I am glad to tell you our *famille* [family] is going on swimmingly. Fanny has quite recovered her looks and spirits. She is going to change her house and take another for two months longer. She is a famous manager; indeed we all quiz her for stinginess. Albinia is still laid close siege to by W[illiam] Lennox, and Mrs Astor is outrageous with her for allowing it, as she says, she is sure, Barnes is to be had. They meet (I mean the Caher & Albinia *au petit comité* ['club']) every evening either at Mrs Astor's, at Fanny's or somewhere, and play at a round game until 1 in the morning.

Everything is perfectly quiet here, and the opposition party are very sore at Richelieu's apparent good footing in his situation. Pray remember me to my aunt and Eliza. Felton is quite hearty. Believe me, my dear uncle, your most dutiful and affectionate nephew,

John Fremantle

An opportunity to purchase a company in the Coldstream Guards was rumoured and John consulted his uncle on the merits of the move, given the complexities of the dual rank system in the Guards. He already was a brevet lieutenant colonel in the army but only a lieutenant in the regiment; purchasing the company would merely remove the 'brevet' as he would become a captain in the regiment and lieutenant colonel in the army; not much return on the additional £2,000* it would cost after selling his lieutenancy. In the event, it did not happen.

---

* Approximately £84,000 in modern terms.

Paris, 26 February 1816

My dear uncle,

I lose no time in answering your letter of the 16th which however only reached me the day before yesterday. It is full of everything kind and amicable on your part, & I again and again reiterate my grateful acknowledgements to you for it. You have waded, and do wade through a great deal of drudgery for us, but I hope we are fully sensible of it. To myself who does not profess to be au fait in such matters, the whole thing appears entirely *aplanir* [smooth].

I have now a very interesting topic to expatiate upon & one which I am sure will interest you; you will perceive by the enclosed letter, that there is a company going by purchase in the Coldstream, which I imagine must be Sutton's.* My answer to Prince† was, at the moment, that I would certainly purchase, this can do no harm.

There is but one consideration on the subject, which is in regard to income, and my money, as you said yourself cannot be laid out to better advantage, than in the purchase of the company, for the income arising from it, which I understand may certainly be averaged at £600 a year. As Prince observes it is not worth my while. It is true in point of rank that it is immaterial at this moment, but I might wait six years for the company without purchase, in the regular routine of the regiment. So much for my idea, but I confess I shall be too happy to be guided by your advice. The sum which Watkins laid out in the purchase of the annuity (called in), I believe of itself will be sufficient, and the money coming from Ireland equally so, therefore there is no fear on that account. The only advantage to me that the company can be is in exchanging hereafter to the command of a corps, which I can never arrive at in the regiment, as I think I shall be a major general before that can happen.

My idea is, to stick myself at the regulation line, and to make the ensign come down with the remaining difference required, a common position in like cases, but pray do not delay in letting me know your opinion.

Little Fanny has a grand ball tonight, to which half of Paris is invited, the duke intended to have had one himself this evening, but would not when he understood that Fanny had sent her invitations. All the Corps Diplomatique have promised me to come. There are two enormous rooms, where *toute sorte de tapage peut se pratiquer* [any sort of din can be played]. The little woman is still very thin but looks very well

---

* Captain and Lieutenant Colonel Francis Manners Sutton did not leave the regiment at this time.

† Lieutenant and Captain John Prince was adjutant.

& mends in spirits. Mrs Astor is still very sanguine in her hopes, but I confess mine are small. I cannot think Albinia has been wise, her head has certainly gone a little turned, with the constant scene of gaiety she has met with, but this is a circumstance which regards herself so much, that I have ventured very little upon the subject with her.

The marriage takes place with the Prince of Saxe Coburg.* I have sanguine hopes, if application were made in time, of having any commitment in his gift, for two reasons. My personal intimacy with him & the friendship he has invariably shown to me, here & at Vienna [&] I never having received anything from government for my services to the duke, like others have experienced. Let me know what you think of my reasoning on the subject.

I never have been on the back of the bay mare since you left Paris till the day before yesterday, and I think her without exception the very thing to suit you. I told you before she had very much improved to the eye. With best love to my aunt and Eliza, believe me, my dear uncle, your most dutiful and affectionate nephew,

John Fremantle

Prince wrote to John from Cambrai continuing the correspondence regarding the company; but others had prior claims, if they could afford it.

Cambrai, 20 February 1816

My dear Fremantle,
You must excuse this epistle being very laconic, as I am suffering from an inflammation of the eyes, which renders writing very painful to me. Now to my business. There is one company going by purchase in the regiment. Bowles† stands pretty openly, but I do not think he can come down,‡ Sandilands§ is also uncertain. May I therefore request of you to let me know your intentions, that I may be guided accordingly. I should think it can never be worth your while. Believe me ever, yours very truly,

Prince

---

* Prince Leopold George Christian Frederick of Saxe-Coburg-Saalfeld married Princess Charlotte Augusta of Wales on 2 May 1816.
† Brevet Major George Bowles, was only a lieutenant and captain in the Coldstream Guards and did not become a captain and lieutenant colonel until 1825.
‡ To 'come down' means to find the money.
§ Lieutenant and Captain Patrick Sandilands did not get a company until he joined the 3rd Foot Guards in 1821.

A further note made it clear that the seller was not known yet, but that the sum expected was large.

> Dear Fre[mantle],
> I was just going to write to you, to tell you this; the price asked is big, I do not know who it is. Yours ever,
> A. W.[*]

The discussion continued regarding purchase, but John now knew that his chances were very slim. He had also decided not to 'tap' Prince Leopold for an award at this time. His hopes for Albinia's marriage were however not as sanguine as his sister Frances believed.

Paris, 11 March 1816, Monday

My dear uncle,

Many thanks for your kind letter of the 4th. I am fully sensible of the interest you bear me in the affair of the purchase of the company, but alas all my hopes are damped on that score, or nearly so, I have not heard from young Prince since. I suppose his letter was to pump me as to my intentions, as he intended to have done so, had it come as low as him. I am fully persuaded it is the best thing I could do with my money, but I heard, a day or two before I received your letter, from Sandilands, who told me that Bowles and Sowerby[†] had the intention to purchase, & he himself had not made up his mind. They are all equally inconceivable to me. Sowerby only got leave to go home, to settle matters with his father respecting his debts, respecting which he has frequently been in disgrace with the regiment, and it sounds very odd that it should now take such a curious turn, as his father on the two last occasions declared he would come forward no more. Bowles & Sandilands I do not imagine have the means.

With respect to Prince Leopold's concern, I think it had better entirely be completely dropped at present, as you say, and I agree, the only object is the increase of the income, which I do not or cannot want now and I might make a mess for myself here, in people thinking I aimed for what was not perhaps fair, as I am very well off, and I never can have any objection at a future period when it may be a greater object, in asking him anything. What do you think of this?

As for Albinia's concern I am very much in the dark since my last, however she seems full of confidence, as does little Mrs Astor, this little woman has been more indefatigable than any creature ever was

---

[*] Second Major Alexander George Woodford, Coldstream Guards.
[†] Lieutenant and Captain Thomas Sowerby gained his company on 14 May 1817.

before her; Albinia has just betted me a guinea that it does, before the 18th April, but we are going on Thursday or Friday next, and B[arnes] will certainly not leave this, without giving her to understand his sentiments if he has any intentions, before this time. As for my part I say he has never ever been particular towards her.

I am just returned with Lady Bengal* from a wolf hunt in the Forest of Bondy, & had a very good run. Felton is quite well, Fanny and her spouse are in great ease. They talk of leaving Paris in the middle of April, and Mrs Astor hinted to me that she would like to keep Albinia in that case, what do you think of that?

You may depend upon it she is a very good little woman, though very young & flighty.

Best love to my aunt and Pussy. Felton has sent to my aunt an *exemplaire* [specimen] of a facsimile of the Queen's letter. Ever my dear uncle your dutiful and affectionate nephew,

John Fremantle

John was very concerned with the influence of Mrs Astor on his sisters, particularly Albinia whose head had been turned by the gaiety of Paris. All attempts at gaining a betrothal however had come to naught, for Barnes had eyes set elsewhere.

The purchase was still not sorted, nor was it clear who sold, but John now held little hope of ultimate success as too many others stood in his way.

Paris, 18 March 1816

My dear uncle,

I did not write to you by the last mail, for I was so puzzled by Albinia's concern that I did not know what to say. I have no hesitation in saying now that I think it will not do. The report went around very much, and came to Barnes, notwithstanding which he attended her the whole evening of our ball on the 16th, but I understand he says he likes her, though he has no decided intention of marrying.

I am by no means, myself, content with Albinia. I wish I had taken your hint some time ago, it was perfectly just, and your idea respecting it quite verified. Her head is certainly going a little round at the constant scene of merriment which surrounds her. I wish to heavens she had a little of Fanny's sedateness. Mrs Astor agrees with me, but if she had not encouraged those half dozen boys to make love

---

* Could he mean Flora Campbell, 6th Countess of Loudoun and the wife of Francis Edward Rawdon-Hastings, Lord Moira, Governor General of India, and as such based in Bengal?

to her, one after another, that it might have done. I have all along said that it was a concern that so deeply interested herself, that if she had not sense sufficient of her own to guide her, that anything I could say to her, could be of no avail; but I must also mention, that I never had any brotherly communication made to me, whatever information I ever got was entirely by my own means, and that with very great difficulty. It was entirely kept between Mrs Astor and themselves and this I cannot help being upset at, they give up everything and every consideration to the society of that little woman, which is un peu trop fort [too extreme]. Mr Astor is as perfect as man can be, but Madame is certainly not quite so irreproachable when I speak of the close connection in which these girls live with her. Fanny is by no means so much bitten, but the other is quite gone. Mrs Astor I am convinced will be anxious to keep Albinia when Fanny goes and I shall be very glad to know what you think about it, for your idea you know is more than law to us all. Apropos your apology to me the other day for what you may think a lecture was very *mal placé* [badly put]; a letter of the sort and your sentiments on anything that passes you, you may be sure is always well received, & I am too happy at any time to have them. This last however afforded a great deal of merriment as it shows how prone people are to do good natured acts, and say good-natured things; things that do pass, things that do not pass, or are likely to do so. That young Ross* who I am supposed to have helped make brash, I do not know by sight, and I certainly never have dined in his company. It is true that Mother Ross and I have had a correspondence, which if you have any curiosity I enclose for your benefit. She may perhaps have been right to be angry with Felton who has known her a long time, but with me, who never heard of her in my life. I cannot conceive what title she can have to take me to task; however reading your letter over again, I am rather frightened at the tone you assume, as it appears that some *mauvaise langue* [rumour monger] with the best intentions I have no doubt been mentioning something to my disadvantage, that I may, in reality, have unintentionally made myself some enemies. I am by no means certain of this, but I should be very glad if you know anything more, to acquaint me of it. You are very much mistaken however, if you think that the *chicoterie* [sic, presumably for *coterie*] you speak of influences me in any way. I have plenty of employment here without mixing in a dispute with any of them.

With respect to the purchase, I understand from Sandilands, who

---

* Almost certainly he refers to Lieutenant and Captain the Honourable Arthur John Hill Fitzgerald de Ros of the Grenadier Guards.

is now in Paris, that I have no chance of it under £3,000* on my part, putting aside an advance piece which I must make the ensign come forward with, as the sum demanded is £500. Sandilands tells me the person selling is not Sutton, but possibly Brand† or Raikes.‡ He also tells me it is very unlikely to come to me as Bowles has gone to England to negotiate, & that Sowerby is also desirous, but I cannot believe either. He, I think from his conversation will not purchase. I am always of opinion myself that even £3,000 in the purchase would be well laid out, the senior ensign cannot purchase, but the second, Gooch,§ will.

All the news I have to tell you is that you will be surprised in a few days by the publication of a letter from our duke to the king giving him a piece of his mind. I cannot suppose you will get it correct, but a good deal mangled and distorted. The trial of the traitors is to come on this week.

The duke has been very unwell; our departure remains as before, no day fixed, but I expect some fine day to be off at a moment's notice. Best love to my aunt and Eliza, and believe me, my dear uncle your dutiful and affectionate nephew,

    John Fremantle

It would seem that the Duke of Wellington enjoyed the intrigues and fully entered into Mrs Astor's machinations; but their indiscrete talk was overheard by Barnes who immediately cooled his relationship with Albinia.

Paris, 25 March 1816

My dear uncle,

I was quite surprised at not hearing from you by the last mail. I have been quite on tenter hooks ever since. This supposed love affair has worked me to an oil. You know however that I never have been very sanguine. The duke was delighted to hear of it, and entered most fully upon it with Mrs Astor some evenings ago at Lady Hardwicke's. She told him, the only obstacle was Hamilton, Barnes's aide-de-camp, who was trying all in his power to prevent it; he immediately said he

---

* According to Burnham and McGuigan, *The British Army against Napoleon*, a captaincy in the Foot Guards officially cost £3,500, but the new captain could sell his lieutenancy for £1,500, making a total net cost of £2,000. The figures here do not correspond with these figures, but did vary unofficially, depending on supply and demand.

† Lieutenant Colonel Henry Otway Brand, future Lord Dacre.

‡ Captain and Lieutenant Colonel William Henley Raikes.

§ Ensign Henry Gooch.

would send him away, but in the mean time I told them both, that I recommended that not being done, as I knew Barnes was very fond of him, besides managing all his horse concerns. He replied however; said, 'O yes!' and *effectivement* [actually] did speak to Barnes, who put it off. The duke, the night before last at Stewart's, was giving an account of this, to Mrs Astor very fully, when on a sudden he looked round and discovered that Barnes had been close to them all the time & she thinks heard the whole conversation, for shortly after he retired with Hamilton. He has been nothing more than commonly civil to Albinia ever since.

I believe that Albinia allowed young Hamilton, who is a very low lived Irish hound, to flirt with her & that he himself is fond of her. I look upon it as entirely over, but little Astor will not give up her hopes. I have however entreated of her not to be so very particular towards Barnes, which she has promised me to comply with.

I have not yet heard whose company it is going for purchase in the regiment, but understand that Bowles is very busy in England, respecting it. I must always doubt his being able to come down with the stumpy [slang, money].

Your mare is improved so much you would scarcely know her, Albinia and Fanny ride her constantly and they are extremely well satisfied with it.

Fanny at present is decided upon leaving Paris to make a tour in the middle of April, but I dare say when Taylor* arrives, they will alter their plans according to his wishes; he is expected here the beginning of next month.

Burgh left Paris yesterday to stand for the county of Carlow vacated by the death of W. Latouche.† Therefore our boutique remain with Percy and myself to assist Felton, it is however quite enough. I understand the Élysée Bourbon is to be occupied by the Duc de Berri upon his marriage,‡ in which case they talk of our going to Davout's house, opposite the Port Louis XVI.

Pray remember me to my aunt and Eliza, & believe me, my dear uncle, your dutiful & affectionate nephew,

John Fremantle

---

* John's stepfather Colonel John Taylor of Castle Taylor in Galway, 88th Foot.

† It was actually David Latouche (son of the governor of the Bank of Ireland), who died on 15 March 1816. His death caused a by-election and his brother Robert Anthony Latouche succeeded him as MP.

‡ In 1816 he married Princess Maria Carolina Ferdinanda Luisa of Naples and Sicily (1798–1870), oldest daughter of the Duke of Calabria, heir to the Neapolitan throne. He did take over the Élysée Bourbon which eventually became known as the Élysée Palace.

In early April John wrote that they were on the verge of leaving Paris for Brussels.

Paris, 8 April 1816

My dear uncle,

I was very much gratified by your last letter, so fully explanatory on every subject. It is very extraordinary, I have never heard anything more respecting the purchase. I have written to Bradford as you recommended, to say I am ready to treat for the purchase, but I do not think it will come down as far as me. As for Old Mother Ross, I have never heard of her, or from her since.

Albinia's concern is quite at an end. Barnes has completely drawn off; I still have the same idea that he has never made up his mind respecting matrimony, although he might have been thinking of it, and he certainly was a little inconsistent. Mrs Astor was in too great a hurry. Fanny has now decided to remain here another month or two, instead of proceeding on her travels, which I am delighted at. It certainly in my opinion is the most eligible place for her, and Danvers who requires society such as he meets with here. He tumbled off his horse the other day & put his shoulder out, but is quite well again.

Our departure from here was fixed for tomorrow, but has been put off for a day or two. We are soon to give up this house, and take up an abode with Mr Bernard again, in the Champs Élysées. In the first instance we go to the king at Brussels, and I suppose will make a tour of the frontier before we go to England.

I have had a great change in my establishment. That ungrateful dog Dukemon has chosen to quit me. I believe because he did not like to ride with my aunt, and I have consequently turned away my small boy, as he has no steady person now to chastise him. However this change, I reckon, will save me near fifty pound a year, I have hired a man I have known a long time, who has lived two years with the Duc d'Angoulême, and who bears a very good character. My state is all in very good order. The ministry chez nous, seems to have taken root again. With best love, believe me, my dear uncle, your dutiful and affectionate nephew,

John Fremantle

Felton has got something the matter with his foot, which came of itself.

In late April John wrote that the duke was at the Hague but that he was busy at headquarters copying Stewart's dispatches from Paris for the duke.

Cambrai, 26 April 1816, Friday

My dear uncle,

You will (I fear) have thought me very shabby for not writing, but the fact is I have always been detained, copying Stewart's letters & dispatches on the day he sends the messengers through, for the duke at the Hague. He will return here on Monday, and I suppose very shortly go to Paris.

Did you receive the books directed to the universities. I gave them to Betsy's* man to send directed to you; in haste. Your ever affectionate nephew,

John Fremantle

A month later, still at Cambrai, John was in charge of headquarters in the absence of Felton Hervey who was away with the duke. The purchase of the company was still rumbling on, the purchase price was now £4,500!

Cambrai, 14 May 1816

My dear uncle,

It is quite Fanny's own fault that the power of attorney was not duly arranged before I left Paris. I told them every day that I was sure it would end as it has done, and I think we shall now be obliged to have another one. Felton certainly was very tiresome about it, but my sisters were still more dilatory. I think they left Paris before it reached there, & I think there is an informality in the witnessing which will render it useless.

I only heard of my grandmother's decease the night before my sisters left Paris; from what Georgiana relates, it must have been at last a happy release.

The duke returns to Paris on the 24th, and takes all his establishment with him, and I suppose he will stay some time. The armies cannot be got together here until after the corn is off the ground at the end of August, when we shall have camps and manoeuvres. I dare say before that period he will go for a short time to England. I shall certainly accompany him in the excursion if I can. Since we left Paris there has only been Felton and myself; Percy is sick in Moulins, and Burgh does not return from Ireland till the 20th. During the duke's excursions Felton has accompanied him, and I have remained chargé d'affaires and have had a good deal to do.

I learnt only yesterday that Bowles has stopped the promotion of the regiment at £4,500, which is reckoned very unfair; at all events I had no chance as Sowerby will decidedly purchase. The negotiation

---

* Uncle Tom's wife, the diarist, née Betsy Wynne.

appears entirely at an end. I can learn from Sowerby who the seller is, and will let you know. With best love to my aunt and Eliza, I remain my dear uncle your most dutiful and affectionate nephew,
John Fremantle

PS I have waited till this instant for the *livre de beurre* [pound of butter] which I was promised would be ready, but will send it next time.

The duke and most of the 'family' was off to Paris again shortly but John was likely to remain. His sisters were in Geneva and Fanny was in financial distress which he could not help, having already given his money to a friend in need.

Cambrai, 1 June 1816

My dear uncle,

I must once more explain to you, respecting the power of attorney,* that the delay has never been occasioned by me. I sent it by Fanny's desire to Paris, and I since learn, it followed them to Geneva, this was owing to their good management, in not letting Westmeath having anything to say to the forwarding it. He was sure to make a mess about it, if it was at all possible.

I heard from Albinia yesterday, of the 24th, they have a very pleasant round of society there. Eustons,† Lloyds and several young men, but she tells me Fanny is in dire distress about her money, and I am sorry to say that from my imprudence's at Paris I am not able to be of any assistance to her, particularly as I have lately listened to a call of a friend of mine.

The duke and all his establishment are going to Paris on the morning of the 5th on that day I shall send my bay mare, and a horse of Felton's from hence to Calais, and if the duke chooses to let me go, I shall come to England for a few weeks. He is only going to Paris for his amusement, and the three other scribes will be there, & I am sure I shall do no good there; but if I find it will not do, I will send you word from Paris and you can send over for the two animals. Pray do not imagine that I wish to be let off my promise, for I will say nothing about her until you ride her yourself again. Felton's is sure to suit you if mine does not.

---

* The power of attorney was to be established to allow the arrangement of Frances's affairs during her absence.
† Henry Fitzroy, first son of George Henry Fitzroy, the 4th Duke of Grafton held the courtesy title of Euston. He was married to Mary Berkeley, but had no children at this time.

I am sorry to say I suffer very much from my eyes more than I ever have done, and I cannot think the reason of it. The scurf adheres so very much to my eyelids, and consequently inflames them a great deal more. Pray remember me to my aunt and Eliza, and believe me, your most affectionate nephew,
John Fremantle

John did actually accompany the duke to Paris and there arranged for the elusive power of attorney to be witnessed and his spare horses to be sent to his uncle.

Paris, 10 June 1816

My dear uncle,
The two horses were to leave Cambrai on the 8th and arrive at Calais on or before the 14th. I gave the man a note to Major Shaw* of the Staff who is stationed there, to ration and take care of them, and also wrote to him from hence yesterday to apprise him of their arrival.

Taylor is going from hence in a week, and he could see them embarked or you can send over to me, and I will order them before, if you think proper. As soon as ever Percy arrives, I shall ask the duke to let me go over.

I have sent the power of attorney, which I found here with Westmeath to Watkins by this post signed and witnessed, I hope regularly. There is no news here, the whole town occupied about Berri's marriage. Pray remember me to my aunt and Pussy, and believe me, your most dutiful and affectionate nephew,
John Fremantle

John wrote of his imminent departure with the duke for home and of a failed plot to kill the three French royal princes.

Paris, 27 June 1816, Thursday

My dear uncle,
At last I have received your letter which I was a long time expecting. Major Shaw sent me your letter and I wrote to him yesterday to send the horses over immediately, however I dare say I shall arrive as soon as them, for the duke goes on Saturday, and I shall go at the same time. At our ball the other night, where the three princes† and Madame de

---

* Major James Shaw of the quartermaster general's office, who later became Shaw–Kennedy and wrote his famous *Notes on the Battle of Waterloo*, published in 1865. He commanded at Calais during the three years of the Army of Occupation.
† The three princes were d'Artois, d'Angoulême and Berri.

Berri were, it appears there was an attempt to burn the premises, for some loose wet cartridges in rags were found fizzing, nearly on fire in a cellar where there were two casks of oil. Luckily the smell attracted attention & when the servant went into the place it was quite full of smoke, and it is supposed in a few seconds more, the fire would have taken.

It was a beautiful fete & it really would have been a thousand pities to have had the harmony disturbed by such a proceeding. Ever my dear uncle, your most dutiful and affectionate nephew,
        John Fremantle

The duke had been prevented from travelling to England by problems with some of the foreign contingents of the Army of Occupation, particularly on this occasion the Bavarians.

Paris, 10 July 1816

My dear uncle,
I certainly have been very remiss lately, but I have at the same time been very busy. I cannot imagine how our new army will continue together, we must have constant bickerings, there has been a very serious difference with the Bavarians respecting their contingent,* and I think all the others will be very hard to keep in order, perhaps the duke may succeed, but I am confident no other person would. It is quite impossible in my opinion that he should come to England for the present, for the machine such as it is, is only kept together by him.

Our departure is decidedly put off, but for how long, we do not know. A week ago all our matters were made, and I expected to be off in a couple of days. The whole of Paris I may say, excepting Richelieu, were in the greatest alarm, I speak of all parties seen, who all agree that it is much better for us to remain until the proper order of things is arranged than to go now with a chance of returning amongst them.

The Westmeaths are here, and my lady is very much feted. Monsieur and the Duc de Berri have both called upon her, and the whole boutique of the Tuilleries have been markedly civil.

Fanny I am happy to tell you is a great deal better, as for Albinia the day is not long enough for her. Mrs Aston and her are inseparable; that little woman it appears cannot live without her. She is always sending for her.

I was present the other morning at a reconciliation between Lady

---

* The governments of the small contingents found the burden onerous and constantly sought to withdraw some of their troops surreptitiously; they also interfered with the local French tax collectors, causing disputes.

Caher and Mrs Bradshaw, which went off remarkably well;* it was brought about by Lady Westmeath. The visit is to be returned, but the terms of the reconciliation are that no intimacy is ever to take place.

The duke has been in better humour lately, but what do you think? That fool Webster is going to prosecute the editor of the newspaper for inserting certain paragraphs. The trial is to come on next month. It strikes me a thousand pities they do not allow the subject to die away. If I am not mistaken, there is much fondness between certain parties.

Adieu my dear uncle with best love to my aunts, Eliza & Georgiana, believe me, your most dutiful and affectionate nephew,
John Fremantle

PS There is a gown here for Eliza which Louis has packed very nicely, but God knows when we shall be able to send it. It is as large as an Imperial.†

Despite the issues raised in the last letter, the duke and hence John, were in England in July, the duke proceeding to Cheltenham to pick up the boys for the holidays.

Hamilton Place, Monday, (dated on the reverse 29 July)
My dear uncle,
I received your note this morning and am not insensible to the reproof contained in it.

I return you the five-pound note you enclosed to me, as had the mare not been here I should certainly have hired a gig and horse, which would have cost me much more. Ever my dear uncle, your most dutiful and affectionate nephew,
John Fremantle

Soon they were back in Paris having toured the Belgian border fortresses.

Paris, Thursday 23 August 1816
My dear uncle,
We have been so constantly on the wing since I left town that it has been quite impossible to send you a line since my departure. I arrived in very good time at Dover, and got my gig on board that evening. The She Worcester‡ was very much knocked up before we reached

---

* Mrs Bradshaw and Lady Caher were sisters; the Lady Westmeath that brought about the reconciliation was Emilia (née Cecil), Mr's Bradshaw's daughter in law.
† A case or trunk made for the roof of a carriage; he means it would fill one!
‡ Worcester had married Georgiana Frederica Fitzroy in 1814; she was pregnant in

Brussels, and it certainly would have gone very hard with her, had we not been able to leave her there during our three days' excursion; we were obliged to start every morning by daylight, and seldom got to our halting place before eleven at night. We travelled over a beautiful country the whole way. I really think the banks of the Meuse for richness and scenery is superior to anything I have ever seen. The duke has been in tearing spirits, and continues in very good humour.

This place is dreadfully stupid; full of [John] Bulls who no person ever saw before, save the Carringtons,* Lord Cotton,† his wife, & a few others, consequently I am not sorry to leave it, which we do on the 1st for our country house, I expect it will be very gay. Adieu my dear uncle, Felton is hurrying me to dinner, ever your most dutiful and affectionate nephew,

John Fremantle

John's correspondence slowed as his workload increased. The duke had been touring the various contingents to review them and to inspect the fortresses. Now he was settled at Cambrai, the duke gave up much of his time to hunting, the business only requiring him at headquarters for a few days a week.

Cambrai, 24 September 1816

My dear uncle,

You must not be surprised at not having heard from me for so long a time, for I have been on voyages ever since and only returned the night before last more dead than alive, having been knocked and tossed about most cruelly over the worst roads that mortal was ever condemned to travel. I am however glad to have made the journey. It was extremely gratifying to see an English general everywhere received and paid the honours of a sovereign by the French & foreign powers. Bitche & Verdun saluted him.

It has also raised my opinion very high of my own country and nation, when I compare them in every way with the systems of the other powers. The Prussians are the best, but they I believe are very inferior. We are to see the Russian corps the beginning of next month. The Duke of Cambridge is coming, and we are to have some grand manoeuvres for him.

1816, eventually giving birth to Augusta.

* Robert Smith, 1st Baron Carrington of Upton and family.

† Sir Stapleton Cotton and his new wife Caroline Greville; Cotton commanded the cavalry during the Army of Occupation. He calls him Lord Cotton as he had become Baron Combemere in 1814.

Worcester & his wife remained here, she must have been bored to death if F[rancis] Russell* had not been here to console her. We go to the chateau tomorrow, and our races commence. The little black mare I expect has a chance for the pony stakes. Felton has two or three horses to run. I understand my sisters are gone to Florence, but although I have written I have not heard from them since I left you.

If you would have the goodness to tell me the name of the agent at Bristol, I would write to him to make him give me a description of the farm. Pray remember me to my aunt and Pussy. I will send you word how our party at the chateau succeeds.

The arrangement at present stands thus, his hounds twice a week, beagles twice a week; twice a week come to Cambrai to do business, & Sunday Lord Hill's greyhounds after church. Ever my dear uncle, your most dutiful and affectionate nephew,

John Fremantle

In his next letter John reported a particularly awkward circumstance, with the duke publicly castigating Doctor Hume, whom he banished and Felton Hervey. A heavy atmosphere was to continue for some time, with the duke severely out of sorts.

John and the others were incredibly busy preparing for a 'Grand Review' of over 30,000 men.

Cambrai, 18 October 1816

My dear uncle,
I received your letter this day week, but I could not answer it on the Tuesday although I was extremely anxious to give you an account of a breeze which has happened in the family. An event the most remarkable I have ever witnessed since my connection with the duke, and I feel you will be glad to hear the rights of the story.

His Grace has not been well pleased I think since the day after his return from the grand tour, but nothing particular occurred till the other evening, when he invited Felton, Hume (the doctor), the Russian, the Austrian, & the Duchess of Richmond† to cut in at whist. The two former excused themselves, and sometime afterwards, they each of them with others, were cutting in at another whist table, upon

---

* Frances Russell, Marquess of Tavistock was a politician, later 7th Duke of Bedford.
† Hume (Drew 1988) was for many years personal surgeon to the Duke of Wellington. The Russian was almost certainly General Michael, Baron Woronzoff who commanded the Russian contingent and the Austrian probably General Johann, Baron Frimont who commanded the Austrian. The wife of the fourth Duke of Richmond, Lady Charlotte (née Gordon), held the famous ball before Waterloo.

which he exclaimed in a voice like thunder, addressing himself to them, that 'it was customary when the commander in chief invited a person to play, not to be refused'. Hume smiled, or appeared to smile, on which he said, 'Yes it may be a damn good joke, but I can tell you, it won't do'; a dead silence reigned for 10 minutes. There were present Sir D[avid] Baird, the Prussian, Lady Jane Lennox,* besides our family. I was sitting on the sofa with Lady Jane; before he went to bed, he told Felton he desired to see all the gentlemen of his family together with Mr Hume the next morning. When we appeared he began by accusing Hume of disrespect, and in the harshest manner dismissed him his family desiring him never to appear before unless sent for; he then read a chapter to us in general, accused us of inattention to a late order he has issued respecting dress & addressed himself directly, in an instance or two of trifling neglect to duty, not to me. From that time to the present hour he has scarcely addressed his conversation to one of us, or one of us to him. Felton is very sore for he imagines that a great deal is meant for him, but Lord Russell, Percy & every one must feel for the way in which he exposed himself before so many foreigners, and are very much disgusted at his procedure towards them. He fancies I think that we were laughing at his being obliged to set down against his will, with the Duchess of Richmond. It certainly did look like it, and therefore I can make every allowance for his feeling offended by it, but I am confident no slight was intended, or had the idea entered any of our heads. So much for that, it is a very unpleasant thing to have happened and he seems very much annoyed. I have several times endeavoured to open a conversation, but he does not answer the question put to him. In the whole business he has evinced a pride, & haughtiness that I always thought foreign to him, or that I should not have conceived could have belonged to the breast of any man.

We are all occupied now about the review, which is on the 21st. The Dukes of Kent and Cambridge are to be here, as all the foreign generals & great people from all quarters. The ground is near Valenciennes. We shall be full 30,000 British. The Danes and Saxons are to be the enemy, and we are to have grand manoeuvring. If it goes off well I hope we shall have a return of good humour from the Great Man. I will write you word about this.

Many thanks for your information respecting Watkins's trip to Ireland. Pray lay out my money as you propose. I shall certainly write to the tiger at Bristol & make him tell me what it is I own. By Watkins's

---

* This was General Sir David Baird. The Prussian was almost certainly General Hans Ernst Karl, Count Ziethen, commander of the Prussian contingent. Lady Jane Lennox was a daughter of the Duke and Duchess of Richmond.

desire before I left England, on my arrival at Paris I drew upon him on Fanny's account for £80 which she owed to a banker there, the draft has been returned, I suppose because W[atkins] was absent. I told him the amount was near £200 which it proves to be, but the banker was in fault for not letting me know both sums, & only gave me the first, which I drew for. This Mr Callaghan, Bradshaw writes me word, is very angry, & it was very wrong of Fanny to have done so for she had never employed Mr Callaghan except in this way. You will see what Bradshaw thinks of it by his letter which I enclose. The Worcester's went away on the 12th there was no g[nashin]g of teeth on Russell's part, whatever there might have been on hers. I think the members of our family were much too scandalous about the business, were I to say I really think all is right. I heard from Albinia two days ago, they were then at Florence, by her account I think going on very well. I am bored to death with his horses (D[anver]'s), I cannot sell them, they are very fine looking but the most determined rips that ever were in the world.

Pray remember me to my aunt, but best love to her and Pussy, believe me, my dear uncle, your most dutiful and affectionate nephew,
John Fremantle

It seems that the duke's humour had soon regained its normal form and the unfortunate incident was forgotten. The review had gone off splendidly and John had enjoyed looking after the Duke of Cambridge. He had however a bad fall and was nursing his shoulder.

Cambrai, 25 October 1816

My dear uncle,
I received your letter of the 20th yesterday. You will have received mine of Tuesday last, giving you a long description & account of the grand breeze. I am now happy to tell you, it all appears to be at an end, and the serenity of the duke's temper seems to be returned to its usual level.

Lady Georgiana Lennox who arrived on Monday, said to him the night before last, on Felton's playing with Lady Jane, 'Why don't you make your aides de camp treat your company with more respect,' upon which he laughed, and said, 'why don't you both fall upon him, you then would surely be more than a match for him,' very good-humouredly.

The royal dukes arrived on the 19th and 20th and the reviews took place on the 21st and 22nd and went off remarkably well, though the weather was extremely bad and the corps were under arms for seventeen hours the last day. The princes were very tired, and I do not think they understood much of the operations. I escorted the Duke of Cambridge from the last stage, in here, and was in attendance the morning he went away at 6 o'clock but he positively insisted on the escort being dismissed. I had a vast deal of conversation with him during his stay, he was extremely affable, and certainly very much pleased at the attention and civility shown him, and gave me an additional message to that effect for the Duke of Wellington. I had a frightful fall the last day which I feel still from my shoulder to the elbow.

Stanhope's court martial* is over, but I cannot imagine what the delay can be in making the sentence known, for it went from hence three weeks ago. It is a sad bad business.

I understand the duke is going to Brussels in a fortnight, and I should think would then soon go to Paris. Lady Hamilton is returned there and a quantity of Mr Bull's family gone there to spend the winter. I dare say it will be very gay.

Lord and Lady E. Somerset† are well, & the whole Richmond family. Arthur Hill‡ arrives tomorrow therefore I expect we shall have high gambols. Best love to my aunt & Eliza, and believe me, my dear uncle, your most dutiful and affectionate nephew,

    John Fremantle

Cambrai, 1 November 1816

My dear uncle,

I have no news to tell you only I am rather surprised at not having heard from you since my account of the breeze which took place.

Sir Henry Wellesley and Lady Georgiana§ only remained with us two days, and proceeded to Paris on their way to Madrid. Lord and Lady Edward Somerset¶ have been with us this fortnight. They are going in a day or two. Our gambols have gone on famously since Arthur Hill's return. We made such a row last night that nothing could equal.

---

* Lieutenant the Honourable Augustus Stanhope, 12th Light Dragoons, was charged with conspiring with others to seduce Lord Beauchamp into a game of cards by which they fleeced him of some £15,000 (£630,000 in modern terms). Stanhope was found guilty of the charge and dismissed the service.

† Major General Robert Edward Henry Somerset had commanded the heavy cavalry in Spain.

‡ Lord Arthur Moyses William Hill, 2nd Baron Sandys.

§ Henry, the Duke of Wellington's younger brother, was ambassador to Spain. His first wife Lady Charlotte Cadogan ran off with Henry Paget (the later Earl of Uxbridge of Waterloo fame) and Henry married Lady Georgina Charlotte Cecil, daughter of the Marquess of Salisbury in February 1816.

¶ Major General Lord Edward Somerset and his wife Louisa Augusta (née Courtenay), daughter of the Earl of Devon.

We are going with the duke tomorrow to meet the Duke of Kent[*] at Valenciennes who dined with his regiment in state. Felton is just returned from the races, not having made a profitable trip. Ever my dear uncle, your most dutiful and affectionate nephew,

John Fremantle

Cambrai, 11 November 1816

My dear uncle,

I take the opportunity of a special messenger going to England to forward to you answer of your letter of the 4th.

I assure you, you are very much mistaken in your surmise about the niece. I think moreover that the scandal from the members of the family was very unfairly and unjustly propagated, and I think you are mistaken in laying so great a stress upon what is termed here follies.

The Duchess of Richmond and the whole family left us on Friday last, much regretted, the old one from the constant sport she afforded, and the young ones for their amusement.

The house was a constant scene of cheerfulness or rather rioting from morning until night, mostly at the expense of the Old Woman. It is filling again very fast, we seldom sit down to dinner under 20 persons.

I have received a detailed statement from Mr Clarke at Bristol of which I will send you a copy another day, as I want to ask your advice upon the subject of it. Ever my dear uncle, your most dutiful and affectionate nephew,

John Fremantle

John now had details of his inheritance, a farm in Gloucestershire, and planned to lease it for seven years at a time. The weather was awful and the duke's humour was no better.

Cambrai, 22 November 1816

My dear uncle,

I enclose you the particulars of the farm in Gloucestershire. Of course I do not pretend to know anything about such matters. It strikes me however that there is no necessity for my having an agent. Farmer Fry, or whoever rents the land I should think could always remit me the amount through Greenwood and Cox.[†]

I shall not answer Mr Clarke until I hear from you, respecting the

---

[*] The fourth son of George III, Field Marshal Edward the Duke of Kent was colonel of the 1st Foot (Royals).

[†] Greenwood, Cox & Hammersley of Craig's Court were his army agents.

new lease, which I suppose you will recommend me to give for another 7 years. I should prefer however letting it from year to year if you see no objection. When I was in England, you said something about the sale of it. This I confess, I should be sorry to do.

I see by the papers and all the private letters seem to confirm the general riotous disposition evinced in England. I hope however, government will act in a determined manner, and not by half measures.

We have been well at the chateau, these last few days. We have had two tremendous nights of hurricane & snow, & the country is in a shocking state owing to it. Hunting put an end to, in consequence. The duke is in very poor humour again, Felton quite well.

Pray give my love to my aunt and Pussy, and believe me, my dear uncle, your most dutiful and affectionate nephew,
    John Fremantle

Postscript: The Duke goes to Brussels on the 13th for a few days. I suppose we shall go Paris very shortly after our return from thence.

His uncle agreed to the leasing plan and a power of attorney was signed; John also discovered that was actually better off than he had feared. The duke was off to see King William I of the Netherlands* in a fortnight.

Cambrai, 28 November 1816

My dear uncle,
I received your letter of the 24th last night, and will attend to your advice respecting the renewal of the lease. I had already Mr Clarke's original paper, what I sent to you was a copy. I now send you the power of attorney fully executed. I hope as long as the occupation lasts, I shall not have reason to touch my funds on the other side of the water, at least I have made that determination, which I have no fear of keeping as I will not frequent the salon on my return to Paris. I drew the other day on Greenwood & desired my friend Mr Davis at the same time to send me my account, believing I was £50 in his debt at least, and was agreeably surprised last night with a letter from him couched in very facetious terms, saying I should find by my account,

---

* At the Congress of Vienna, Stadtholder William Frederick of Nassau, who reigned in Holland, had Belgium (or the southern Netherlands) added to his domain and he was raised to king. This new kingdom was termed the 'Netherlands'. However, this unhappy amalgamation of a Catholic, French-speaking Belgium with a staunchly Protestant, Dutch-speaking and republican Holland made for an uneasy marriage. In 1830 Belgium finally revolted and the two countries split again in 1839 with their own monarchs.

that I was more than that sum on the credit side. I can't tell you how it revived me.

The king returns to Brussels from The Hague on the 9th December & I expect the duke will go there then for a week. I shall certainly go at the same time. We have had the Asgill* at the chateau; she treated poor Lord Lynedoch† worse than a dog, and made herself otherwise extremely ridiculous. We christened her Elle Merciless. Lady Frances Cole‡ is the only visitor there now.

Mrs Wells was only a few days at Valenciennes and has left it, these two months, John Wells is now with her at Brussels, not very well.

I have also had a long letter from Albinia, since Trip destroyed himself.§ It is a horrid thing, but I must say I think the world and the community in general could very well spare him.

I have purchased a pair of very fine long legged grey horses, they are of a breed extremely quiet, strong enough for your carriage, and my aunt I am convinced could drive either of them. If you should ever fancy such a thing, pray let me know and I will send them over. With best love to my aunt and Eliza, believe me, my dear uncle, your most dutiful and affectionate nephew,

John Fremantle

Suddenly, much sooner than expected, Wellington was off to Brussels and John was to follow him as soon as he could.

Cambrai, 3 December 1816

My dear uncle,

I have only a moment to tell you we are all on the move this morning after breakfast. The duke announced his intention of going to Brussels and started accordingly. He desired the duchess to go to England tomorrow, he returns on Sunday next.

Felton was very unwell the day before yesterday with rather a severe attack of fever, this morning he rode from the chateau all in the damp & is gone with the duke to travel all night. I think we shall be on the road to Paris towards the 20th of the month.

I start for Brussels tomorrow. With best love to my aunt & Eliza,

---

* Major General Sir Charles Asgill's wife Jemima Sophia (née Ogle) who was a close friend and held a frequent correspondence with Lord Lynedoch.

† Lieutenant General Sir Thomas Graham, Baron Lynedoch.

‡ General the honourable Sir Galbraith Lowry Cole had missed the Battle of Waterloo, marrying Lady Frances Harris, daughter of 1st Earl of Malmesbury on 15 June 1815 in England.

§ Baron Trip committed suicide in 1816.

believe me, my dear uncle your most dutiful and affectionate nephew,
John Fremantle

Two weeks later John was back at Cambrai, having furtively smuggled Lady Hamilton's diamonds across the border to avoid customs dues.

Cambrai, 17 December 1816

My dear uncle,
I have written all the news I have to my aunt who was so very anxious about Felton, whose account will amuse you.

I have had a very unpleasant commission at Brussels viz. to get Lady Hamilton's diamonds which are tremendous out of a banker's hands. I had great difficulty in making the man deliver up his charge, & still greater anxiety in getting them across the frontier.* However I have succeeded happily with all but one case, by going through in my buggy at night. You may conceive how nervous I was. I drove that gig in tandem, it was as black as possible and I once lost my way. Adieu my dear uncle, believe me always, your most dutiful and affectionate nephew,
John Fremantle

Without warning, the duke left for England to pay a fleeting visit on the Prince Regent, almost certainly regarding the political unrest in England, but he still intended to be in Paris by 1 January.

[London] Thursday, 2 o'clock p.m. (dated on the back 20 December)
My dear uncle,
Alava,† and Arthur Hill, and myself, are just arrived with the duke. I suppose he will go down to Brighton tomorrow if the prince does not come to town. I must of course accompany him if he does; I thought it was best to come with him as Felton declined it. We are to leave this so as to arrive at Paris on the 1st. All our baggage was to leave Cambrai on the 26th as was the original intention. Ministers went over for him to confer, therefore I do not suppose they will let him away so soon. I should think they must be in a bad way. Ever my dear uncle, your most dutiful & affectionate nephew,
John Fremantle

---

* This was presumably to avoid custom dues at the border.
† Miguel Ricardo de Álava y Esquivel had originally served as an officer in the Spanish Navy at the Battle of Trafalgar; later he became the Spanish representative at Wellington's headquarters throughout the Peninsular War and was then appointed Spanish ambassador to the Netherlands.

The duke stuck to his plans and even arrived at Paris early and both the duke and Alava had been particularly pleasant on the trip. The French welcomed the duke with great warmth, but turmoil had erupted in French political circles once again.

Paris, 13 January 1817

My dear uncle,
We arrived here most prosperously on the 31st at night, the duke having been in the greatest good humour all the time. Alava was delighted with Brighton, and the prince was exceedingly civil to him. I do not understand that there is to be any change at present in our cabinet.

I found all our boutique here quite well. Felton was taken ill as soon as he arrived at Brussels but recovered as usual next day. I cannot learn that anything particular took place that would interest my aunt on his score. I thought him looking ill when I first saw him, but he has picked up in his looks wonderfully since.

The French ministers and people have been particularly civil to the duke, and I think upon the whole receive us better than I should have expected, an interesting discipline comes on today in the Chamber of Deputies, '*sur la liberté individuelle*' [for individual liberty], and I should think more squabbling will ensue. For my own part I do not think the present session is likely to turn out less turbulent than the late one, I do not find any person of any party speak in a satisfied tone. Old Talleyrand's house is much pleasanter since his disgrace.* The people who fill it are all going from different motives.

The shoals of [John] Bull & Co. in Paris is something terrible to look at. The duke declared he is afraid to open his house in consequence. We have been very gay and it promises to continue so. I sat next but one yesterday at Monsieur de Roges' to Mademoiselle Ruffo with whom I made a stronger acquaintance in a shorter time than I ever did with any young lady before. She has invited me to dance with her at Stuarts this evening. She desires to be particularly remembered to Eliza. With best love, believe me, my dear uncle, your most dutiful and affectionate nephew,
John Fremantle

The duke held a number of very glamorous balls, which kept John extremely busy. The American Caton sisters arrived from England; little

---

* Charles Maurice de Talleyrand-Périgord, 1st Prince de Bénévente was banished from court for a few months when he criticised the elections for the Chambers of 1816 for electing a very pro-royalist chamber.

did he suspect that they would all become very familiar with this family.*

Paris, 5 February 1817

My dear uncle,

I was so dead knocked up the day after our Ball I could not write to you, it was extremely brilliant and I bustled about to keep things going at a tremendous rate; now our fancy ball is fixed for the 17th, therefore from the 7th until it is over I shall have no peace, for all the people fancy that I have the power to invite and pester me with millions of billets which I am in most part obliged to answer, and the civility of all is something quite laughable. Mrs Wells† arrived the day after I wrote to my aunt, she is quite delighted. I had ready for her a very nice apartment at a very cheap rate, the corner house in the Boulevard de la Madeleine.

The duke and all of us have been very busy in ushering about Mrs Patterson‡ and her sisters. I do not know whether you were acquainted with them in England, but I confess I have been very much *épris* [the prize] with the young one Miss Louisa Caton. There never was so naïve a little creature.§

We have been extremely gay, the ladies have been quarrelling for their days of entertainment, we have Lady Mansfield¶ and Lady Conyngham** in reserve for Thursday and Tuesday next.

I see by the papers you have been giving Lord Cochrane†† a dressing [down]. I am delighted at it, as in my opinion nothing can be so disgraceful and low-lived as his conduct.

---

* For details on the Caton sisters, see *Sisters of Fortune* by Jehanne Wake, Chatto & Windus, London 2010.

† John's Aunt Sarah (née Fremantle), having married Vice-Admiral Thomas Wells.

‡ Mrs Marianne Patterson (née Caton) was the daughter of a wealthy American tobacco plantation owner in Maryland and was married to Robert Patterson (the brother of Betsy whom Jerome Bonaparte had married but was forced to divorce by Napoleon). Marianne had come to Europe in 1816 with her two younger half sisters Elizabeth and Louisa Catherine and their beauty soon gave them access to London society. Marianne was to marry Wellington's older brother Richard in 1825.

§ A swift judgement that he was quick to change!

¶ Lady Frederica Murray (née Markham), was the wife of David, 3rd Earl Mansfield.

** Lady Elizabeth Conyngham (née Denison), was the wife of the 1st Marquess Conyngham.

†† Admiral Thomas Lord Cochrane had been found guilty at a trial for Stock Exchange fraud in 1814 and was imprisoned for a year, sacked from the Royal Navy and his knighthood was removed by the king. He was however re-elected as a member of parliament on his release from prison and quickly become a champion of the repressed and presented petitions to parliament demanding reform and brought forth the plight of the poor at every opportunity.

Our household goes on in the good old way. The duke in famous order, Arthur Hill* goes home in a day or two for his election, that is the only change likely to take place.

Lord Carrington's Sir Smith saw Lionel† at Munich ten days ago, and gives a capital account of him, in famous spirits, and delighted being chief. I dined there the day before yesterday, they are very civil to me.

I am happy to tell you I have kept my resolution nearly; last night being the first time the salon has had me within its walls, since my arrival. I was carried there with others, but came away within the half hour, content with leaving my 10 napoleons‡ behind. I feel myself rich and very happy and nothing but the salon can make me otherwise. I hope I shall soon hear from you.

Pray give my best love to my aunt and Eliza, and believe me, my dear uncle your most dutiful and affectionate nephew,

John Fremantle

The news of political unrest in England concerned John who held very conservative views. They also had moved to new offices in Paris.

Paris, 10 February 1817

My dear uncle,

I have received yours of the 1st and I must tell you how much I am pleased with your reasoning. I confess when I was in England I was inclined to laugh at all the fears I heard set forth, but this last business appears too wanton not to excite alarm and it continues in a way that leads me to think the 'mal persons' are not entirely confined to the lower orders; liberty is a very precious gem, but when carried to licentiousness it is very bad and I think no thinking person ought to attempt to improve on British liberty; so much for my politics. We hear on this side, that your party are coming round.

I gave you in my last a long account of my occupations and amusements here; I am now in the full heat of the invitations for our fancy Ball on this day week. I wish it was over with all my heart. Nobody is lodged in the same house with the duke. Felton, myself &

---

* Lord Arthur Hill won his election and became an MP for Co. Down.

† Almost certainly he refers to Robert John Smith, only son of 1st Baron Carrington, who was to become the 2nd Baron Carrington in 1838. He was MP for Wendover at this time. Lionel Hervey was now one of the legation at the court of Maximilian I King of Bavaria, at Munich.

‡ A napoleon was a coin worth 20 francs; therefore the 200 francs (10 napoleons) he had spent was equal to £8 (approximately £340 today).

the office are in the Rue Mont Tabor close to [Rue] Mondovi, where you lived. I rather think we shall go next week down to Mont St Martin* to hunt for a few days. Felton was not very well yesterday and is ailing, today with fever but nothing of consequence.

Louis Dixhuit who you enquire after so tenderly I am happy to tell you is charming well again, he never lost his appetite. I have not heard of the quarrel you talk of between the French & Swiss Guard. The hatred of the former nation towards Mr Bull I think increases every term.

I have not heard from my sisters for an age although I wrote to know what I should do with the 60 guineas I sold a horse of theirs for.

Nothing can equal the gaieties here, balls continually, Mrs Wells and family enjoy themselves very much, the latter is very much admired here.

Pray make my best love to my aunt and Pussy, and believe me, my dear uncle your dutiful and affectionate nephew,

John Fremantle

Postscript: my eyes are very much mended since the application of the salve.

John was forced to reassure his uncle that the visit to the gambling house was a one off and that his finances were still sound.

Paris, 24 February 1817

My dear uncle,

What could have possessed you when you wrote your last note? What I told you about the salon was the exact case, but I assure you at the time I mentioned the circumstances of my having been there I chided myself much, at only having been there once and do still, as I have no intention of giving way to the habit. It makes me feel as airy and comfortable as possible the idea of being so well in my finances, on the 1st of March I shall have 75 Napoleons to receive, don't owe a sous; all my servants 5 in number settled with to the end of February. You must also have misconstrued my letter. I must have made a great mistake, I meant to have told you, that by the constant application of the salve to my eyes they were considerably better, and I should be very glad to have some more.

I am sorry to tell you that Mrs Wells has been thrown out of her

---

* His house at Mount St Martin was a country retreat with ample hunting, away from the pressures of Paris.

carriage this morning. Fanny, Henry Wells,* and Mr Disbrowe† were driving in the Place Saint Germain when they were *accrocher*'d [struck] by another carriage, upset and the whole party thrown out except Fanny who remained inside, and has only hurt her hand. Mrs Wells has been bled, Henry has hurt his side but not materially. Disbrowe got up and stopped the horses, the coachman having been thrown from his seat. I will let you know on Thursday how they all are again.

Felton is quite well again, his illness only lasted him two days. Our Ball went off better than it was possible to have been expected, nothing could be more magnificent or brilliant, and every person delighted.

The duke the world says, is badly *épiné* [thorny] with Mrs Patterson, I think he seems to like her myself. Her sisters are also great favourites, they are all going to England in the middle of March. We are all on the best of terms with His Grace. I should not be at all surprised if he went to England in the summer, for I hear nothing mentioned of the duchess's appearance here, which was likely she would have done after her boys' holidays. Whether he does or not, I shall ask leave for a month.

I am afraid we shall be obliged to part with Webster. The duke you know is a queer person and likes that place to be filled as it always has been by a sergeant. He will be a very great loss to us, James Butler has often spoken to me about such a person, and if he is now in want of one, I can recommend Webster most strongly in every way, his place here is worth £100 a year. Give my best love to my aunt and Pussy, and believe me, my dear uncle your most dutiful and affectionate nephew,
John Fremantle

In his next, John informed his uncle that Felton was to marry Louisa Caton, sister of Mrs Patterson, in London on 24 April.

Paris, 20 March 1817

My dear uncle,
I am very glad, I have never mentioned anything respecting Felton's *amour*, for fear my opinions might have been erroneous. He never told me of it till last night, but I had learnt it a few hours before from Mr Patterson. The family start tomorrow, therefore you will soon be able to judge for yourselves.

She is a very charming girl, I think. She is not exactly what I should

---

* Henry and Frances (Fanny) Wells were John's cousins being his Aunt Sarah's children. Eventually Henry married his sister Albinia, and Frances married Felton's brother Lionel.

† Lieutenant and Captain George Disbrowe, 1st Foot Guards.

chuse [*sic*] as a wife, very naive and natural, extremely good natured, sensible, and good hearted few accomplishments, and has been a favourite child. This is still secret, but the duke is coming over in April, and I shall of course come with him to assist at the ceremony.*

The young lady was given out as a fortune, she has now not a sous, but will eventually have £50,000, but between you & I, all things considered, if she had the money what they call on the nail, I should think her dear at the money but they are each equally in love, which is a great blessing, & Felton swears he will not play anymore & he never has been for the last five weeks. He is in high spirits & looking very well.

I will write to you more fully next post on this subject, & assure Eliza I will do the same to her, but really have not time now, for the fellow is waiting to close the bag. Fanny Wells has lots of supplicants, Sir Manley Power,† Mr Rice,‡ and Mr Wall, also over for her. Adieu my dear uncle, believe me always, your most dutiful and affectionate nephew,

John Fremantle

In the following letter, John explained fully how he had met Louisa Caton and that Louisa had openly stated that she was marrying beneath her!

Paris, 24 March 1817

My dear uncle,
I was so perplexed last mail that I had not collected half what I wanted to say to you respecting Felton's fate; you must know that two days after the arrival of the Patterson family, they were present at a dinner of forty persons at the duke's. Miss Louisa Caton was sitting on the right of the centre opposite the duke, & I was sitting on the left of the centre on the same side as the duke. I had never seen the young lady before, but something occasioned a laughter between us which was kept up all dinner time, so much so as to attract the attention of Stuart & Madame [D'Lechitz?], who quizzed me a good deal about it.

After dinner I talked to the young lady, and found her just as extraordinary to talk to, as she was to look at. I reported all this right and left and everybody there was anxious to converse with this oddity, but at that stage it was more for the purpose of laughing at, than laughing with her. I used to visit frequently at the house for a week, and when I ceased, Mrs Patterson rather upbraided me for it,

---

* The wedding was set for 24 April 1817.
† Lieutenant General Sir Manley Power.
‡ Probably Mr Edward Royds Rice, who married Miss Elizabeth Rice in 1818.

and I gave her clearly to understand that I did not feel myself equal to any change, and that I feared to trust myself, or something to that purpose. As soon as I understood that the business was settled, which it was before one had time to look about one, between Felton and her, I thought it incumbent on me to go and put as good a face on the thing as I could, although as an admirer of Felton's, I must think with any other friend of his, that he has thrown himself away, but however he says very fairly that he [is] now able to judge and chuse for himself.

I could not help being very much mortified the day before they went away, being for a few moments in the room alone with Miss Louisa, when she began telling me, that she had already told Felton, she did not consider him, her superior in any point of view except in years, that they were the first people in their country & he was not in his by any means, that she was sure she should not have done it, had it not been for the duke who was always extolling and praising him to her. I was so thunderstruck at this, that I had not recovered my senses sufficiently to reply (very luckily), when Mr Patterson came in.

On the morning of their departure Felton and Miss Louisa Caton went 10 miles together in the curricle, and I went in the Patterson carriage, and Mr P[atterson] was so indelicate with his hints respecting the elder Miss Caton and me, that her indignation was at last roused to such a degree, as to tell him, that these sayings & witticisms might do very well in America where he was known, that of course I J[ohn] Fremantle could not misunderstand them; that in England and amongst English people, it was not received; it was very disagreeable to her, and she begged he would discontinue. A dead silence and all looked foolish; I yesterday mentioned this latter part to the duke, and he ended by saying after having asked what Mrs Patterson had said (meaning Miss Caton), 'that's a devilish nice girl too, that is, thinks I to myself' when I told this to Felton he laughed, significantly.

Adieu my dear uncle, remember me affectionately to my aunt and dear Pussy, and believe me, ever your most dutiful and affectionate nephew,

John Fremantle

A two-month gap appears in his correspondence during which they returned to London and witnessed Felton's marriage; but by May, John was back in Cambrai. It would seem that John had nearly missed the duke on his return and had received an admonishment from his uncle.

Cambrai, 20 May 1817

My dear uncle,

I was up to my elbows last Friday, and though extremely anxious to send you a line was absolutely prevented. I know Felton wrote to my aunt a few lines, which I was glad of; many, many thanks for this additional mark of your kindness. I assure you I feel very grateful for it. It is what I have often thought of speaking to you about it before & I will write to McMahon as you desire.

I perceive by your letter that you think I committed some 'extravagance' in not being ready for the duke when he started, but I knew that he had promised to go to Lady Castlereagh, and I knew at the opera of his movements until within half an hour, and when I found out there, that he was not quite decided about going to Lady C[astlereagh's], I set off to Apsley House,* and stopt [*sic*] him at the corner of Hamilton Place. We then went to Pole's and remained there half an hour, having taken up Alava and Percy at Pole's. Madame [Louisa] has entertained the company at the chateau very much. It is impossible not to be very much amused with her. I must tell you of a scene which I think will divert you, though perhaps Mrs F[remantle] might think it too much. On the first evening, the house being very large, she did not know her way to bed, and the duke took her. The instant they were out of the room, the duchess asked Felton whether Mrs H[ervey] would not require her maid; he made no answer she then desired me to ring & Cathcart to call the servant. We are all capital good friends, the duke has been very civil to me he offered me a horse the other day which I declined, as I had already too many. I forget what you said the determination of my sisters was about returning whether to come by Paris to remain, and about what period. I shall be much obliged to you to let me know this, and also where I am to direct to them.

The duke, Burgh, Felton and his [new] wife, started this morning for Brussels. I was left here to send forward Stewart's letters and the English mail today. I shall take those of Friday myself, and return with him. Believe me, my dear uncle, with best love, your most dutiful and affectionate nephew,

John Fremantle

Postscript: William Russell has written to the duke to announce his intended marriage with Miss Rawdon.†

---

* Wellington had bought Apsley House from his brother Richard in 1817.

† Major William Russell, 102nd Foot, became an aide-de-camp to Wellington in 1817. He married Elizabeth Anne Rawdon on 21 June 1817.

A short note told of their imminent arrival in England once again. He does not mention it, but Wellington was due back to partake in the celebrations at the opening of Waterloo Bridge across the Thames on 17 June 1817.

Cambrai, 10 June 1817

My dear uncle,
I have not time to answer my aunt's letter which I received last night on my return to the chateau. We leave this on the 12th & I suppose I shall be in London on the 14th. Will you desire Stag to procure for me a lodging, and you will oblige me much by sending to Vernon's stables where I believe Lady Glengall's* horses stand and have my mare brought to Woodgate's on the 13th. Ever, my dear uncle, your most dutiful & affectionate nephew,
John Fremantle

PS I am bringing home a wild boar, which was found in the woods just cubbed, 17 days ago, if you do not want it I will give it to Frederick.

A few weeks later John was back at Cambrai, recounting a fine dinner at Bromley and details of his return journey.

Tuesday, Cambrai, 7 July 1817

My dear uncle,
Nothing worth relating passed at our dinner at Bromley. After dinner I was much edified by the conversation of those wondrous statesmen Castlereagh, Poole,† Long‡ & Bathurst, it chiefly turned upon flies and fishing; we slept at Rochester that evening, and embarked in Smith's vessel at one on Sunday, and landed at five, we set off from Calais before our servants arrived by the packet which sailed with us. I therefore could not deliver your letter to Souville,§ but I called upon him at his house, himself and wife were *à la campagne* [in the country], but the servants told me Thomas had called there on his landing, and that he had left Calais a week ago, we arrived at the chateau yesterday

---

* Lady Glengall was his Aunt Emilia, formerly Lady Caher, her husband becoming 1st Earl Glengall from 22 January 1816.
† This would appear to be John Poole, the great playwright. It is noticeable that there is a gap in his prodigious writing between 1816–18, when he may have undertaken a Grand Tour.
‡ Charles Long was paymaster of the forces.
§ The previous Baron Souville had been governor of Réunion and had died in 1810 in a duel.

evening at 8 o'clock & found the duchess, her three boys* and Cathcart all well; we are just arrived here for the post. Pray let me know if any of my concerns transpire. I hope Knightly has not forgot the boar, he said he would send for it in a fortnight after he left Town. Pray remember me to my aunt and Eliza and believe me, my dear uncle, your most dutiful and affectionate nephew,

John Fremantle

It would seem that John had been concerned over some indiscretion he had committed while inebriated in London and was relieved that there were no serious consequences. The duke however seems to have been in a very good frame of mind.

Cambrai, Friday 11 July

My dear uncle,

I have heard from Town, and everybody as gay as possible; I am not at all unhappy, on the contrary, I bless the cup which gave me liquor, which prompted me to so rash an act, and for fear I should ever commit another such one, will you believe I have only tasted one pure glass of wine (Sauterne with the duchess) since the 4th July this you will not be sorry for. I really think it agrees better with me, I do not know how long it will last. The more I think of it the more I am impressed with the idea that all has been for the best. I do certainly not think I am fit to sit down yet en famille. You will easily imagine however, that I am extremely anxious to know whether anything has transpired. I expect Mrs Fox† will let me know in a day or two. What do Eliza and my aunt think? If Eliza ever hears of it, she will tell Louisa & then my life will be become a burthen. I fear this beyond measure. We are going to Brussels on the end of the month, and shall be at Paris on the 26th August.

I left the half of the lease in your room. Will you have the goodness to take care of it. Is it not very odd that Mr Clarke has never sent me the remainder.

The duke is in famous ease, good spirits, and great good humour prevails. Pray give my best love to my aunt and Puss and, believe me, my dear uncle your most dutiful and affectionate nephew,

John Fremantle

---

* The Duke and Duchess of Wellington had two boys; the third boy could have been William Richard Arthur Pole-Tylney-Long-Wellesley, son of William Pole Wellesley and Catherine Tylney-Long, who would have been four years old at the time.
† Almost certainly the widow of the Right Honourable Charles James Fox MP, Mrs Elizabeth Bridget Fox (née Armistead).

It would seem that his indiscretion had been a drunken proposal of marriage, but luckily for him, it would appear that it had not been taken seriously. He also had to deal with squabbles between Felton's servants.

Cambrai, Friday 18 July 1817

My dear uncle,

Yours of the 14th I received last night and with the greatest possible satisfaction. I hope nothing has transpired, but I confess I have my doubts & fears, however a great many people will be leaving London, and the history will blow over & be forgotten. I am still in the same mind, and think myself very fortunate in having escaped, for I cannot fancy I could ever reconcile to myself a person, who would let such an animal as Delegate Burke* talk to her for a second time and she used to suffer him to flirt with her I understand. There is nothing here which has happened yet in the shape of news.

As Felton is to be with you on the 21st, pray tell him there is a blow up amongst his stable people. I have had all the parties before me, the cook knows nothing of the quarrel, and was rather affronted at my supposing she was likely to know. The groom & the lad of the 18th Hussars can't keep their horses together at all, and as I do not chuse [*sic*] to send the lad away & replace him by another, and can't send the groom off, I have judged it best till I hear from Felton to put the old black mare & Merriman with the lad under Scovell's† charge, who will have an eye to them all.

The men complain of each other, and I conclude are both to blame. The lad used to be a very decent one, but his appearance has been much altered, indeed he has imbibed the head quarters principles, the sink of all domestiques, except old Webster and my groom.

We go tomorrow to Paris for a week and are to be at Brussels on the 27th. The King of the Prussians is to be at Sedan on the 16 August. The reviews take place there and at Ligny.

Has Knightly sent for the pig? Pray give my kind love to my aunt and Pussy, and believe me, my dear uncle, your most dutiful and affectionate nephew,

> John Fremantle

Postscript: Mrs L. F.‡ promised to write to me but I fear some of my

---

* This is likely to be Sir John Ignatius Burke of Glinsk, 10th Bart or his brother Joseph who succeeded him.

† Lieutenant Colonel George Scovell, assistant quartermaster general at Waterloo.

‡ This almost certainly refers to Lieutenant and Captain William Augustus Lane Fox, 1st Foot Guards and his soon-to-be wife, Caroline Douglas; whom it would

letters must have fallen into Mr L. F.'s hands on account of the Mrs, for I am sure she would have written. There was no person in mine but a vast deal of ambiguous matter.

John's relationship with Louisa Hervey was clearly strained and he would be avoiding her wherever possible.

Cambrai, Friday 1 August

My dear uncle,

I received your letter of the 28th last night, and I value it so much that I at once ventured to disobey one of your injunctions which was to destroy it. I think it so valuable a piece of instruction that I have resolved to keep it till I shall hear from you again. I told you long ago what you now tell me respecting Felton's wife. I look upon it as the greatest calamity that she ever entered at once our public & private family, but what can't be saved, must be endured, & I will bear with her as well as I can. I am aware I have a temper, and that it will be often tried; at present all I can permit is that if she leaves me alone I will never trouble her. It is of no use to tell you that I will promise to correct her, I will try and if she behaves well, I will. You may depend upon it, I will keep you and my aunt informed of any machinations that are practised. The duke writes to her almost every post. Pray when do you hear the others are likely to go, and what news about Blücher,* you know I am most anxious respecting her prospects.

I am very glad you have heard from Tom and that he has arrived safely at Florence. Bradshaw told me at Paris there is no probability of my sisters coming for some time. Old Danvers is gone to meet them at Bologna where young Danvers has an aunt married to a Sicilian.

The duke will not return here before Wednesday next. I expect William Russell & his wife here tomorrow, or next day. The duke has lent them his house at Cambrai till theirs is ready.

Pray give my best love to my aunt & Pussy, and believe me, my dear uncle your most dutiful and affectionate nephew,

John Fremantle

---

seem was guilty of holding an indiscreet correspondence with John at the least.

* Mentions of 'Blücher' from this point on cannot refer to the Prussian Field Marshal who had retired to Germany and was soon to die. It is a nickname for a female who was very close to the Duke of Wellington at this time. It is almost certainly the nickname of the widowed American Mrs Mary Anne Patterson, sister of Louisa who is referred to, whom the duke appears to have loved deeply. She eventually married the duke's brother Richard.

John next wrote from Paris having been to Brussels and the review at Ligny. It is clear that his uncle shared his concerns over Louisa and John promised to report any new intrigues.

Paris, 18 August 1817

My dear uncle,

I received your letter the day before I set off for Ligny. Poor Felton arrived on the evening of the 12th about 11 o'clock, he appeared to suffer dreadfully, and I took him to bed immediately. There is no doubt of its being an attack of the gut, but Campbell who I heard from yesterday says that he is much better. Percy and myself are in the house here, but are to turn out if Felton is able to come with his wife, which however I doubt very much.

We go back again about the 1st of September. The King of Prussia who is here is to be at Sedan about that time to review that part of his army stationed there. The review at Ligny went off remarkably well, only the duke was not there in time to receive His Prussian majesty, owing to his having come a day sooner than was expected.

I had only time to see Louisa the one evening. We set off the next morning at 8 o'clock, she got up, and remained with the duke half an hour before we started, she was looking very well and I think fatter than usual.

I think we shall do very well without an explanation, if ever I find that she acts according to my opinion unfairly, I will not to fail to let you know, and will promise you to act in the meantime with all proper forbearance, if any intrigue is practising. There has been the devil to pay lately about letters miscarrying. Burgh & myself have each had a rise out of the duke owing to two unfortunate circumstances, where however there was no great blame to be attached.

The girls are here looking very well. Fanny not a bit fatter than formerly, young Danvers is very much improved in appearance and they tell me also in temper. I dined with them yesterday.

The father attacked me about the signing of these papers which he has brought out. I understood from him that they are concerning the estate which young Danvers gave up, which they have now found purchasers for, but that the deed was neglected previous to the marriage. All the trustees to the marriage are to sign, that is young Bradshaw, and me. Young Danvers tells me, that Wainwright, Watkins and yourself have appeared, but it strikes me as odd that he should have left England without getting your signature, & that Bradshaw should have gone without signing also. I said yesterday that I was quite agreeable, but shall remain till I hear from you, which I request you will let me do

as soon as possible. Pray give my best love to my aunt and Eliza, and believe me, ever your most dutiful and affectionate nephew,
John Fremantle

Another letter from Paris tells of another amour, but there was serious competition.

Paris, Thursday 21 August 1817

My dear uncle,
I did not mention in my last that I had destroyed your former letter according to your wish. I heard from Louisa yesterday, a long letter full of commissions, the latter part perhaps may interest you, therefore I enclose it. I made no answer to it that signifies. Whatever Campbell communicates to me, I will acquaint you with. It is very possible they may be afraid of her marrying this De Sauveur,* whose attentions she never seemed to dislike, and that they might wish my suit in consequence, but it won't do in any way I am not sufficiently reprise to think it worth my while.

The King of Prussia, and all his tribe dined here this morning at 2 o'clock, his usual hour, to our great discomfiture.

Lady Hamilton went to England this morning on her way to Scotland for two months. For goodness sake send me word whether I shall sign this deed of Old Danvers. He tells me it is not valid till you have signed it, but I do not like to do it till I hear from you. The duke also recommends me not to sign. Pray give my best love to my aunt and Eliza, and believe me, ever your most dutiful and affectionate nephew,
John Fremantle

The note he enclosed with this letter is signed by Lady L[ouisa] Hervey:

Undertake to settle this business for me. I cannot tell you the name of the man or where he lives. Lady Hamilton was with me and she undertook to have it sent to me when it was finished. Should Lady H[amilton] have paid the 40, instead of the 25 I wish nothing to be said about it; there will remain nothing to do, but to repay her the money, which you will do out of what you will get from Amadeus. She wrote to me about it, and I told her I thought it a great imposition,

---

* This refers to Miss Emma Tylney-Long who never actually married. It is clear in subsequent letters that John had attempted to woo her but a Portuguese gentleman of some worth, named De Sauveur also courted her at this time. She was William Pole-Tylney-Long-Wellesley's sister in law.

and that Hervey was going to Paris and would see the man. At all events bring me my comb; it was given to me by Mrs Fremantle, and the man had only to make it a little larger. Sir Colin [Campbell] tells us that Long Wellesley wishes you to marry his sister in law and says you have a very good chance if you would only come over and make this agreeable to her. You have a rival in some little Portuguese, whom they are afraid she will marry. Long Wellesley* said he was ready to pay her 52 thousand pounds,† which Hervey thinks would be a good thing, and is worth trying for. But Sir Colin has a message for you on the subject, which he only waits to see you to deliver. Mrs L[ong] W[ellesley] was very anxious for it also. Adieu and believe me, ever yours very truly,

    Lady L[ouisa] Hervey

Written on the back of the enclosed letter:

I have written to Amadeus to bring the money to you.

A week later John had finally finished his time with the Prussian king and his entourage. The duke had gone to review the Austrians and John had to set off after him post haste when the mail had arrived. It would appear that Miss Long Wellesley had been the recipient of the drunken proposal in London and that she had declined; but John had made it known through Campbell; that when thoroughly sober, he still had sincere feelings for her; if she would have him. He also reported regular exchanges of very strong words and a battle of wills between Felton and Louisa.

                        Mont Saint Martin, 1 September 1817

My dear uncle,

I have received your two letters only four days ago, but I have been going for these last three weeks *à la suite du Roi de Prusse* [in the entourage of the King of Prussia] and was heartily tired of it. He left us thank goodness the day before yesterday after the reviewing at Valenciennes at which he was very much pleased. The duke went off yesterday morning with Felton, Campbell, & Percy. The latter wished to see the Austrian troops, which as I had already seen them, I let him go, but I am obliged to set off this afternoon as soon as the mail comes in with the letters.

---

* William Pole-Tylney-Long-Wellesley, who later became the 4th Earl of Mornington, renowned for his dissipated lifestyle. He is often referred to as 'Wicked William'.

† This would equate to approximately £2.2 million today.

I shall not overtake him before he reaches Sarreguemines* & as I intend to ride post, I expect to be pretty well fagged before my return; It will be very near 400 miles. I hope to be back on Friday night.

I brought the deed from Paris with me until I should hear from you respecting my signing. I will sign & send it when I come back, as it is now in Cambrai.

With respect to the other concern, your advice about which I am so much obliged to you for, the only step that has been taken is the following. Louisa & myself have not exchanged words about it, she appears to have totally forgotten the matter, since her comb, which was the matter of her letter has reached her safe.

I asked Campbell what his message was, he told me that one day riding with L[ong] W[ellesley] they were talking about the young lady and myself. He said he had been telling her that if she did not make haste she would be an old maid, & went on to say since Fremantle was off and on, he then talked of this Portuguese Mons. de Sauveur, who I know has been paying his addresses to her. He was in Paris when we were and gave out that he was going home immediately to be married to her. Campbell told me that he was sure they all expected me to propose. I am sure from this that L[ong] W[ellesley] is ignorant of what passed.

Campbell is a great favourite of the family. He wrote to L[ong] W[ellesley] by my wish & his own to say that he was sure I was more attached than I liked to own, and a great deal more other stuff as from himself. With all due deference to you, I think this is a much better stage to let it be in, viz. to get his written answer before I take any decided step, for you seem to forget, that what I received was very decided, and it has since been repeated to me through Mrs Fox. I told Campbell that probably the family was anxious to get me or any other Englishman, fearing she might fancy this Portuguese. Long W[ellesley] was furious at the idea, and said he should be most happy to see her married to any Englishman, a gentleman & had no objection to me, that probably he should have a good deal to pay for the money, but that he could get it etc. I fear I have now bored you a good deal, but hope you will excuse it. I shall be most anxious to hear from you and will let you know the purport of Campbell's answer.

I think Felton has been very imprudent to go on this trip. He looked wretchedly thin, Louisa is very well. I hear they have had a tremendous breeze concerning her going to the reviews, & that she has shown a great deal of bad temper about Lady Burgh taking precedence of her. Felton has however been very firm and decided throughout.

---

* Sarreguemines is 10 kilometres south of Saarbrucken.

She said she would never let him alone till he had turned away all his present servants, got a fit carriage for her to ride in etc. he replied he was glad she had told him so, for now he certainly should not turn one of them away! The Duchess told me all this in the strictest confidence. What can be done to remedy the precedence of these knightly wives, they even look very angry. Felton told her it was like the butcher's and baker's wife, that if ever she mentioned it again he should take her into Cambrai and leave her there. That she was not fit society for gentlewomen, etc.; her and I are upon civil terms. I never say to her more than is necessary. I expect my aunt and Georgiana here from Spa on my return.

Adieu my dear uncle, best love to my aunt & Pussy, ever your most affectionate nephew,

John Fremantle

John wrote a week later, feeling let down by Felton and badly treated by the duke over a minor misunderstanding.

Cambrai, Tuesday 16 September 1817

My dear uncle,

I started last Tuesday at 3 in the afternoon to overtake the duke with Stewart's dispatches, he left the chateau at 6 in the morning for Colmar. I overtook him at Sarreguemines, where I arrived in 39 hours from hence, being 250 miles. I reached that place at 3 a.m. Thursday; he was in bed, & I went to his room [&] awoke him; he desired me to put them down. I did so, and went to bed. At 7 Felton came into my room and gave me a parcel of tooth brushes I had put in the bag, but did not give me any instructions. When I got up at 9 o'clock, I found them all gone to the Bavarian review. They were not to return, I therefore started as soon as ever I could procure post horses, and returned here on Saturday morning, riding post the whole way and rather angry that no word had been left for me.

We have this day heard from him. He has written to Louisa to say that in consequence of my coming away, he had been obliged to send one of the foreign officers back with the dispatches. I am sorry to say this shows how prone he is to find fault with me, for mark the difference, two others have been dispatched, but out of four ADCs who remained not one went, they allowed officers of the Staff Corps to go instead of them. I am also affronted that he should mention these sort of things to Mrs Hervey. I understand he also says I shall pay the expenses of the officer who brought them back. This is immaterial, it is his style that wounds me. I don't see likewise why it should be necessary to send back a foreigner, as he had two [aides de camp] with him besides Felton, and also an officer who accompanied General Barnes.

My aunt and Mrs Fitzherbert slept here last night and proceeded this morning on their road to Paris. Georgiana and the whole party seem delighted with their trip to Spa, she is looking remarkably well. Pray give my best love to my aunt and Eliza. I went into Felton's room at Sarreguemines, he told me the journey had done him a vast deal of good, that he was considerably better since he had begun the journey.

Ever my dear uncle your dutiful and affectionate nephew,
John Fremantle

Three days later John wrote in lighter vein having found that the duke had laughed off the incident. Louisa however continued to intrigue and bluster.

Cambrai, Friday 19 September 1817

My dear uncle,

As I am sure my last letter will have made you very anxious, I took not a moment to tell you of the duke's return on Wednesday night; he attacked me immediately half in joke and half in earnest about going away. I told him I came, and that it was he who went away & left me no orders, I told him I was quite unhappy to come back empty handed etc and the business ended very well. Next morning, Louisa boasted before the duchess & others three or four times over, that she had made the duke promise not to be angry with me, nobody answered her. When I heard this I thought that I should have burst with rage, but the duchess & I agreed that it would mortify her vanity more, by taking no sort of notice of her, this costs me much, but as yet I have not said a syllable to her. Everything that you have foretold is coming to pass & I am sure with plenty of rope she will hang herself. The whole household will soon be about her ears.

Cathcart and Hill have been busily employed writing a play during his absence, which the duke knew about before he went away, they thought of erecting a stage on the top of the house, i.e. between the roof and the top, which is all wood work; he would not allow our servants to inhabit it for fear of its being set fire to. Louisa wrote the duke word that they had begun their work without waiting for his leave & he said 'I'll Theatre them'. They are naturally very angry at her going out of her way to tell a mischievous lie, and the duchess also.

The duke always writes to her and pays her the greatest attention. We shall have famous sport when the Lennox's come, and I will not fail to send you a bulletin, in the mean time I shall be very impatient till I hear from you.

I send you the deeds by this post, signed and witnessed. Campbell on his return showed me his answer. It shows me still more clearly that he L[ong] W[ellesley] is not in the whole secret. He says the young lady he thinks is favourably inclined towards me, but that I managed my amour in a singular manner.

Pray remember me to my aunt and Pussy. Felton is surprising well after his journey, he has both his boots on today. Believe me, my dear uncle, your most dutiful & affectionate nephew,

John Fremantle

PS Our reviews begin here in three days. On looking at the deed again, I find there is no place on the back of it for people to witness your signature. If there is anything wrong, you can rub, or scratch my name out.

John was in soul-searching mood in his next letter, as he believed that although forgiven for the recent incident, that his standing with the duke had been in decline for some time. Louisa seemed to be upsetting everybody and now even the duke took delight in playing jokes at her expense.

Cambrai, Friday 26 September 1817

My dear uncle,

I have just received your letter, and it has done me much good. They always fortify me, and I am delighted always to let you know the worst of any case that occurs. This breeze has entirely blown over. Though, I must tell you I do not think I am so well with the duke as I have been. I am aware I did enjoy his favour and partiality and my belief is I lost it on our arrival in Town previous to Felton's marriage. With respect to the dispatches, what he expected was, that I should have followed him to Haguenau and have brought the dispatches back, this would have added a hundred miles to the five I made before my return & I confess I did not think he would have expected that, when in an hour he might have easily sent them to Sarreguemines where I waited 6 hours after he had left it.

You know Mrs Hervey has been trying heaven and earth to go to all the reviews; they, I mean the duke & Felton have blinkered her heretofore, but yesterday she went to the Saxons with Felton & Burgh in the D[uke]'s carriage, rode by the duke's side all day, breakfasted at the Saxon general's afterwards; she was so tired then, that she would not go to the prefect's party at Lille in the evening. I rather think she is bored, because she does not go tomorrow to see the Hanoverians at Conde.

I foresee she will go by the run very soon. The duke occasionally gives her japes, which she is not at all aware of, as do several others, she has disgusted besides myself, Campbell, Hill, Percy today, and young Cradock* by an impertinence some days ago. I have not said a word to her respecting her officiousness in my case, but will when a good opportunity offers.

Pray give my best love to my aunt and Eliza, and believe me, my dear uncle, your dutiful & affectionate nephew,
 John Fremantle

I have got the music, and will send it by the first good opportunity. I think between ourselves, the duke will go over [to England] in the winter.

His letters continue to tell of Louisa's rapid fall from grace and the ill feeling shown between husband and wife.

Cambrai, Friday 5 October 1817

My dear uncle,

Again let me thank you for your letter of the 23rd. Do not be the least alarmed respecting your apprehension of any anger that may have been evinced in it. Believe me, I am always glad to receive any advice that you think necessary, and in this instance I assure you I felt considerably relieved by it. I am sorry to say I cannot alter my opinion with respect to the duke's affection or manner towards me. It certainly is very different, but I shall endeavour to follow as much as possible your precepts and steer a clear course. She is losing herself in the eyes of all the young men in our family every day by some *bêtise* or *gaucherie* [foolishness or awkwardness], or impertinence or another; yesterday Felton was obliged to set her down in a very abrupt manner in the middle of dinner at the chateau.

Our Russian review takes place on the 11th and the British on or about the 16th. The Duchess of Richmond arrives tomorrow with Lady Georgiana. Lord & Lady Anglesey† on the 9th with two of his

---

* This would appear to be the young son of General Cradock; John Hobart Cradock (later changed to Caradoc), future 2nd Baron Howden who became a politician and diplomat.

† The Earl of Uxbridge had been made Marquess of Anglesey in 1815, he was married to Lady Charlotte [née Cadogan], ex-wife of Henry Wellesley.

young ladies, and we are to have a great many others. Pray give my best love to my aunt and Eliza, and believe me, your most dutiful and affectionate nephew,

John Fremantle

Have you received the deed?

The duke continued to favour beautiful young ladies, but one of them, Lady Georgina Lennox, caused great embarrassment by halting a full review in front of all the allied sovereigns when she came off her horse!

Cambrai, Friday 17 October 1817

My dear uncle,

I received your letter yesterday, it appears by it you were actually informed of every hour's occurrence in our family here. Your advice is most wholesome and I will use my endeavours to follow it.

Our reviews thank goodness are all at an end, the party in the duke's carriage were always Felton & his wife, & Poole, or some other youth (a visitor). The Duchess of Wellington always took the Duchess of Richmond, our Lady Lennox & Lady Edward Somerset. Lady Anglesey and ladies went in their own carriage. The duke always went to the ground with Mrs Hervey, Lady Georgina Lennox & Lady Jane Paget at his side, the two former always close to him. The last day a ridiculous circumstance occurred; as we were going down the line, ADCs preceding etc in grand parade, Lady Georgina's stirrup broke as her horse was going over the little ditch and she slipt [*sic*] off, but the duke & Lord Lyndoch dismounted, and the whole cavalcade was stopt [*sic*] until the groom brought another stirrup leather; there were present by special invitation, the Austrian, Russian, and Prussian commanders in chief and a prodigious number of foreigners of all nations.

I ought to mention to you that in an explanation which took place some time ago between our Duchess and Mrs Hervey on account of the coldness of the former towards the latter; Louisa said she was aware of Percy's change of manner, and of my dislike. The Duchess assured her that she had never heard me express anything of the sort, but that she knew I was devoted to Hervey.

I should be very glad to go to Paris for a short time to see all the family, but I dare say the duke himself will go for the opening of the Chambers on the 5th November.

Give my best love to my aunt and Eliza, and believe me, ever my dear uncle, your most dutiful and affectionate nephew,

John Fremantle

I sent the deed long ago under cover to Planta, Downing St directed to you Stanhope St. It must be at either one or the other now.

John wrote that he was not attending the duke to England because of illness but continued to write regarding the situation at headquarters. Louisa continued to lose favour within the 'family', to the point of open hostility and mockery.

Cambrai, 5 November 1817

My dear uncle,
I received your letter the day before yesterday; you will be surprised no doubt at my not attending the duke to England, but the fact is I am not in a state to travel, having been indisposed ever since the review.

I must now let you know something more concerning our family, but I beg that if you converse ever with Felton on the subject you will not give him the smallest clue to imagine that I have been gossiping.

The duke has twice found fault with the duchess for asking questions of the aides-de-camp respecting him, the fact is that she never knows what is about to pass in the house, any more than you do, except by what she hears by accident, or is told. I am convinced that he cannot bear anybody to pay any attention to, or to notice her, or to use Alava's expression, '*il serait content qu'on lui fouettasse*' [He would be happy that someone would whip her]. I cannot say whether he imagines that I have been gossiping, his manner is very fair towards me, but from being confined to the house, I have been more with her certainly than any other.

I do not think Louisa is in such favour as she has been, he laughs at her, and his kindness I think proceeds from pity, for to prove to you, that what I say of her does not proceed from ill will or ill nature, you must know that a week ago, after several times having broached the subject, she must have a ride in the rug,* and said something amounting to the duke ordering the ADCs to draw her, upon which A[rthur] Hill said very stoutly that they would not. The rug was produced, the duchess (ours), Lady G[eorgina] Lennox, and Louisa were there, and upon asking who would ride, Louisa volunteered, but there was a general cry for the duchess first, Lady G[eorgina] Lennox got in second. Louisa went away, but Felton went and fetched her. Four of the horses went away immediately and she was left (with Campbell and Felton) to be drawn, when I saw what was happening I went to act as coachman, but no entreaties from our duchess could prevail on

---

* One of the parlour games at headquarters entailed drawing the ladies upon a rug throughout the house!

A[rthur] Hill, G[eorgina] Lennox, or the rest to go and assist. She then came into the drawing room and told the duke, she had not had a coachman, upon which he said immediately 'I'll be Coachman'; but she stammered & said she had no horse. Lady Georgina Lennox tells me, she told the duke, that she was not liked & that one and all had declared that they would not draw her. I feel convinced, as he likes a friend of his to be popular, that he will never support her against the whole, and that she will eventually go by the run, *id est* [that is], when sake's sake needs no longer avail. She has certainly had her sway, for no woman has ever bullied him in the way this one has done.

There was a terrible to do, about Felton's going to England. She would not hear of it till the duke reasoned with her. There is a fire under the ashes between the Duchess of Richmond and her; this will be a famous opportunity for me to pay her a little court and I intend to push a patrole her way; if she behaves decently I have no objection to be on friendly terms, but my temper will never bear disdain.

The whole party were engaged the night before last at a game, and when Louisa being asked to join it she saw this occasioned a hoarse laugh; no it was vulgar, apropos, it was cross questions & crooked sentences, of course they were all cuts upon America, and she was driven to bed. So much for the gossip, but I do expect, as you foretold, that there will be a grand blow up, by means of Beldon,* Richmond, Louisa and the rest. If we do not go to Paris soon after his return, I think I had better make myself scarce for a short time. I can easily put it upon the plea of health, change of air, what do you think? I have no where particular to go to.

Louisa tells me Puss is going to be married to Jenkinson.† Pray give my good wishes & hopes that it may prove true. She also tells me Emma Long is going to marry de Sauveur. Is this true? Don't be alarmed, I am not unhappy. Best love to my aunt, with best love, believe me, my dear uncle, your most dutiful and affectionate nephew,

John Fremantle

John had been quite unwell and had not travelled with the duke, but was now improving. The rug pulling had been improved by the introduction of a mule and the use of crackers had further enlivened things. He was also trying to build bridges with Louisa, but she was now out of favour with almost everyone.

---

* I have been unable to identify this person.
† Elizabeth never married.

Cambrai, Friday 7 November

My dear uncle,

I am very much obliged to you, for your tender enquiries. My last letter will have explained to you the cause of my not attending the duke on these two last trips. I certainly have suffered a great deal, but I hope I am now turning the corner, and shall soon be quite sound again. I am just arrived from the chateau, and intend to lay myself up entirely for a week.

Since my long gossip of Tuesday, I have only one funny anecdote which I cannot avoid mentioning. Ar[thur] Hill's mule has been trained to draw the rug you have heard so much of.

Last night the duchess, and Lady G[eorgina] Lennox were drawn by him to perfection, and Louisa was persuaded to try afterwards, she had no sooner seated herself, when said mule let fly such a volley as made her and all the ladies take to their heels at their best pace.

The night before last Ar[thur] Hill desired me to give a letter to the Duchess of R[ichmon]d, which I did very innocently. It contained one of these crackers, called Cossacks,* which are sold in the fair here. It went off, and the duchess also, into one of the most violent fits of laughing hysterics ever witnessed. I am happy to say she does not think me guilty. I wonder it did not kill the old woman. They have teased her this time worse than ever.

Give my best love to Puss and my aunt, and pray write to me, and believe me always, my dear uncle, your most dutiful and affectionate nephew,

John Fremantle

I wrote to Felton last Tuesday to tell him, that as there was now a good opportunity I intended making my approaches to Louisa, and should be delighted if I succeeded in being on anything like terms with her, that I was sorry I had always remained so heretic; that it was not my fault, was I right to say so? I sat next to her yesterday at dinner, and had a good deal of conversation. She said yesterday 'Who'll walk to the stable with me, you? None of you seem very fond of going with me.' Nobody answered, I was not there. She took the parson with her. Her nickname is Chitty with an S.

His relationship with Louisa steadily improved, but he conceded that she was a clever intriguer and cared little about the views of the rest of the 'family' as long as she had the duke on side.

---

* This describes Christmas crackers, which according to the *Oxford English Dictionary* were originally called 'Cossacks'; although this proves that the *OED* statement that they were invented in England in 1840 is in error.

My dear uncle,

I received your letter last Friday, but I could not answer it in time as I was very busy. It puts me so much in mind of Lord Chesterfield, and amused me very very much,* but you may depend upon it I will use my utmost endeavour to follow your precepts. I am perfectly aware of my want of command of temper, and will try and conquer it. I am sure a great deal can be done by taking pains with oneself upon any particular point, and whenever you will tell me of any failure, which you alone can do, I shall be most thankful, and will pay the strictest attention to it.

The letter, which I mentioned to you to Felton, came back here and was opened by Louisa, but, I did not tell you the beginning. It ran thus 'I am delighted you succeeded in your determination about accompanying the duke, it would have been too ridiculous had you given way'. I have had very little communication with her, but I do not think her averse to being on fair terms, therefore I will go on *peu à peu* [little by little]. She is certainly devilish clever. She does not care one iota for the dislike of all the whole family; on the contrary, it enhances her more with the duke, and she does not take the least notice of any of us and carries everything with a d[amne]d high hand, exposing herself occasionally.

I have undergone a very severe penance, but I hope another week will see me again in the field. Have you received one half of the music which I sent by Colonel Blair† last Friday? I will send the other half by the first safe conveyance. Pray give my best love to my aunt & Eliza, and believe me ever, my dear uncle, your most dutiful and affectionate nephew,
John Fremantle

I am grown thin, thinner I mean, have a whopping post.‡

John's next letter gave further information regarding their amusements during the long hours of darkness in the late autumn. The duke and duchess had also had a fall-out.

---

* Philip Dormer Stanhope, 4th Earl of Chesterfield (1694–1773) was a British statesman and man of letters; he was famous for his wit.
† Lieutenant Colonel Thomas Hunter Blair was major of brigade to Major General Frederick Adam.
‡ A lot of mail to deal with.

Cambrai, Friday 23 November 1817

My dear uncle,

Many thanks for your kind note of the 16th, I am quite recovered now, but am very weak. I went out hunting yesterday for a short time, and found myself very much fatigued by it. I wrote you a long letter on Tuesday,* telling you all the news I was master of here.

The great amusements of the chateau now are 1st rowing, and talking tawdry to the Duchess of Richmond, who enjoys it extremely. 2nd the preparation for two plays, one of which is to be acted the day after tomorrow. I confess all the preparations bore me extremely which you will be very much surprised at; I acted at a late one, as they were disappointed at one of their members, but I never will again.

There is also a box, called a Love Box, which everybody has written something for, in feigned hands, this is to be opened tomorrow. There are many squibs and home things in it; I expect before they are done some fingers will be burnt, and I shall endeavour to keep as much aloof as possible.

The duke was in very low spirits yesterday evening after the post came in, whether at letters he did receive, or for what he expected and did not receive. I think he has been very civil to me lately when I have addressed him.

Felton was unwell yesterday, and Louisa and the doctor prevented him riding into Cambrai, which he wanted to do. Louisa let out the other day that we were all going to England in a fortnight, and recovered herself immediately. You may depend upon it, the duke's motions there will be very much influenced by the Pattersons.

Apropos, the duchess went to the duke's room the other day, in order to speak to him, she found Louisa seated on one chair, Mrs Patterson's picture on another, and the duke. On seeing this she turned back, they called after her, but she would not go in.

The duke, sometime afterwards went to her room, to know what was wanted. Louisa has twice taken the duchess to task for not coming in, at which she is of course very angry. Felton has never said one word to me about the letter which Louisa opened. The other half of the music went yesterday by Campbell, who is gone over for a week. I desired him to let me know if the report was true about Miss Long's marriage.

Adieu my dear uncle, believe me ever with best love, your most dutiful and affectionate nephew,

J. Fremantle

---

* This would have been dated Tuesday 21 November, which is now missing.

Plays and boar hunts filled their hours and the news that Miss Long Wellesley was still unattached was excellent news to John.

Cambrai, Tuesday 3 December 1817

My dear uncle,
I have received yours of the 25th, and am very much obliged to you for your advice, and good nature. So much time has elapsed now since the arrival of Felton, and as he is going away the day after tomorrow, I think the subject on which I wrote to you, had better die its own death; he appears to me as cordial as ever he has been lately, I mean in the last six months.

Our play went off admirably the other night, and everybody was delighted with it. The Duke of Richmond, Lady Mary and Lady Jane Lennox arrived a few days ago in addition to our party. The same scene still continues with the duchess, she is roasted from morning till night, and upon my word I do not think she dislikes it. The chateau is very gay, and the boar hunt affords great sport; every person goes out with a spear, and the duke has as yet been the one who has come first in contact with the animal. He stuck one on Saturday fairly to the ground.

Campbell is returned this moment from Town. He tells me he left the music at your house, the other half went three weeks before by Colonel Blair. I shall be glad to hear that you have received it. Campbell tells me [he] asked Shawe, who had lately come from Lady C[atherine] Long's* as to the truth of the report of my little friend's marriage with De Sauveur. Shawe told him he did not think there was any foundation for it therefore that's all very good. Pray give my best love to my aunt and Pussy. I never have been able to learn how the Boar gets on. Pray, pray [sic] let me know. Ever my dear uncle, your very affectionate nephew,
John Fremantle

John was now fully recovered from his illness, having prescribed his own medicine. His relationship with the duke was quite normal and he was back in charge with others away.

Cambrai, 16 December 1817

Many thanks, my dear uncle, for your tender enquiries. You must

---

* Lady Catherine Tylney-Long, Emma's sister, was reputed to be the richest commoner in England until she married 'Wicked' William Wellesley, the duke's nephew. At her death the duchess became guardian to her children.

know the doctors attempted to cure me without mercury but luckily for my own peace of mind, I treated myself without their instruction, on my own.

I am now however perfectly well, in good spirits and all alive, and have taken to riding, and hunting as before etc. I must say, I am not so fat as I was, *mais avec le temps cela viendra* [but in due course that will come].

Do not be alarmed at my mentioning to you that the duke never addressed me except on business for you know that he never addresses any person who does not address him. Felton being away & Burgh living at Cambrai, makes me No. 1 at the chateau and I always do the business with him as such, and I think he seems as usual with me. I accompanied him to Maubeuge to go there with Campbell and Lennox, and you may rest assured that no pains shall be wanting on my part now to re-establish myself in his good graces. So much for that, if anything occurs, you shall be kept informed, apropos you accuse me of being a gossip; that I must say in my own justification that the only reason I left off my correspondence with my aunt was my fear my committing myself with histories about Louisa, of which I could furnish her volumes. Louisa told me you are building near Englefield Green a house for yourself. What did she mean by that?*

I am glad you liked the music. Pay Felton five pounds for it and ask him to pay for the stockings he sent me. He did some commissions in Town for me very obligingly. With best love, my dear uncle to my aunt & Eliza, believe your very dutiful and affectionate nephew,

J. F.

John wrote during the Christmas season, to assure his uncle that the rumours of a liaison were not true and that the ladies at headquarters were all envy and jealousy.

Cambrai, Friday 26 December 1817

My dear uncle,

I have just got your letter of the 22nd and I was not at all surprised at your fears, as I perceive the gossip of the chateau has reached you. You know it is quite sufficient to sit twice next a woman, and converse with her, for a history to be made by old Mother Richmond or Hill who really is quite as bad, this is the case I am sure, from little insinuations, which have been made to me by both of them. However I cannot tell you the load I feel relieved of by the departure, and you may take my

---

* This might indicate that there were thoughts of rebuilding at Englefield Green, but it did not come to fruition.

word for it, there shall be no correspondence, as I am happy to inform you we had a coolness a week before she went away, and parted very ill.

No words can convey to you a just idea of the scenes of gambols going on here. Old Richmond is pinched black and blue all over, and Lady Georgiana is beset by Percy & Cathcart, having young Uxbridge & Charles Fitzroy as cats paws.

Lady Ch[arlot]te Greville came two days ago, you must know the two families are at daggers drawn with each other, and it is consequently great fun to watch the different feelings of envy and jealousy of Old Richmond at the attention paid to Lady Charlotte in preference to her daughters.

We go to Paris on Sunday, but shall return in a week, till the end of January. I have written twice to Felton, but I have not heard from him in answer. He wrote to me about some commissions he did for me.

With respect to the duke, I am very well satisfied, but, as I have never disguised anything from you, you must know, that I think since my confinement, that Percy is more better with him than I am, and partly owing to Lady C[atherine] L[ong], but at the same time he is so very avantageux [favourable] that I have no fears of him, and I think he will throw himself over. Adieu my dear uncle, with best love, believe me, with every affectionate regard, your very dutiful nephew,

John Fremantle

In January he wrote that he was soon to arrive in England and that many still blamed him entirely for the failure of his attempts to marry Miss Long Wellesley.

Cambrai, 13 January 1818

My dear uncle,

My numerous tribe of relatives petitioned the duke to leave me behind at Paris, which he very good humouredly allowed me to do, and I could not refuse. However I returned yesterday and found everything in status quo and the duke in great good humour. I am not at all sure that I have not been mistaken in my suspicions.

You will not be sorry to hear that Mrs Pole told me the other day in Paris, that she was quite surprised to hear at Brighton previous to her coming to this side of the water from Lady Wellesley and Worcester that it was entirely my own fault that I had not married Miss Long [Wellesley]. We had a great deal of conversation about it, however I shall see you in a few days, and we will talk it all over. Adieu my dear uncle, believe me always, your most dutiful and affectionate nephew,

John Fremantle

His next dealt mainly with his inheritance of land in Ireland from his grandmother and its finances.

Tuesday, 27 January 1818

My dear uncle,

The history you read in the papers regarding our little Duchess is all false. There is no more the matter with her than I mentioned to you. The reason that Felton and I did not accompany the duke was that he took Poole, and Mr & Mrs Arbuthnot.*

I saw Watkins yesterday, and remained with him an hour, but he did not appear to me to understand a great deal more of the business than I did myself; he is to call upon me this evening when he says he shall be more *au fait*. He does not know whether [Kilmaclancy?] belongs exclusively to me, or to myself and sisters, but that is not material, he says he hopes in the spring to get the two years' rent which are due. The deed he says is at your house. I have a year and a half's annuity due, which is 6 months in arrears, during which arrears he receives compound interest for. This, John Butler disapproves of very much, he says it will certainly be paid off in six months.

We were to have gone today, then tomorrow, now it is next day. Therefore it is quite impossible I should be able to come down. Pray give my best love to my aunt & Puss, and believe me, my dear uncle, your most dutiful and affectionate nephew,

John Fremantle

A short note announced their arrival in London and much on the travelling arrangements.

Monday, 2 February

My dear uncle,

We arrived here safe and sound on Saturday night. On Thursday morning at 6, Felton started with Louisa to fetch Blücher. We followed 10 minutes after, and remained about a quarter of an hour at Thomas's door for the three to come down; nobody got out of our carriage. Felton who was to have come with us, went in his own carriage but at Rochester, Louisa sent him to our carriage, to say she was frightened at going so fast with him, and would come with the duke, which she did accordingly. Hill could not help telling her, that she would go equally fast with us. From Calais, Hill & myself travelled in Felton's carriage and the duke and Felton sat with their backs to the horses in the duke's

---

* Charles Arbuthnot, the diplomat and politician, and his wife Harriet, were to become very close friends of the Duke of Wellington.

carriage. But what amuses me most is that the duke says it is much warmer going in that manner.

Felton moves into his billet in a few days, but Louisa has declared she will not have it. Pray give my kind love to my aunt & Pussy, and believe me, my dear uncle, your very affectionate and dutiful nephew,
        John Fremantle

PS Do you call this a gossiping letter!!!

Only a week later, John wrote from Paris with news of a failed assassination attempt upon the Duke of Wellington.

Paris, Thursday 10 February 1818

My dear uncle,

You will of course be anxious to know the particulars of the event which took place the night before last. The duke was returning home the night before last between 12 & 1 when a fellow fired a pistol at him from behind the sentry box as he was entering his own *porte-cochère* [covered carriage porch] in his carriage. The sentries (as is usual) being under the *porte-cochère* when a carriage enters. The footman or no person ran after the man and so he escaped. The villain is said to have had mustachios and as it is supposed he will have shaved, all persons are taken up who have shaved off their mustachios during the last week 'whip all the boys'. We believe the fellow was bribed by a set of refugees in the Netherlands, and we have great hopes of discovering them. You, of course, will hear all the lies here respecting it, but the above is all we know, the *bleu* [the Napoleonists] is very active.

Felton went into his billet a few days ago and it is a very comfortable one, of course Louisa is not content with it.

We have volumes to write therefore excuse any more, give my best love to my aunt and Eliza and believe me, your very dutiful and affectionate nephew,
        John Fremantle

Out of the blue, his uncle was to receive a secret letter from John explaining his many troubles: a widow with two children whom he had befriended wanted to marry. He was not inclined to marry her, but news of this might seriously damage his chances with Miss Long Wellesley, who apparently might say yes if asked.

He was also in trouble with the duke and had argued terribly with his aunt; he needed his uncle's sage advice.

Paris, Monday 3 March

SECRET

My dear uncle,

I have been in a world of troubles for a long time, in brief there is a Mrs Spalding here, a widow with two children, with whom I have been a very short time acquainted, but who it is evident to me is willing to marry me.

She was a Miss Eden, she lives in Hill Street. This is all I know about her, except that she is said to have a fortune. I am sorry I have given her the encouragement I have, but some evenings ago I told her to inquire about me and not to be in a hurry about anything. The word remember has never been in question, and I am by no means in the mind yet, and can't help regretting my little [Emma] Long, in short I am in the agonies of the damned. Lady Fitzroy has found out this & I know she is interested about me, I have told her the above and she says from what Mrs Pole told her she thinks Miss E[mma] L[ong] would. Pray write to me anything that you can.

The duke got into a violent passion with me the other day, and abused me a good deal for nothing at all, I believe he is sorry for it. I have had a royal quarrel with my aunt of Glengall & I think we are torn for ever likewise; is not this a pretty production? Ever dear uncle your most dutiful and affectionate nephew,

John Fremantle

PS Fanny is a little indisposed, *bouleversement de l'interior* [upheaval of the insides], but has got very fat of late.

On the last page of the letter in his Uncle William's handwriting he has written his answer. He clearly felt that John was hot-headed and declined to admonish him at his age, but he leaves a clear impression that he is disappointed in him.

Stanhope Street, 16 March 1818

My dear John,

After a silence of about 2 months your letter of the 9th* has just reached me, which is so strange both in matter [&] manner that I can only make a short answer to it.

It is truly heartbreaking to me to find you continue to incur the duke's anger, I know not whether he had or had not reason for abusing you as you term it, he does not abuse others of his family, *mais fais*

---

* This must be an error for the 3rd as all of his comments refer to the contents of the secret letter of that day.

finis [it is finished]. In losing the help you now enjoy, it will not be me, but you who become the victim. Never again shall I offer a rebuke, at your age and with your experience, it is neither advice or censure that can aid reflection.

With regard to the other part of your letter, it is for you to judge; ignorant as you profess yourself to be, and as I am both as to fortune & connexion I cannot give you an opinion.

I really don't understand what you mean to say regarding Fanny, but I am very sorry she has been ill. As to Lady Glengall you have long known my opinion of her, but I should not have recommended to you to volunteer an additional enemy by joining in (as I have heard) sending a public insult to a lady and that lady a near relation. Adieu my dear John, wishing you always prosperity, I grieve to see is so destroyed by imprudence, your affectionate uncle,
W[illia]m

Soon he was writing a little easier, as the threat of marriage had faded. The duke was also fully occupied in completing the final measures before the Army of Occupation left France.

17 March 1818

My dear uncle,
I fear my last letter will have caused you a little uneasiness, but I am happy now to tell you, that I am much more at rest, and have no intention of taking unto myself a bride.

The duke is so much absorbed with these liquidations that we see very little of him. He has had a very bad cold lately, and so have I, a horrid one. His attention to Felton is very remarkable, his wife still makes a fool of herself and is much disliked. But Blücher is very popular, I must say with everybody. Felton has told my aunt a very curious anecdote of Louis XVIII.

Pray give my love to her and Pussy and believe me, ever your most dutiful and affectionate nephew,
John Fremantle

A pained note, from a clearly hurt John, would indicate that he had just received his uncle's reply and did not like it!

Monday, 23 March 1818

My dear uncle,
I regret to find, that the object for which I have strived all my life has been of no avail. I shall ever remember with gratitude all you have

done for me and must forgive your letter on that account. Though I am convinced I never shall forget it all my life. It is the only one I ever received, that did not reach my heart. This I am sorry to say has incited quite different feelings, ever your most affectionate nephew,
John Fremantle

However, a few weeks later, still at Paris, John writes as though nothing had happened and was happy to make arrangements for purchases for his uncle. The duke was still immersed in the reams of bills for the Army of Occupation which had to be signed off.

Paris, 13 April 1818

My dear uncle,
I have received your note, and will procure for you the lithograph prints of Bourgeois before the duke leaves Paris, which I believe will be in five or six days. He wishes if possible to be in Town for the Drawing Room,* but it will be very close shaving if he does it.

I think he can scarcely finish his business with the commissaries liquidators by that time. It has been a very arduous undertaking for him but he will get through with *éclat* [brilliance] I think.

Felton is going to England with the duke, and although the women say they are not, I think it will end in their going also. Felton just said that he had told the duke that Percy wished to go and upon some question during the conversation about my going, he said probably I should be required to remain. This is a sort of thing which annoys me beyond expression, why he should put himself out of the way to assist Percy's convenience and leave me totally out of the question. If I do stay I shall be devilishly mortified. Percy's business is to effect an exchange in order to put some money in his pocket which he has lost at play.

Blücher is all the go now. He calls there every day and takes her out riding. The other is as jealous as possible. Poole and Mrs Poole went away this morning, Burghersh and Lady Burghersh† remain a short time longer. With best love to my aunt and Eliza believe my dear uncle your dutiful and affectionate nephew,
John Fremantle

I made no sort of remark to Felton.

---

* The King's Levee.
† Colonel John Fane, Lord Burghersh, and his wife Lady Priscilla (née Wellesley-Pole), he was now minister to Tuscany.

It appeared likely that he was to remain in Paris for a while yet, although the duke had completed all the paperwork to every one's satisfaction.

Paris, Monday 9 April 1818

My dear uncle,

The orange trees went on the 18th and I send you the bill according to your desire. The lithograph prints are beautiful and as I am not certain of coming to England myself, I shall forward them to Calais this evening by the messenger, to be taken up there by either Felton or myself, or who ever goes. Our departure is postponed for a week.

The liquidations thank goodness are at an end, and the French are quite in love with the duke for having consulted their interests so much in the arrangements he has made. We have been so busy lately that I have seen very little of the Americans, all the English here detest them for taking up so much of the duke's time.

Fanny has been very unwell, she suffers much from a general weakness, and fainted the other day. She intends going to Spa, which I hope will do her good. Pray give my best love to my aunt & Eliza, and believe me, my dear uncle, your most dutiful and affectionate nephew,

John Fremantle

His next letter again betrays John's hot-headedness, when he perceived an injustice had been perpetrated against him by Felton.

Paris, Monday 12 May 1818

My dear uncle,

I am very much obliged to you for your letter of the 4th. I see Felton has thought it necessary to make an explanation respecting my not coming. The fact is this, ten days before the duke went, during a conversation about England wherein Percy said he had business, Felton said he had told the duke so. I said I expected to go also, and Felton thought it would be necessary for me to remain, and there things remained for some days afterwards, when Felton allowed me to send my clothes to Calais and as if on purpose, and in a very aggravating manner, a night or two before they started, told me he had known positively for some days that there was no likelihood of my being of the party. Of course I took fire at this.

He may have spoken very fairly and kindly to you about it, but his act I never can think either the one or the other, besides why should he put himself out of the way to do a thing for the one, and give himself trouble to disoblige the other, for there never was a day that he did not hear me talk of going and he had not the grace ever to tell me I am sorry to say & I told him so, that I had long thought he had been anything but friendly to me. Believe me, my dear uncle I am as much averse to quarrelling as any man, but it wounds me to find everybody taking part against me, everybody is willing to condemn me unheard.

Be assured you shall not hear of any disputes, for if I find I cannot keep my place & live happy, I have made up my mind, I'll go. Louisa volunteered a long conversation with me upon the subject, in which she said she had told Felton he was very wrong. I cannot tell you how all this worries and bothers me, for although Felton & myself have often had trifling disagreements, yet I always thought he had been my friend.

The baggage arrives tomorrow at Cambrai & so do I. I have this instant got a note from my groom to say that one horse had kicked another, and is dead. This animal cost me a world of trouble to dress, and my neck was endangered for 4 months by it, but I had completely subdued him. Misfortunes never come singly. I wonder you have not received the plants.

I suppose Campbell did not like the responsibility of taking the lithograph prints over. He was to take them from Calais where I had sent them with my clothes.

I am very sorry for my aunt & poor Randall's misfortune. Burghersh is gone, but when I spoke to him about the star he did not seem at all conscious that he was the bearer of it. Adieu my dear uncle with best love to my aunt and Eliza, believe me always, your very dutiful and affectionate nephew,
    John Fremantle

Postscript. L[ord] Essex* and I have been great cronies here.

A short note a few days later indicated that on their return from England, the spat with Felton was already forgotten.

Sunday, 16 May 1818

My dear uncle,
I have only a moment to tell you that they arrived on Saturday night, Felton and I saluted each other very cordially, and are for aught I know very good friends.

The duke goes tomorrow to Brussels the women go too. I do not wish and I think it will be convenient that I should remain here. I have been very busy these last two days. Ever my dear uncle in great haste, your most dutiful and affectionate nephew,
    John Fremantle

---

* George Capel, 5th Earl of Essex.

Back at Cambrai he awaited the duke's return after a visit to Brussels.

Cambrai, 22 May 1818

My dear uncle,

I received yours this morning, and am very much obliged to you for it indeed. All I am anxious to convince you of now, is that the disappointment of not going to England the last time which I knew was only to be for five or six days, cost me not a moment's uneasiness, but certainly saved me a hundred pounds, but what mortified me bitterly was Felton's manner and behaviour to me. I could only write you a line or two last time as the bag was shutting, but I cannot say he appears otherwise than well disposed towards me, now, but for God sake let this matter drop, it annoys me beyond measure to think of it.

The start to Brussels was capital. The duke appointed 7 o'clock, but did not appear till past 8, and the women were very angry. Then there was a mess about Louisa, riding backwards or forwards. Blücher can't ride backwards & Louisa wanted the duke to ride forwards, but he would not. He must sit opposite Blücher. Campbell, Cathcart, and Cradock had ordered horses and were to go in my carriage, only Cathcart was ordered to Maubeuge; then Campbell would not go, and young Cradock rode courier. It never was a question about my going, I took it for granted I should remain to send the dispatches after, and asked for orders accordingly.

We expect the Grand Duke Michael* in a few days at Maubeuge, and are to have a grand review of all the troops for him. The duke returns for it.

I have just heard from Fanny, she leaves Paris for Boulogne this day.

I am infinitely obliged to you for your offer but I am in no want of horses, having too many already. I regretted the loss of the one I mentioned, because I had had so much trouble with him, but I believe it to be a lucky riddance, for the chances are that the animal would have seriously injured somebody if it had lived.

I have ordered two young boars & sows to be procured. If Selina wishes to have hers replaced, let me know, & I will order a fifth for her. Pray give my kindest love to my aunt and Pussy, and believe me, my dear uncle, ever your most dutiful and affectionate nephew,

John Fremantle

Two weeks later, John wrote of a near escape in a driving accident, but he was fit enough to escort the duke to Brussels shortly afterwards.

---

* The Grand Duke Michael was the brother of Tsar Nicholas I.

Cambrai, Tuesday 9 June 1818

My dear uncle,

The arrangements which I had made for accompanying the duke to Paris, were unfortunately put an end to by an upset from a gig which I met with coming out of the town of Maubeuge, a heavy cart having been purposely driven against me by its conductor. I was jammed between the gig with my chest against a window stand and suffered violent pain in consequence, however I have been bled, blistered, and physiced [*sic*], and feel quite relieved by it, although of course am a good deal reduced. I do not expect the duke back for a week, but if he comes in two days, I shall be quite ready to attend him to Brussels, where I imagine he will be detained a week, I believe on a visit to the Prince of Orange.

I am sorry it has disappointed Felton who intended to have remained at Cambrai, and has been obliged to go to Paris instead of me. I did not think he was looking very well at Maubeuge, but it is possible he might have been fagged with the heat. The Grand Duke I hear was very well pleased with our troops at Valenciennes, which were shown to him, and they say, looked remarkably well.

I see no probability of my being able to visit you this summer, for Burgh must certainly wait for the general election, and the duchess wrote to Campbell the other day to say that Percy was by no means better. I have long thought myself that he was in a very bad state.

I have long been expecting to hear from you, but Felton told me you were out with the yeomanry. If it has been as hot on your side as it has here, I pity your complexion.

Louisa had a very nice little party last night and both her & Blücher are looking quite blooming. Give my best love to my aunt and Puss.

I have not heard of Fanny for two days, nor do I know whether she is arrived at Boulogne or not. Believe me, my dear uncle, your most dutiful and affectionate nephew,
        John Fremantle

As the summer progressed, Louisa apparently grew fatter and her intrigues were incessant.

Cambrai, 12 June

My dear uncle,

Many thanks for your kind enquiries, my letter of Tuesday will however have given a full account of what happened to me. I suffered horrid torture in my head from that till yesterday, but am now charming well again. Louisa is very sorry for my accident as it caused Felton to go to Paris. She is growing as fat as a pig, from lolling on the couch with her feet up all day long, with Blücher opposite to her in the same way. She is dying to have a finger in the house & had actually entered into the matter with Baring,* and is now vexed to death that Felton will not stand the nonsense, she talks of nothing else and is laughed at abominably for it. She has a party this evening. Old Campbell is gone to Paris although very unwell from a bad fall from his horse, I believe to do business in the loan way.

Steele† is lately returned from Town, no talk of promotion he says. I had a very entertaining note from Hill the other day. Pray write me word how Percy is, best love to my aunt & Eliza. Believe me ever, my dear uncle, your most dutiful and affectionate nephew,

John Fremantle

With every passing day, John's frustrations with Louisa increased.

Cambrai, Tuesday 16 June 1818

My dear uncle,

I have been boiling with passion for this last half hour. I received a letter from Felton by the messenger dated yesterday from Paris, telling me he had sold my horse and nothing else.

I went over to Louisa and was accosted with 'you are to start to Paris immediately'. I read the duke's notes in which he says he cannot possibly return before Thursday or Friday, but to start me as soon as she gets this note, in case he may be detained longer.

You may conceive how angry this has made me, but as I consult my inclinations I am off like a shot. I expect he will be there a fortnight and my belief is that Felton will not come down.

The devil take this woman It was owing to her not knowing her mind, that Cradock and I were obliged to go to Maubeuge in our own way. She found out in the morning she had a sore throat. The duke & Felton consequently went alone, we having gone the evening before. Adieu, my dear uncle in great hurry. Believe me, most affect[ionate]ly yours,

John Fremantle

John rushed to Paris and found the duke in excellent mood; he suspected that he lingered at Paris to avoid Louisa, but also to continue more agreeable female liaisons!

---

* Alexander Baring, MP and financier, in charge of the Hope & Baring bank. A deal was negotiated by which the bank loaned the French government the sum required to pay the outstanding indemnity to the allies, allowing the occupation to finish early.
† Lieutenant & Captain Thomas Steele, Coldstream Guards.

Paris, Monday 22 June 1818

My dear uncle,
I started last Tuesday evening as I told you at 6 p.m. and travelled till 10. Set off again at 9 and arrived here at 5 o'clock on the evening of Wednesday, having come a *franc étrier* [at a gallop] the last 45 miles, and thank goodness was not the least the worse for it, indeed the bleeding has done me so much good that I recommend everybody whom I hear complain, to undergo the same discipline.

Felton left this morning after I came, and rode down all the way, it rained torrents, and I very much fear his being knocked up, but you will probably have heard from him since. My opinion is that the duke sent for me, in order that he might remain here without being bothered by Louisa from Cambrai about Felton. He is as happy as possible, nothing to do, but to amuse himself with Lady C[harlotte] Greville, who all the other English women are furious with for monopolising all his attention.

He starts tomorrow, as he has being doing every day since I came. I hear he intends going to England in July, when you may depend upon it, it shall not be my fault if I do not come too. Adieu my dear uncle, with best love, believe me ever, your most dutiful & affectionate nephew,
　　John Fremantle

John wrote again on their return to Cambrai indicating that he was hopeful of joining a planned excursion to England.

Cambrai, Tuesday 21 July 1818

My dear uncle,
I received your letter before the last mail was sent off, but we were so hard set, that I had not time to write. Percy met Cradock & myself at Paris when we went the last time with the duke, and everything I am happy to say went *à l'aimable* [to our mutual satisfaction]. We returned here on Wednesday last, and are likely to stay till the end of the month, when I believe there is a trip to England in meditation, whether I go or stay is yet an enigma, but if it depends on myself, I shall certainly be of the party.

Burgh having been elected,* I imagine will return very soon. I shall be very glad when he returns and also to go to England this time, for I shall be very happy to have a little more conversation with you on the old subject. Things do not altogether go on as I like.

All the Greville family arrived last night, to stay a week on their

---

* Burgh was returned for Carlow County in 1818.

way to Spa, which I am very glad of. I like Lady Charlotte myself of all things, and the duke is always in such good spirits when she is with him. You remember I have always said that the other chick could not last long, and it is evident to all that they are going downhill.*

The little one thought proper to ask the duke the other day how old Lady Charlotte was, if though young she was not old enough to be a grandmother and this some never do.

I wish I had met Lord Essex again at Paris, he is quite delightful, and was exceedingly civil to me and I should be much obliged to you on the first occasion to tell him. I enquired according to his desire at Cambrai for the plants, but could not find his man. I have lost his letter now and do not remember what the plants were, would you ask him?

I have procured with a great deal of difficulty a boar and a sow, 4 months old of the wild species, they are now here quite tame, ask Knightly whether he chooses to have one.

I do not think my sisters will come here at all. Everyone who has seen Fanny says she has benefited very much by the sea bathing. Mrs Wylly† offered to take Albinia to stay with her when Fanny went to England, but she thought it prudent to decline. I should have been very glad that she had accepted it, but perhaps it is as well as it is.

Pray remember me kindly to my aunt & Puss and believe me, my dear uncle, your most dutiful and affectionate nephew,
 John Fremantle

Percy was hoping to gain a majority by exchange but John also felt that he would like the opportunity to be offered to him to make such a move. He had also fallen out with Felton again.

Cambrai, 25 August 1818

My dear uncle,

I received your letter yesterday, but can do nothing to remedy all that has happened between Felton & myself till they return, which will be the 1st week in next month; in the meantime I must inform you that I have just heard Percy is trying to get the majority of the 18th Hussars which will be vacated by Colonel Hay,‡ who is certain

---

* Relationships slowly waned between the duke and Mary Anne Patterson as it became clear to her that the duke would never undergo the scandal of a divorce to marry her.

† The wife of Lieutenant Colonel Alexander Campbell Wylly, 7th Foot, Assistant Adjutant General at Waterloo.

‡ Lieutenant Colonel Philip Hay, 18th Hussars, was actually acquitted of the charges brought against him of misappropriating funds and was allowed to continue in the regiment; blame being put upon Lieutenant Colonel the Honourable Henry Murray

to be broke by the general court martial about to sit upon him for various misdemeanours. Now Percy has never been a month longer with a cavalry regiment than myself, and I surely have a prior claim to him from service, he was a prisoner from his own fault during the war in Spain[*] and received a brevet of major as soon as it was over notwithstanding. You know everyone composing the duke's Staff got the step of regimental lieutenant colonel from that of captain, excepting myself, who happened unluckily to be a lieutenant in the Guards.

I can only say, I should consider my fortune made, if I could get this. It must not go in the regiment, and I should be ready to undergo any drill they chose to practise on me, pray write to me, and believe me always, my dear uncle, your most dutiful and affectionate nephew,
    John Fremantle

PS If you could in any way prepare Torrens with this, I will write to him to the same effect by the next post.

A month later, the ill feeling continued.

Cambrai, 15 September 1818

My dear uncle,
I am sorry I have nothing satisfactory to acquaint you with, regarding the difference between Felton and myself. He remained here two days after his arrival previous to his going to Spa. We had had a correspondence, by which it appears he intended me to be satisfied by his addressing me as if nothing at all had happened, which after insulting me most grossly was what I never could submit to, particularly as I know it would have to be done over again at some other time, and I wrote him word that I thought half measures always a bad thing and had much better be left alone, consequently for the two days he was here we had no sort of communication. I understand they are to remain at Spa till the sovereigns meet at Aix [la Chapelle].

Our reviews went off famously, everybody in the greatest good humour, the Duke and Duchess of Kent I trust were content. I expect His Grace will go to Paris between this & the 20th previous to his going to the congress which is fixed for the 27th.

I heard from Fanny the other day who says she is very ill at Boulogne. I wish to goodness she could be persuaded to leave that horrid place.

---

for the failures. See *A Collection of Charges, Opinons and Sentences of the General Courts Martial . . . from the year 1795* by Charles James, T. Egerton, London 1820.
[*] Henry Percy was actually in the 14th Light Dragoons from June 1810 and was made a prisoner of war during the retreat from Burgos.

I want them to come here *pour cause* [for a reason], Barnes is always asking after Albinia.

Pray give my best love to my aunt & Eliza, and believe me ever, my dear uncle, your most dutiful and affectionate nephew,

John Fremantle

The next letter follows after a two month gap. The Congress of Aix-la-Chapelle* began on 1 October 1818, where the four main powers agreed to remove the Army of Occupation from France. This treaty was signed on 9 October, but discussions continued until 15 November, in an attempt to get a pan-European agreement on a range of issues. The Duke of Wellington and Castlereagh attended the Congress for Great Britain and presumably the constant travelling and inordinate correspondence involved prevented John from writing regularly.

This note was sent to Sir Charles Stuart, Ambassador to France regarding the copying of his dispatches to the duke at Brussels and a second copy to Aix-la-Chapelle.

Friday [Undated – Cambrai, 13 November 1818?]†

Dear Sir Charles,‡

Scovell & myself held a council of war on the arrival of your messages, at which it was decided that we should copy the dispatches and send them on both ways. It has not delayed the messengers at all, for arriving earlier than usual, they would have been obliged to wait until the mail bag was made up here, as the duke sleeps at Brussels tonight. We sent one of the messengers there to him, he however will arrive in time at Calais to bring the next bag up here; if not we have desired [Juilian?] to forward it.

This is a royal stupid place, no inducement to put one's head out of doors. I have business luckily to keep me employed for a good week or ten days. The surplus of Paris.

You will have some visitors soon at the boxes of the theatres. Lord & Lady Euston, & Lady Isabella Fitzroy who are going up the road from hence.

I sent a packet of letters last week under cover to Sir Stuart§ begging him to forward them to my sisters. I am afraid he has not done so. As some of them were of consequence, dare I ask you to enquire whether they are still at your house?

---

* The French name for Aachen.
† Courtesy of the National Library of Scotland, reference MS 21321 ff. 102–7.
‡ Sir Charles Stuart was married to Elizabeth Margaret (née Yorke).
§ Probably the Honourable Major William Stuart, Grenadier Guards.

Pray make my best respects to Lady Elizabeth & believe me, most faithfully,
John Fremantle

Another hasty note mentioned that John would remain at Cambrai for a few days after all of the army had marched for home by 20 November.

Cambrai, Friday evening [13 November?]*

Dear Crosbie,†
I shall remain *here by the duke's desire* till the 22nd in order to forward any letters that may arrive for him and apprize you accordingly. I imagine he himself will be here on that day. I have however received no directions by what means I am to forward them, as all the sergeants, and orderlies will have quitted on the 19th. Ever yours most sincerely,
John Fremantle

He found time to resume his correspondence with his uncle while he awaited the final march of the troops. With the end of the Army of Occupation, the duke would no longer require his large 'family' and John was perfectly happy to return to his battalion; indeed he seems to view the prospect with some relief.

Cambrai, Tuesday 17 November 1818

My dear uncle,
Your letter of the 9th returned from Aix this morning by young Hutchinson, whither he had been sent on some communications respecting the evacuation. The troops march tomorrow but I have received directions to remain 3 or 4 days in order to keep up the communications between Paris & Brussels & Aix. I have written to Lord Clancarty & Burgh to tell them that I intend to leave on Saturday unless I hear from the latter that it is wished for me to stay longer, the post days from Paris being Tuesdays and Fridays. I have not yet determined whether I go to Paris or straight home. If the duke comes through here & I ought to go with him, I will, otherwise I do not wish it. I am to take Albinia up at Calais. Louisa & Blücher are here [&] are going with the duke to Paris, the house of the former much put out of joint of late by her impudence, and assurance.

I am fully sensible of the good nature expressed in your letter, I have not written for a week, I had nothing pleasant to say to you. I will not

---

* Courtesy of the National Library of Scotland, reference MS 21321 ff. 102–7.

† Lieutenant Sir William Edward Crosbie 6th bart. 21st Foot; he had been wounded at Bergen op Zoom.

dwell on the subject now as we are so soon to meet. I went over to Valenciennes during the review and the duke was very civil, and [I] returned here afterwards where I have remained ever since.

I think you are mistaken respecting a foreign force in the Netherlands. If however there is to be one, the commissioner you may depend upon it will be appointed from home, or by Lord Castlereagh. I thank you at all events for your idea, but to tell you the truth I am fully prepared to join my battalion and am determined not to be disappointed at whatever arrangements may take place. Pray give my best love to my aunt and Pussy and believe me, my dear uncle, your very affectionate nephew,
    John Fremantle

John continued forwarding information.

Cambrai, Tuesday Evening [17 November?]*

Dear Sir Charles
I send you a copy of a note I have received from Lord Clancarty† this morning, regarding the communication. The troops evacuate this place on the 19th. Ever yours most faithfully,
    John Fremantle

His next letter announced his imminent arrival in London, his role being virtually complete.

Cambrai, Friday 20 November 1818

My dear uncle,
I write in order that you may know I am still in the land of the living. I shall remain I think till Tuesday, as I have heard from Burgh that the duke will possibly pass by here on Monday, on his way to Paris. If the duke does not pass before that time, I shall proceed on the shortest road to London, as I shall then think he will have taken the other road from Aix-la-Chapelle.

I have been very much surprised at the general civility the people have outwardly shown to me since the departure of the troops. We all expected it would be very much the contrary.

Believe me, my dear uncle, ever your most dutiful and affectionate nephew,
    John Fremantle

---

* Courtesy of the National Library of Scotland, reference MS 21321 ff. 102–7.
† Richard Le Poer Trench, 2nd Earl of Clancarty, 1st Marquess of Heusden, was ambassador to the Netherlands.

Ten days later a note announced his arrival in London.

Whites [Club], 30 November 1818, 5 p.m.

My dear uncle,

I landed here about an hour ago, and propose paying you a visit tomorrow. The duke's papers arrived in the river yesterday and must go down to the custom house in the morning to see about them, so you may expect me at dinner or else by the mail at night. I do not expect the duke for four days and must be back for his arrival. Best love to my aunt and Pussy, your most dutiful and affectionate nephew,

John Fremantle

LATER YEARS

Within a fortnight John was back on duty with the 1st battalion of the Coldstream Guards, taking a detachment to Deptford.

Monday, 14 December 1818

My dear uncle,

I received your note at Hatfield on Friday upon my arrival there, and I am greatly obliged to you for the anxiety it expressed about me. I will endeavour as far as it lies in my power to follow the principles laid down by you.

I find however that I am ordered to Deptford tomorrow with a detachment. Ever my dear uncle your dutiful and affectionate nephew,
John Fremantle

The same day, Uncle William received a letter from John's second cousin John Butler, who was concerned for John's welfare. Clearly, the fall out with Felton was now serious and it had subsequently affected John's standing with the duke. Once again his quick temper caused most of the problems.

From J. Butler[*] to William Fremantle,
Park Lane, 14 December 1818

My dear William,

On Saturday evening I had a visit from John Fremantle who I did not then think had arrived in England. He looked well, but I thought depressed in spirits, bearing etc. & later in my little back room my conversation naturally led to his actual position & future view & I learned with the most sincere regret that both mine & the other were the very reverse of what I could wish & indeed far nearer than what from my previous knowledge of things I had anticipated. He was unreserved

---

[*] John Butler was a merchant in the City of London and first cousin to William Fremantle.

and communicative to the fullest extent & gave me the opportunity to offer to him my sentiments and opinions on the subject at large. I availed myself of it, by putting before him in the strongest colours what must be the inevitable consequence to himself of pursuing a line of conduct so wholly destructive of those prospects he might otherwise so reasonably encourage that it was morally impossible he could make head against the phalanx he had thought fit to oppose, that submission & yielding were the only means left to him for regaining the height from which he had thrown himself, & that however humiliating this might feel it was still a trial less severe than the mortification he would inevitably experience from the taunts & slights of the lesser people whom he certainly has not counted in provoking & who would be delighted in an opportunity of retaliating. I then strongly urged the misery & unhappiness which his proceedings which must necessarily involve you in under the particular circumstances in which you were placed & that the gratitude he owed to your impartiality called upon him to adopt at once a different line. I should not do him justice if I did not say that this view of the subject seemed sensibly to affect him. He indeed admitted the full extent & justice of all I had put before him, but the pill was very hard to digest & I could not get from him any positive assurance that he would try to swallow it.

What I strongly urged was an immediate letter to you or a candid explanation with Mrs F[elton] to bring a reconciliation with Sir Felton (which as he has been a little violent), I think he would not refuse, then with a different turn of conduct also would probably restore him to that ostensible footing with the duke as would at least leave the world in ignorance that he was much otherwise; in that quarter likewise he had been & this for the present is all that is necessary. I have given you in as concise precise as I could the substance of my bit of the conversation & I was in hope that I had succeeded in producing a determination to act somewhat in this way with his promising on his going away to consider it over & and see me on the following day, but as he did not call & I have not since heard from him I am fearful my efforts have failed to second my wishes on a subject in which I am truly interested for himself whom I sincerely regard, more particularly for you whose domestic happiness and comfort is so much involved in it. I could not therefore resist calling upon you for a few lines to tell me whether you have heard from or seen him, as I cannot but be anxious for his taking serious steps at least to prevent his sinking in public opinion. His disposition I really believe to be good, but his temper is such, it cannot be moved or driven though it may be worked upon by conciliation and you who have been to him as a parent will

I am sure feel that it is not of moment provided the effect desired is produced (whether it is effected by mild means or otherwise). I say this much because he seemed to think & feel that you had received him very cruelly at Englefield Green; although I did not mean to wade much & indeed I am not very fit to wade at all, I find I have scribbled through a sheet of paper, but I entreat of you that as soon as it is read you will burn it & not mention to the party to whose concern it relates that you have ever heard from me on the subject. You know that I ever am most affectionately yours,

    J. B.

He remained at Deptford throughout Christmas.

Saturday morning 26 December 1818

My dear uncle,
Yesterday being Xmas Day it was necessary I should attend church at Deptford with my detachment. I was at the duke's the day before though I did not see him. He went out of town early.

I fear I cannot serve God and Mammon and please you. Ever my dear uncle, your most affectionate nephew,

    John Fremantle

Unfortunately it is at this point that John's regular correspondence with his uncle ends, however he was to continue his career in the army and we can gain occasional glimpses of his life through a few odd letters that are to be found in various archives around the country and other publications.

John was appointed to the Staff in Jamaica on 25 August 1819, where he was meant to be serving as deputy adjutant general, however he was still in London on 15 December 1819 writing formally to the Duke of Wellington requesting permission to wear a foreign award.

54 Lower Grosvenor Street, 15 December 1819

My Lord,
Having received from Count Einsiedel* the Military Order of St Henry,† conferred upon me by His Majesty the King of Saxony, I request your Grace will obtain permission for me to wear the award.

I have the honour to be, with the greatest respect, your Grace's most obedient honourable servant,

    John Fremantle, Lt Col, Lt & Capt. Coldstream Guards

---

* Count Detlev von Einsiedel was the Saxon minister at the Congress of Vienna.
† The Military Order of St Henry was a military order of the Kingdom of Saxony, with four classes.

One reason for his delay in sailing may well be that Felton Hervey Bathurst had died suddenly on 24 September 1819. Despite their recent issues it would seem unlikely that John would not have attended the funeral.

John must have sailed for Jamaica in early 1820 and got to know a fellow traveller well on the passage, one David Lyon, brother of his future wife. However he was certainly not in Jamaica for any appreciable period, having landed back at Falmouth on 1 March 1821.

He returned to his battalion in London and a letter written by the Duke of Wellington in the summer of that year indicates that he had met John recently and would push to help him gain substantive rank at the least to major; his ranks being brevet; his official rank being only a lieutenant and captain. It seems likely that John was contemplating exchanging regiment in order to gain his promotion or another Staff appointment, but was advised to stick it out with the Coldstream by the duke.

Brussels, 11 August 1821*

My dear Fremantle,
I received here last night your letter of the 3rd. Before I left London I had a conversation with John Fremantle respecting his situation, which I confess I think as good as it can be made as far as regards his duties, but he ought to make up his mind. However I told him I consider the matter well in all its bearings, and to let me know positively what he wished, and that I would apply to the Duke of York.

It will be impossible in the first instance to get for him anything better than a majority, but we can get him promoted from thence to a lieutenant colonelcy.

I confess however that I think he is wrong, and that he ought to make up his mind to perform his duties as subaltern of the Guards till he can get his company, or can be employed in some manner more agreeable to him.

You may rely on it that I shall be happy to do anything in my power for him as well for his sake as for yours. Believe me, ever yours most sincerely,
    Wellington

It would seem that John had ignored all advice and had sought another Staff appointment. The duke was as good as his word as can be seen from an extract of a letter from Wellington's brother Lord Wellesley, who was taking up the post of Lord Lieutenant of Ireland, to Lord Buckingham regarding the post of aide-de-camp.

---

* Courtesy of Buckinghamshire Archives reference D/FR/48/9/10.

. . . My brother Arthur has mentioned Lt Col Fremantle to me with great regard. I shall be very happy if it is within my power to promote his wishes; but in the very extended state of my own engagements I cannot make any decision before my arrival in Ireland.

W[ellesley]

This undated draft in William Fremantle's hand stating the current state of John Fremantle's position clearly refers to this period of his life and is contemporary to the duke's letters. It must have been prepared in 1821 as part of the concerted campaign to gain John his substantive rank.

The state of Lt Col Fremantle is this:

He has been 16 years subaltern in the Coldstream Guards, and is now second in succession for a company either by vacancy or purchase. There are three additional captains now seconded who by the regulations are entitled to a company previous to the advancement of a subaltern. In case of purchase, the purchaser is by the new regulations to give a greatly advanced price (and is not so immediately to be put on half pay and thereby excluded from further succession in the regiment)

Under these circumstances can it be worthwhile for Lt Col Fremantle to purchase who has had brevet rank since the year 1814?

On the other hand if he retires on half pay as captain, he excludes himself from ever commanding a regiment, it being the regulation of the army not to allow officers to return to the army from half pay, but on the permanent rank of their half pay, be their brevet rank what it may.

The object therefore of Lt Col Fremantle is either to procure a Staff employment in England which will enable him to continue as subaltern in the Guards & wait for accidental promotion in his regiment, or to procure a majority from which he is ready to purchase a lieutenant colonelcy in the line.

The latter would be the most desirable object to Lt Col Fremantle for even if a difficulty existed in purchasing the step of Lt Colonel, it would be infinitely better for him to retire on half pay as major than as a lieutenant in the Guards.

The Duke of Wellington must be aware that by the new arrangement Lt Col Fremantle cannot even with the most favourable result, have the hope of succeeding to a company in the Guards under ten years, unless he were to purchase, but then he would have to tempt an officer to sell

---

* Courtesy of Buckinghamshire Archives reference D/FR/48/9/9.

at the advanced sum of £6,500, *and be reduced to half pay forthwith.*[*]

The duke again wrote to his old friend, William Fremantle.

London, 2 December 1821

My dear Fremantle,
I wrote to Lord Wellesley on Saturday & saw him and spoke to him this day concerning the appointment of your nephew to be his aide-de-camp. He is very anxious to defer all arrangements respecting his family till he will arrive in Ireland; & he will decide nothing till then. I think you will do well to get Lord Buckingham to speak or write to him upon this subject. Ever yours, most sincerely,
Wellington

On 22 July 1822 John gained further promotion by brevet to colonel, exacerbating his position, but the situation was relieved immediately by his purchase of the rank of captain & lieutenant colonel on 1 August 1822, finally giving him substantive rank beyond a subaltern.

In 1824 Canning proposed sending John Fremantle with diplomatic papers to Mexico, unpaid, however it came to nought.

Uncle William wrote to the Duke of Buckingham:

3 March 1824

. . . By the bye, my nephew, John Fremantle, came to me the day before yesterday to tell me that Canning had offered to send him confidentially to South America, furnished with letters to Henry, and other duties; that he was to have no appointment whatever, but his expenses were to be paid, and he was to be remunerated on his return if they were satisfied with his conduct. He likes the trip very much; I own I should not be particularly pleased with a little excursion to Mexico and back again; however *on ne peut pas discuter des goût* [No accounting for taste]. Adieu my Duke, ever most faithfully yours,
W. H. Fremantle

. . . My nephew just tells me that his intended expedition has got wind and that it is all off, and he is not to go.[†]

The drive for a Staff appointment continued, John sought and gained a post with Sir Charles Stuart on his mission to Brazil and Portugal in 1825.

---

[*] These last seven words are underlined with 'not so' written beneath in an unknown hand.
[†] *Memoirs of Court of George IV*, vol. II, pp. 53–4.

During 1823 Portugal had requested British mediation with Brazil, and it was only after long tortuous and often futile negotiations that George Canning decided, in the interests of all the states concerned, to dispatch a special mission to Portugal and Brazil to arrange the terms. Sir Charles Stuart, a diplomat of great experience, was selected for this task. In addition to negotiating the recognition of Brazilian independence from the mother country, Stuart was empowered to obtain from Brazil the prolongation of the trade treaty with Great Britain, originally signed in 1810 and due for revision in 1825. Until such time as Brazilian independence was a recognized fact this would suffice; then a more permanent commercial agreement between Great Britain and Brazil could then be negotiated. He wrote to apprise his uncle of the success of his private campaigning.

79 York Street, 7 February 1825

My dear uncle,
In the event of the circumstance of my being named to accompany Sir Charles Stuart being a matter of any interest to you. I take the opportunity of mentioning that it has just reached me. At the same time, I cannot describe to you how bitterly I lament the necessity I have felt myself under of taking these steps without any previous communication. Hoping that I shall do justice to [your?] good opinion and kind help on this occasion. Believe me, my dear uncle, ever your fond and affectionate nephew,
John Fremantle

He received a congratulatory reply. The correspondence of his uncle also shows that William gave John £200* to kit himself out as ADC to Sir Charles Stuart on the mission.

My dear John,
I had been informed of your nomination to accompany Sir Charles Stuart which I was very glad to hear & hope your military service will make advantage from it. I find he goes in the *Wellesley* 74 & is expected in about ten days or a fortnight. What other persons belong to his mission, I have not heard. No previous communication with me would have assisted your object. Feeling the warmest interest in your business I have only to say you have nothing to lament in not having previously communicated with me upon it. If I can assist you in any way in your outfit you have only to name it to me. Every affectionately,
W. F[remantle]

---

* This would equate to approximately £8,500 in today's terms.

William also wrote to the Duke of Buckingham:

7 February 1825

... Sir Charles Stuart has been forced upon the king for this roving mission. ... My nephew, John Fremantle, goes attached to the mission; I never knew that till this instant. I suppose it is to make up for the disappointment in having suspended his former appointment to South America.[*]

Although Sir Charles Stuart succeeded in achieving his first objective, the recognition of Brazilian independence by Portugal, his mission was not an unqualified success. He exceeded that part of his instructions relating to the commercial relations of Great Britain and Brazil by signing two permanent treaties, one concerning commerce and the other for the abolition of the slave trade which, though ratified by Dom Pedro, were quite unacceptable to Canning who was forced to disallow them. Stuart was recalled in the summer of 1826 and returned to Europe by way of Lisbon.[†]

The mission was expected to be short, therefore Uncle William wrote to the duke again to gain another appointment for John as an aide-de-camp, but the Duke of Wellington was clear that he could not interfere in such matters.

London, 7 March 1825[‡]

My dear Fremantle,

I am really the last person to whom application ought to be made [to] recommend an aide-de-camp to another. There are numbers (among others your nephew) who have heard me say frequently that I should just as ever think of recommending a wife of a man as an aide-de-camp. I did try to experiment once with my own brother and you know the result. Yet the aide-de-camp of the Lord Lieutenant of Ireland is a very different person from the aide-de-camp of a general officer of the Duke of York. I cannot but think that I stand in relation to the latter in a very delicate situation. I am obliged to recommend to him nearly every officer in the army; and the relatives of every officer in the army. He has a few offices at his disposal principally about his own person; and I am not to allow him who knows the army & particularly your nephew as well as I do, to choose for himself, but I must go out of my

---

[*] *Memoirs of Court of George IV*, vol. II, p. 209.

[†] The manuscript papers of Charles Stuart, Baron Rothesay are housed at the Lilly Library, Indianna Library, Bloomington, USA.

[‡] Buckinghamshire Archive reference D/FR/48/13/47.

way & contrary to my own practise repeatedly stated [&] recommend an ADC to him!

I am certain that you must see that I cannot with propriety interfere in such a case. Believe me, ever yours, most sincerely,

Wellington

We gain another glimpse of John around 1827, when without warning, John was suddenly appointed to the duke's Staff again when he became commander-in-chief.

Windsor, Sunday 21 January 1827

My dear uncle,

The Duke of Wellington has appointed me to the only vacancy he has had as aide-de-camp, as I have never seen him for two months or written to him.

I hope that will be a convincing proof to you that he does bear me in mind, ever you affectionate nephew,

John Fremantle

Uncle William was surprised and delighted to hear the news.

My dear John,

I am extremely surprised to hear the Duke of Wellington has again placed you in his family, I hardly know any event which could have given me greater pleasure, as it proves his regard towards you & confirms what he stated to me some years since at Stratfield Saye.* It is more gratifying to me for not having made any personal application to him. Ever affectionately,

W. F[remantle]†

However, the reply from John was not particularly gracious to his uncle, upbraiding him for assuming that his personal intervention with the duke had helped gain his reappointment, rather than John's own merit.

Tuesday 6 February‡

My dear uncle,

I received yesterday the letter you sent to town when I was at Lord

---

* The estate at Stratfield Saye was bought for the Duke of Wellington by a grateful parliament in 1817 and remains the country seat of the family. It cost £263,000, which would equate in modern terms to approximately £11 million.

† Buckinghamshire Archives reference D/FR/49/4/5.

‡ Ibid., reference D/FR/49/4/7.

Clarendon's. There is a passage in it however, that appears to imply that it was the Duke of Wellington's promise to you (as you term it) that actuated him in this instance. If that is what you mean to convey to me, I beg you distinctly to understand that I by no means coincide with that opinion. In the first place it was unfair towards me you ever bringing on that conversation with him, and it has always struck me that his answer to you was nothing more than repelling the accusation you made against him of placing me aside. I feel that I am more fully borne out in my conjectures as I learnt the day before yesterday that Armstrong did not resign till the day before the funeral. The intention of appointing me was announced the day after it, but when it became a question of filling up the vacancy, although there were numerous applications the duke immediately said 'Fremantle is my first object'.

I cannot also help feeling, that if you did consider he had pledged himself towards you, you have been wondrously supine upon the occasion, in as much as it never once occurred to you ever to give me a particle of advice how to act, on the contrary it is since the Duke of York's death that you proposed my going to the Havannah though I make no comments at the moment, you are wrong in supposing me to be such an idiot as not fully to appreciate such remarks.

I am fully aware, it was you in the first instance who introduced me to the duke's notice, but I must again and again repeat my belief that he is aware that I always performed whatever duty I was called upon, with assiduity & attention & in a way to merit his good offices; for I know that within these last four years he said he had brought me up and considered me as one of his own kidney.

It disturbs my peace of mind, to bring these matters before you, but I have long brooded over these and I feel myself imperiously called upon to do myself justice.

The salutation you made me when I came to take leave of you before I went to South America was not lost upon me. I have thought of it ever since and I tell you distinctly that the footing you wish to place me on I do not value & I had rather be without it. Believe me ever, my dear uncle, very affectionately yours,
    John Fremantle

John also wrote around this time to Sir Charles Stewart regarding Lord Hertford.

Sandbourne, Friday [1827?]*

Dear Sir Charles,
Lord Hertford† has the gov[ernmen]t in his right hand therefore less
I will say to you how much he is obliged for your letter. He thinks he
never was entitled to the privileges of a returning resident ambassador,
so he has not brought back a bottle of wine, of liquer, and he has sent
for some furniture which he has given directions to pay the duty. He
brought 4 or 5 glass tables in the frigate, and he does not think he could
get in another without asking a favour which he says he has too much
abhorrence of Lord Goderich‡ policy towards the Turks to be able to
make up his mind to do him a favour.

Lord H[ertford] says he never had any chimneypieces, except those
you saw buy, and which are up in Piccadilly. Lord H[ertford] says you
must remember he did not buy a twentieth part of those which were
on the grass in the Champs Élysées. Believe me, my dear Sir Charles
most faithfully yours,
John Fremantle

Best remembrances to Lady Elizabeth.

We gain another glimpse in 1828 when we find John at Calais standing in
as a second in a duel between his old friend Long Wellesley and a Mr de
Crespigny, a champion steeplechaser.

Newspaper report of 1828§
On Thursday, a duel was fought on the sands at Calais between Mr
Long Wellesley and Mr de Crespigny. The dispute originated in a
remark made by Mr Wellesley respecting some parts of the conduct of
Mr de Crespigny's father.¶ He was requested to retract it; and on his
refusal a challenge was sent to him by the two Mr de Crespigny's, when
all the parties started at full speed from Dover to Calais. Colonel John
Fremantle of the Guards was second to Mr Wellesley, and Colonel

---

* Courtesy of the National Library of Scotland, reference MS 21321 ff. 102–7
† Francis Charles Seymour-Conway, 3rd Marquess of Hertford, Vice Chamberlain
of the Household.
‡ Lord Goderich was prime minister in 1827; he was pressurising the Turks to stop
attacking the Greeks. This was formalised by the Treaty of London when Britain,
France and Russia pledged to support the Greeks if there was not an immediate
armistice.
§ From *Memoirs of Sir Claude Champion de Crespigny, Bart,*edited by George A. B.
Dewar, London 1896.
¶ This refers to Heaton de Crespigny.

Brooke,* also of the Guards, attended his antagonist. The duel was fought on the sands immediately after the arrival of the seconds. Both parties fired together on a given signal at the distance of ten paces, and neither of them happening to be wounded, the seconds immediately interfered. A question here arose with respect to the second challenge, as to how far it was or was not to be accepted, when Captain Brooke decided that Mr Long Wellesley had done as much as he was required to do. The parties then separated and returned from Calais on Friday morning to Dover, where Mrs Bligh† at the York Hotel was waiting with great anxiety the arrival of Mr Wellesley, and, accompanied by him and Colonel Fremantle, she has since left Dover for London.

Uncle William received a letter from the Portuguese Ambassador announcing the award of the Grand Cross for John.

London, 7 November 1828

My dear sir,

It affords me particular pleasure to inform you that I have this morning received an answer to my letter addressed to the Baron de Queley under date of the 17 September. What follows is a translation of his answer.

'I had the honour to acquaint His Majesty with the contents of your letter dated the 17 ultimo. His Majesty was pleased to give his immediate orders relative to the Grand Cross, which he was pleased to confer when in England to the persons mentioned in your letter and you may assure them that His Majesty regretted much that they had not yet been forwarded, the more so as His Majesty on his arrival in his kingdom gave the necessary orders for their committal, which order he has renewed to be forwarded as soon as possible. Do me the favour to acquaint them with what I have written and at the same time remember me to those gents most respectfully.'

Do you think I may communicate the above to Lord Stuart Charles [sic], I have the honour to be with respect my dear sir, your much obliged,

F. T. Sampoya

In late 1828, there is a short series of letters from John to William regarding

---

* Captain and Lieutenant Colonel Thomas Brooke, Grenadier Guards.
† Long Wellesley had begun a relationship with Helena Patterson Bligh, the wife of Captain Thomas Bligh, Coldstream Guards, whom he married in 1828.

his whirlwind romance with Agnes Lyon a sugar plantation heiress with a considerable dowry.

21 December [1828]

There was no post yesterday. I received a note from Miss Wynyard in answer to mine stating HRH's desire to see me tomorrow at one o'clock.

I read the enclosed yesterday to Miss Lyon and when arrived at the part 'supposed to have a large fortune' she said 'how much am I reported to have?' I replied '50 or £60,000', to which she made no answer. She observed to Miss Taylor who was standing with us that she liked my letter very much. Ever again my dear uncle, most affectionately J. F.

Since writing the above I have had an interview with Mrs Lyon, as she was writing to her eldest son at Paris. She said she should be glad to tell him what income her daughter when married was likely to have. I told her I had about £600 a year with which she declared herself satisfied & dismissed me saying her daughter had £52,000 3 percents. Miss told me her father left £600,000 between 4 sons and £200,000 between 4 daughters, one married Lord Kilmaine,* a 2nd Mrs Wedderburn of Stanhope Street,† a 3rd Mrs Massy.

It would seem that his proposal was accepted much more quickly than he had hoped!

Brighton, 28 December 1828

My dear uncle,

It was utterly impossible for me to have mentioned the subject of my former letter at an earlier period for I assure you I was as much surprised when the *éclaircissement* [enlightenment] took place as you were at hearing of the event. I thought Miss Lyon was well disposed towards me but I was not prepared for her making up her mind, on so short an acquaintance.

I have seen some of her letters from individuals connected with her, and have been very much gratified and indeed cannot help feeling proud at the character which these people say they have always heard of me, one of them traces many events of my life, & notes me as being known by all the potentates and their ministers as the confidential servant of the Duke of Wellington.

---

* John Cavendish Browne, 3rd Baron Kilmaine married Elizabeth Lyon on 4 January 1822.

† Isabella Lyon had married James Wedderburn of 'Spring Garden' Jamaica in 1817.

Nothing can be pleasanter than the Lyon family, every day brings an improvement on acquaintance and to me personally increased delight; our ideas perfectly coincided in my minutia, we are not to start with any show or attempt at expense, nor are we to decide about a house till I see what arrangements I can make about my regiment in Ireland next year; Miss Lyon is quite determined upon going with me as she wishes eventually to be established in town. I have suggested the neighbourhood of Belgrave Square which she liked very much. Mrs Lyon provides linen, and enough [households?] to make a beginning. I shall see the father's will tomorrow, I understand the money to be tied up in Chancery; 25,000 to be mine if I outlive my wife, 15,000 is otherwise disposed of if there are no children, and 10,000 are at the disposal of my wife, so that all trouble with the lawyers will be avoided.

I am much obliged to you for your offer and hope you will be the trustee to my marriage settlement. I have written to my friend Briscall to do the job for me and I hope it will take place very soon after David Lyon comes from Paris, he leaves on the 5 January. I have received the kindest letter from the duke and from all his family and the warmest congratulation from all my friends. Be so good [as] to tell Albinia I will write to her tomorrow and thank her for her letter. I am much obliged to my aunt & Eliza for their congratulations. Fanny has a nasty cough. Believe me, my dear uncle, your very affectionate nephew,

John Fremantle

Once again we find John apologising for a previous response to his uncle.

2 January 1829

My dear uncle,

I confess to you that your first letter cast a considerable gloom upon my spirits and has reminded me that there is still something wanting to complete my happiness. I am fully sensible that I have often unduly held myself towards you and that I was manifestly wrong in doing so, but I thought you were too severe in your censure towards me. Pray remember, however, the many mortifications and disappointments I have undergone and the pinnacle from which I fell. I owe everything in life to you, you are the only person in the world for whom I have the slightest awe. Without you I feel I can do nothing and unless I can be restored to your confidence neither wife or fortune will ever avail me.

I received your letter before I left Brighton yesterday, I return there on Sunday and will write to you. In my letter to Tom of this day I have given him a little of my mind. I hope you will find I have not been unfair towards him.

Believe me ever, my dear uncle, your truly affectionate nephew,
  John Fremantle

His uncle, as always, forgave his errant nephew.

4 January 1829

My dear John,
I only write these lines to say I received your letter & can assure you
that I never have & never shall withdraw my confidence from you,
whenever you think it worth your acceptance & that most sincerely do
I wish you happy & prosperous in your future life & station.

With regard to what you observe about your letter to Town, I can
give you no opinion for I can assure you that I never conversed with
him in my life, nor has he ever spoken to me about you & it is not
therefore likely that I should see your letter to him.

I shall be delighted to hear from [you] when you write.
Yours affectionately,
  W. F[remantle]

On 17 January 1829 John Fremantle married Agnes Lyon from Goring on
Sea, Sussex, a plantation heiress worth £52,000. The service was conducted
by a personal friend, Samuel Briscall MA, rector of South Kelsey, ex-
chaplain of the forces during the Peninsular and Waterloo Campaigns and
the personal chaplain of the duke. The Duke of Wellington attended the
wedding at St George's, Hanover Square, which he described as 'corking'
and signed the register as first witness, just days before he moved the
Catholic Emancipation Bill in Parliament.

John was promoted colonel in the army on 22 July 1830 and was
also made aide-de-camp to King William IV who had only gained the
throne the month before. Unfortunately, a few years later he was to
draw criticism from the king for his failure to accompany his battalion to
Ireland. He wrote a rash letter to Sir Herbert Taylor, military secretary,
explaining the delay that had occurred in his travelling to Dublin.

Dublin, 20 March 1837

Sir,
I have been informed that at the last two levees His Majesty has desired
to know, whether I had complied with his commands, delivered to me
in person.

I deem it therefore proper to state, that as soon as I received those
commands, I lost not a moment in retiring to Dublin.

I avail myself of this occasion to assure His Majesty, that for a period upwards of 31 years, during which I have 20 times crossed the Bay of Biscay, 4 times crossed the line and that the fortune of war has on two occasions enabled me to exhibit the trophies of the enemy at my sovereign's feet. I can fearlessly say that I have never permitted myself to make a convenience of the service. I am never so happy as when I dutified [*sic*] with my regiment, and I feel the same pride in it, that my king & master can do for his crown & sceptre.

I have felt the deepest regret at the remark, made by my king to Lord Hill, respecting our answer I made at his levee. I simply told my king the truth, but I could not on that occasion, enter into a detail of my private affairs, viz. that I had intended to ask permission till June in order to settle the property of New Lodge, which I am to deliver up at that period. My absence is likely to occasion me a pecuniary loss, but after what has occurred, I shall dismiss the subject from my mind, my sole object being to do myself justice in the eyes of my sovereign, & if I did not do so, I should not feel satisfied to retain the command of a battalion of this bodyguard.

Sir, I am incapable of making to my king, an improper answer. I have the honour & c.,

John Fremantle

A frosty official reply was received from General Taylor.

Windsor Castle, 27 March 1837[*]

My dear colonel,

I have been favoured with your letter of the 21st instant, which I have had the honour to submit to the king. I was not aware of the enquiry, which you were informed the king had made, nor had he spoken to me on the subject of your proceeding to Dublin, to take charge of your battalion, but upon this occasion His Majesty asserted that he could not admit to be while in Ireland, a nominal command.

The king was however pleased to add that if urgent private business should require your presence in England for a few weeks, you might apply for leave through Sir Edward Blakeney. Believe me, &c.,

J. H. Taylor

Realising the seriousness of the business, John had retired to Dublin immediately and wrote to his uncle, concerned to discover how much damage he had caused.

---

[*] Buckinghamshire Archives, reference D/FR/49/10/7C.

Dublin, 30 March 1837[*]

My dear uncle,

I have been laid up with influenza & stomach since I came, but not having my uniform or baggage till yesterday. I passed my time directing everything from my barrack room window and have found pleasure in perceiving the readiness with which the trifling alterations I wished to make were attended to.

My first act of authority was after a communication with the general, to dispatch a young man (son of Lord Cavan) to England, who was about to contract a very ineligible marriage and have received from Lord Cavan a letter from thanks for the same, which I discovered from a lady who I sat next to at dinner, that I had here too officious, but she 'was unmarried'. The general here speaks highly of the regiment and McDonnell who passed through here yesterday on his way to attend the queen told me it was the general opinion. I showed to him the letter I addressed to Sir H. Taylor and his answer. I believe he was always well disposed towards me, while in the regiment and that feeling is not likely to be lessened by my having been able to do an act by a young officer in the regiment since I came, who proved to be his nephew but I did not know it. McDonnell told me he was glad to have seen the regiment and he should know what to say if the king made any enquiries.

I have dwelt upon the subject of the king's communication to me, till I dare say, you will be annoyed by it, but I have done so under the impression that if undone now, his torment or relation would continue so long as I held the command. It was unbecoming of him to treat me as a young malingering officer.

I enclose you copies of the two letters and I shall be glad to know your opinion. I confess to you I was on tenter hooks, as to know any letter would be received. Give best love to all your house, believe me, my dear uncle, your most dutiful & affectionate nephew,

J. Fremantle

I have only to add that if I Johnny can be back in time from his father's funeral, to do our concerns at New Lodge. I have no desire to come over. I am very happy & comfortable here.

A confidential letter from his uncle rebuked him for his rash letter to the king's representative.

---

[*] Buckinghamshire Archives reference D/FR/49/80/7A.

Stanhope Street, 8 April 1837

My dear John,

I have just received your letter of the 6th and feeling how greatly you deceive yourself as to the position in which you stand with the king, I cannot forbear to write to you on the subject, desiring you to consider this letter as most strictly *private and confidential.*

I will not pretend to say why or wherefore, but I can assure you that the king's mind is still under impressions highly unfavourable to you & not lessened by the last communication you made to His Majesty through Sir Herbert Taylor, and knowing as I well do, the excitement of the king's mind on any subject which immediately operates upon it, I am quite satisfied that nothing but time (which may & must prove the injustice of his prejudices) will remove them & until this arises, no step which you or any friend of yours would take, can alter the state in which these impressions exist. It is because I feel deeply for your interests that I tell you this, & urge you to no further communication with Sir Herbert Taylor or with any other public functionary on the subject.

I am giving no opinion on what has passed, if I had been counselled previous to your writing to Sir Herbert Taylor, I would have tendered to you, as I always have done (when previously asked) my best advice, but as in your letter to me of the 6th you 'Thank God it is all at an end', I am to conclude you think & wish to be so, and most happy I should feel if I could confirm such a wish, as the same time, if you can be induced to leave matters where they are, I am persuaded, as I have before said to you, that the king's mind naturally kind, will never in the end be led to acts of injustice by the excitement of the moment. That you have some enemy approaching His Majesty I cannot but think and whose object is to drive you from the regiment. Your service in the army & your character as an officer cannot however be overlooked, so long as you allow not your temper to get the better of your judgement. You are now in command of your battalion, you have the means of showing your talents for command. You have no one object on earth that ought to interfere with this duty, & which the king requires from you and as your best friend (if you mean, or wish to continue in the service) I should recommend you to remain quietly on your post till the regiment returns to England.

As to the insignificant personal object of a sale at New Lodge, or any other personal matter, they are not worthy of a moment's consideration & unless you are prepared to go on half pay or to quit the army, any proposition of exchanges or removal would be only accomplishing the object which your enemy, whoever he may be, has in view.

Again I must repeat that these opinions are strictly confidential & you will take them as they are meant in friendship & in the best wishes for your welfare & reputation. Yours affectionately,
W. Fremantle

Previous to writing the letter & before the fate of the one battalion was known, the king had spoken to me in very indignant terms at the general behaviour of Colonel Fremantle & of his having written a very improper letter to Sir H. Taylor

Perhaps luckily for John, King William died soon after and on 20 June 1837 Queen Victoria gained the throne and ignoring previous issues, John was confirmed as an aide-de-camp to her majesty.

However, only two years later, on 31 December 1839 John became a lieutenant colonel in the Coldstream Guards and retired on half pay unattached, but retained the office of aide-de-camp to the queen. In 1841 he was promoted a major general in the Army.

John and Agnes had a happy marriage and the couple raised five children: Augusta Wilhelmina who eventually married Lieutenant General Julian Hall; Arthur James Lyon, who married another Hall, became a general and is particularly famous in the United States for his eyewitness journal of the American Civil War;* Fitzroy also became a general and married Julia Campbell; John Charles was a lieutenant in the Life Guards but died at the age of 32 unmarried and Delvin became a lieutenant in the Royal Navy and married Emma Isaacs but also died early at the age of 31.

John Fremantle died peacefully at Tilney Street, London on 6 April 1845 and was buried in the parish church of St Marylebone, Middlesex on 12 April 1845 in a service performed by Thomas Woods Goldhawk MA. The church register that day records five other burials, all from the local workhouse, including a three-month-old baby.

His obituary was published in the *Gentleman's Magazine* of June 1845 (page 650) and the Annual Register of 1845, appendix (page 268). A memorial to him was erected at the Royal Military Chapel, Wellington Barracks, Birdcage Walk, London. Unfortunately it was completely destroyed by a flying bomb in 1944. However, we are lucky to have a record of the memorial:

---

* Published as *Three Months in the Southern States, April–June 1863* in London 1863.

In memory of Major General John Fremantle, C.B., who entered the Coldstream Guards on 17 October 1805, and took part in the expedition to Germany under Lord Cathcart; the expedition to and storming of Buenos Ayres under General Whitelock; the Peninsular War and the campaign of Waterloo, including the passage of the Douro, Battle of Talavera, Battle of Busaco, Retreat on Torres Vedras, Battle of Fuentes d'Oñoro, Siege of Ciudad Rodrigo, Battle of Salamanca, Siege of Burgos, Battle of Vitoria, Battle of St Marcial, Passages of the Bidassoa, the Nive, and the Nivelle, Battle of Orthes, Battles of Quatre Bras and Waterloo. He served as both adjutant and commanding officer of the Coldstream, and was aide-de-camp to the Duke of Wellington from 1812 to 1817. He died in London on 6th April 1847 [1845], aged 55 years. Placed by his son, Colonel Arthur Lyon Fremantle, commanding Coldstream Guards.

BIBLIOGRAPHY

Anon. *The Army List*, War Office, various edns

Anon. *The Royal Military Calendar*, T. Egerton, London, 1820

Anon. *The Gentleman's Magazine*, June, London, 1845

Anon. *The Waterloo Medal Roll*, ed. C. J. Buckland, Naval and Military Press, Dallington, 1992

Beamish Ludlow *History of The King's German Legion*, vol. 2, Thomas and William Boone, London, 1837

Bryant, Arthur *The Great Duke*, Collins, London, 1971

Buckingham, Duke of *Memoirs of the Court of George IV 1820–30*, vol. 2, Hurst & Blackett, London, 1859

Burnham, R. and R. McGuigan *The British Army against Napoleon*, Frontline Books, London, 2010

Chandler, David *Dictionary of the Napoleonic Wars*, Arms and Armour Press, London, 1979

Couzens, Tim *Hand of Fate: The History of the Longs, Wellesleys and the Draycot Estate in Wiltshire*, Bradford on Avon, ELSP, 2001

Dalton, Charles *The Waterloo Roll Call*, Eyre & Spottiswoode, London, 1904

Drew, Robert *Commissioned Officers in the Medical Services of the British Army*, vol. 1, 1660–1897, The Wellcome Historical Medical Library, London, 1968

Edwards, Peter *Talavera: Wellington's Early Peninsular Victories 1808–9*, Crowood, Ramsbury 2005

Fletcher, Ian *The Waters of Oblivion*, Spellmount, Tunbridge Wells, 1991

— *For King and Country: The Letters and Diaries of John Mills, Coldstream Guards, 1811–14*, Spellmount, Staplehurst, 1995

— *A Guards Officer in the Peninsula: The Peninsular War Letters of John Rous, Coldstream Guards 1812–14*, Spellmount, Staplehurst, 1992

Fremantle, Anne *The Wynne Diaries 1789–1820*, OUP, London, 1952

Glover, Gareth *A Young Gentleman at War: The letters of Capt. the Hon. Orlando Bridgeman, 1st Foot Guards 1812–15*, Ken Trotman, Godmanchester, 2008

— *A Guards Officer in the Peninsula and at Waterloo: The Letters of Captain George Bowles Coldstream Guards 1807–19*, Ken Trotman, Godmanchester, 2008

— *It All Culminated at Hougoumont: The Letters of Captain John Lucie Blackman Coldstream Guards, 1812–15*, Ken Trotman, Godmanchester, 2009

— *Eyewitness to the Peninsular War and the Battle of Waterloo: The Letters and Journals of Lieutenant Colonel James Hamilton Stanhope, 1803–25*, Frontline Books, London, 2010

Gore, John *The Creevey Papers*, B. T. Batsford Ltd, London, 1963

Hall, John *History of the Peninsular War*, vol. VIII, Greenhill Books, London, 1998

Hamilton, L. Gen. Sir F. *Origin and History of The First or Grenadier Guards*, John Murray, London, 1874

Mackinnon, Colonel *Origins and Services of the Coldstream Guards* (2 Volumes), Richard Bentley, London 1833

Miller, David *The Duchess of Richmond's Ball, 15 June 1815*, Spellmount, Staplehurst, 2005

Muir, Rory (ed.) *At Wellington's Right Hand: The Letters of Lieutenant-Colonel Sir Alexander Gordon, 1808–15*, Army Records Society 21, Stroud, 2003

Mullen, A. L. T. *The Military General Service Roll 1793–1814*, London Stamp Exchange, London, 1990

Myatt, Frederick *British Sieges of the Peninsular War*, Spellmount, Tonbridge Wells, 1987

O'Byrne, William *A Naval Biographical Dictionary*, John Murray, London, 1849

Oman, Sir Charles *A History of the Peninsular War*, 2 vols, Clarendon Press, Oxford, 1902 and 1930

— *Wellington's Army 1809–14*, np, London, 1913

Park, S. J. and G. F. Nafziger *The British Military: Its System and Organization 1803–15*, Cambridge, Ontario, 1983

Reid, Stuart *Wellington's Officers*, vols 1–3, Partizan Press, Leigh-on-Sea, 2008–11

Robertson, Ian *Wellington at War in the Peninsula*, Pen & Sword Books, Barnsley, 2000

Siborne, H. T. *The Waterloo Letters*, Arms & Armour Press, London, 1983

Veve, Thomas Dwight *The Duke of Wellington and the British Army of Occupation in France, 1815–18*, Greenwod Press, Westport, 1992

Ward, S. P. G. *Wellington's Headquarters*, OUP, Oxford, 1957

Watson, Steven *The Reign of George III, 1760–1815*, Oxford History of England series, Clarendon Press, Oxford, 1960

INDEX